SON OF THE ROUGH SOUTH

PublicAffairs · New York

SON OF THE ROUGH SOUTH

An Uncivil Memoir

KARL FLEMING

ESERT LITERARY SOCIETY

SPONSORED BY
Northern Trust AND season
in the sun

Published in the United States by PublicAffairs™,
a member of the Perseus Books Group.

Book design by Mark McGarry
Set in Sabon

Library of Congress Cataloging-in-Publication Data
Fleming, Karl
Son of the rough South: an uncivil memoir / Karl Fleming.—1st ed.
p. cm.
ISBN 1-58648-296-3
1. Fleming, Karl. 2. Civil rights workers—United States—Biography.
3. Journalists—United States—Biography. 4. African Americans—Civil rights—History—20th century. 5. Civil rights movements—United States—History—20th century. 6. Civil rights movements—Southern States—History—20th century.
7. United States—Race relations. 8. Southern States—Race relations.
9. African Americans—Civil rights—Southern States—History—20th century—Press coverage. 10. Southern States—Race relations—Press coverage.
I. Title.
E185.98.F55A3 2005
070'.92—dc22
[B]
2005043158

FIRST EDITION
10 9 8 7 6 5 4 3 2 1

To All the Reporters Who Did the Right Thing

Contents

Acknowledgments

This book would never have been written without the unswerving love, support, and keen editing eye of my wife, Anne Taylor Fleming.

I also owe a huge debt to my longtime friend and colleague David Halberstam, who, among many supportive gestures, read an early draft and helped me give this work a more focused narrative definition.

I would also like to thank a long list of other reporters, photographers, and editors who helped me along the way, and/or who stood side by side with me through the difficult and dangerous days of the civil rights movement in the South: Hugh Aynesworth, Nicholas Von Hoffman, Nan Robertson, Tony Lewis, Jim Fulghum, Wilson Minor, Jack Nelson, Gene Patterson, Ray Jenkins, Russell Baker, Osborn Elliott, Van Gordon Sauter,

Jim Cannon, Ben Bradlee, Gordon Manning, Vernon Jarrett, Lester Bernstein, Gay Talese, Ed Kosner, Bob Sherrill, Joe Cumming, Dorothy Gilliam, Bill Emerson, Herb Kaplow, Bill Kovach, Richard Valeriani, John Herbers, Hodding Carter, Haynes Johnson, Gene Roberts, A. J. "Jack" Langguth, Dan Rather, Murray Fromson, Earl Caldwell, Ed Guthman, Charles Moore, Ernest Withers, Flip Schulke, Matt Herron, Jim Bellows, Jack Laurence, and John Seigenthaler. I owe a special debt to longtime *Newsweek* writer Peter Goldman, who always distilled my raw civil rights reporting into elegant prose, and to the *New York Times* reporter and my traveling companion in many a dangerous situation, Claude Sitton, who set an example for great reporting and who tried, sometimes successfully, to restrain my wilder side.

My special thanks go also to a few of the many brave warriors of the civil rights movement who helped me and inspired me: John Doar, John Lewis, Vernon Jordan, Julian Bond, James Meredith, James Bevel, Sam Block, Aaron Henry, Bob Moses, Jim Lawson, Bernard LaFayette, Lawrence Guyot, Wyatt Tee Walker, Fred Powledge, Andrew Young, and James Forman.

This book is not intended to be a precise historical catalogue of events. It is, instead, my very personal memory of what happened in my life, colored no doubt in some cases by my own particular way of looking at things. All of the stories in this book and the names of nearly all of the characters in them are real and I have tried to be as factual and accurate as possible. I have, however, changed the names of a few people whose only fault was getting caught up in my life. I have used the words "colored," "Negro," and "black" in this book commensurate with their use at the time written about.

I want to thank a few writers whose fine works on the civil rights movement I used to verify some dates, facts, and figures: Paul Hendrickson, David J. Garrow, Diane McWhorter, Seth

Cagin, and Philip Dray. I also owe a debt to my late childhood friend and fine reporter-editor Charlie Clay, whose novel *The Alien Corn* helped sharpen some of my memories. I also am indebted to my longtime friends and early readers Victoria Brown and Judy Kessler for their help with research and photographs.

I am also grateful to my writer friends at the Sun Valley Writers Conference, and especially to its founder, Reva Tooley, for their inspiration and support.

And of course I am hugely grateful to Peter Osnos, publisher of PublicAffairs, for his vote of confidence in me; to my editor, David Patterson, for his consistent encouragement, diplomacy, and fine skill; and to Robert N. Solomon, for skillfully handling my business matters.

And, going all the way back, my gratitude to my sister, Ethel Gray Little, and my childhood friends Paul Smith, Wade Holmes, Charles Aguirre, Bill Long, Colin Maultsby, Mildred Carney Holt, Donald Styron, Jewell Hayes, and Billy and Peggy Griffin for enhancing and correcting some of my larval memories.

And finally my deep gratitude to my sons, Charles, David, Russell, and Mark, for their love, integrity, and unflagging support during my long effort to finish this book.

Chapter 1

Down in Watts

ON MAY 17, 1966, after I had spent years in the South reporting on the civil rights movement and living with the constant threat of being beaten or killed by white people, I was beaten and almost killed by black people on an angry street in South Central Los Angeles.

An Associated Press photograph of me bleeding and unconscious on the sidewalk ran in newspapers and on television all around the country with the caption: "NEWSMAN BEATEN IN WATTS DISTURBANCE—Police officers bend over Karl Fleming, 38, Los Angeles bureau manager for *Newsweek* magazine, after he was beaten in a flare-up of Negro disturbances in the Watts section of Los Angeles last night. An officer said about 20 Negro youths attacked Fleming...."

This happened at dusk on an acridly hot and smoggy day in

front of a liquor store in the treeless black ghetto known as Watts. Ten days before, a white cop had shot dead an unarmed black man named Leonard Deadwyler, who was speeding his wife to the hospital to have a baby. Deadwyler had tied a white hand-kerchief to his radio antennae, the universal signal in his native Georgia of an emergency, and apparently mistook the pursuing police siren as an escort. Next thing, the cop got him to the curb and ended up shooting him in the chest. On the day I was hurt, there were angry demonstrations in protest but they produced nothing but frustration. At one point a crowd of 600 was driven away from the Seventy-Seventh Street precinct station by cops on the roof leveling rifles at them. The protesters' pent-up rage finally boiled over a little later when one of them kicked in the window of a white-owned liquor store at Eighty-Fourth and San Pedro. Hundreds rushed in, grabbing bottles and smashing every-thing in sight.

I'd been following the demonstrations all day, carrying my .35 mm. Pentax camera—from old habit—and my reporter's note-book. I was across the street when the crowd exploded. I'd learned the hard way that a camera was a lightning rod for trou-ble in these situations, and I had just run back to lock mine in the trunk of my car when it was lights out for me.

I'd had a vaguely ominous feeling all day that something bad—other than a riot—was going to happen. I'd awakened exhausted and on edge with a nauseous hangover after a night of hard drinking (my accustomed way of quieting my nerves) at the Cock N' Bull (Richard Burton, Elizabeth Taylor, and John Carradine hung out there a lot) on the Sunset Strip. Once more, I had driven home on Sunset Boulevard in an alcoholic blackout, thrown up black bile, and passed out on the bath-room tile.

Just before I was attacked there was a brassy, electric feeling in the sour air—as just before a thunderstorm in my native South, or just before other riots I had experienced. I could feel it in my teeth akin to the sensation of biting aluminum foil. But this time there was something very different going on with me.

In my immediately previous years, I'd been in many risky racial situations—including a huge white riot. I'd been threatened, followed, phone-tapped, spied on, hit, and even shot at by whites who hated black attempts to gain equality and hated the few reporters who were writing about their efforts to do so. So there was nothing new to me about being in danger. I was as alert to it as a bird. I was used to around-the-clock tension and in a weird way almost addicted to its adrenaline rush. But I had expectations for a new life when I went out to Los Angeles in early 1965 to be *Newsweek*'s bureau chief.

I had spent part of 1964 in Texas reporting on the trial of Jack Ruby, the man who shot Lee Harvey Oswald (my time there included the dubious distinction of having Oswald's mother spend the night in a Dallas hotel suite I shared with a friend from the *New York Times*), and standing in as the White House reporter for *Newsweek* when LBJ went down for weekends at his ranch on the Pedernalas River near San Antonio. Before that, I'd covered John F. Kennedy's assassination and its aftermath and I'd covered the assassination of the three civil rights workers— Andrew Goodman, James Chaney, and Michael Schwerner—in Philadelphia, Mississippi. From Selma, Alabama, beatings to Birmingham, Alabama, bombings, from Greenwood, Mississippi, threats on my own life to watching cops club children and old people carrying American flags in a march in Jackson, Mississippi, from being shot at in the riot that followed James Meredith's admission to Ole Miss, I'd seen enormous cruelty, brutality, and bloodshed, and I was sick with it all. I slept too little, drank too much, and hovered daily in a jagged state between depression and rage. I was sensitive and cynical, anxious and bellicose all at the same time. I was pretty burned out.

So the move west, aside from being a significant promotion (L.A.'s four-man bureau was *Newsweek*'s largest except for Washington) and a big raise (to $26,000 a year), promised surcease, a chance to calm down and to spend more time with my wife and four young sons. I wouldn't have admitted it—partly because civil rights had been such a big story and I had been such a committed part of it—but the idea that I would be through with violence, certainly at least racial violence, was a big relief. Outwardly, I was still the same crew-cut, 210-pound, cigar-smoking, Jack Daniels–gulping, profane, cynical, take-no-shit-from-nobody, gruff, tough-guy reporter I had learned to be over the years. But I had brought out my wife and four sons and bought a low-slung modern house for $42,000 in the ocean-front suburb of Pacific Palisades, and I had let my accustomed guard down a bit. At least a little of me was ready to lead a less nerve-rattling life.

I felt totally out of place in Los Angeles. To the rest of the country—and to me—it was America Lite, alien to life and reality as I knew it. My serious reporter friends from political and civil rights beats kidded me that all I'd be writing about now was pale health nuts, sun-tanned surfers, oily radio evangelists, right-wing crazies, little old ladies in tennis shoes from Pasadena, and brain-less movie stars. There'd been a time when many writers I admired, Fitzgerald, Hemingway, Faulkner, Dorothy Parker, Robert Benchley, Nathanael West, James M. Cain, and the great Raymond Chandler, had hung their writing hats there. But that was in another, and better, day. Now the great studio heads were dying off and the perfidious agents were rising to power, so that Hollywood at this time, one of my reporter pals told me, was "where all the assholes go for the finals." Tinseltown, it was called. "You get beneath the surface tinsel in Hollywood," Oscar Levant had said, "and you get down to the real tinsel."

Indeed, the early January 1965 day I arrived in Los Angeles I rented a Hertz car at the airport and drove to the Beverly Wilshire Hotel in Beverly Hills, near where the *Newsweek* bureau was situated. As I pulled up to park, the young attendant peeled off a white glove to reveal manicured nails—and he let me know in a minute that he was really a screenwriter. In the hotel lobby as I checked in, gas logs were weakly flickering in a faux fireplace. Next day I drove out Wilshire to Santa Monica and took a walk on the palm-lined palisades overlooking the Pacific, a radiant blue sky hanging over the shimmering ocean, with the alligator snout of Point Dume jutting out north and the etched hills of Palos Verdes to the south. Near the statue of Saint Monica there was a nativity scene in a straw hutch, the baby Jesus cradled by a Mary with vermilion-lacquered nails and rouged cheeks. These impressions confirmed everything negative I had heard about "Los Angeles The Damned," as my journalistic hero H. L. Mencken had described it.

Anyway, whatever Los Angeles represented, my heart was still in my native South, where I had spent most of my tempestuous life, where I felt closely attached to the land, to its buttery moons, its honeysuckle nights and languid days—and to its people, including its black people. Here in Los Angeles I had no feel for or connection to the blacks who lived in the vast flat ghetto off the Harbor Freeway, its hot streets peppered with glowering unemployed young men and equal numbers of garish liquor stores and bereft-looking storefront churches.

Down South, the lives of blacks and whites, despite official segregation, were intimately intertwined due to dependence on each other in their work lives and mutual ties to the land. But though Los Angeles's blacks (or "Negroes," as they were then called) titularly had more "rights," the city was in real senses more segregated than Mississippi. South Central L.A.'s 450,000 black people were spread out over fifty square miles. Its epicenter, the community of Watts, was, despite its rows of neat houses, trimmed lawns, and palm trees, the biggest ghetto in America, and white attitudes toward it were just as blatantly racist as in many places in the South. Watts was as invisible, as remote, and as exotic to white Los Angeles as some country in Africa. Not a single Los Angeles radio or television station or mainstream newspaper had a black person on its staff, not even the giant *Los Angeles Times.* The news from Watts was nil, its only point of interest to the outside world being the so-called Watts Towers, a maze of filigreed spires of scrap iron and broken glass put up by an Italian immigrant.

As part of learning about my new beat, I got the sheriff's department public relations man to drive me around South Central and was stunned when he repeatedly said "nigger" as casually as any redneck counterpart in deepest Mississippi. When I visited the Seventy-Seventh Street police precinct station in the heart of Watts I saw a prominently displayed picture of Eleanor Roosevelt hanging on the wall with the inscription "nigger lover" beneath it. Billy clubs were laughingly known among LAPD cops as "nigger knockers." South Central's big public housing projects had large numbers painted on their separate building roofs—like prison camps I thought—for easy identification by police in helicopters.

Black resentment against the cops, I soon learned, ran deep and wide. Almost without exception, whenever I asked South Central's residents what their gripes were, they immediately started in on the cops. The men complained almost universally of being dragged out of their cars on the slightest pretext, "proned out" on the ground, and otherwise humiliated in front of women and children.

"How do you think it feels to be a father with several kids," one said, "and police stop you on a minor traffic violation. The next thing you know they've got you out of the car with your hands flat on the hood and they're searching you while all your kids are watching?"

Resentment against nonresident merchants ran deep, too—and it carried a heavy strain of anti-Semitism. "They come down here and take our money all day, and then drive home at night to Beverly Hills in their Jew canoes [Cadillacs]," one resident told me.

The police were led by an authoritarian ex-Army officer, Chief William Parker. He was coldly unsympathetic to black complaints. His cops were clean-cut and military trained, unlike the slack-bellied, undisciplined redneck cops I had seen in action all over the South. The L.A. cops rode around behind sunglasses in air-conditioned cars and emerged in their crisp black uniforms only to confront and arrest—like an occupying army in a conquered and hostile country.

One third of South Central blacks were unemployed, and those who worked did so mainly as busboys, dishwashers, janitors, and maids. Only one in ten had a white-collar job. Half of Watts's people were on welfare. A fourth lived below the poverty line. A third came from broken homes. Half were dropouts from school.

Untold numbers were seething with pent-up rage, though this had not been reported at all in the white establishment media. That rage finally ignited on the hot, smoggy evening of August 11, 1965, over an arrest of a black man on a minor traffic violation and an ensuing argument between the arrestee's mother and a cop. Somebody threw a rock at a cop. Others joined in. The violence spread like a wind-fueled California wildfire and quickly became the granddaddy of all urban racial uprisings—the so-called Watts Riots.

The Wednesday that the riot broke out, I was vacationing in Newport Beach, California, in a rented beach house with my wife and sons. I heard on the radio that violence had begun and I was trying to ignore it—having spent so much time away from my family on racial stories in the immediate years before. But then Phil Hager, the No. 2 man in my bureau, telephoned and said this was big and serious and didn't look like it was going to stop. A thousand people were involved. So I knew I had to go, right then. I got out of my bathing suit, quickly dressed, and got into my car. Approaching Watts on the Harbor Freeway North I could see many huge funnels of flame and black smoke rising beside planes gracefully descending through the glide path to the L.A. airport.

I turned off the freeway onto Manchester Avenue and ran into pure bedlam. I could hear the crack of gunfire, burglar alarms clanging, the crash of breaking glass. Police cars, fire trucks, and ambulances were being stoned as they drove into the riot zone. Hundreds of shirtless blacks in "doo rags" over their hair raced through the streets, carrying prizes from white-owned stores that had been looted and set afire. "Burn, baby, burn" and "Kill, kill," they shouted. Shotgun-wielding cops and sheriffs fired at them as they ran. Many markets, shops, and liquor stores were blazing, set afire by blacks hurling Molotov cocktails. Scores of automobiles had been overturned and were on fire. I saw a makeshift sidewalk police command post, parked my car, and walked fast toward it. Suddenly I was confronted by three young black men with blazing eyes.

"The fuck you doing down here, Whitey?" one of them yelled.

"I'm a reporter," I said, flashing my notebook.

"You gonna be a dead muthafuckin' reporter you don't get your honky ass out of here," he said. I retreated quickly toward the cops.

"You'd better stick close," a cop warned me. "They're pulling any white people out of their cars and beating the shit out of them. They beat one guy 'til his eyeball fell out."

By midnight 10,000 people were rampaging in a battle zone ten miles long and five miles wide. It was an orgy of released rage. So many white businesses were burned along a six-block stretch of 103rd Street that it was quickly dubbed "Charcoal Alley." Black businessmen wrote "Blood Brother" and "Soul Brother" on their windows in hopes of being spared. Along one block of Central Avenue every business was burned except the Soul City Record Shop and Marie's Beauty Bowl, both marked to indicate black ownership. A young black man named Ferman Moore, just out of high school and working part-time at the House of Burgers, told me he laughed out loud when he smelled the aroma of hams and spices cooking in grocery stores set ablaze. He said that was after police had ordered him out of his car on the way home from work the night before and hit him with a rifle butt.

"When I woke up next morning, all of Watts was rebelling and everybody was in it," Moore said. "Everything was on fire. The police were shooting at groups of people standing on the streets. I don't know who you are. I don't care who you are. Boom!"

That was Friday morning, by which time 10,000 National Guardsmen had been called in to help beleaguered cops and deputies. They all were taking a lot of sniper fire. One had been killed and two wounded. They set up roadblocks and put a sign at one intersection that said, "Turn Left Or Get Shot."

On Central Avenue I watched cops march a group of mostly old couples and children in pajamas out of a second-floor apartment from which sniper fire had been reported. The cops forced them onto their faces on the pavement and sprayed automatic rifle fire into the building. "What about our rights?" an old man protested.

"You goddamn niggers gave up all your rights this week. One fucking move and I'll kill you," a cop said.

Up the street I asked a young black man pausing with a stolen TV set why he was looting. "You jes take and run," he said. "And when there ain't nuthin' to take, you burn. You burn Whitey, man. You burn his tail so he knows what it's all about."

I had seen scores of black protests in the South. But they were carefully organized and deliberately nonviolent. This was massive, spontaneous, violent revolution, its ragtag soldiers unafraid of the authorities and uninhibited by church influence or the pleadings of their so-called leaders. The rioting went on for five days, near the end of which Martin Luther King Jr. came out to plead for an end to the violence. I had heard him rouse respectful church audiences to march nonviolently to jail many times in the South. He was able to get black people to turn the other cheek to beatings, dogs, and firehoses. But here in Watts I heard him mocked and jeered even before he opened his mouth as he tried to reason with 250 angry blacks in a faded two-story meeting hall in the middle of the riot zone.

"I had a dream. I had a dream," one of the listeners mocked. "Hell, we don't want no damn dreams. We want jobs."

"We must join hands..." King tried to start. Someone shouted, "And burn!" The crowd cheered.

King and other national black leaders tried to meet with pomaded Los Angeles Mayor Sam Yorty but he refused. He said Communists were behind the uprising and added that critics of the cops were part of a "worldwide subversive campaign to stigmatize all police as brutal."

Police Chief Parker was even more intractable. He said the trouble started when "someone threw a rock and others joined in like monkeys in the zoo." Black criminals were the cause, he said, and they just made the cops scapegoats to cover their crimes.

The rampaging went on, day after scalding day. I called home every few hours to reassure my wife and children. I stayed on the streets from dawn to dusk and went to the *Newsweek* office at Wilshire and Western to write at night. I drank coffee, ate sandwiches, and caught naps on my sofa. In all, I and the three reporters helping me filed—over Western Union's "Night Press Rate Collect"—more than 100,000 words to New York on the riots, enough for a book. It became two straight cover stories, with no bylines. Except in the places where we lived, and worked, news magazine reporters were all but anonymous.

When the toll was added up, thirty-four were dead (all but four black), 1,000 wounded, 4,000 arrested, 209 buildings destroyed, and 787 damaged by fire, adding up to $200 million in property damages. "It cost $200 million and thirty-four folks were killed," said one unremorseful black man. "I hope Whitey got the message."

One message was unmistakably clear to me: Whites were not welcome in Watts right then. Not even white reporters. Maybe especially white reporters. We were part of the white establishment, and the establishment was at the center of the problem. Though the federal government moved in with millions of dollars and started programs designed to alleviate problems—and soothe feelings—black anger festered while Los Angeles appointed John McCone, former head of the CIA, to head up a bipartisan investigation of the riot's causes.

So out of touch was white Los Angeles with its black citizens and their gripes, and so stunned were whites by the riots, that fear of a violent black invasion consumed Beverly Hills and the San Fernando Valley, the bastion of middle-class whitedom. Gun sales to Los Angeles whites rose to unprecedented heights. Off-duty cops made a bundle lecturing white groups on self-defense. Construction of security-protected high-rise condominiums along

Wilshire Boulvard, theretofore almost nonexistent, boomed as affluent, panicked citizens sold their homes. High fences went up quickly around private homes, the first "gated" communities were built, and security companies had a field day. The LAPD quickly began building new walled-in precinct stations that looked like military fortresses.

One person keenly interested in all this, and one of my favorite people, was Osborn (Oz) Elliott, the patrician, Harvard-educated editor of *Newsweek*. Despite his upper-crust background, he nurtured a meritocratic atmosphere at *Newsweek* where an extremely gifted group of reporters, writers, and editors could do their best work. He led *Newsweek* to the forefront of reporting on the civil rights movement—which its rival *Time* ignored at first and then reported from a distance and with distinct distaste.

Oz also liked to laugh and drink, and I was just the man for that. He came out after the riots settled down. I took him on a tour of Watts and other places, so he could talk to black leaders and white business leaders and get a better feel for the city. We went out to Palm Springs for a weekend at the Racquet Club and social engagements arranged by *Newsweek*'s stringer. This included a dinner with the songwriter Jimmy Van Heusen, who lived in a house perched on the side of a hill that had a cantilevered swimming pool with an electrically operated cover. We had a dinner, served by a black female cook, of pork chops and sweet potatoes, washed down by many bottles of Dom Perignon. Van Heusen played the piano, sang bawdy songs, and generally reveled in his remote and secure home far away from the black hordes. We arose with hangovers the next day for a lunch with Frederick S. (Fritz) Lowe, the Austrian-born composing half of Lerner and Lowe (*Camelot, My Fair Lady*), who lived as a bachelor in a glassed-in box of a house in Palm Springs. Lowe had been awarded a honorary doctorate from nearby Redlands University, which was displayed on a wall along with many show business photographs. After we'd had several Bloody Marys, his white-jacketed factotum announced, "Lunch is served, Dr. Lowe," and as we sat down, Lowe brandished a silver .357 magnum pistol and launched into a tirade against blacks that ended with him saying, "If they come, I am ready."

California was already changing fast, the culture moving from liberal to conservative. There was widespread fear, confusion, and anger among middle-class whites over what had happened in Watts, over mass student "unrest" at the University of California at Berkeley ("Don't trust anyone over 30" was the student battle cry), over anti-war demonstrations, and over passage in 1963 of a state anti-discrimination "open-housing" law. Suddenly, affable old Irish Governor Pat Brown, under whose leadership California had built the finest education, highway, and water system in the world, seemed too liberal, permissive, and out of it. All this, plus more white resentment, especially in the sprawling white San Fernando Valley in Los Angeles, over "forced busing" of black students to white schools, played into the hands of second-tier actor Ronald Reagan, who had in January 1966 announced he would run against Brown for governor. Reagan had been the host of a television series called *Death Valley Days* and a ranter against "big guv-mint" and high taxes for the show's sponsor, General Electric. Now he went on the attack against student demonstrators and welfare abusers. Most people on welfare, in fact, were white.

The violent black anger that surged up again nine months later when Leonard Deadwyler was shot in Watts played into Reagan's hands as well. As for me, driving down there once more on this hot, smoggy afternoon to cover yet another "incident," a lone white man in a Brooks Brothers suit, white shirt, and repp tie, driving a sedate black Chrysler that *Newsweek* leased for me, made me, to say the least, more than a little tense. For the first time in my life, I was frightened of black people, rattled and apprehensive—feeling as if I had no place to run if there was trouble.

Besides the general hostility toward whites that I knew awaited everywhere, something else had put me on extra edge: I had been fingered as a white intruder in Watts at a rally that morning in Will Rogers Park to protest the shooting of the black man by a cop. The person who fingered me was none other than my old friend—or so I thought—from the South, Stokely Carmichael. He had recently been elected chairman of the Student Nonviolent Coordinating Committee (SNCC) in Atlanta and was in Los Angeles trying to guilt-trip money out of white liberal movie stars.

Carmichael was a fiery speaker with a staccato style, just the man to stoke black anger. I had known him since he came South from Howard University at age nineteen with the Freedom Riders and stayed on to help SNCC try to register black voters in Alabama. I was in the Atlanta bureau of *Newsweek* then and was the magazine's point man on the civil rights beat. SNCC's headquarters were in Atlanta and I often met with Carmichael and other SNCC workers at a black restaurant on Auburn Avenue, where they lobbied me to cover their activities. *Newsweek* and the *New York Times* were the only publications then paying much week-to-week attention to the civil rights movement, so the SNCC kids treated me in a friendly and confiding way though some of them, including Carmichael, tried to make me feel guilty for being a part of the white establishment media and, for that matter, merely for being white. White people had a debt to pay after all they'd done. The black kids were careful and wary though, because both I and my friend Claude Sitton, the Atlanta-based reporter for the *New York Times* and also a white Southerner, were tough-minded reporters who cut them no slack.

I'd worked on four Southern newspapers before going to *Newsweek* and my private sympathies were entirely with the black people. I had from my earliest days seen the humiliation and cruelty visited upon them. I was sometimes sick with shame and anger at what I saw and what I knew was happening out of my sight. I was proud to be a reporter who aspired to the ideal of "common sense, fairness and human decency" articulated by another of my journalistic heroes, the English essayist George Orwell. But I'd been taught by my mentors to be "objective," that is, to report both sides factually and truthfully. There is such a thing as objective truth, and it should be pursued as the ultimate goal of the reporter. Report the facts, and let the chips fall where they may. And I'd run across this from the Associated Press, which was the model of objectivity: "A burro is an ass. A burrow is a hole in the ground. A good reporter should know the difference." I'd learned to be skeptical of all politicians left and right, to not accept their assertions at face value—though many of them were charming rogues you'd like to get drunk with—and I more or less agreed, cynical young man that I was, that Mencken was right when he said that "the only way to look at a politician is down." I liked the idea of being thoroughly independent, idealistic, and an outsider, of having disdain for money, power, and celebrity, and contempt for the people—Sinclair Lewis's Babbitts—who chased those things. Reporters were outsiders, a special breed, poorly paid and proud of it, poorly schooled, usually, but highly educated in the school of hard knocks—hard-drinking, hard-living "ink-stained wretches" on the side of the underdog and the outcast but ruthlessly fair. Most of them wanted to write a novel someday. They looked at newspapering as a calling, not a job. They considered themselves—to the extent they admitted being part of any class at all—members of the working class. They were *reporters*. A *journalist*, said Mencken, was a reporter "with two pairs of pantaloons."

In this spirit, I'd written some things the young civil rights workers whom I admired didn't like. For one thing, I reported factually on the tension between the aggressive black kids whose mentors and heroes were Malcolm X and the African philosopher Franz Fanon, whose fiery *The Wretched of the Earth* was a sort of handbook for black militancy, and the more patient, go-slow, older NAACP-bred "Negroes" like Martin Luther King Jr., whose passive resistance approach came out of the black Baptist church and the teachings of Gandhi. The kids were impatient with religion and the legal gradualism practiced by the NAACP. They contemptuously referred to King as "De Lawd." And the older and more conservative blacks shook their heads disapprovingly and told the kids they were too rash and reckless, that they didn't know much about actually living in fear of white violence—that if you wanted a pie from Mister Charlie you had to get it one slice at a time.

Mainly college students, the young black activists were smart and sophisticated enough to know that national media attention helped their cause, and they were more than aware, based on painful experience, that the visible presence of a *Newsweek* reporter at their church "mass meetings" and their courthouse voter registration marches lessened their chances of being beaten by white mobs and jailed or perhaps killed by redneck cops.

Carmichael himself was long, intense, and skinny, with ebony skin, huge eyes, and tall white teeth. He was usually got up in blue jeans and a white shirt, a slight deviation from the usual SNCC uniform of jeans and blue denim shirts. He was brash and charismatic, so cocky that his friends said he looked like he was strutting even when he was standing still. Despite being jailed more than thirty times in Alabama and Mississippi and beaten up by white cops a lot, he used a Confederate flag as a handkerchief. I admired his guts, if not his judgment. Many blacks in the South had been lynched, castrated, or shot to death for far less.

I had reported on Carmichael in Alabama, where he was an extremely effective organizer and the major force in increasing black voter registration. It was there in early 1964 that, impatient with the gradualism of King and his nonviolent movement and with white volunteers, he formed an all-black voter registration group in Lowndes County and used a black panther as its symbol—the precursor of the Black Panther Party born in 1966.

I had talked to him a lot in early June 1964, when he and hundreds of other volunteer kids, black and white, gathered for a week in Oxford, Ohio, to train for "Mississippi Freedom Summer," the hoped-for final assault on Mississippi, the state that had said "Never." From there I flew down to Jackson, Mississippi, to set up some kind of base camp for the summer with Claude Sitton when a call came that the civil rights workers Chaney, Goodman, and Schwerner (I had accidentally captured Goodman in one of many pictures I had taken in Ohio) were missing after they had visited a rural black church that had been burned out and its congregation beaten by the Klan. The kids were in a station wagon driving back to Meridian—their home base—when they were waylaid by Klansmen with the connivance of the Neshoba County sheriff and his deputy. Months later a paid informant told the FBI what happened: The kids were savagely beaten and then shot to death and buried in an earthen dam. I rented a car and rushed to Philadelphia, Mississippi, when I got the news of their being missing—Claude and I were the first reporters there. Carmichael was one of the dozens of civil rights workers who poured in, along with a lot of national media attracted by the novelty of two northern white kids (Goodman and Schwerner) being killed.

After that Carmichael became more and more bitter and soon

led a move to expel whites (they were mostly Jewish college kids from New York, Chicago, and northern California) from the movement. He had decided to go another way.

In June 1966, Carmichael participated in a Mississippi "Walk Against Fear" led by James Meredith, the black man who integrated Ole Miss in 1962, Meredith was shot, and when the march reached Greenwood Carmichael was arrested—for the twenty-seventh time, At a rally he cried, "We've been saying 'Freedom' for six years. From now on we are going to say 'Black Power!'"

But during all this time and before, I had felt perfectly safe with and around Southern black people—and the militant Northern kids who had put their lives on hold to help them. When they held mass meetings in their churches and sang "We Shall Overcome" and "Which Side Are You On?" I was more than welcome. I always sat in the front row and took notes without any objections arising. I was welcomed into black people's homes to interview them and the civil rights workers who were staying with them. I had joined them in ducking behind sofas in such houses when shots were fired through the front windows by segregationists.

Throughout the early Sixties, there was plenty of reason for white reporters to be afraid. A white reporter from Agence France-Presse was shot in the back and killed during the riot that greeted Meredith's entry into Ole Miss. (It required the force of U.S. marshals and the U.S. Army to get Meredith onto the campus and into a dormitory room.) I myself was tear-gassed and had four bullets stitched in a white wood column six inches from my head that night as I watched the Ole Miss riot from the entrance of the administration building.

Later in 1962 I had been threatened with hanging during a voter registration march in Greenwood, Mississippi. In 1963 I'd had a shotgun shoved into my belly by the head of the Alabama Highway Patrol in Birmingham. On several occasions I'd been followed on lonely rides at night by rednecks in pickups with whiplash antennas and rifles on racks behind the seat. I'd had my typewritten stories sabotaged at local Western Union offices (some were in the backs of drug stores) when I transmitted them "Night Press Rate Collect" to New York. I'd had voices come on my motel phone when I was talking to the home office in New York and call me a son-of-a-bitch nigger-lover. A friend from *Time*, Sim Fentress, was thrown through a plate glass window in McComb, Mississippi. Another friend, Wilson Minor, *Newsweek*'s Mississippi-born "stringer," or part-time contributor, a mild-mannered Jackson-based reporter for the New Orleans *Times-Picayune*, had been threatened by the Klan and had crosses burned on his lawn. Through all this, though, I often reminded myself that the people in constant and more serious danger were the local blacks who dared to speak up, for they had to live there all the time, and the young "outside agitator" civil rights workers who constantly faced jail, beatings, and death. Reporters were not the heroes. We could leave. I could go home to Atlanta for weekends, sometimes after filing my stories Thursday night. But the black people had to live there, all the time.

The hard-nosed and audaciously violent "segs" who made and carried out these threats against reporters were well-organized, mainly through a well-funded band called the White Citizens Council. They knew the identities and whereabouts of every outside reporter who came into the segregated states. They branded me and the few other reporters regularly on this dangerous beat as members of the "nigger-loving Yankee Jew-Communist press." To be an alien reporter in the remote towns of Mississippi, Alabama, and Louisiana where the young black "outside agitators" were causing trouble was to be almost totally isolated behind enemy lines, linked to the outside world only by a long distance line that I always assumed was tapped. My nerves were constantly on edge. I drank a lot of Maalox and a lot more bourbon. That I had grown up in segregated North Carolina and had a redneck crewcut and deep Southern accent made it even worse. Not only was I a troublemaker, I was traitor as well, for my reporting, objective though it might be, was perceived as betraying "our Southern way of life," which was of course just a romanticized euphemism for segregation.

To blacks in the South, I was one of the good guys, someone to trust and shelter. To blacks in Watts, I was just another faceless exploitive whitey, someone to hate, and hurt. This reversal was a bitter shock, and unnerving, too. And it was much on my mind the first time I saw Stokely Carmichael out of the South.

On a morning eight months after the first big riots of 1965, Carmichael mounted a concrete bench and exhorted a crowd of 300 blacks in Will Rogers Park to go downtown to City Hall and demand that the cop who had shot Leonard Deadwyler be arrested and charged with murder—an audacious statement even in Los Angeles. That failing, he said, blacks would exact an eye for an eye. Then he spotted me at the back of the crowd.

"And we need to stop these honky reporters from coming down here and exploiting us," he cried and pointed at me. "They never show up except when they have a chance to make black people look bad. Where were they all these years when the cops have been intimidating, beating, and murdering our people? Where were they when we needed jobs and better education? Where were they when these white merchants were down here exploiting our blood brothers and driving home to Beverly Hills in their Cadillacs? These honky reporters make money off of our troubles, and then they go away. I'll tell you what, these white reporters ought to have to pay us money to come down here and write up what we are doing and saying."

Maybe he was being flippant. Maybe he thought this was

funny, a private joke between him and me. He had a taunting sense of humor. I knew that. But if he was teasing me, I was not enjoying the ribbing. Angry faces turned and glared at me. Mine was the only white face around. I could hear some of them muttering "honky muthafuckah"—the same menacing words I had heard in Watts the previous summer when I was subjected to black anger for the first time.

I prepared to get myself out of there, quick, but luckily Carmichael redirected his fulminations to the cops and urged the crowd to march immediately to the Seventy-Seventh Street police precinct station twenty blocks away. I followed at a safe distance. When the marchers arrived the cops had barricaded themselves inside with doors locked, blinds drawn, and guns on the roof. Nobody would come out to address the blacks' demands. After an hour of yelling at the silent police building, somebody suggested the marchers carry their protest to a building on Eighty-Fourth Street near Manchester that housed several civil rights organizations—the Urban League, the NAACP, SNCC, and CORE. There they might regroup and find a new direction. But that building turned out to be closed for the day and suddenly there was no place else to go—no place for the anger to be discharged and satisfied. And that was when the rock went through the window of the liquor store and the crowd erupted and I was coming back down the street after putting my camera in the trunk when I lost consciousness.

"He ain't dead," somebody said.

"Muthafuckin' honky, fuck him," somebody else said.

"Busted that muthafuckah's head wide open," somebody said.

I heard these voices faintly, as from behind a wall. There was a strange humming in my head and no feeling in my body. Slowly through a clearing haze I saw angry black faces staring down at me. And then I realized it was me they were talking about. As my head cleared a little more I could see I was splayed out on my right side on the sidewalk, my right arm straight out above me. Beyond my hand on the dirty pavement I could see my reporter's notebook and beyond that a small rivulet of blood—my blood— and a five-foot length of dirty four-by-four. There was blood on my white shirt, on my repp tie, and down the sleeve of my striped Brooks Brothers suit. One of my shell cordovan shoes was off beside my right foot.

A skinny black man in a baggy blue security uniform bent over me. "The ambulance is on the way. Don't try to move," he said. Everybody else had become very quiet, looking down at me, this alien white face.

A cold surge of fear and anger suddenly swept over me. I was dying, I thought. And for what? Perhaps the God I didn't believe in, who I was contemptuous of, the alleged omnipotent puppeteer who had figured so large in my life, was playing another one of his cruel cosmic jokes. I had imagined my death before, romanticized it even—shot down in Mississippi or Alabama in a bad moment or maybe hauled out of my motel room in the night by the Klan or killed face to face with some violent white mob. And wondering in these musings—realistic as they were—how I would behave when the moment came, hoping I would be brave and defiant, like Horatio at the bridge, and certainly with a sense of pride for being on the right side of a noble cause—something in fact worth dying for.

The joke was that I was dying instead in ridiculous ignominy, like another of my adolescent heroes, Cyrano de Bergerac, felled not in glorious battle but hit over the head by a stick of wood, his tossed from a second-story window, mine wielded from behind by some nobody who didn't know who I was and what I had stood for and fought for and couldn't have cared less. And not sur-

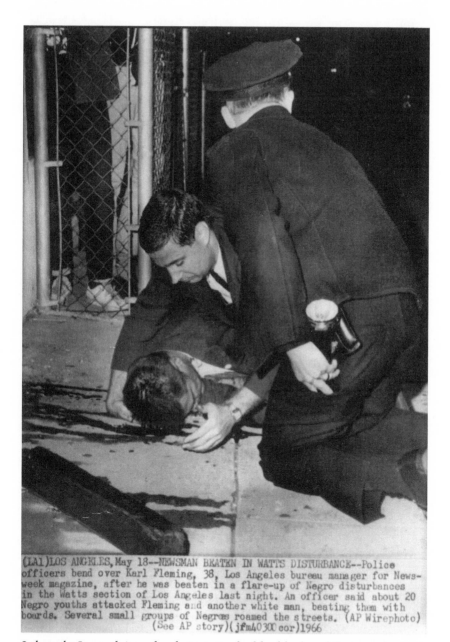

I thought I was dying after being attacked by blacks while reporting on the 1966 Watts riots in Los Angeles.

rounded by the colleagues I had worked with, laughed with, cursed with, drank with, and admired, but totally alone and thousands of miles removed from my roots and my past. My sons would be home now with my wife, playing in the streets or in the canyon a block from our house. Suddenly I missed them with an intense ache. I felt cold and alone. I thought of the Camus line at the end of *The Stranger* about facing death and surrendering to "the vast indifference of the universe."

Only I was not surrendering. I was scared for sure but defiant and angry though not certain who or what to be angry at as the ambulance came and I was loaded into it. I was still dazed as the siren wailed and I was carried to Daniel Freeman Hospital, onto a gurney, and into the emergency room. Then I was out again. I awoke next morning in a hospital bed, sore all over and with a crushing headache. A surgeon came and told me I had a serious skull fracture, that both my upper and lower jaws were broken, and that I had multiple deep bruises from being kicked. He showed me several inch-long slivers of wood he had picked out of my skull and said I was lucky to be alive.

"Well, thank God they hit me in the part of my body where I am least vulnerable, my hard head," I said.

He laughed and said "Yeah, you'd have to have a hard head to be in that part of town yesterday. I saw your picture in the paper this morning."

There were many requests from the media to see me. There was black-on-black violence in Watts and all across the country every day, and violence against blacks by whites and by white cops, all largely ignored by the media, but a white reporter being attacked was big news.

This was confusing. I knew I should be angry at the people who attacked and beat me. But how could I, this disparity of my special attention being so unearned? Thus when the media came into my room that afternoon I gave them what I was sure they were not expecting.

How did I feel?, they asked.

"It's been a feast of chuckles all day," I said.

And what did I think of the people who had attacked me?

"If I was a young black man growing up on the streets of Watts, seeing what they had seen and going through what I know what they went through to survive, I might feel like hitting some white guy in the head, too," I said.

But in fact I was more than a little uncertain about why I did not feel more anger at my attackers. Others questioned my posture, too, including a right-wing columnist for the *Los Angeles Times* who branded me a reverse racist.

Was he right? For sure I had in the past experienced no trouble being angry at whites for what they did to blacks—and had said so privately many times, though I was careful to be meticulously objective and balanced in my reporting.

I had puked in shame and rage after seeing big-bellied white cops snatch American flags from children's hands and club their parents as they marched in their Sunday best, in Jackson, Mississippi, to protest Medgar Evers's assassination.

I had been sickened as I watched Public Safety Comissioner Bull Connor of Birmingham, Alabama, loose dogs and fire hoses on children and mothers who were peacefully marching across a public park to seek desegregated lunch counters and fairness in hiring and voting.

I had felt nauseous anger when I picked out of dusty debris a Sunday school program with the face of Jesus crayoned black the afternoon of the day the Klan bombed the Sixteenth Street Baptist Church in Birmingham and killed four little girls.

I had watched in shame one summer afternoon as a young black Student Nonviolent Coordinating Committee volunteer named

Lawrence Guillot took off his denim shirt in a Mississippi country churchyard to reveal a bloodied and bruised back that he'd gotten from cops who'd beaten him in a jail cell for not saying "Sir."

I had turned my head in revulsion as Sheriff Jim Clark and his "mounted posse" in Selma, Alabama, clubbed and kicked those who came from a church rally to the courthouse to register to vote.

I understood the poor white rejects who did all these savage things—the ones so eaten up by hopelessness and impotence that they violently insisted that virile young black men ("bucks," they called them) bow before the term "boy." These rednecks (a literal description of the sun-reddened necks that white tenant farmers got from bending behind mule-drawn plows) were, after all, the sanctioned, indeed encouraged, licensees of the Southern white power structure. They were selected, appointed, applauded. But I was disgusted by what they did, especially those who hid behind badges, guns, clubs—and the pulpit.

It was harder to feel angry at the young black men of Watts who had attacked me and rebelled so terribly against the world in which they felt trapped. They had grown up walled off from the rest of the world in their freeway-encircled ghetto, without fathers, without education, without jobs or hope. Most of them, I strongly suspected, had never had human contact with a white person, and if they had, it had likely been with a white cop bent on showing them who was boss. In hitting me, I knew, they had attacked a symbol and not a person. Therefore, how could I take it personally? So went my thinking as wellwishers, friends, and colleagues came to visit. Among them was Frederick S. (Fritz) Beebe, the publisher of *Newsweek*, who flew out to express the magazine's care and concern. He engaged a limousine to bring my wife to the hospital every day, handed me a check for $2,000, and told me to take my family on vacation when I got out, to stay gone as long as I wanted and send for more money if I needed it.

Cards and letters came in from all over the country, from old friends and reporter colleagues, a governor and a Communist leader, a couple of U.S. senators, and black soldiers in the civil rights movement, all of whom I'd written about. In its next issue, *Newsweek* unprecedentedly devoted its entire "Top of the Week" page to my incident, saying, "That he was beaten by Negroes in the streets of Watts was a cruel irony. Fleming had covered the landmark battles of the Negro revolt from Albany, Ga., to Oxford, Miss., to Birmingham, Ala., and numberless way stations whose names are now all but forgotten. He ducked bullets and brickbats, whiffed tear gas, brazened out threats on his life—and never was seriously injured. And, a North Carolinian by birth, he reported the black man's march down Freedom Road with insight and compassion. No journalist was more closely tuned into the Movement; once when a *Newsweek* Washington correspondent asked the Justice Department to name some Dixie hot spots, the Justice man replied, 'Ask Fleming. That's what we do.' And none did more to bring the story of the Negro revolt to the public in such vivid, thorough detail."

I choked back tears when I read that, as it occurred to me that this was the first time I had cried since I was a small child. I had not known, or had not let myself know, that anyone cared that much for me. I had pushed myself up through hard Southern soil and along the way I learned early to take care of myself, to depend on nothing and nobody. I had run too hard to stop and cry. And anyway, real men didn't cry, and I was a tough guy who prided himself on being so. But the blow to my head had jarred loose my carefully developed tough-guy carapace and exposed a little of the more tender part of me. I had no idea what to make of that.

I did, at least, understand that my answer about how I felt regarding the black people who tried to kill me was odd, especially given where I had come from. After all, I was a poor white kid who came up in the completely segregated rural South, where whites and blacks picked cotton and cured tobacco together, but drank from separate water buckets and went their own ways at quitting time. Everybody around me had casually used the word "nigger," told "nigger" jokes, thought of black people as slightly less than human—tamed animals, or children, really—and treated them accordingly. That blacks and whites would in any way "mix," even at water fountains or bus stations, or that they were in any sense "equal," was literally unthinkable. So by all genetic and social rights I should have been a stereotypical Southern cracker and should perhaps have been out burning crosses at night and not looking for the nearest Western Union.

But I had felt different, as far back as I could remember, like an outsider and an underdog. So I identified with black people, even before I was old enough to understand that I was doing so, even when I barely knew that blacks were in my world. I was very young when I first had these feelings, perhaps no more than five years old. And as I lay there at thirty-eight years old in that Los Angeles hospital, looking at my life's beginning—like peering down the long reverse end of a telescope—I realized that my always-present anger, an anger that often boiled over into hatred, which I had thought was purely about racism, was really about another issue of which racism was just one manifestation: the strong who held down and tormented the powerless. I hated bullies. That's what it was. Perhaps I had an instinctive sense of fair play, but it was bullying that I had recoiled at and rebelled against. And I could remember with painful detail the exact day those feelings were born.

Chapter 2

Handsome Little Man

ON THE UPPER INSIDE of my left ankle is a faint scar, almost invisible now after so many years, a tic-tac-toe pattern of tiny lines with puncture marks at the intersections.

This scar is the faded evidence of a blood transfusion I had when I was four months old. That was right after my mother hurried me to the county hospital with a high fever. I was so sick the doctor told my mother, "You better send for this baby's father right now."

My father was an insurance salesman and he was off crisscrossing the dusty dirt roads of the Carolina lowlands in his Model A trying to sell life insurance policies to farmers. This was in 1927. The Great Depression had come early to the South, and nobody had any money.

So she sent him a telegram at the Florence, South Carolina,

hotel where he was staying. When he arrived at the county hospital, which was in the little farm town of Whiteville, North Carolina, near the coast, sixty miles from Florence, the doctor came out to the waiting room and said, "This baby needs a blood transfusion or he is going to die."

"Well, I can't do it," my mother told me my father said.

"There was this Eye-talian man sitting there," my mother said, "and he said, 'I'll give this baby some blood' and Fleming [which was what she called my father] said, 'We don't want any of your goddamned Wop blood.'"

"So I told the doctor, 'I'll do it. I'll give my baby all the blood he needs,'" my mother said.

"Mizris Fleming, you can't do it. You're so weak and run down you ought to be in the hospital yourself," the doctor said.

"Well, I don't care. He is my baby and I am GOING to do it," she said.

So, she said, they laid us out on adjoining beds and made the surgical cuts—from whence came my scar—so as to attach rubber tubes between us through which they pumped her blood into me. And she said that right away I began to get better. What exactly was wrong I was never to know, because my mother could not or would not tell me—as she could not or would not explain the large scar on the bottom of my scrotum that I found when I got old enough to begin to investigate my body. (To this day I do not know what caused this particular scar.)

Within weeks of the blood transfusion, when I was six months old, my father died. He was fifty-four. He had a heart attack in a Florence hotel room where he was staying and where he was, according to my mother, on another bender with another insurance agent.

It was a warm late winter day and my mother was sunning me on the front porch of the rooming house (a private house with rooms to let) where we were staying when a Western Union messenger walked up with the bad news about my father. And it was at that very moment, my mother said, that I laughed out loud for the very first time.

It would be many years before I began to perceive the dark implications of her stories about my father and to begin to doubt her credibility as a witness to our impecunious and unhappy past.

My father was twice as old as my mother when they met and had four grown children from a previous marriage. His first wife had died, from what my mother could not say. He had begun courting my mother, Nettie Lewis, after following his insurance route to the family house "out in the country" from Whiteville, North Carolina, where she was living with her parents. Her father, son of a Civil War veteran who was fading away in an old folks home across the nearby swamp, managed a sandy vegetable farm for a rich widow lady. Its main crops were cucumbers, watermelons, cantaloupes, and corn.

Their house, on a dusty dirt road far removed from any neighbors, was of unpainted pine wood. It perched on stump stilts, with chickens running underneath and doodlebug holes in the dirt. There was a swing on the front porch but no screens on the doors or windows, and of course no electricity or running water. There was a well in back with a bucket that was let down on a chain and pulley. The water had a metallic taste and it turned teeth rusty. There was an outhouse, a henhouse up on pine posts, a small barn and a shed for the two mules and the plows, and a yard devoid of grass but decorated with two old tires out front with geraniums planted in them.

After the breakup of her only real romance, my mother had moved back in and was helping with the cooking, laundry, and other housekeeping chores. She had four older brothers and a sister, but they had moved away to non-farming jobs. Her youngest brother had gone on and joined the Army, which was what many men did back then to escape the drudgery and poverty of tenant life. She herself had left home to clerk at a drugstore in Whiteville, was living in a rooming house, and was seriously "going steady" with a handsome World War I veteran named Lance Clemens. There was an unspoken expectation that they would get married. But one day she saw him walking along the railroad tracks with a girl who had a reputation of being "fast," and when he arrived Saturday night to take her to the dance at a tobacco warehouse, she told him it was over. "That was the end of him," she said.

It was soon after this that my father started coming around. My mother had deep-set brown eyes, delicate skin, high cheek-bones, and a good chin. She was tall and slender, awkward-gaited, spoke in a guileless soft and cracked voice, and must have exuded an air of pliant innocence, although I would come to realize that this appearance was deceiving.

He was gray-haired and wore glasses, dressed in suits, and had a gold pocket watch and a fob in his vest even on weekdays out in the country among the farmers. And he had a car, a Model A Ford, in a time and a place where the common conveyance was a mule-drawn wagon.

His main attraction, though, and the final reason my mother said she succumbed to his importuning and married him, was that he promised her he would help her finish school. She had had to quit in the third grade, she said, because her parents were too poor to buy the few textbooks required.

That promise, she said, was not kept. Instead my father wanted her with him constantly and would drive her around on his insurance route along the sandy roads. Sometimes he accepted chickens and hams and mason jars of preserved vegetables and jellies in lieu of the cash premiums—even fifty cents or a dollar

The only picture I ever had of my father, probably taken in 1926, the year he died and the year before I was born.

that the farmers did not have—hoping to recoup the money owed to the insurance company some other way. On Saturday nights, if there was any money, they would go dancing at Moose clubs and roadside supper clubs.

At some point he had owned a house, in Greenville, North Carolina, the coastal plains tobacco town where he had grown up and raised his first family. His father had been a substantial farmer who died of food poisoning, trichinosis, after partaking of a tin tub of free pork barbecue set out by a tobacco-buying ware-house to attract farmers and their cured crops.

What happened to the Greenville house I never found out. My mother was secretive and incurious about both her own past and my father, except for details of our history that embellished the image she had of herself as self-sacrificing and unfortunate. I knew of only one photograph of him, a Kodak box camera shot which I still have, in which he is standing in a suit wearing glasses and a snap-brimmed hat beside a picket fence in front of a wooden house—what house I never knew. My mother said all of their other mementos burned up in a fire—what fire I could not get out of her.

Her reluctantly imparted memories of him were almost com-pletely negative—mainly about how he had let her down in many ways. At some point after they were married—after he'd reneged on helping her continue her education—she said she told him she wanted to have a baby. He responded that he already had a bunch of children and didn't want any more, especially what with times being so tough.

"So what happened after he said he didn't want to have a baby?" I once asked her.

"I got pregnant," she said. I never challenged her as to whether this—my being conceived and born—was accidental or deliberate on her part. In any case she made it very plain that my father had not wanted me. Whether this was resistance to the burden of more children when he must have already been beaten down by hard times, whether his drinking had become truly serious, or whether he had soured on the marriage to my stiff and stubborn mother I never knew.

She and my father lived in a series of boarding houses until he died. She told me she did not attend his funeral, as she "didn't know any of his people." And this insurance salesman died, she said, leaving not a cent of insurance money. To survive she tried selling dishes and Bibles door to door but was dismally unsuccessful. She was becoming more and more desperate when my father's best friend, another insurance salesman named McDuff Laughinghouse, who was the same age as my father, began nagging her to marry him.

Finally, with nowhere else to turn and with no idea how to take care of me, she said, she relented and married Laughinghouse, three months after my father's death. We then moved into an apartment near the train station in Fayetteville, North Carolina, atop a neighborhood grocery store with a Nabisco sign over the door.

This was the locus of my earliest scattered memories—and of the last happy one with my mother for many years. One sultry summer night, with fireflies winking and train whistles moaning far away, she took me to an exhortatory revival meeting in a big tent beside the railroad tracks. There were wooden chairs set up in rows on the grass under the canvas and a wooden pulpit in front. People fanned themselves and mopped their faces with handkerchiefs in the stifling heat. My mother had taken a dime out of her powder-smelling purse and put it in the collection basket, the sweating preacher had said his last amen, and we were walking away to the receding strains of "Nearer My God To Thee," with the yeasty smell of baking bread in the air. She was wearing a white hat and a polka-dot summer frock, carrying her black purse and a Bible, and she took my hand and smiled at me as we walked along. I felt warm and safe in that moment. It seemed like we were going to be all right.

Fayetteville was a small mercantile town, completely segregated, of course, as was the entire South, with an old brick slave market in its center and the Fort Bragg army base on its outskirts. Its annual Fourth of July celebration featured a contest in which a watermelon would be placed on the cobblestones under the four arches of the slave market, and "colored" contestants would futilely—amid wild laughter at their flopping, overall-clad bodies—try to run a gauntlet of high-pressure firehoses to retrieve the melon for a five-dollar cash prize. Something about this made me uncomfortable. Why didn't they have white men chasing watermelons?

My stepfather had thick gray hair, a permanent stubble on a glowering face, and an explosive dislike of me. By the time of my early memories he was beginning to decline in health, with Bright's disease—which affected his kidney functions—and was at home a lot instead of out selling insurance. When my mother was away from the apartment, he chased after me with his leather razor strop and beat me when he could catch me. This was not often, because I was nimble and I quickly learned to scamper out of his reach and take refuge under the oilcloth-covered kitchen table.

He called me "The Little Prince" and "Mama's spoiled little sissy boy." She called me "my handsome little man," and it must have been obvious that she cared more for me than for him.

One evening when I was four years old, my mother cooked for supper, along with cornbread and some other vegetables, "a mess" of collard greens, seasoned—as was the Southern custom, which was born more of necessity than of taste—by a big chunk of pork fat. This was called fatback, or "Hoover ham." This was the only meat served at most of our meals (except for the rare fried chicken) and I didn't like it. In fact I was repulsed by its greasy and rubbery texture.

My stepfather served me a big chunk of this meat with the collards. I leaned my left arm forward on the table to block his view of me and proceeded carefully to eat around this nauseous wedge of fat, hoping he wouldn't notice. But no such luck.

"I guess The Little Prince is too good to eat what the rest of us eat," he snarled at me. "I apologize. We should have got you a porterhouse steak with onions."

I didn't say anything. My mother sat with her head silently bowed as he launched into a tirade about what a spoiled brat I was and how, by God, I was going to eat that piece of fatback if it was the last thing I ever did.

"Put it in your mouth! Chew it up and swallow it, " he yelled, slamming his fork down.

I put it in my mouth. It was fat and slippery and disgusting. I tried chewing, through tears, but the nausea rose and I ran from the table into the bathroom and vomited. My mother didn't say anything.

After that I stayed out of the house as much as I could. There was a gravel apron in back of the apartments and a chinaberry tree that I climbed and daydreamed in and watched the robins and woodpeckers flit in and out of the branches. I played alone. I had no friends and didn't know how to make any. A group of rowdy boys, older than me, played together nearby but ignored me until one day they called me over and led me into a garage behind the apartment. They formed a circle around me and one of them unbuttoned his pants and pulled out his dick as two others grabbed me and forced me to my knees in front of him.

"Suck it! Suck it!" they all shouted, as the two forced my head down. I didn't know what to do. I wanted them to like me. I was frightened and uncertain, so I put it in my mouth. There was a salty, fishy taste and I ran away silently and ashamed as they jeered, "Dick sucker, dick sucker."

"What's wrong, son," my mother asked when I ran inside.

"Nothing," I said, and went in the bathroom and closed the door and brushed my teeth with the salt and baking soda we used as toothpaste and sat on the toilet silently crying.

Soon after that my stepfather got more ill and couldn't work at all, so we moved 100 miles east into a three-room shack owned by his family on Mauls Swamp, "out in the country" near the tiny village of Vanceboro, North Carolina, near the Carolina coast. His father and mother lived up the dirt road a quarter-mile away in the main family house—"the Laughinghouse place." Two brothers lived nearby in houses they had built—one of them the first brick house for miles around—on the 500 acres that comprised the farm property.

The house we moved into was one of those crude old lodgings of unpainted plain pine wood with a tin roof called a "shotgun shack," meaning you could fire a gun through the front door and the charge would go out the back without hitting anything. Many years before it had been the main family house. By the time we got there the Laughinghouse farmers were using it as a packing shed for tobacco between the time it was harvested and cured and graded and taken to market. The house sat back fifty feet from the road on a rain-pocked dirt plot. It had no electricity, plumbing, or running water, merely a potbellied wood stove in the middle room for heating, a wood range in the kitchen for cooking, and a rusty hand-cranked pump on a little side porch outside the kitchen door. When we moved in the family let us borrow a used bed, a cot, a rocking chair, a wooden kitchen table and three chairs, and a few kerosene oil lamps. They also put up for us a fenced-in chicken house and a one-hole outhouse stocked with a wooden tub of corn cobs.

My mother and stepfather slept in the middle room with the stove and I slept in the front room on the cot. At night in winter my mother would heat a brick on the stove and put it under a homemade patchwork quilt at the foot of the bed. My mother and some of the ladies from the Methodist church had made the quilt from feed sacks and cotton stuffing grown on the Laughing-house farm and with covering patches from feed-sacks.

On summer evenings my mother would sit on the side porch and shell beans or shuck corn while I played alone in the yard. The only book we owned was my mother's worn illustrated Bible, and the only printed material that ever arrived was the Sears, Roebuck catalog that came each fall, full of toys and things I had never seen. I marveled at but did not dare hope to get for Christmas the Genuine Top Grain Leather Holster With Decorated Belt And Two 8-Inch Clicker Type Steel Guns priced at 79 cents, the Speed King Racing Car for 59 cents, the Colored Humming Top for 10 cents, the Airplane Kit Complete With Balsam Wood, Glue, Rubber Bands, Insignia, Paper, and Instructions, "Designed By A Leading Authority," for 89 cents, the Famous Hurst Gyro-scope Top for 19 cents, the Marx Climbing Tractor for 89 cents, the Acrobatic Monkey for 25 cents, or the 50 Genuine Akro Agates for 29 cents. The Lowest Priced Reversible Electric Train Sets On The Market for $4.29, the Electric Lighted Speed Boat for $1.39, the Smart Looking Tubular Tricycle for $3.59, the Roller Bearing Scooter for $1.98, and the Streak-O-Lite Wagon for $4.79 were simply beyond the dreaming of. There was no money for presents or a celebration of Christmas except for Sunday school and church services devoted to telling the story of the three wise men following the star and Mary and Joseph and the baby Jesus born in the manger.

Each Sears catalogue, from which nothing was ordered, finally was consigned to the malodorous and fly-infested outhouse as temporary and luxurious replacement for the corncobs.

We had no neighbors, so I continued to spend my days alone, doing my chores or daydreaming in the woods behind our house, in the summer picking wild huckleberries and blackberries and wildflowers for my mother.

My half-sister, Ethel Gray Laughinghouse, was born August 29, 1931, in the Mauls Swamp house where her father—my tormentor of a stepfather—was becoming sicker day by day. Soon he was totally bedridden. I was not unhappy at this development, because it meant he was no longer a threat to me. My mother told me that I was now the man of the house, her "handsome little man." His worsening Bright's disease prevented his passing urine, and his stomach would swell enormously until the doctor came weekly and punched a stainless steel catheter into his belly and drained the accumulated liquid into a porcelain slop jar. Certain duties had come with being the new man of the house. And one of them was that I had to carry, bumping, struggling, and spilling, the noxious pail of piss out to the outhouse and empty it down the hole. Every now and then I helped my mother get him off the bed and into a chair, and then held up one side of the mattress and then the other while she struck matches and burned the fat bedbugs that clung to its undersides and the springs.

My days and my mother's and sister's started just after the rooster crowed. I dressed hurriedly and went out on the porch to prime the pump while my mother lit a fire in the kitchen from the pine wood I had cut and lugged in. In the winter the pump's rusty throat was frozen and there was always a tongue of ice hanging from its spout. I would melt the ice with a pitcher of hot water that my mother had heated on the stove. Then as the day went on I fed the chickens, gathered the still-warm eggs, cut kindling from pine hearts, and dug sweet potatoes out of the cone-shaped, pine-covered potato hill that my stepfather's brothers had prepared and stocked. I helped my mother build a fire under the big outdoor cast-iron kettle—loaned by the Laughinghouses—to boil and wash our clothes, punching them with a long wooden stick, and helped her hang them on the line to dry. In the afternoon I chopped and pulled weeds in the vegetable garden. Every evening I walked the lonesome quarter mile up the sandy road, with the crickets chirping and the frogs croaking in the ditches and a moldy smell of rotting grass in the air, to the Laughinghouse place to lug back a bucket of "sweet" milk, and occasionally buttermilk—"clabber" it was called—into which we broke up cornbread and ate with a spoon, or which my mother used to make biscuits.

We had no money at all. Nobody had much. The farmers in that part of the South were all but self-sufficient, buying only sugar, flour, tea, fertilizer, and farm equipment. None of them was affluent enough to hire tenants, so there were few black people around, and none that I saw. My stepfather's parents supplied us with fatback, lard, ham, and sausage from their smokehouse, canned vegetables and fruits, preserves and jellies, and burlap bags of shelled corn with which I fed the chickens.

The elder Laughinghouses had a Ford pickup truck and every Sunday morning they picked us up and drove us, crouched in the back, to the crossroads tin-topped unpainted wooden Epworth Methodist Church. I sat with my mother on the plain pine benches and listened to the sweating preacher warn us over and over against the devil's many cunning traps there to lure us into sin on this earth and thus condemn us to eternal damnation in the next. Earthly existence was a passage full of toil and tears, but a better life awaited us in the hereafter if we would confess our sins, repent of them, and walk in the footsteps of the Redeeming Jesus.

There was an old upright piano in the left corner beside the rude pulpit, a small choir, and a chalk board with the title of the sermon and the names and page number of songs to be sung that day from the musty Cokesbury Hymnals that sat in racks on the backs of the pews. Often at the end of a fearsome sermon the choir would sing "Softly and Tenderly," as the minister called for all the unsaved sinners among us to come to the crude altar, kneel and be saved and blessed in the name of Jay-suss Christ.

> *Softly and tenderly Jesus is calling.*
> *Calling for you and for me.*
> *Patiently Jesus is waiting and watching.*
> *Watching for you and for me.*
> *Come home. Come home. Ye who are weary come home.*
> *Earnestly, tenderly Jesus is calling.*
> *Calling, O sinner, come home.*

One September morning soon after I turned six years old my mother and I stood by the road waiting for the school bus to take me to my first day of school. I was barefoot and wearing a pair of patched overalls and a faded cotton shirt. She said I was now going out among people who had a lot more than we did. And some of those people might make fun of me. But even though my clothes had patches in them, they were clean. There was no reason to be ashamed of being poor. We might be poor, but we weren't trash. Times were bad and a lot of good people were poor. We could be proud of who we were. She didn't have anything to give me. All she could do was try to be the best example she could and not do anything herself that she wouldn't want me to do. "Just always remember that what you have in your heart is more important than what you have in the bank," she said. She made it sound as if there was something almost noble about being poor.

I sat silent and alone on the bus. When we got to school and my first class began, I was overwhelmed by uncontrollable diarrhea, no doubt from extreme anxiety. The teacher sent me to the bathroom to clean up. I waited on the schoolyard in solitary shame until classes were over and sat alone in the back of the bus as other children looked at me and whispered and giggled behind their hands. I didn't make any friends at school. Because of what had happened in that garage in Fayetteville, I was afraid of other boys and fearful of being laughed at.

Often feeling fear, rarely feeling joy, I continued to be a serious child, just going through the days trying to be the good little man that my mother urged me to be. But I was mysteriously affected by the church sermons and especially the songs about the gentle Jesus who nestled in his arms the little children who came unto him, who healed the sick and raised the dead, who forgave everyone, even those who crucified him on the cross, who multiplied the fishes and loaves to feed the multitude. I was confused, though, because God, the Father of Jesus, the God of the Old Testament, the omnipotent king of kings who was in charge of the heaven we could go to if we were good, was harsh and quick to visit horrifying punishments upon those who defied his stern directives. I could feel the preacher's burning eyes on me as he warned that the day of awful judgment was soon at hand, when the sun would turn black, the moon would turn to blood, the stars would fall from heaven, burning mountains would be cast into the sea, and mighty men would cower in caves, "for the great day of His wrath is come." God's avenging angels would wreak hail and fire mingled with blood upon the earth, trees, and all green grass burnt up, vast numbers of people and creatures perishing as the angels cried out, "Woe, woe, woe to the inhabitants of the earth."

I was further frightened and perplexed by the contradiction

between the vengeful, mean-spirited Father and his forgiving Son as shown in my mother's Bible. The New Testament had reassuring pictures of a haloed Jesus cradling infant lambs and blessing fishes and little children. The lurid Old Testament was filled with bloody sacrifices, plagues, battles, flashing scimitars, avenging angels, spear-pierced bodies, writhing serpents, and other horrors visited upon sinners, of which I might have been.

As a good and obedient little boy I didn't ask questions about any of this. I accepted what I observed: that everyone seemed mournfully and passively resigned to lives of sun-up to sun-down labor and deprivation here on earth—but that they plodded along with the faint hope of peace, plenty, and eternal rest in the hereafter. When someone died—assuming he was saved—he went to a better place, the preachers all said, his final reward.

One rainy, cold March afternoon when I got off the school bus my mother met me on the porch and said, "Duff is dead." She kept me out of the bedroom where his body lay on the bed. Before dark two of his brothers came with a two-wheeled mule cart and took him away in a pine box as my half-sister and I stood on the porch and silently watched. He was buried in the family cemetery in a thicket of pine trees and honeysuckle behind the main house. I didn't go to the funeral and neither did Ethel Gray. She was now three years old. She had silken blonde hair, deep-set brown eyes like our mother, pale skin, and a shy manner.

It soon became clear to my mother that she could not take care of us. The Laughinghouse family offered to take us in, but she didn't want that. She said she had better dreams for me than to be a farmer, and, anyway, she did not want someone else to be the parents of her children. Somebody at the Vanceboro Methodist Church mentioned orphanages to her and told her that was a possible way of relinquishing us, perhaps temporarily, until she could get back on her feet.

There were nine orphanages around North Carolina then, and all of them were full. But the Masons had an orphanage in the town of Oxford, one hundred miles west from Vanceboro, and they had a place for one girl. Soon a case worker came and filled out a questionnaire, which many years later I exhumed from the Oxford Orphanage archives. My mother was listed as having a bad heart and gall bladder trouble, which she told the interviewer "developed during two years of nursing her husband, looking after two children, and trying to do so much work."

My mother told the interviewer that my stepfather before he died had graded tobacco that was brought to the house by his brothers to try to make some money, that he was a Presbyterian and was industrious and thrifty before "financial reverses," that he possessed neither real estate nor insurance, that he didn't drink, take dope, or gamble, that our home was "a happy one with real affection shown."

"Is the home a scene of constant strife?"

No, the caseworker reported in her questionnaire. "Impressed me as being very pleasant."

"Mother's occupation?"

"Is not strong enough to work, at present."

"Wages?"

"Is on relief."

"Chief reason for desiring children admitted?"

"Death of the father, and inability of mother to support children."

"What method of correction of children is used?"

"Says very little. Was in home when children were there, and both seemed quiet and well behaved."

"Are they easily controlled?"

"Judging from observation, yes."

"What is the type of associates?"

"Good, but very limited. Children stay at home with mother."

"Do they attend Church and Sunday School?"

"Yes."

"What are her amusements and recreation?"

"None, other than playing with her brother."

"Are children allowed to roam the streets and do as they please?"

"No."

"What discipline is maintained in home?"

"Mother is very indulgent, she claims."

"Are the children properly fed and clothed?"

"Yes, with aid of Welfare, and relatives, mostly Welfare."

"What is their attitude about entering the orphanage?"

"Little girl too young to realize meaning. Boy wants to come."

"Does child sleep alone?"

"Yes. Mother, age 35, sleeps with boy."

"Is there any apparent reason why the child should fail to respond to the Orphanage program of life and training?"

"No, judging from observations in two visits, would think she would respond nicely, especially as she is very friendly type. Little boy quiet and serious type."

Summarizing, the caseworker said that "the mother is very anxious for the children to be admitted, but was interested in the rules governing adoption, as she was not willing to consent to this. She, while physically unable to do any work other than her housekeeping, is still bright and cheerful, full of energy and vitally interested in all things pertaining to her children. The little girl is a nice-looking child, the dainty type, and vivacious, like the mother, while the little boy is a very quiet and more serious type of child."

A car with a man in it came and took my sister off to the Oxford Orphanage on September 5, 1935, within a week of her

fourth birthday and my eighth. We had stayed together constantly, outside, away from our mother, during the days leading
up to her departure. She cried a lot and I tried to comfort her, but
didn't know what to say, for I was aware the same fate lay in
store for me soon and that we had no idea when we would see
each other again.

My sister, pale and frightened, had her clothes in a big paper
bag when the man with the car came up to the porch. My mother
was crying. I hugged my sister and then she left. My mother went
into the house. I went out to the chicken house and stood there
feeling cold, lonely, and scared. Now alone with my mother, I
lapsed into even further isolation. My sister had been my only
companion. But my mother had told us she had no other choice
but to send us away, and I didn't know anything to do except
agree with her.

After that, my mother said, it was unclear how we would survive. We were getting twenty dollars a month in welfare money,
but that was insufficient. President Franklin Roosevelt's relief
programs were beginning to come to the South, and home
demonstration agents came around with free mason jars and
instructions on how to safely put up vegetables. That late summer
and fall after my sister left, my mother and I picked vegetables
from the garden her dead husband's family had planted for us
and whose weeds I had hoed. She wore a calico bonnet and an
apron over a print dress made from feed sacks. I wore overalls
without a shirt and was barefoot and on the lookout for snakes
and hornets while I filled my tin bucket. We fired the kitchen
wood stove day after day and put up 300 quarts of tomatoes,
butter beans, snap beans, soup mix, carrots, black-eyed peas,
Kentucky Wonders, field peas, okra, and corn, these to be cooked
through the winter months. Later in her life she would remember
this period as the happiest of our short lives together—she and

her little man harvesting and canning vegetables. I was content, too, except that I missed my sister. The mysterious specter of my being sent away hung heavily in the air but I tried not to think about it.

Craven County, in which Vanceboro was situated, had ruled us a "destitute" case. Country people were prideful and stubbornly resisted charity except in the most extreme cases. But my mother accepted the help on the grounds that she had done the best she could. The Laughinghouses provided assistance, but they were having their own family troubles, including the death of a teenage daughter of my stepfather's brother, Clinton, and Queenie Laughinghouse, who lived in the brick house down the road from the main Laughinghouse home. The daughter had a reputation for being wild and was killed when she ran the family car into a tree on the road running through Vanceboro. At that time, everybody buried their dead in homemade pine caskets on their own places, little graveyards back in the woods. My mother said Miss Queenie insisted on burying her daughter right behind the house under a cedar tree with a stone marker. The neighbors thought this strange, but she explained that "at least I know where she is now."

My mother kept us pretty much removed from the Laughinghouses and their dramas, however, except for church and, sometimes, Sunday dinner, followed by my gorging along with their children from a giant scuppernong grape bower in their yard. As my mother worked in the garden and kitchen alone, she sometimes sang, mostly mournful tunes. Her favorite was "A Letter Edged in Black":

> *I was standing by my window yesterday morning,*
> *Without a thought of worry or of care,*
> *When I saw the Postman coming up the pathway,*

With such a happy face and jolly air.
He rang the bell and whistled as he waited,
Then he said, "Good morning to you, Jack."
But he little knew the sorrow he had brought me,
When he handed me a letter edged in black.
With trembling hand I took this letter from him,
I broke the seal and this is what it said,
"Come home, my boy, your dear old father wants you,
"Come home, my boy, your dear old mother's dead."
I bowed my head in sorrow and in sadness.
The sunshine of my life it all had fled,
When the Postman brought that letter yesterday morning,
Saying, "Come home, my boy, your mother's dead.
"The last words your mother ever uttered,
"'Tell my boy I want him to come back,
"'My eyes are blurred, my poor old heart is breaking,'
"So I'm writing you this letter edged in black.
"Forget those angry words that we had spoken.
"You know I didn't mean them don't you, Jack
"May the angels bear as witness, I am asking
"Your forgiveness in this letter edged in black."

It was at these moments that I felt some embryonic pang of guilt, that somehow I could and should do more to make her happy. Often I picked wisteria and mimosa blooms and brought them to her where she put them in a mason jar of water on the kitchen window. Soon my mother's health began to fail even more. With help and relief money from the Vance County Welfare Department, we moved out of the shack on Mauls Swamp and into a three-room apartment on the second floor of a white wooden house near the Vanceboro elementary school. She wanted to get away from the Laughinghouses, lest somehow we be drawn further into their web, which seemed to lead nowhere but to the farm and tobacco and peanuts.

Vanceboro was an all-white farm village of 500 people beside a slow-moving river with cyprus trees growing in it that turned the water to the color of strong iced tea. It had two filling stations, a drugstore, a garage, a dry goods store, a feed and seed store, two churches, a hardware store, a lawyer's and a doctor's office, one restaurant, and a tiny wooden movie theater that had "bank night" once a month and a drawing with a $5 jackpot. Somebody introduced us into the nearby Methodist Church where the minister, a gray-haired and kind-faced preacher named the Rev. Henry Lewis, and his wife, Minnie, befriended us. Minnie wore rimless glasses on her always-smiling round face and costumed herself in modest shin-length cotton dresses. The Lewises got my mother a job helping out at Miss Ada Smith's sewing shop next to the parsonage, and I began to run errands for the pastor and his wife. One day early in that period he gave me a nickel for an errand I had run and went with me to Jordan's Drug Store on Main Street, into whose cool, medicine-smelling interior we walked and went over to the fountain counter where the reverend introduced me to a hitherto unimagined delight, a "fountain" Coke.

I still had no friends. I remained afraid of other boys and their laughing at me. I played alone either outside our apartment, swinging Tarzan-like from a wild grapevine that hung from an oak tree, or across the street from the church in a kudzu patch, imagining I was a missionary among the African savages—the Methodist Church minister occasionally having taken up special collections to save these benighted souls in the dark continent. I listened all the while for the sound of a pewter bell my mother rang when she wanted me to come home.

When we went to church I began to hear whispered conversations between my mother and her few friends, the gist of which was that her life was going further downhill and she didn't know what to do. At home, Mother sighed and lay down on the bed a lot. One day I heard her talking to Miss Ada Smith and Mrs. Lewis about what to do with me. My mother said the Laughinghouses had offered to take me but she couldn't stand the thought of that, which was why she had sent Ethel Gray to the Oxford Orphanage. Mrs. Lewis said something about a Methodist orphanage up in Raleigh that might take me. Of course, I was scared and alone on the edge of these conversations and didn't know what to say and so said nothing.

Soon Mrs. Lewis wrote to the Rev. Albert Sydney Barnes, superintendent of the Methodist Orphanage. I excavated her letter from the orphanage files many years later:

Dear Brother Barnes,
We in our church have such a needy case and I hope you can do something to help. A woman by the name of Laughinghouse whose husband was sick in bed a year before his death, was left with no health and two children. Mr. Proctor has taken the little girl. The little boy is a handsome little man, my little errand boy. His mother cannot even earn enough to keep herself. She looks to me like her days are few. Can't you crowd him in somewhere? If you say so we will take him to you. I do hope you can take him. Mr. Lewis is not home this morning but he is as interested in and anxious about this boy as I am.

On October 14, 1935, my mother walked me to a Vanceboro doctor's office and the doctor gave me a physical examination as part of my application to be admitted to the Methodist Orphanage. I was pronounced healthy and normal. The doctor's record, which I looked up years later, showed that I had been vaccinated against smallpox and typhoid fever at school and had not had any of the diseases of the day—syphilis, enuresis (bed-wetting), smallpox, whooping cough, tuberculosis, epilepsy, scrofula, measles, mumps, scarlet fever, or kidney trouble—except diphtheria.

My mother did not discuss these preparations with me. She became still more quiet, as if readying herself for the coming fracture, and at the edge of her silence I withdrew even further.

The Rev. Mr. Lewis said on the official orphanage application that I was a member of his church and answered "Yes" to the question of whether I was "reasonably bright and capable of receiving an education."

"Why?"

"Because he is equal to or above the average."

"Do you believe this child to be destitute and worthy of aid?"

"Yes."

There was, too, a section on the two-page application for my mother to fill out.

"Real and personal property?"

"None."

"Insurance received?"

"None.

"I hereby certify that the above information is true and accurate to the best of my knowledge, and that I bear to the child the relationship of mother. I also hereby certify that I am in the rightful custody and control of said child, and I hereby agree that the authorities of The Methodist Orphanage may have full control and management of said child while it remains at the Orphanage."

The application also called for my mother to agree that "I hereby covenant and agree, to and with the Trustees of the Methodist Orphanage, that the superintendent of said orphanage and corporate authorities thereof under provisions of laws and by-laws and regulations legally established, may in his discretion procure for the said child a suitable home, or permit him to be adopted by some white person to be approved by the superintendent, who shall take such legal precautions as in his discretion may be necessary, or may place him in a reformatory should he become ungovernable or should he have a vicious influence over other children."

But the Rev. Mr. Barnes assured my mother by letter that I would never be put up for adoption, and on October 19, just after my eighth birthday, she, bent and crying, signed the official application in the pastor's little office. I sat silently watching, overcome by a dreadful foreboding, of what I knew not, except that it sounded as if I would be cleaved from her for a long time and maybe forever.

A few Sundays later, I climbed up into a chinaberry tree in front of the Methodist Church, after the eleven o'clock services were done, and watched as my mother talked to a man I had never seen, a big white-haired imposing man with a bulbous nose and thin lips. He wore a white suit with a red rose in the lapel and gold-rimmed glasses. After a bit the man shook hands with my mother and got into a shiny black Pontiac and was driven away by a teenage boy. This man was the Rev. Albert Sydney Barnes, superintendent of the Methodist Orphanage in Raleigh, 100 miles west. They were agreeing that I would go there as soon as there was an opening.

Chapter 3

Orphanage Boy

I T WAS A COLD, melancholy day, December 27, 1935, two
days after Christmas, as quietly the old gray Plymouth went
along through the bleak Carolina countryside, past tobacco barns
with Clabber Girl Baking Powder and Smith-Douglas Fertilizer signs
on their sides, past crossroads stores, wooden churches, and fields of
dead corn and broom-sage, carrying me, my mother, and the Sunday
School teacher who had volunteered to drive us to the Methodist
Orphanage. Hardly a word had been spoken the whole trip.

We made our way through Raleigh, past the domed marble
capitol with its gray Confederate statues and squirrels and
pigeons on the lawn. Finally we turned onto the orphanage campus off Glenwood Avenue and headed slowly up a winding red
clay road cut though a grove of oak, hickory, and dogwood trees.
The trees were black and shiny with rain.

I rode in the back with my pasteboard suitcase beside me, wearing a white shirt and a wool tie and a scratchy hammer-and-nails suit that the ladies' sewing circle of the Vanceboro Methodist Church had bought for me. My mother wore her blue Sunday dress with the white collar.

We went silently at a funereal pace up past a row of old two-story brick dormitories and stopped at last on a macadam apron in front of the big three-story brick building whose faded cement cornerstone read: "Methodist Episcopal Orphanage. Founded 1900." A teenage boy with oily black hair came out and introduced himself as Ben Moore. He said he was there to escort us to Mr. Barnes's office.

My mother held my hand as we went into the silent lobby and climbed marble stairs to the second floor and went along to a corner office where Ben Moore knocked and a deep voice said, "You may come in." Once we were inside the room, Mr. Barnes shook hands with my mother and sat down gravely on a wooden swivel chair in front of a rolltop desk. Paintings of important-looking men hung on the walls, with little brass plaques on them. My mother and I took our places on hard wooden chairs as Mr. Barnes, wearing a blue suit, black shoes, and gold-rimmed glasses, told my mother, "We are going to take good care of your boy. He will be raised in a fine Christian atmosphere and he will receive a good education. So you do not need to worry about him. Right now, one of the older boys here will take him down to the infirmary. He will get a physical examination. He has to stay in quarantine for a week and then he will move into the Brown Building with thirty other boys."

My mother was crying quietly into a handkerchief as Ben Moore came to lead me away.

"You be a good boy now, Son," she said.

"Goodbye, Mama," I said. I didn't cry or anything. I felt dead and numb and very alone. This would be the first time I had ever been separated from her for more than a few hours since I was born.

"You'll get used to it here. We all did," Ben Moore said as he led me away to the infirmary.

The infirmary was a grim old two-story brick building set well away from the other cottages in a grove of oaks and pines. The Vann Building, which housed Mr. Barnes, his secretary, an auditorium, and our school classrooms, was at the center of the campus at the top of the hill. Four girls' and four boys' buildings spread out in a wide V on either side. Behind the Vann Building was the dining room, the laundry building, and a rectangular swimming pool that was emptied in September and filled at Easter. The Baby Cottage, housing children two to six, sat by itself behind Mr. Barnes's residence near the orphanage entrance. The infirmary was run by a dumpy red-faced nurse named Mrs. Fogleman and her assistant, Stick Watson, a former orphanage girl herself, who was skinny and had long buck teeth. They led me to a big room containing four white iron hospital beds and sat my suitcase on one of them. There was nobody sick at the moment, so I was totally alone. At noon I heard the dong of a bell and Stick Watson came in and said she was going to dinner in the dining room and would bring me something. But I wasn't hungry. There were a few old magazines on a table in the hall—*Collier's, Boys' Life,* and the *Saturday Evening Post*—and I took them back to the bed. There I spent the next seven nights in solitary tears, picking at my meals that were fetched from the main dining hall by Stick Watson. The room was unheated. I was cold and it took me a long time to go to sleep.

The morning after the first night I had oatmeal and a glass of milk and was told to go past the laundry and report to somebody called Muh Brown. Her real name was Mable Brown, Stick

The Baby Cottage children called the orphanage superintendent Daddy Barnes. The older boys and girls called him Old Man Barnes.

Watson said, but everybody called her Muh. The "Muh" was short for mother. She was the longtime matron of the Brown Building (no relation to her), into which I would move after my quarantine. "You're going to be one of my little boys now," Muh Brown said.

She was a merry elf of a woman, about forty, with a tiny wrinkled face and a gentle voice. She gave me a spring-toothed rake and directed me to the wide dirt yard between the Brown Building and the Vann Building and told me to rake up the leaves into piles. All the other children were in school. It was cold, windy, and damp and soon my legs and hands were red and chapped and my thighs raw from the rubbing of the new suit that I had arrived with. I raked leaves into piles every day, crying and feeling lonely, frightened, and forsaken. One day Muh Brown led me into her apartment and gave me a cup of hot chocolate. She sat down in a rocking chair and began knitting. She told me not to worry. Everything would be all right in a little while when I got to know the other boys. She herself had been at the orphanage practically her whole life, she said, since she was four years old. She finished the orphanage high school, she said, had no place to go and no job or the prospects of one. Her parents were dead and there were no other relatives or friends on the outside. So they let her stay at the orphanage, first helping out in the dining room and then the laundry, until finally they made her a matron. She cried a long time after she came there as a little girl, she said. When she left home to go to the orphanage, she said, her mother told her to go to the window every night before bed, look out, and recite, "Goodnight, mother, sweet as a rose. How bad I miss you, God only knows."

By the end of my quarantine, during which I had spoken to no one but Muh Brown and Stick Watson, the legs of my new suit were shredded and my thighs were red and raw. When I moved into her building, Muh Brown threw the suit and my other few clothes into the trash and I was issued the customary Brown Building clothing: a pair of black brogans, two pairs of socks, three pairs of cotton BVDs with flaps in the back, two cotton shirts, two pairs of corduroy knickers and a black wool zip-up jacket. These were our "everyday clothes." We also had "Sunday clothes": a brown wool sweater, a white shirt, a little striped tie, a new pair of corduroy knickers, and a pair of black slippers. Thus accoutered and quartered, I was now officially a "Brown Boy." You were designated a "Borden Boy," or a "Brown Boy," or a "Page Boy," according to the building to which you were assigned successively according to your age, excepting that when you progressed to the Cole Building, the last stop before graduation, you were known as a "Big Boy."

In my status as a new Brown Boy, I was assigned a cubicle in the clothes room in one corner of the basement and a footlocker across in the basement playroom beside the boiler room. The floor was concrete and rows of sewer and water pipes ran along the ceiling. It was in the basement that we boys, thirty-five of us between the ages of eight and twelve, were sequestered during bad winter weather. Beyond the boiler room and coal bin was the tub-room where we bathed with white Poco Soap ("It Floats"), two to a tub, every other day. We each had an assigned nail on the wall for our toothbrushes, wash cloths, and towels.

One half of the main floor was given over to Muh Brown's apartment. The other half housed one dormitory and our study hall, which contained six oak tables with wooden chairs, two steam radiators, and a bell-shaped Atwater-Kent radio on which we listened to *The Lone Ranger*, *The Shadow*, and *Mr. District Attorney* on Sunday evenings. The upstairs was sectioned off with four more unheated big rooms holding between six and eight beds each. The beds were steel-framed, flat-springed affairs with thin cotton-stuffed mattresses covered with white cotton sheets and patchwork quilts but no pillows. All the rooms had gray, unpainted oak floors. Every Saturday morning we scrubbed them, as well as the toilets, tubs, and sinks, with brushes and rags on our hands and knees.

There was a front porch, which we boys were not allowed to use, with white banisters, a swing, and a rocking chair. It was reserved for Muh Brown and her occasional guests. There was a concrete back porch, too, but it was too small for much of anything except Muh Brown's rocking chair.

My first night in the Brown Building we were ordered to bed by Muh Brown's brass bell at 8:30 P.M. We undressed to our underwear, kneeled down by our beds and repeated with Muh Brown:

> *Now I lay me down to sleep.*
> *Pray the Lord my soul to keep.*
> *If I should die before I wake,*
> *Pray the Lord my soul to take.*

Then Muh Brown turned off the light and told us to be quiet. There was a scattering of whispers and giggles and then all was still as I settled into my cold bed. I began to cry, quietly, in fear and loneliness. I missed my mother and my sister, who was forty miles from here at the Oxford Orphanage. They seemed so incredibly far away. Somebody yelled, "Cut out the boo-hooing," and finally I slept.

Entering the Brown Building began a daily routine that was to last as long as I was at the orphanage. An iron bell mounted on a wooden pole outside the laundry building donged at 6 A.M. We rose, dressed, brushed our teeth, washed our faces and combed our hair, and walked to the old brick dining hall for 6:30 breakfast. The breakfast menu changed but once a year. It was oatmeal in winter and corn flakes and skim milk in summer, with the occasional variant of stewed government surplus prunes, which consumed in sufficient quantity (Dickie Tharrington held the record with sixty-seven) would produce projectile diarrhea, otherwise known among the freely cussing boys as "The Flying Shits." The girls wouldn't eat them, so there was always a plentiful supply.

The dining hall was an enormous vaulted cave of a room with three tall arched windows on each side. Wooden tables and chairs—six to the table—accommodated all 300 children in the orphanage plus the nine matrons and the administrative staff. Girls sat on one side, boys on the other, grouped according to the buildings they were in.

All of the matrons were well-meaning "old maids" or Methodist widows. Each of the matrons sat with her boys' or girls' sections in the dining room. In addition, "big girls" were assigned to each younger boys' table, to help police our conduct and teach us table manners. The teachers and administrative staff had their own tables.

The dining room sat on a slightly sloping hill, with the cold storage rooms, the boiler room, and the ammonia-smelling ice house in the basement in the rear. The huge kitchen was on the level with the dining room. Above the kitchen were the quarters of the "dining room girls" and their matron and the chief cook, Miss Lizzie Sanders. Miss Lizzie was red-haired and red-faced and was famous for her curt manner and for cowering under her bed during thunderstorms.

Each meal was preceded by a blessing, which was as unvarying as the food—"For these and all Thy gifts we give Thee thanks and praise," intoned either by one of the matrons or teachers at breakfast and dinner (noontime) or, invariably at supper, by Mr. Barnes himself or some visiting dignitary. Often there came a Mr.

Craft, a roly-poly Bible and religious book salesman with wavy brown hair slicked to the side, who played a spirited Methodist tune on a brass trumpet. His blessing always ran, "E-a-t–s-l-o-w, workfast. Amen."

The noon meal in winter consisted of vegetables that had been purchased in cases of three-quart institutional cans—green beans, corn, lima beans, and tomatoes, plus, from our own farm, baked sweet potatoes or boiled Irish potatoes, turnips and their greens, and hard-baked corn sticks made from yellow corn, ground at the nearby Lassiter's Mill.

Supper was the same, except that three nights a week it consisted solely of peanut butter, molasses (which for some old unknown reason was called "zip"), and sliced "light" bread which was baked in the kitchen. All meals, three times a day, were accompanied by skim milk. This came about because of financial rather than health reasons. The orphanage operated a sixty-cow dairy on its 300-acre farm five miles from the main campus, but sold off the cream to the Pine State Creamery on Glenwood Avenue every day, leaving for our consumption what we sneeringly referred to as "blue john," which was served plentifully in pewter pitchers. I was lucky enough to have a catholic appetite or perhaps, like some of the other boys, I had been too poor to learn to turn up my nose at any food. Quantity was the only issue, and we, clinically speaking, were well-fed—and always hungry.

Because of the farm and because we boys and girls delivered virtually all of the labor, the orphanage ran on a small budget—$35,000 the year I got there. Mr. Barnes raised most of this money traveling the Methodist church circuit around Eastern Carolina with an a capella quartet of orphanage voices, two boys and two girls.

Occasionally when one of the cows got old and was butchered

we got beef stew. And at hog-killing time when freezing weather came on, we got a kind of pork liver stew. Otherwise we had no meat except on rare special occasions such as every Easter, the biggest holiday of the year. The older boys helped in the annual winter killings of the hogs and their butchering and the salt-curing of the hams and shoulders, which were given away by Mr. Barnes to members of the board of trustees and other friends of the orphanage. The tenderloins and bacon also went to the trustees and contributors—rich people who we never saw. The "side meat" was kept for seasoning our vegetables.

The dining room was closed on Sunday evenings. At our dormitories, we each got a paper bag with a peanut butter and "relish" sandwich, plus a wedge of pound cake. There was fierce competition and traditional rules about the fair division of food at the boys' tables. One boy was designated to divide each table's bowl of peanut butter into equal shares, and whoever said so first got "first extra," meaning any that was left over after the apportioning. It was advantageous to have a girlfriend who was a "dining room girl," one of the dozen older girls resident in the dining hall who waited tables, for she would liberate leftover peanut butter and bread from the delicate girls who didn't eat much and deliver it to her heart throb. Thus a boy who had a girlfriend in the dining room was the envy of all. But I was too young and too new for that.

The peanut butter came in fifty-five-gallon steel drums and the molasses in wooden barrels. There was no limit on the amount of "zip" one could have. It was served in aluminum pitchers, but its consumption depended entirely on the amount of bread available with which to sop it up. It was not unusual for a boy to wolf down a dozen slices of bread, assuming they were available. If any bread was left over, it could be pinioned under the tabletop with a knife until the next meal.

In summer there came a cornucopia of fresh vegetables from our farm—beets to squash—all seasoned in the accustomed Southern style with fatback. The Page Building Boys and big boys from the Cole Building grew the vegetables, the Brown boys picked them, and the dining room girls prepared them.

I ate hardly anything my first days. Nor did I speak. I moped forlornly around with my nose running unwiped, my shoes untied, my socks fallen into them, and my shirttail always out. Forthwith my nickname became "Slouchy." My Brown Boy mates were tough and self-reliant. I had never been around anyone like them.

My doleful isolation continued through the bleak winter, when I gradually melded into the routine of the Brown Building and surrendered to the inevitability of my fate—to the oft-repeated injunction that life in the orphanage was "root, hog, or die." I slowly began to be accepted by the other boys. My mood and my deportment improved, and my nickname changed to "Pretty Boy." I had no sense of being physically attractive, but apparently I was—with deep-set brown eyes, fair skin, a small nose, and in general a well-formed face. One of the older girls called me "John Payne," after a movie star of that era. I didn't like any of this at all but I couldn't do anything about it and I dared not say why: that it reminded me of being laughed at and humiliated by the boys who did what they did to me in the garage. I feared being a sissy. All this got better when within a few months, I became almost as scruffy and profane as everybody else. After that I became and remained simply "Karl Payne."

Many of my colleagues got nicknames, which stuck to them forever. There were two brothers, for example, named John Roach and James Roach. The redheaded and skinny John was discovered to have head lice upon his return from a summer visit with his family and was immediately branded as "Cootie." His freckled, pale-haired brother, James, had constantly runny eyes and was nicknamed "Snot-Eye." There were two dark-skinned Rogers brothers, James and Maurice, and they were nicknamed "Big Nigger" and "Little Nigger." There was Rudolph Valentino Perry. Using a pole made from a tree limb, he had tried to vault over a six-foot fence surrounding a small flower garden beside the Brown Building, ripping the crotch out of his Sunday pants and exposing an unusually large pair of testicles. He henceforth was called "Nutsy." There was Willis "Stone" Moore, who had a grip like a vice, and Calvin Coolidge "Stony" Heath, who was a fiercely tough football player. There was Cecil "Greasy" Brooks, who was constantly oily from working on the tractor and other farm implements. There was Martin Luther "Preacher" Weeks, after the Protestant reformationist. There was Warren "Gumps" Dudley, who looked like Andy Gump in the funny papers, and brothers Howard "Monkey" Jordan, a fearlessly agile tree climber, and Jimmy "Shorty" Jordan, he of short stature. There was Edgar Allen "Cockeye" Smith, he of off-kilter eyes. There were brothers Charles "Big Jeebie" and Russell "Little Jeebie" Clay, who had large noses reminiscent of the Jeebie characters in the comic books; Ralph "Skinny" Bostian; and Logan "Pussy" Leathers, so named because he had a scar on his left shoulder, the result of a fall from a tree, that allegedly looked like female genitalia. There was Frank "Sleepy" Williams, who appeared half asleep all the time. There was Walter Pate "Pooty" Parker, a virtuoso of flatulence, and Willard "Lightning" Parker, he of turtle-like gait. There was Jim "Skunk" Bradford, who had odiferous feet. There was Grange "Chin" Lee, whose chin projected out like a lantern. And there was my personal nemesis, John "Fatty" Clark.

The lumpish Fatty was only a year older than I but considerably bigger. He was a veteran orphanage boy, having been sent there at age three with an older brother. He had graduated from the Baby Cottage to the Borden Building and then to the Brown Building by the time I arrived. He was derided as "Lard Ass" and "Whale Tail" as well as "Fatty," and in the Borden Building he had been a particular victim of a dreaded "big boy" football star named Leon "Link" Tilley, who was the matron's assigned factotum. Tilley physically tormented his charges, including lining them up and making them fight elimination fights. Every Christmas morning we went to the dining room and found our only orange of the year on our plates. But the Borden boys didn't get theirs. Tilley set a bushel basket beside the fire hydrant in front of the Borden Building and as each boy dropped off his orange in the basket, for Tilley's private consumption, he marked off his name from a list. No one told on him, though, out of fear, along with the strong prohibition against squealing.

By being assigned to the Brown Building right off, I escaped the cruelty Tilley visited on Fatty Clark and others. But I soon had my own fearsome tormenter, Fatty Clark himself. Something about me set Fatty Clark off, and he would punch me, wrestle me to the ground, and pummel me, or "kick my ass," literally, practically every time he saw me. I had no idea what I had done or what there was about me that aroused his wrath. Perhaps it was because I was the newest kid in the Brown Building. Perhaps it was the way I looked—shy and sensitive. Perhaps there was something wrong with me, the same thing that had made the kids who forced me to "suck it" choose me as their victim. I didn't know for sure what it was. All I knew was that I walked everywhere in fear of him. And what made it worse was that there was no one to turn to for help. The other boys who at first I thought and hoped might have come to my aid merely shrugged and went

about their own survival. That was the code. Row your own
boat. Peck shit with the other chickens. Root, hog, or die. Out-
doors, I could outrun Fatty and keep sprinting until he tired out,
because he was sluggish and ungainly, but confined inside, or on
the truck going to the farm, there was no escape.

I quickly learned that there could be no appeal to higher
authority, such as to Muh Brown or to Mr. Barnes, who had
promised my mother he would take care of me, for protection or
justice in such cases, because "telling on" somebody was strictly
against the orphanage's long-practiced unwritten code of conduct. It was considered the worst possible act of cowardice and
perfidy. This was a lesson I learned indelibly one day during my
first months at the orphanage after Fatty Clark began to beat me
up. Every day there were mid-morning chapel services conducted
by Mr. Barnes in the big auditorium of the Vann Building. To the
right of the stage, which was framed in wine-colored velvet cur-
tains, was a tiny, concrete enclosed courtyard between the auditorium and a wing of the building where classrooms were located,
constructed so as to let light into the auditorium. During chapel
one morning there was a percussion in the courtyard so loud it
rattled the windows. I looked out the window and saw Fatty
Clark running. He had clearly set off a big firecracker in the
courtyard and had been seen by others—though not by Mr.
Barnes—for there was much whispering and giggling. Mr. Barnes
indignantly denounced the criminality of defiling a religious service and vowed to catch the culprit. "I will give him a thrashing he
will never forget," he sternly announced.

When dinner convened that night, Mr. Barnes again angrily
denounced this unknown miscreant, and said he was offering a
five-dollar reward, payable immediately in cash, to whoever
would reveal the name.

"I'm going up there and tell him it was Fatty Clark," I firmly declared to my table. All of my pent-up hatred of Fatty Clark took form in this sudden resolve. To be sure, five dollars was much more money than I had ever dreamed of, but vengeance was my motive.

The "big girl" assigned to our table was a pretty brown-haired senior named Josephine Peppers. "You don't want to tell on him, Karl Payne," she said. "If you do, you will become known as a tattletale and none of the other boys will have anything to do with you from now on. Do you remember the Sunday School story about Judas telling on Jesus and how despised he was? Even convicts in prison won't squeal on each other. Just remember, everybody everywhere hates a tattletale. So you just keep still."

So I forced myself to keep quiet. Instead, I vowed to myself to kill Fatty when I got big enough to do so. Everybody else kept quiet, too. So Fatty was never caught. Nobody in the orphanage liked bullying, or bullies, and for that nobody much liked Fatty Clark. He was a laughed-at pariah, sullen, and a loner. But nobody interfered with his bullying. The code decreed you were on your own to work out your own problems. There was only one loophole, and that was that the code also said you could have a protector in the form of an older boy, and soon I acquired an inadvertent one. His name was Ed "Snake" Driver, so nicknamed because of his ink-black hair, pointed pockmarked face, and serpentine black eyes. Both of his parents were dead and he had been at the orphanage since the age of four. He lived in the older boys' Cole Building, but was the assigned "big boy" factotum to Muh Brown. His chief duty was to feed the boiler-room furnace with coal, clean its ashes and clinkers (which were used to fill in potholes in the dirt driveways), and to bank the fire at night.

Muh Brown soon appointed me Snake Driver's deputy, and this allowed me the right to take refuge in his sanctum, the boiler room, and to come under his special protection. Snake was an ill-tempered and lazy boy who spent most of his days in a wicker chair with a busted-out seat in front of the boiler reading the funny papers and pornographic "Big Little Books" featuring lascivious Olive Oyls, Betty Boops, and Wonder Women and slavering, hugely endowed Popeyes, Moon Mullinses, Flash Gordons, Li'l Abners, Supermen, and such like. Some unknown "big boy" had gotten them somewhere and smuggled them onto the campus after a vacation, and they had become discolored and dog-eared from being passed from hand to hand.

After I became Driver's aide de camp, I quickly saw that when Fatty chased me all I had to do was scamper into the boiler room, where Snake invariably sat loafing, and he would yell at Fatty, "Get your fat ass out of here and leave this kid alone." Snake's protection of me was based entirely on his self-interest, and not because he felt sorry for me or because he abhorred bullying. In fact, he paid no attention to me at all except to order me to do his chores.

The orphanage boy code also decreed that you did not steal from your peers. It was perfectly OK, therefore, to leave your locker unsecured. The code also decreed that you share special gifts such as packages from home, that you did not shirk your work so that its burden fell on someone else, that you did not tell lies to each other, that you did not cheat at games, that you did not cry when you got hurt—either in a fight or an accident—that you did not appeal to the authorities under any circumstances, that when caught red-handed by the people in charge you took your punishment like a man, and—this one above all—you did not act like a coward. This meant principally that in a fight you did not hit someone from behind, below the belt, or when they were down, or in any other way behave in a sneaking, sniveling, craven, or furtive way. You fought standing up, facing your enemy. That was the way you were supposed to face all of life's adversities.

My bullying nemesis, Fatty Clark, second from left, pitching hay on the orphanage farm, 1941. I vowed I would someday kill him.

There was a definite and well-understood pecking order among the boys. Everybody knew who could beat whom. There was a fair amount of arguing and drawing lines in the dirt with a stick and daring an adversary to cross it and face fearsome consequences. I didn't like to fight. I never had. I didn't know how. My mother had told me the way to deal with unkindness was to turn the other cheek, as Jesus had done. Besides, I was scared. So I tried not to provoke anyone into challenging me. For a long time, I didn't fight back when Fatty Clark beat on me. One day in the basement he started hitting me and said he would continue to beat me until I cried "Uncle." This and "I give up" were the accepted expressions of surrender. But I didn't and wouldn't say either. Instead, some awakening stubbornness made me put myself into a fetal ball on the concrete floor and engage in passive resistance. Everybody was watching.

"Give up?" he yelled.

"No, I won't," I said. I wasn't crying. He was on top of me straddling my back and pounding away. He kept on beating me and ordering me to give up as everybody watched. I kept saying "No I won't," until finally he simply got too tired to continue and gave up and walked away. I knew when I got up that I had won a victory of some kind. None of the boys said anything but it was clear that they looked at me with a new respect. Nobody except Fatty bothered me any more after that. That was when the taunts of "Pretty Boy" stopped.

I was finally liberated from Fatty's terror one summer day when we were working on the farm, and he began chasing me around the milk barn. Suddenly I stopped and picked up a big rock and turned and threw it at him. It hit his left wrist, and he cried out in pain. From that day on, he never picked on me again. And neither did anyone else, although later on I got in a few fights that others started—and won them all. I discovered that pushed far enough, I had an eruptive temper and would strike back in a way that frightened attackers.

No one talked about where these unspoken and universally adhered-to rules came from. I supposed that they had been gradually worked out since the orphanage was founded at the turn of the century. The code helped identity each of us as "orphanage boys," and we were proud of that, proud of our toughness, our ability to take it, and proud of our self-imposed system. Boys on the outside were soft, we believed. Our athletic teams routinely beat those of much larger schools. Occasionally some "town tacks" who didn't know any better tried to take a shortcut through our campus on the way home from the nearby Needham Broughton High School. They were invariably challenged about being on our turf, and fought and driven off if they didn't depart at once.

The Brown Building boys were like all of the children, all white, of course, and all from Methodist churches that supported the orphanage. About half of the orphanage's children had a living mother. Rarely there was a father, and the others had had no living parents. Many poor people of that era died from complications of extreme malnourishment, and there was a long list of diseases, some now rare, that commonly carried people off, principally smallpox, diphtheria, scarlet fever, rheumatic fever, rickets, spinal meningitis, lockjaw, food poisoning, heart attacks, cancer, pneumonia—and tuberculosis, or "consumption" as it was commonly called. Extreme poverty, though, was the principal reason why most children ended up in our orphanage. Except for orphanages such as ours, no real support systems existed where death and poverty had rendered many families without even the most basic needs of food and shelter. Adoptions were practically unheard of. Since poverty was so widespread, "another mouth to feed" was the dire announcement that accompanied many an unplanned child into life.

Frequently there were four children from the same family at the orphanage, rarely five, and commonly three. In rare instances a family would recover somewhat financially, and the children would be returned from the orphanage, never to be seen or heard from again. But most were there until they graduated from high school, and we all understood this. Gradually their connections with their families dimmed or disappeared altogether, and the orphanage became the family.

When you went to the orphanage, there was no contact with the outside world at all in the first months, except by mail. After a year, there theoretically could be a week's summer vacation to be spent with one's family, assuming there was a family, and assuming that it was not too poor to bear even that expense. Many children had no place to go and stayed at the orphanage all year round, year after year.

My half-sister was transferred at age four to the Methodist Orphanage five months after I got there and was assigned to the Baby Cottage. I saw her only at meal times when the Baby Cottage children came in a group with their matron—like a mother quail with her babies—and then very briefly. And I didn't know what to say when I did see her. Beyond that, I was caught up in my own survival and unhappiness, and her presence reminded me of our having been wrenched away from our mother.

Our school—grades one through eleven—operated as a separate entity within the Raleigh Public School system, and our teachers came daily from outside, although one or two were matrons as well as teachers. The classrooms were all in the Vann Building. Upon my arrival at the orphanage I was assigned to the second grade, though I had tested well above average for my age. My teacher was a fat and ill-tempered martinet named Miss Hester. She was famous and hated for disciplining her boys by thrusting their heads down through a bottomless cane chair and beating them on the butt with a yardstick. Girls were immune from her corporal punishment. A female miscreant was forced to write "I will not talk in class," or whatever the crime was, 100 times, or more if she was a repeat offender. Miss Hester was famous, too, for her parsimonious preoccupation with bathroom functions.

"May I please go to the bathroom, Miss Hester?" someone would reluctantly ask.

"Number one or number two?"

"Number two, Miss Hester."

"Go ahead then, but remember toilet paper costs money, and money doesn't grow on trees. Mr. Barnes has to go all over the country and beg for money so that you can be here, so do not to use more than two sheets of toilet paper. You should be thankful for what you have. And don't be lollygagging in there either. If you do I will come and get you and you know what that means."

At mid-morning everybody in school filed into the auditorium for a fifteen-minute chapel service presided over by Mr. Barnes. An older girl would read a selection from the Bible. We would join in a group song out of the *Cokesbury Hymnal*. Then Mr. Barnes would launch into a gloomy prediction of our doomed futures unless we evaded the many sneaky snares of the devil. Given our inherent wickedness, especially we boys, it was clear that only hard work, regimen, discipline, robust food, heavy doses of cod liver oil and religion, and relentless policing of that most tempting and alluring-sounding sin, lust, could save us from the cunning of a scheming Satan. Above all, an idle mind was the devil's workshop.

On Sunday mornings we put on our knickers, shirts and ties, and wool sweaters and walked to the gloomy old Jenkins Memorial Methodist Church near our campus for the eleven o'clock service. The sermons were unrelentingly harsh, promising fierce punishments for mysterious and unspecified sins, mainly of a carnal nature—whatever that meant—and even the sin of thinking bad thoughts. But with redemption and the renunciation of sin from thenceforward, heavenly bliss was available for those sinners who would surrender themselves to Jesus.

There were 300 of us in the keep of the orphanage, and the necessary constant inoculation against our sinful proclivities was carried out with Sunday School, church, Sunday evening service, bedtime prayers, morning chapels, "grace" at every meal, and two solid summer weeks of menacing nightly exhortations from visiting revivalists.

When it rained or when it was too cold to be sent outside, we Brown Boys were confined to the basement, where I began to emerge from my emotional paralysis and to join in the traditional diversions—skinning the cat on the overhead pipes; building little tractors out of old thread spools, rubber bands, matchsticks, and Octagon soap; pitching pennies to a line on the floor drawn with chalk; or cutting coupons out of old magazines and sending them off, plastered to a penny postcard supplied by Muh Brown, for free samples of Ovaltine, Lifebuoy soap, Listerine, and Vicks Vaporub. We drank the exotically astringent Listerine—unaware, of course, that it contained alcohol—and ate the Vicks, which allegedly cured colds if rubbed on the chest, and used the jars for carrying contraband peanut butter out of the dining room.

Infrequently there was a light snow, and if anybody had any money—perhaps a dime or quarter sent from home—he would be cajoled into buying a pound of sugar and a bottle of vanilla extract (each cost a nickel) from a little store at the bottom of the Long Hill near the orphanage entrance. Then we would sneak milk from the dining room and make "snow cream." Some winter mornings we awoke in brilliant sunlight with hoarfrost on the baseball diamond and all the bare black tree branches encased in glistening ice, which crackled and snapped and showered to the ground when the wind blew.

When it was not raining in the winter and the leaves in the oak grove were temporarily raked up, we were sent outside, where we played the traditional games that had been handed down and perfected over several generations of boys: "fanning out" with a tennis ball and a broomstick, hell-over, hide and seek, marbles, fox and the wall, kick the can, and horseshoes. Sometimes I took shelter from the cold by climbing through the coal bin window and huddling among the lumps in the warmth from the furnace.

Soon after my arrival, the Raleigh Lions Club contributed money for the building of an oval concrete skating rink between the Brown Building and the dining hall, next to the swimming pool. A few boys had skates, sent to them by their families. A few had homemade scooters built with old skate wheels—found in trash piles in the woods—and nailed to the bottom of two-by-fours. Mostly we used the rink for seeing who could circle it running the most consecutive times. I was good at this because I was stubborn. In general, commercial toys were a rarity among us. Nutsy Perry had an old bicycle left to him in an uncle's will, and Little Nigger Rogers won one in a citywide marbles contest. We all carried our cache of marbles in our pockets and competed in rings drawn in the dirt with a stick. You got to keep the marbles that you could knock out of the ring while keeping your shooter inside. The shooter of choice was a "steelie," a steel ball bearing, of which Little Nigger Rogers had several—and a vast hoard of marbles he had won from us less skillful players.

In school I was an indifferent student. I was so enveloped in my unhappiness and my differentness that the dry mandated rote memorizing lessons could not ignite my imagination. My grades were mostly C's, with an occasional D in arithmetic and an A in

English. But I soon discovered that I liked reading and began to spend my free time in the musty third-floor library. I had it to myself and it became my secret refuge. I read voraciously, often in solitude, for the orphanage boys were generally uninterested in or actually hostile to books. I was swept off into imaginary worlds by *Robinson Crusoe*, *The Voyages of Dr. Dolittle*, *Tom Sawyer*, *The Bobbsey Twins at the Seashore*, *Huckleberry Finn*, *Uncle Tom's Cabin*, *Silver Chief: Dog of the North*, *The Deerslayer*, *The Last of the Mohicans*, *Heidi*, and dozens of other books. I was especially moved by anything written by Charles Dickens, Mark Twain, and Jack London, stories about outcasts, underdogs, and bullying.

This was my first exposure to non-pedagogical and fictive writing, and from then on I lived much of my time in solitary imaginings of worlds far beyond my reach—about which I talked to no one. Reading made my conviction grow that I was very different from the other boys. I had a secret self that I did not openly even hint at because of fear of being laughed at and tagged a "sissy," which was, tattletales excepted, the worst thing you could be in the orphanage. In my barricaded heart I felt lonely and alone much of the time. I had a secret place to which I retreated quite often—a perfumed bower beneath a weeping willow tree beside a brook below the barn, where I lay in green clover amid wild violets and listened to the robins, redbirds, bluebirds, thrushes, flickers, and woodpeckers talking in the trees and to the water gurgling over the rocks. I lay dreamily on my back and watched the towering clouds sail slowly along through the azure sky. At these moments I was overcome by a mix of ecstasy, loneliness, and hunger—for what I did not know.

This wastefulness and dreaminess I kept carefully hidden. I gradually adopted the tough exterior braggadocio of my peers: "I'm gonna kick a mudhole in your ass and stomp it dry" or "I'm so tough I've got muscles in my shit." There was also a lexicon of familiar taunts and insults, for example, "If I had a dog with a face like yours, I'd shave his ass and teach him to walk backwards" or "I saved your life this morning. I killed a shit-eating dog." Such talk was confined entirely to us boys. No one would have dared use "bad" words around Muh Brown, out of respect for her rectitude, or around "Daddy" Barnes—as the smallest children were encouraged to call him—or around girls, who were considered almost alien creatures and whose company we rarely shared anyhow.

As I increasingly took on the coloration and manners of a seasoned orphanage boy, I began to erase the conscious memory of my previous life. Occasionally I got a one-cent postcard from my mother or, more rarely, a scrawled letter with a dime taped inside. The short message was always the same: " Dear Son, I am doing fine and I hope you are fine. I hope you are doing what Mr. Barnes tells you to do. I hope I will get up there to see you soon. Love, Your Mother." She sometimes said she couldn't afford to come, or that she was sick, or that there was nobody to give her a ride. Only when her cards or letters came did I felt a stab of pain, confusion, and wonder as to why she had given Ethel Gray and me away.

My spirits lifted when spring burst upon us with the explosive flowering of the dogwoods and azaleas and the budding out of the oak and hickory trees. Spring's arrival was officially celebrated on Easter Sunday. This was the most important day of the year, even bigger than Christmas, at the orphanage, it being Christianity's most exultant event, but for the children it was most popular for its uncustomary secular delights, the main one being that when we returned to the campus after church, we got to take off our shoes and go barefoot until school started in September.

At church, the ladies from the town were arrayed in fine new dresses and hats and the men in their best suits. We orphanage boys and girls were in our new-smelling summer Sunday outfits for the first time. Tradition decreed that you wore a red rose pinned on your chest if your mother was alive and a white one if both parents were dead.

Easter was also time for the annual orphanage reunion, when the former residents returned for a long weekend. Extra tables were set up in the dining room. The returning alumnae always numbered 200 or more, and we had to double up in our beds to make room for them. For the noon Easter dinner, we got our best meal of the year: plenteous helpings of traditional Eastern Carolina chopped pork seasoned with vinegar, salt, and hot peppers, Brunswick stew, cole slaw, potatoes boiled in catsup and water, cornsticks, and sweetened ice tea, followed by, miracle of miracles, vanilla ice cream. And you could have all you wanted.

After dinner, everybody gathered in front of the Vann Building. The "old" boys and girls had hidden hundreds of candy Easter eggs in the huge grove and at the ring of a bell we raced downhill (the "big" boys and girls were excluded) for the annual Easter egg hunt. In time-honored fashion, we Brown boys had cut the pockets out of our corduroy knickers, which fastened close to our calves with elastic, so that we could fill both legs with candy. What followed was an orgy of boy gluttony.

And it wasn't over then. In the early evening, following an afternoon of fond laughter at "Do you remember when?" stories among the "old" boys and girls, there was, in place of the usual bag supper, the annual wiener roast. A wood fire was built in the incinerator behind the infirmary, and everybody gathered around its glow for hot dogs, marshmallows, and lemonade. Again, it was all you could eat and drink—and the lemonade was strong. That first year, my contemporary Dickie Tharrington ate sixteen hot dogs, a supposed record, at least for our age group.

As we cooked our wieners, wedged them into rolls, slathered them with French's mustard, and sprinkled them with raw chopped onion, and toasted marshmallows on sticks, we could see some of the old boys furtively disappear into the shadows on the periphery of the fire. We could hear them laughing and then they would ease quietly back into our mix, smelling of whiskey and wearing sheepish grins. Girls, though, did not drink. Leaving aside that drinking was a sin for everybody and a crime for us orphanage children worthy of being "sent away," it was even in the outside world thought unladylike to drink, and certainly not to be done in public. I wondered if I would drink when I got to be a man, and whether these old boys were indeed going down the slippery path to Hell and into the Lake of Fire as Daddy Barnes so regularly warned.

On Easter Monday morning, everybody went to the red clay baseball diamond in front of the Page Building for the avidly contested annual game between the resident orphanage team, dressed in its striped cotton suits with "MO" across the chest, and the old boys, dressed in street clothes. The old boys were the stars of past teams and they usually won.

After the game, the old boys and girls gradually drifted away, and by the next day our lives had returned to normal. Muh Brown resumed benevolent control of her domain, keeping watch over us from her rocking chair on the back porch of the Brown Building, knitting, and mending clothes. Though she was soft-spoken and kind, she ran a tight ship. Breaking the rules meant certain punishment—sitting on the stairs alone inside as the other boys played, or, for more serious crimes such as "telling a story," standing on one foot with your face against the wall in the study hall.

As it got warmer and the days got longer we began, with permission, to roam farther from the Brown Building.

"Muh, can we go to Peter Deep," somebody would ask.

"Yes, but listen for the bell," she would say.

Then we would run down the hill behind the dining hall through a hay field to a brook whose deepest pool came just about up to our crotches—thus "Peter Deep," although at this time of our abject innocence we did not make the connection between the water's depth and the most common euphemism for our "privates." We caught crayfish and made them fight each other while dragonflies—"snake doctors" we called them—flitted overhead and daddy longlegs darted on the water. We collected "frog jelly," the gelatinous substance in which eggs were suspended, in jars, sat the jars on shelves, and waited for the tadpoles that morphed into frogs.

To otherwise entertain ourselves, we slid down hills on pieces of tin and cardboard, caught rats and made them swim in the millpond until they drowned, and climbed through big underground culverts. We set bottles on posts and had contests shooting rocks with our homemade slingshots. We played baseball with old balls whose leather covers had been knocked off and which we covered with "sticking plaster" swiped from the infirmary. In the woods we dug tunnels with tin cans and made underground hideouts with walls and ceilings supported by pieces of scrap wood and corrugated tin. Into these we carried contraband food—perhaps peanut butter saved for one of us by an older sister or girlfriend. Sometimes we had Pepsis ("Pepsi Cola Hits The Spot, 12 Full Ounces, That's A Lot!") or Dr Peppers and Hobo Buns purchased at the Milky Way just beyond the orphanage fence on St. Mary's Street with nickels and dimes acquired by saving tinfoil from empty cigarette packs—found on adjacent streets—until it became a big enough ball to sell at Weinstein's junkyard at five cents a pound. We made magnifying glasses out of the concave bottoms of Coke bottles and used them to burn our initials into wood and to light piles of dried leaves.

In the leafy trees down behind the campus barn, which housed Pat the mule—another eight mules lived at the farm—tools, a hay rake, and a wagon, we walked the swaying limbs of the oaks and maples and swung from long wild grapevines with Tarzan yells.

Some days we lined up and bet pennies as to who could piss the farthest and sang a song about a lady with prodigious projectile talents:

> *Did you ever see Lilly make water?*
> *She pisses a beautiful stream.*
> *She pisses a mile and a quarter.*
> *She's a regular old pissing machine.*

Girls were a subject of endless conversation and wildly inaccurate information among the vastly older boys of eleven who were resident with me in the Brown Building while I was still a "new boy" and a larval Lothario. Occasionally while exploring the woods across St. Mary's Street to make forts out of abandoned car bodies or to forage for wild plums and huckleberries, we came upon used "rubbers" where amorous couples had parked their cars on sandy paths. We poked at these exotic and repulsive yellowed objects with sticks, and our older colleagues commented that "somebody got some." There was also speculative talk among these older colleagues of a rubber called a "French Tickler," though no one knew exactly what this was or what it was for, except that it was involved in some way with the exciting but sinful world of sex.

As spring passed into summer, we Brown Boys were boarded onto the big Dodge farm truck after breakfast and hauled to the 250-acre orphanage farm, five miles distant from the campus beyond a suburban mill village on Highway 401 called Carolee. On the farm we raised vegetables for feeding the people at the orphanage and hay and corn for the mules, cows, and pigs. The corn for the cows was cut off at the ground while still green. It was hauled on the mule wagon from the fields and fed several stalks at a time into a chute with blades driven by a belt attached to the tractor, and the resultant silage was pumped up into two giant silos attached to the cow barn. It was used for the winter feeding of our sixty Holstein cows.

The corn for the mules and pigs was allowed to dry out, and we plucked the ears with chapped hands in early winter and tossed them into a two-mule wagon. They were stored in a corn-crib attached to our big barn and we shucked them by hand as needed through the winter.

During the summer days we shed our shirts and picked bushel baskets of tomatoes, butter beans, corn, string beans, carrots, squash, mustard greens, turnips, and cucumbers for the orphanage kitchen. These were brought back at noon, and the dining room girls shucked the corn and shelled the beans in the afternoon. We weeded the crops with short-handled hoes and distributed "soda" (ammonium nitrate) along the rows of corn out of three-quart cans with dime-size holes punched in their bottoms.

In dry spells we put a wooden barrel onto a one-horse wagon, filled the barrel a gallon at a time from the creek that ran through the farm, and watered the vegetables by hand using old three-quart cans.

On many days during my first summer I was the water boy for the older boys who performed the more senior farm jobs—plowing, baling hay, building fences, and digging stumps in new ground. There was a natural spring in the woods by Brickyard Hill to which I went with a zinc bucket and a dipper. I was supposed to sit at the edge of the woods with a full bucket until someone cried "Water Boy!"

By early summer our footpads had thickened and toughened.

In the afternoons after our farm work we roamed in small packs barefoot far from the campus to pick blackberries. We went door to door trying to sell them for ten cents a quart and twenty-five cents a gallon with only occasional success. What we couldn't sell we ate, or we squeezed them through a piece of cloth into a bucket, added sugar, and made what we called wine.

Sometimes after a successful blackberry sale, we made lemonade. With sugar at five cents a pound, and lemons two for a nickel, with a dime we could make a whole gallon jar of lemonade. This was anemic stuff but popular, for lemons were a rarity. Sometimes we cooked a pound of sugar in a three-quart can until it caramelized and hardened into "rock candy" that we carried in our pockets, gathering lint. We also foraged for red and yellow wild plums, which grew in profuse thickets in many areas within walking distance of our campus. There was also the knowledge, passed down for years, of the location of every apple, peach, pecan, and pear tree within five miles of the orphanage boundary, and we raided them ruthlessly and without conscience—barefoot Robin Hoods in short ducks.

The orphanage did not have any fruit trees save for a forlorn apple tree in the middle of the skating rink whose fruit we captured long before it was ripe. There was a balding man named Fred Fletcher who lived with his wife in a brick house across the small creek that bordered the orphanage property on Glenwood Avenue. He was a local celebrity, a radio announcer with WRAL, and a great friend of the orphanage. More important to us boys than his celebrity was the fact that he had a large apple tree in his back yard. One summer day when the apples were ripe, three slightly older boys, Paul Smith, Greasy Brooks, and Leche Aguirre talked one of my classmates and friends, Bill Long, then age eleven, into climbing Fred Fletcher's tree and throwing down apples to them. Fred Fletcher was not at home, they assured Bill, but they promised that in any case they would stand guard, while at the same time gathering the bounty that Bill would throw down.

Paul Smith clinched the deal when he told him, "You're a better climber than we are, and besides, Fred Fletcher doesn't care if we have a few apples."

So Bill clambered up the tree and was happily eating an apple and dropping others to the ground when Fred Fletcher threw open his back door brandishing a shotgun.

"Don't move an inch. I've got you covered with this shotgun," he yelled. Terrified but thinking fast, Bill yelled back, "It's against the law to shoot a man when he's in a tree."

Fred Fletcher burst out laughing, called his wife to the door, and told Bill Long, "Tell my wife what you just told me."

"It's against the law to shoot a man when he's in a tree," Bill said.

Fred Fletcher laughed again—and so did his wife—but said. "All you boys come with me. I'm taking you to Mr. Barnes."

Mr. Barnes's house was near Fred Fletcher's at the foot of the hill. "I ought to thrash every one of you," he said when Fred Fletcher told him what happened. Instead, he sentenced them to mow Fred Fletcher's lawn and wash his windows for six months. During this time Fred Fletcher would occasionally emerge from his house and get Bill Long to repeat what he'd said, and then he'd laugh again.

Watermelons were a rare delight, available to us only on July 4 when we had the annual Watermelon Feast beside the swimming pool. Two dozen melons were lined up in a row and, after Mr. Barnes said a blessing, they were sliced and apportioned by dormitory. We boys were able to gorge ourselves because only a few smaller girls partook. Eating watermelon was considered déclassé by the "stuck-up" big girls. Some unknown friend of the orphanage always donated these melons.

On summer evenings the big boys got exclusive use of the swimming pool, forty feet wide and a hundred feet long, with a diving board at the deep end and a baby pool at the other, because they worked on the farm all day. We little boys swam at allotted hours during the day, wearing hand-me-down white-belted scratchy wool suits. We learned to swim the traditional orphanage way—by being tossed into the deep end by older boys. It was sink or swim. Girls swam separately, during the late afternoon, and the older boys gathered along the iron rail around the pool and furtively ogled the shapelier ones, their "curves" encased in one-piece suits. Once a month the pool was drained, and it was a Brown Boy chore to get in and scrub its algae-greened walls foot by foot with brushes as the water level lowered.

At night after supper, the swimming pool being closed to us, we played hide and seek, fox and the wall, and other games, and caught in our hands the yellow-winking fireflies that lazed through the honeysuckled air. We captured slow-flying stinkbugs and flew them over our heads on thread tethers tied to their legs.

There was very little mingling between boys and girls. For one thing, there wasn't much time for it. Dating, or having a girlfriend, was not officially forbidden, but there were few real opportunities for such an arrangement. Being caught alone with a girl at night was a serious offence. In my early years at the orphanage, it was viewed as grave and incorrigible enough to warrant being "sent away" to the legendarily dreaded state-run Jackson Training School, whose viciously wielded paddles were reputed to leave the initials "JTS" engraved on your butt.

Some years before my arrival at the orphanage, girls who were caught alone in the company of boys at night were locked in closets and their heads shaved. Late in my era, some dating was countenanced but it was chaperoned by matrons in the "sitting

rooms" of the big girls' dormitory. All that took place was whatever furtive "necking" could be done in semi-public. There was
not in the whole history of the orphanage a known case of a girl
getting pregnant and actual sexual intercourse was in fact
unheard of. If anybody was doing it, it was a closely held secret.
And with good reason, for that sin would have meant instant
expulsion.

My tenth birthday, August 30, 1937, was also the date of a
much ballyhooed heavyweight boxing match between champion
Joe Louis, the Brown Bomber, and Tommy Farr, a British chal-
lenger. It was such an exciting event that the Brown and Page
boys had been allowed to assemble together in the study hall of
the Page Building to listen to it on the radio. But early in the fight,
the matron came in and said that all Brown Boys were to go back
immediately to their building and that Big Jeebie Clay, Billy Bates,
and Maurice Evans were to report immediately to Mr. Barnes in
his office in the Vann Building. They were twelve years old. What
could this all about, we wondered? Interest and conversation
quickly shifted away from the fight, for this was an unprecedented summons.

The whole true story of what had happened to prompt Mr.
Barnes's next frightening moves has never been known. What we
heard was that the three boys went off to pick wild plums and
came back on campus just at sunset, up through Peter Deep
behind the dining room and beside the laundry. There was a hole
in the laundry's brick wall where the steam pipes from the Vann
Building boiler went in, a hole big enough to crawl through.
Peeking through this large hole in the bricks they spotted a girl
named Dorothy Rochdale, who was a grade ahead of the three
boys and two years older, having at one point failed a grade. She
had been Billy Bates's girlfriend and on occasion had smooched
with him. Billy crawled through the hole and went into the drying

rooms where she was folding clothes. She was apparently being made to work late as a punishment. When Billy didn't reappear, Jeebie and Maurice crawled through the hole to see what was happening, and saw Billy writhing on top of her on the floor. They went in and when Billy got up, first Jeebie and then Maurice got on top of her, too, before Billy pulled them off. Dorothy apparently became scared that things had gone too far and jumped up and ran away, whereupon the boys became frightened, too, and fled.

What details may have filtered up to Old Man Barnes was not known by the boys but when they got to his office he was in a rage. He told them he knew what they had done and that it was one of the worst things that had ever happened in the orphanage, something indescribable and unforgivable. He said he was going to teach them a lesson they would never forget, but he would go easier on them if they confessed. Billy Bates admitted he had been the ringleader, that he had "done something" to Dorothy Rochdale. Jeebie and Maurice admitted they had "tried to do something" but that nothing really had happened. Dorothy Rochdale, though, had been frightened enough to go to the infirmary. What the "something" was no one knew, perhaps not even the boys themselves. We were all very innocent. In any case, Old Man Barnes listened to their account with a grim face and sternly told them to go back to the Brown Building and wait for him.

"When we get there and I ask you what you did in the laundry, say 'I did something dirty to a girl' and that's all. Nothing more and nothing less." he said.

When the rest of us got back to the Brown Building, Muh told us to go to her room and sit on the floor. Shortly Old Man Barnes walked through the door brandishing a long oak paddle fashioned from a chair rung and ordered the three accused to line up in front of him. They stood there, heads down. Old Man Barnes ordered us to bow our heads in prayer. He closed his eyes, turned his head upward, and in a fierce voice said that the ugliest kind of sinful occurrence had brought us together. He ordered us to close our eyes while he prayed for guidance.

"What these boys have done is an abomination in Thy sight, O Lord, an affront to all that is holy and decent, and to everything we hold sacred in Thy name, especially womanhood.

"Be with us, dear Lord, and guide us and strengthen our hand as we deal with these sinners in Thy name and for Thy sake. In Jesus' name we pray, Amen."

Muh Brown was crying softly. Mr. Barnes then took off his white linen suit coat and, with sweat rolling down his angry red face, he one by one beat the boys relentlessly on the back of the legs with the oaken chair rung until the blood ran down. None of them cried out. There was no sound except for the awful whacking of the paddle on their legs and Old Man Barnes's labored breathing. We other boys watched in dreadful fear. I had to turn away.

After he was done, Old Man Barnes announced that Billy Bates and Maurice Evans were to be sent away and that Jeebie Clay was to be confined to his bed for two weeks. Billy and Maurice were gone the next day, never to be heard from again. Dorothy Rochdale disappeared, too. Jeebie was hurt so bad he had to spend a week in the infirmary.

Why Billy and Evans were not sent to the Jackson Training School instead of being permanently expelled, no one knew. And where they went exactly we didn't know. Maybe it would have taken a court action to send them to the training school, and maybe they hadn't done anything criminal. (Despite rumors, no one in the long history of the orphanage ever had ever actually been sent there, so far as we knew. Only two orphanage boys had ever gone to prison. At age sixteen, they had teamed up and were drinking with some "town tacks" when they stole some dynamite from our farm and blew up the small earthen dam at Boone's Pond on the outskirts of Raleigh as a prank. They also stole a car.)

What happened in the laundry made the fear of being sent away hover even more menacingly over us all. A solemn quietude persisted for several days. Muh Brown hardly came out of her room. But I was in no danger of being expelled because I was always the good boy my mother had asked me to be—polite to adults, conscientious about carrying out my assigned tasks, obedient if inattentive in class, and quiet in church.

Meantime, I had not seen my mother since that bleak day in December when she said goodbye and I went off to quarantine. I didn't want to think about her.

School began soon after my birthday and the laundry room incident. This signaled the official end of summer play, and work on the farm. And we had to put our shoes back on. That was bad, but what was worse was that Muh Brown lined us up in the study hall and administered us each a tablespoon of greasy, nauseating cod liver oil. This was supposedly a prophylactic against colds. We got a piece of hard candy as a chaser. Into mothballs went our summer clothes and out came the winter ones again—knickers, long-sleeved shirts, sweaters, and black brogans.

Soon excitement I did not at first understand began to build in the Brown Building. All the boys began talking about doing something called "making a wish." Little Jeebie Clay explained to me what that was. You could write a "wish" on a piece of paper for a Christmas gift not exceeding $1 in value, and the wish would be fulfilled. The women's groups of the Eastern Carolina churches that supported the orphanage were the source of this largesse. A dollar was a large sum, and the range of things you could "wish" for was quite wide: a two-battery flashlight, a Scout knife, an aviator cap with goggles, a Marine Band harp, a magnifying glass, a gyroscope, model airplane kits, Tinkertoys, crossword puzzles, a tool set, a microscope set, a Dick Tracy cap pistol, various kinds of toy trucks and cars, a yo-yo, and several kinds of pound boxes of candy: chocolate covered cherries, Snickers, B. B. Bats, Mounds, Peter Pauls, or Baby Ruths. Most of the boys, I learned, wished for candy.

As Christmas approached, I was painfully conscious of the fact that two days after Christmas was the first anniversary of my arrival at the orphanage. But as Christmas morning arrived I was excited. We went to breakfast in the dark to find an orange on our plates—the first physical evidence that this was indeed a special day.

When we got back to the Brown Building Muh ushered us into the study hall, where on a wall molding she had hung us each a small mesh stocking, full with nuts, candy, and a tangerine. We dressed in our Sunday clothes and trooped excitedly into the auditorium at 10 A.M. A giant Christmas tree stood in the center of the stage with a mountain of presents around it. We sat down and squirmed with excited impatience as Mr. Barnes rocked back and forth on his heels and admonished us to remember the true meaning of Christmas, and the orphanage Glee Club sang "Away in a Manger" and "Oh, Holy Night."

A visiting dignitary always dressed up as Santa Claus, and my first year it was a portly, gray-haired man named Josephus Daniels. He was the owner of the *Raleigh News & Observer*. He had formerly been undersecretary of the Navy under President Franklin Roosevelt and at this time was Roosevelt's ambassador to Mexico. "Ho, ho, ho," he said awkwardly, and began picking up presents from under the tree, calling out the names and handing them out. It was a long process, for there were 300 names. When mine was called I nervously mounted the steps to the stage, walked self-consciously across, and took my present and a little gift bag Santa Claus had for everyone. Opening of presents was not allowed until the whole process was finished.

As I had hoped, my silver flashlight with an adjustable spotlight worked perfectly. The gift bag contained a trove of delights—striped candy canes, hard candy, an apple, a tangerine, English walnuts, pecans, nigger toes (Brazil nuts), almonds—plus a tiny Mexican donkey woven from hemp.

After we returned to the Brown Building, bartering began—with the admonition of "don't try to Jew me down"—and I had several offers to swap things for my flashlight. I declined. I took it to bed that night—with a stomach crammed with goodies—and shined it under my tented sheet and made spots on the ceiling. It was my first Christmas present.

I had gotten a Christmas card from my mother. She said she wasn't well and was sorry she didn't have any money for a present. I had no money either, but I sent her a penny post card wishing her a Merry Christmas. Soon after that I got a letter from my mother announcing that she had been diagnosed with tuberculosis and was being sent to a TB sanatorium in Southern Pines. Her letters then became even less frequent and I tucked her further away into the fenced-off recesses of my mind. I saw her once in the next four years. One Friday when I was eleven the orphanage's football team had a game at Sanford, fifty miles southwest of Raleigh, and Mr. Barnes had me ride in the truck with the players and dropped me off to spend the day with her. She was ensconced in an antiseptic-smelling, long hall of beds—an elongated sun porch—dressed in pajamas and a robe, with a sputum cup on the little table beside her bed. She looked pale and defeated. I didn't know what to say to her and stood awkwardly by her bed.

"How are you doing in school, Son?"

"Fine."

"Are you doing what Mr. Barnes tells you to do? Are you being a good boy?"

"Yes, Mama."

"I don't know when I am going to get out of here. They say it will be a good long while. I don't know why I have had such a terrible life. If I ever do get well, and you grow up, we're going to get a little white house with a white picket fence and a big garden. I never had a home but I have always dreamed of having one where I could cook and raise vegetables and flowers and you could be the man of the house."

I felt a fist of dull pain in my stomach and all I could think about was when would the truck come to take me back to the orphanage. I wanted to run. I felt like I was bad. What kind of son wouldn't feel love for his mother, and want to be with her, especially a mother who had sacrificed so much and had such an unfortunate life?

I forgot about her again when we got back to the orphanage. Protective layers were growing one by one around my heart, like onion skin. I resumed what had become a familiar and comfortable routine, working, going to school, playing with my friends, and going to church. I was hardly ever alone except when I sought solitude. I didn't feel so lonely any more. The other boys seemed to accept me. I had made two special friends, Cootie Roach and Little Jeebie Clay. Muh Brown was very kind to me, so as time more quickly passed I was in some ways, like my friends, beginning to feel a certain fierce pride in being an "orphanage boy."

Chapter 4

Big Boy

I HAD BEEN in the Brown Building almost four years, had finally learned to be comfortable and secure there in the warm discipline of Muh Brown and in the acceptance of my peers, when right after my August 30 birthday Muh called me into her room, hugged me, told me to pack up all my clothes except what I was wearing, and leave them in my locker. I was moving up to the Page Building, the next-door repository for intermediate age boys. I felt very sad. Muh Brown had become my substitute mother. She had loved and comforted me and made me feel special, although there were many other boys in her charge. She was the person I felt closest to in the orphanage, the only one who had seemed to take a special interest in me. She said I would be all right, that I would always be her little boy. There were tears in her eyes, and I began to cry, too. She smiled and said I wouldn't have to wear short ducks and knickers anymore. I would now be wearing long pants with the other bigger boys.

My new matron was Mrs. Eudell Smith. She was not like Muh Brown at all. She had coal black hair, dark eyes beneath penciled brows, and her bosoms bulged out of white blouses. She was just this side of thirty. She was the wife of the new football, baseball, and basketball coach, Fred Smith. He was a heavy-bearded giant of a man (six foot, three inches, 225 pounds) with a hoarse high-pitched voice who had been a college football star. He and his wife had been college sweethearts at Appalachian State Teachers College in the mountains of North Carolina. They had two sons, ten and twelve, whom they carefully kept away from us boys. Their sons attended city public schools away from the campus.

The Smith family lived in a suite at the front of the Borden Building. Unlike Muh Brown, Mrs. Smith was aloof and did not much involve herself with us boys. She left the discipline to her husband, who besides being the coach was also the seventh-grade teacher.

I quickly learned that some of my peers were taking turns sneaking into the hall during the day, when Mr. Smith was absent in teaching or coaching, and peeking through the keyhole of their apartment hoping to see some part and perhaps by some miracle all of Mrs. Smith naked. This was a vain hope, as it turned out, although Mex Aguirre rushed excitedly back to the basement locker room one day to brag that he had seen her in her bra and slip.

The boys who participated in this spying did so with extreme caution, with a lookout posted at the back door, for quickly after his arrival Fred Smith came much to be feared. He had a violent and combustible temper. He hit Fatty Clark over the head with a hard-backed arithmetic book—for talking in class—so hard that the book collapsed on all sides and knocked Fatty out of his seat. He frequently skipped past the formality of the usually imposed punishments, such as confinement in the basement or the surrendering of certain privileges, and went straight to physical slaps or blows. This was unusual. Theretofore Mr. Barnes had been the only one at the orphanage to mete out corporeal punishment. No one reported Mr. Smith, of course, but there was the hope that Mr. Barnes would somehow find out and get rid of him. He was universally disliked.

I did not participate in the surveillance at Mrs. Smith's door, or in other escapades that I usually might have been inclined toward, because, leaving aside other inhibitions, I upon arriving at the Page Building rapidly slipped into a silent melancholia. I missed Muh Brown and my friends terribly. The old feelings of dread and cold that I had experienced in my first weeks at the orphanage came right back. I stopped eating and stopped playing and talking, stayed by myself when possible, and soon began to seriously lose weight. Somebody must have told Mrs. Smith of my state, for she called me in and ordered me to go to the infirmary. Mrs. Fogleman and Stick Watson had by then moved on and the infirmary was now being run by a rosy, warm, widowed nurse named Mrs. Wall, who had two daughters of about my age. She examined me and took me downtown to the official orphanage physician, Dr. Bell. They didn't find any medical problems, but Mrs. Wall said she temporarily wanted to keep me in the infirmary for a while for "observation." I was put in the same ward where I had been quarantined my first week and where I had recovered from a tonsillectomy my third year there (every child was knocked out with ether in the infirmary and had their tonsils removed). She brought her daughters and read books to us, and even took us downtown to the S & W cafeteria where she said I could walk through the food line and pick out anything I wanted. It was my first restaurant meal, and I gorged on meat loaf, baked chicken with stuffing, mashed potatoes and gravy, candied sweet potatoes, and black-eyed peas—topped off by a slab of apple pie and ice cream—while Mrs. Wall looked on with fond amusement.

Under her solicitous care, I immediately began to get better and to put on weight. After ten days she sent me back to the Page Building carrying a hand-written note addressed to Mrs. Smith. I peeked at it along the way and it said in part that "what this child needs is a lot of T.L.C." I had no idea what that meant. Vitamins, maybe. But life soon return to the norm—structured, disciplined, impersonal—and I regained my sense of belonging. As before, Mrs. Smith rarely spoke to me or to any of the other boys. Everybody said she was stuck up.

In the summer, the duty of the Page Building boys was to board the truck after breakfast, go to the farm, and chop the long rows of vegetables with hoes to get rid of weeds. The big boys plowed, milked cows, baled hay, cut ditch banks, put up fences, pulled corn, and removed stumps. When late fall came, we smaller boys had to rake leaves in the huge oak, dogwood, and maple groves on the campus. This was in the afternoon after school. We worked in teams, moving the leaves into parallel rows with spring-toothed rakes, from which point they were hoisted onto the orphanage's big Dodge farm truck with tall sidegates by means of a vast scoop made with two poles and a sheet of canvas. The truck was then driven to the farm where we spread the leaves in the barn where our milk cows were housed and fed during the winter when the pastures were frozen.

By early spring, before planting time, the leaves and manure had become compacted into three feet of ammonia-smelling com-

My sister and I at the Methodist Orphanage when I was twelve and she eight. Girls and boys were kept separated and I did not see her often.

post, which we pitchforked into a mule-drawn manure spreader whose gear blades flung it out over the fallow fields in preparation for plowing. Later in the spring, we went to the farm every day after school and planted vegetables. When it rained we swam naked in the swollen creek by the bridge and got in mud fights, or stacked bales of hay in the barn loft and made secret mazes and tunnels and placed bets on who could stay hidden the longest.

In our summer off-time, which was Saturday and Sunday afternoons, we roamed the woods beyond the campus looking for dogwood trees with symmetrical forks with which we made the slingshots—"bean-shooters" we called them—that all orphanage boys carried. The dogwood was the only tree with wood hard enough and perfectly symmetrical branches from which to hew a staff. The rest of the slingshot was string, strips of rubber from an old inner tube, and a leather pocket fashioned from a shoe tongue. Every boy carried his bean-shooter in his hip pocket and a load of rocks in a front pocket—ammunition at the ready with which to shoot at birds and squirrels or bottles atop posts. Some boys were astonishingly accurate with these bean-shooters, even deadly enough to kill an occasional squirrel in a tree, which was immediately skinned and cooked on a shovel in the furnace, producing a stringy and bitter but exotic meal.

Part of the fighting code was that bean-shooters were forbidden as too dangerous for man-to-man combat—even in skirmishes against the small band of despised but respected black boy warriors who sometimes ventured into the woods between the orphanage and the small "niggertown" on Oberlin Road. (Years before in such a fight, the lore had it, an orphanage boy had an eye put out by a rock from a bean-shooter.) These battles were fought over who would rule the woods. These interlopers called us "soda crackers" and we called them "niggers." This was with never a thought of racism. We had no idea what racism was. Such a thing was never discussed. We felt superior, certainly in matters martial, to all outside boys, because we were tougher.

Smoking was another badge of advancing manhood, and we aped the older boys by puffing dried corn silk and a wild bitterly acrid plant called "rabbit tobacco," wrapped in strips of newspaper. In the evenings some boys roamed Glenwood Avenue and St. Mary's Street searching for cigarette butts tossed from cars. The popular brands—Lucky Strike, Camel, and Chesterfield, cost twenty cents a pack, but there were others, Sensation, Spud, Wings, Cavalier, that were only fifteen cents. Shortly after I became a Page Boy we began getting ten-cents-a-month allowance. The big boys got twenty-five cents. But the sacrifice of your allowance for cigarettes, as measured against the lure of a twelve-ounce Royal Crown cola and a Moon Pie or a hobo bun, was unthinkable.

At about this time in my development, Mex Aguirre and Pussy Leathers summoned me one day up into a tree house. They asked me if I knew how to "jack off." I blushingly confessed I did not, whereupon they brandished stiff little dicks and demonstrated. My face was hot with shame but I did not want to be different or be laughed at, so I followed their lead. I soon felt a stinging sensation in the groin, but no discharge. I was still too young, they said, to "shoot off"—ejaculate.

In the summer, after I was thirteen, we got to go to the movies every two weeks, if we had the ten cents admission and this privilege had not been withdrawn as punishment for something. We walked in chaperoned groups downtown to the Capitol and Wake theaters, along Glenwood Avenue, past houses whose lighted windows revealed families seated at the dinner table or listening to the radio in the living room. At such moments I was swept over by a strange longing—and anger at the people inside.

Three months and a week after my fourteenth birthday, I was

in the bathroom getting ready for church on Sunday morning, December 7, 1941, when someone ran down the hall shouting that the Japs had bombed Pearl Harbor. What did this mean? We all gathered around the radio and heard President Roosevelt talk about "a day that will live in infamy" and say that we were now in a state of war with Japan. We had known nothing about the Japanese except for seeing bubblegum wrappers that pictured slavering Japanese soldiers skewering babies and killing old men and women with bayonets in some place called Manchuria. Soon we got word that many of the "old boys" were signing up for the service—most for the Navy, for some reason—and some of our seniors were dropping out of school to enlist, and coming back to visit in their spiffy uniforms.

As the war effort cranked up, we worked in the fields on the farm alongside Highway 401 and watched Army convoys go by, lorries loaded with soldiers and trucks hauling guns, and Army Air Corps planes flying in formation on training missions from Fort Bragg, which was fifty miles away. It was a point of pride that none of our seniors or old boys waited to be drafted. They joined up. And not a single one was turned down, either, proof that the orphanage's plain diet and hard regimen had produced healthy bodies. But Coach Fred Smith didn't join up or make himself available for the draft. He got a job as a locomotive fireman with the Seaboard railroad. Such jobs were considered vital to the national defense and thus qualified one for a draft deferment. It began to be whispered among the boys that Fred Smith was a "draft dodger." That was a bad thing to be called. The war was unanimously supported. One day on the back porch Froggy Tharrington, who had come up from the Brown Building right after me, muttered, "Draft Dodger," as Fred Smith came up on the porch in his overalls, his face blackened with coal smoke.

"What did you call me?" he turned to Dickie and said.

"Draft dodger," Dickie muttered.

Fred Smith rushed at him like a maddened bull, knocked him down, pinned him to the concrete, and began to beat him with his fists, breathing heavily and sweating. Dickie took the hard blows to his head and back silently, bent in a fetal position. When it was over he gave Fred Smith a defiant look and got up and limped away. A week or so later, Dickie got sick with a 104-degree fever and was diagnosed with spinal meningitis. He died at Rex Hospital on St. Mary's Street near the orphanage three days later. We were immediately quarantined in our building for two weeks. Nobody else got sick, and a lot of the boys connected Dickie's death to the beating and blamed Fred Smith. This was the first time anyone close to me had died. I was angry at the injustice, and angry at our impotence to do anything about it. So were my friends. Charlie Clay said to us Fred Smith should be arrested, but of course no one spoke up, and so none of it reached Old Man Barnes.

There was a funeral service for Dickie in the auditorium, presided over by the Rev. A. J. Hobbs, pastor of the Edenton Street Methodist Church, where we were now attending services every Sunday. Hobbs was a bald, pink-faced, and hog-jowled man with a purring and obsequious manner. We Page Boys were sequestered in a special section in the auditorium, because of the quarantine. I was chosen to be one of the pallbearers, and I sat beside Hobbs in his black Buick as we rode to the Oakwood Cemetery near the state capitol, where the orphanage had a special section, for Dickie's burial.

"Why did God make Dickie die?" I asked him on the way.

"God moves in mysterious ways," he said. "He has his purpose, but we can't always know it. We just have to have faith that God knows what he is doing."

I didn't respond but his answer didn't satisfy me at all, and this marked the beginning of my clearly formed doubts about God and religion. If God was all-powerful and in control of all events, like a puppeteer, then what kind of puppeteer was he that he killed innocent boys—or for that matter let them get beat up? What kind of God—although this I could only allow myself to feel and not allow myself to think—would take a little boy like me from his mother and put him in an orphanage?

I did not let anyone else in on these nascent doubts. I thought I was the only one among us who had them, for no one else expressed anything but obedient if silent piety and acceptance of the religion that was crammed constantly into us. I didn't want to be seen as different, though I was increasingly convinced that I was.

I had not seen my mother for two years when she was released from the TB sanatorium and came for Easter, wearing a white hat and a blue dress. She looked older and thinner and even more unhappy, and suddenly I felt guilty for not thinking about her more and not writing her more letters. She ate with Ethel Gray and me in the dining room and later sat and talked with us on the grass in the grove of trees in front of the Vann Building. I was silent and uncomfortable and wanted to run away and play with my friends, especially when she began to talk about giving us up, and how it was a sacrifice forced upon her, the low point of her terrible life.

"I didn't have any choice," she said. "You know, son, I would lay down my life for you."

When she left in mid-afternoon, I was relieved.

Not having Muh Brown's tenderness in my life any more, I sought more and escape in the orphanage library. I began to read more serious and grown-up stories—*Les Misérables, Don Quixote, Hard Times, The Red Badge of Courage, Two Years Before the Mast, Moby-Dick, Ivanhoe,* and *The Courtship of Miles Standish.*

I liked poetry, especially the epic kind, and I was the only one in my class who memorized and recited in full "The Walrus and the Carpenter," "The Rhyme of the Ancient Mariner," and "The Cremation of Sam McGee." I also memorized and amused my friends with a scatological version of that Robert W. Service poem, which ended with "and there on the floor, with his asshole tore, lay Dangerous Dan McGrew."

Scatology and profanity in all its forms were officially forbidden, of course, but "cursing" was a badge of toughness and looming manhood, and all of us used it with exuberant defiance around each other. Old Man Barnes was particularly intolerant of profanity and to be caught by him—if he happened to wander into an off-color conversation—would bring down a severe punishment, such as digging up an oak tree stump in your spare time. This would require several Saturday afternoons of hard labor with a grubbing hoe for digging and an axe for cutting the roots.

Old Man Barnes was extremely watchful over the girls. Infrequently big girls would sneak out of the Burwell Building at night and meet their boyfriends in the grove. So Old Man Barnes patrolled the grove with a big four-cell Eveready flashlight hoping to catch them. He also would show up at the Cole Building unexpectedly at night and do bed checks, shining his flashlight onto each blanket, hoping to catch some sexual adventurer at large. The older boys, and some of the girls who had been the object of his special attention, were cynical about his preoccupation with sex. Some girls told some older boys, and they told us, that Old Man Barnes would "feel them up" (touch their breasts) while pretending to count their ribs.

His obsession wasn't limited to girls and what we might do to or with them. He frequently interrupted our study halls at night, dismissed the matron, and lectured us severely on the evils of "self-abuse." He quoted the Scripture's urging that if "thine eye offends thee, put it out; if thine hand offends thee, cut it off," whose application to this issue, he said, meant plunging your "tallywacker" under the cold water tap. He said you could always tell a boy who abused himself, for he would be pale, weak, and guilty-looking. It stunted growth, he said, along with undermining good moral character.

Of course, everybody masturbated, in solitary shame. On moonlit nights I would lie awake and see the blankets rising and falling on other beds. There was no homosexuality as far as I was ever aware. If anyone had any such tendencies, they were never exhibited. Blustering insults of "you queer" and "suck me off" were exchanged but no one knew exactly what a "queer" was or what they did. All we knew was that being "queer" was shameful in the extreme, even worse than the mysterious "muff diver."

When I was fourteen we had a Sunday school teacher at the Edenton Street Methodist Church named Mr. Hudson. He wore black suits and his thinning gray hair was pomaded and combed over to the side. One Sunday he invited me and two of my classmates, Bill Britt and Adrian Clewis, to go swimming at the downtown YMCA. Mr. Barnes gave his approval, and next thing we knew the three of us were swimming nude, and Hudson was posing us naked beside the pool and taking our pictures. He gave us each a set. I blacked out the genital areas of mine. Unfortunately for him, word of the pictures got back to Mr. Barnes. That was the end of the swimming at the Y for us. And Mr. Barnes immediately banned Hudson from the campus and he disappeared from the church. We had no idea he was after us sexually.

Our awakening interest was in girls. In the back of the dining room there was an outside steel stairway with a landing at the top where the dining room girls sometimes gathered to gossip, and I furtively lurked with my buddies Little Jeebie Clay and Cootie Roach under the landing, hoping to be able to look up their dresses. We never could. And as we rode to and from the farm on the truck we clung to the side-gates and peeked over, hoping to see a woman driver with her dress up around her thighs. Sometimes to our great excitement that actually happened.

Soon after her release from the TB sanatorium my mother married a man named Sherman Johnson whom she had met there. I got a letter from her informing me of this. He was a nice and kind man, she said, a widower with three grown children, and he looked forward to meeting me. They moved to the town of Wilson, about fifty miles east of Raleigh, and into a tiny unpainted wooden house at 301 Pine Street, a twenty-dollar-a-month rental house already tenanted by my mother's sister, Belle, and Belle's husband, Walter Sills, who was paralyzed as result of a fall from a house roof and permanently confined to bed, unable even to speak.

My Aunt Belle was a coarse-faced and potato-shaped woman with rough red hands who, as I look back, looked like she belonged in a Brueghel painting. She bore no resemblance whatever to my mother. She earned meager wages walking to sick people's houses and doing their cooking and cleaning. She and Uncle Walter lived in two rooms on one side of the house and my mother and her new husband in two rooms on the other. In back was small kitchen with a wood stove and a bathroom with a toilet and a tub with only a cold water faucet.

My mother wrote and asked Old Man Barnes if I could come for a weekend. Since I had not seen her for a long time, he agreed. Mr. Barnes drove me to the bus station, bought me a Trailways bus ticket, and waited while I boarded. Listless mothers and children and old people occupied the seats and though there were a few stops along the way, it was a silent two-hour trip. A few colored people sat in the back. My mother met me at the Wilson terminal. Her house was only six blocks away. They had set up a cot for me in the little hallway by the back door. For my welcome home dinner, my mother cooked fried chicken, mashed potatoes, gravy, and biscuits—which except for the Easter barbecue dinner was the first such lavish typically Southern dinner I had had since I went to the orphanage. Aunt Belle made me her special sweet potato pie. I devoured the food, but felt like I was among strangers. I didn't know what to say, especially to my mother's new husband. He was a stocky man, gray-haired, and silent and didn't seem to know what to say to me, either. My mother seemed happy.

On Saturday afternoon of that weekend, my mother and I walked downtown. There was a nice man who worked at Moss Brothers Clothing Store on Goldsboro Street who wanted to meet me, she said. She had met him through some friends at the Moose Club, told him about me, and he had told her he might buy me something. His name was Jollie Cramer. He was wearing a white shirt and tie and tan pants over a small, delicate frame. He was black-haired with dark eyes and looked to be about thirty-five. He said that he owned a farm outside Wilson and that he had a wife and a son and daughter of about my age. He farmed tobacco but in the idle winter months sold clothes at Moss Brothers. He gave me a necktie.

A few weeks after my return to the orphanage he wrote to Old Man Barnes:

Guess you will be as [sic] little surprised to get a letter from some one you never have met. You have a boy in your school that I met and I think he is a swell kid. Its [sic] Karl Fleming. I would like to give him a little gift and would like for him to come down here for a few days if you could arrange it for him. I would like to give everybody in your school something but you know how it is with we poor folks. Any time you can arrange it for him to come will suit me. Let me know soon. Thank you.

Old Man Barnes replied, "I appreciate the fact that you want Karl Payne to visit you, but I regret that it will be impossible for him to do so while school is in session. Our children visit only in the summer, and they have only two weeks to visit then. I shall be glad for you to send Karl Payne a gift any time you care to do so and I hope you will come to the Orphanage and visit him, and see our other children, campus and buildings. We are always glad to have our friends visit our orphanage."

That summer I went half-heartedly back to Wilson on vacation. I had no friends there, no one to play with. My sister did not go with me. I felt bad about her not coming. I was seeing her more regularly and had become her protector. But my mother said she didn't have room for us both. I slept on the cot again, and during the day sat on the porch or did chores for my mother: going to the corner store for a five-cent block of ice for tea or getting a "bladder" of Sweet Railroad Mills snuff for my mother. She had agreed that I could go stay a couple of days with Jollie Cramer and play with his children. After church and dinner on Sunday, he came by and got me in his pickup truck and drove me out to his farm about ten miles out of town.

That first afternoon he said he wanted to show me his farm. As we drove along a dirt road through a corn field, he started talking about sex and how normal it was to jack off, that it was just a normal urge and there was nothing wrong in doing it despite what the preachers all said. Then he unzipped his trousers and took out his prick and began masturbating and said he would give me one dollar if I could come before he did. So I did it, feeling a mixture of guilt, excitement, and avarice. He gave me one dollar.

That night, he had somehow arranged with his wife that at bedtime he was my sleeping mate alone in a double bed. There was a pendulum clock on the mantelpiece and oil lamps. After the lamps were turned off I went to sleep but was awakened by hands creeping down below my waist. I moved slightly away, thinking it was an accident. But the hands came after me again, this time lower. So I moved farther away, and again there was sighing and his hands on me.

"You don't have to be afraid or embarrassed," he said. "This is what men do sometimes. It's just that people don't talk about it. But you don't have to be ashamed or anything."

I couldn't think of anything to say. I didn't understand what was going on. For all I knew he may have been right. But I didn't like it. His hands on me and his insistent breathing was disgusting and repulsive. I slipped out of the side of the bed and went and sat silent in a rocking chair. He begged me to come back to bed but I wouldn't and I stayed in the chair until daybreak. After breakfast I asked him to take me back to my mother's house.

"Didn't you have a good time, son?" my mother asked.

"It was OK," I said. I didn't tell her or anyone what had happened. Although it had been a horrible night, I didn't know if he had done anything wrong. I thought perhaps I had. I was embarrassed about jacking off in the truck with him. I felt guilty and dirty. And when I went back to the orphanage I became a little more withdrawn and secretive and spent more time in the library and on my own daydreaming and reading books.

My grades in school didn't improve much, but I became the person my classmates would come to when they wanted to know how to spell a word or what a word meant. This was because my English papers always got an A and because I always knew the answers to teacher questions about grammar and literature. I gained a little literary reputation when the *Raleigh News &*

Observer ran an essay contest for high school students on "What Raleigh Should Be Like After The War," and I won first prize, a twenty-five-dollar savings bond. I was also elected president of my sophomore class and head of the student council.

Although the orphanage code of ethics prohibited us stealing from each other, candy and chewing gum that could be swiped from the Walgreen's drug store and the Woolworth's on the way to the movies was considered fair game. In our minds such brigandage was a Robin Hood act. When I was fourteen I got caught, along with Cootie Roach and Little Nigger Rogers, by the manager of the Woolworth's store on Capitol Street and turned in to Old Man Barnes. Fearing that we were headed down the path toward criminality, he assigned us a big stump to dig up. And he wrote a letter about me to the Rev. Henry Davis at the Vanceboro Methodist Church:

> Karl Payne has a way of letting things that do not belong to him stick to his fingers occasionally. A few weeks ago he slipped away from the Orphanage campus on Saturday afternoon and went downtown to one of the 5 and 10-cent stores and swiped one or two articles. I think a letter from you urging him never to be guilty of such conduct any more would have tremendous influence over him.

The Rev. Mr. Davis responded to me:

> Dear Karl Payne,
> I heard something about you the other day that caused me a heartache. I heard that you had taken some things that did not belong to you. I believe that if you did, you realize it was a mistake, and I want you to know I trust you and have confidence in you, and believe that you are going to make a sure enough man

out of yourself. You are going to grow into a man I will be proud of, the orphanage will be proud of and your mother will be proud of.

You know what a good sport is? Well, I want you to be a good sport. Now I know you do not have much money to spend. So I want to make a proposition to you. If you really need money for something, you write me and I will do my best to send it to you. The next time you think of taking something that does not belong to you and you cannot buy because you do not have the money, think of this: "Mr. Lewis will get this for me, if I really need it, so I will just wait." Now you know, Karl Payne, that I do not have a whole lot of money and I can't buy you just anything. That would not be good for you, even if I could. But I want you to know I am your friend, but I cannot help you unless you help yourself.

Mr. Barnes, your house mother, your mother, your friends at Vanceboro and many people you do not know want to help you if you help yourself do the right thing. These folks cannot help you if you do wrong. You have a good home, good food to eat, warm clothes, and lots of boys and girls do not have these things. Since I have known you I have grown to love you, and have expected good things of you. I do not believe you will let me down.

I was overcome with new guilt and shame, and I replied:

Dear Rev. Davis,
I am sorry for what I did and I promise I will not swipe anything again. I know I let you down and I promise I won't do it again.

Yours truly,
Karl Payne Fleming

But on another level I was beginning to feel more rebellious against Old Man Barnes and what I thought to be his hypocritical parsimony and against the outside world of privilege and wealth. Nutsy Perry, he of the protuberant teeth and wild look, thus became one of my rebel heroes. He had achieved minor fame by hanging by his hands out of the second-story window of his eighth-grade classroom until the teacher, Miss Monnie McDonald, tearfully begged him to come back in and promised not to punish him for shooting spitballs at Cora Mae Fitz. He said it was a false accusation.

Now, one summer day, he, at age sixteen, revolted against the whole economic system, specifically against what he considered unfair labor practices, in a more dramatic way. He fled to the woods beyond St. Marys Street, took up residence in a rusted-out abandoned car body, and refused to come back. He contended that the orphanage was exploiting us, making us work long hours with no remuneration—except for room and board—and that we should be paid minimum wages of thirty-five cents an hour. He wrote these demands in a letter to Old Man Barnes and asked Pee Wee Edwards to deliver it through the mail slot in Barnes's office door. These ideas, exploitation and rebellion, had not occurred to any of the rest of us, but thirty-five cents an hour sounded like a much better deal than the twenty-five-cents-a-month allowance we were getting, so he had wide support for his cause, though no one joined his strike.

Old Man Barnes denounced Nutsy at chapel services and said that those who aided and abetted him would face the severest retribution and that Nutsy better come back and face the music. But it was summer and the nights were warm and Nutsy had a girlfriend, Ruth Judd, who worked in the dining room, and she kept him well supplied with peanut butter, molasses, and milk, delivered daily by a co-conspirator. Nutsy sent word that he was prepared to hold out indefinitely—especially inasmuch as he had attained celebrity and was being cheered on by those of us less bold.

Finally, after two weeks, Old Man Barnes, apparently fearful that the story of Nutsy's rebellion would get into the newspapers, was forced to sue for peace and sent word that Nutsy could come back without punishment. He made, however, no other concessions, and our work hours and conditions continued as before. But Nutsy remained a hero.

Soon I got another lesson in labor-management practices—and racism. Tom Russell was a taciturn Scotsman with a young daughter and a German police dog. Under his supervision was a graying "colored man" of about forty named Tom Roach, who lived in a warren of shacks on a muddy alley in Buttermilk Bottom behind the Raleigh municipal auditorium. We picked Tom Roach up and dropped him off every day going to and from the farm. He was a skilled fence-builder, ditchdigger, and plowman with a keen eye for laying out straight lines—and was always assigned to plow the first row in the middle of a field, from which point we boys would take over. He wore old overalls, a battered felt hat, and busted-out shoes.

In the early winter every year, there came the yearly killing of eight to twelve hogs, which had been fattened up on garbage hauled in barrels from the dining room. Mr. Russell would stand at the edge of the pen and shoot the hogs one by one between the eyes with a .22 rifle. Tom Roach would be standing in the pen and would cut their throats one by one with a long butcher knife as they fell and bled with their legs kicking. At first I was sickened by this spectacle but hogs were not sympathetic creatures, and many of them would attack you if you accidentally fell into their pen. Besides there was nothing that smelled worse than pig shit and the stench of it on your brogans would linger for days. I soon became inured to their deaths.

A huge cast-iron vat of boiling water heated over a log fire awaited, and one by one the dead pigs were plunged in to loosen their wiry hair. We boys them scraped off the hair with the sharp edges of tin can lids. The pigs were strung up on a block and tackle, and Tom Roach gutted them, their steaming entrails spilling out onto the ground. Just before quitting time at the farm, Tom Roach washed out the hog entrails with a hose, loaded them into burlap bags, and carried them home—to boil them and make "chittlins." I felt sorry for him as he trudged wearily along the dirt alley with the bag over his back. We hauled the carcasses back to the campus, where they were butchered in the cold storage room.

Mr. Russell smoked a particularly noxious brand of cigarettes called Piedmont. Tom Roach smoked, too, but rarely had cigarettes because he had no money. When we would pause for a break in work, Mr. Russell would light up, very conscious that Tom Roach wanted to smoke. He never offered Tom Roach a cigarette, and would wink knowingly at us boys while Tom Roach shuffled uncomfortably until he got up the nerve to ask:

"Missuh Russell, could you spare a smoke, suh?"

"Well, Tom, I don't know. Are you sure you want smoke to one of these?

"Yassuh, Missuh Russell."

"Ok, Tom, well, why didn't you say so?"

"Well, I don't know Missuh Russell. I'm sorry, suh."

"Ok, Tom, you go ahead and smoke one," he said, proffering his pack.

I inwardly cringed at these exchanges, without understanding exactly why. I felt humiliated and embarrassed for Tom Roach, for his being made to crawl and cringe in order to get a single cigarette. This fueled my nascent sense of social and racial injustice. The other boys invariably laughed, although perhaps they were uncomfortable, too. No one talked about it. This was the first time I related to a real person I saw every day being subjected to the cruelties perpetrated by some human beings in books I had read, like Mark Twain's Jim in *Huckleberry Finn* and Dickens's *Oliver Twist*. I thought Tom Roach had about him a kind of patient nobility and fortitude, but he did not get even the respect that was given to our mules. Besides the books, perhaps my feelings came from my own having been bullied and laughed at, I thought, or perhaps my values in this regard came from my mother. I realized when I thought about it that she never used the word "nigger" and often said she didn't understand why some people thought they were better than others, whatever their color. Where her own opinions on this came from I did not know, and she never talked about it. I realized that she was different, though, and perhaps my differentness came partially from her, despite the widening gulf that I was digging between us.

When I became fifteen and moved up to the Cole Building, I became a "milk boy," a member of a six-boy crew that milked our cows twice a day. Of all the jobs we had to do, this was the most despised. It meant rising at 3:30 A.M. and riding the truck to the farm, in winter cringing on the floor under the rolled-up greasy truck tarpaulin to ward off the cold. Except in the deep winter months when they were in the barn, the cows would be standing silently in the wet pasture, and we would get out on the road, climb the barbed wire fence, and herd them up to the milk barn and into their assigned places. The cow barn was attached to the two huge round silos that we filled in late summer with shredded green corn. It was a long, flyspecked hall with thirty stalls on each side with spaces for each cow marked by rusted steel collars that locked around the cows' necks. A concrete ramp ran down the middle, with a trough behind the cows to catch their effluence. We wiped off their teats and swollen bags with

My sister waiting tables for Baby Cottage children in the orphanage dining room, 1944. She sometimes saved extra food for me.

wet chlorined rags and milked them into gallon buckets by hand while they munched. At 4 P.M., we stopped whatever other farm chores we were doing and milked them again.

We had Holsteins because they produced a large amount of milk. Next to the milk barn was a room where the milk was sterilized by steam and the cream skimmed off. We dropped off the cream twice a day at the Pine State Creamery, and the skim milk was served in the dining room.

Old Man Barnes had his own private cow, a brown Guernsey named Daisy. Her milk was creamier than that of the Holsteins, and we were required to milk her into a special one-gallon can, which we dropped off at his house at the foot of the hill on the campus. Frequently we put a straw into his can on the way back to the orphanage, siphoned off and drank the cream, and substituted the less rich milk from the five-gallon cans. We were proud to put one over on him.

The worst part of this worst job of being a milk boy—even worse than getting swatted in the face with the cows' wet tails, kicked, or spattered by cascading cow piss—was dealing with the prodigious amount of manure manufactured by these despised creatures. Cows in our opinion were the stupidest of animals, even dumber than chickens, but in our resentful minds they were smart enough to maliciously wait to relieve themselves until they got into the barn. Afterwards, their immense issuances had to be shoveled into a wheelbarrow and wheeled outside to what gradually grew into a sort of manure mountain. The hateful job of "taking up crap" was simply rotated daily. In early spring, just before plowing, it was hauled to the fields in a mule-drawn manure spreader along with the compost from the barn.

Just when I reached milk-boy age, we got a new farm boss, Mr. Pierce. He was a tall, prim, but well-meaning Puritan who wore severe steel-rimmed glasses, spoke in a clipped, high-pitched voice, and periodically ignited in anger. What most provoked his anger was our profanity. Shocked by the extensiveness of our profane vocabularies and our jubilant use of them, almost an art form in its imaginative sweep, Mr. Pierce became almost apoplectic with rage when he heard us. His jaw tightened, his face turned red, and he would yell, "All right, you boys, cut it out!"

Cursing was obviously in Mr. Pierce's gloomy view a sin that perched us, perhaps irretrievably, on the slippery slope downward to the fiery furnaces of Hell. But his teeth-tightening anger had absolutely no effect on our raw language, so one day, at rope's end, he said, "All right, you boys, the next one I catch cursing will have to take up crap for a week." This was a threat, to be sure, with teeth in it, especially for me. Perhaps as a way of convincing others, and myself, that I was as tough an orphanage boy as anyone, I was an accomplished user of profanity. And a habit so deeply ingrained and enthusiastically practiced was not easily broken. Within twenty-four hours, I was caught and sentenced on the spot, which provoked whoops of laughter from my unindicted co-conspirators.

They hung around in the barn after milking and kidded me unmercifully as I loaded and reloaded the noxious wheelbarrow. As the hateful days wore on, I bore my sentence stoically, and was near its end and ready for parole when Mr. Pierce caught me cussing again. And then the next week he caught me again. And then again. And again. This hateful cycle continued unbroken for seventeen weeks, by which time I rebelled inside, like Paul Newman in *Cool Hand Luke*, and began to wear my sentence with defiant pride. How many wheelbarrow loads, how many tons, I hauled from this Stygian stable I do not know. But as the manure mountain grew outside the barn door, it became in my unredemptive mind an encrusted monument to noble boys everywhere who were oppressed by joyless and narrow-minded grownups.

For his part, Mr. Pierce was by and by a beaten man. He finally gave up and without a further word to me gruffly announced the reinstatement of the rotation system. From thence forward he looked at me with a mixture of pity and disgust. The sheer magnitude and incurability of my criminality was obviously too far beyond any cure or punishment that he could offer, and he surrendered me to my fate.

In due course, now that I had attained "big boy" status, I become a plowboy. We had nine mules, and I rode one of them bareback from the barn to the fields and walked all day behind a plow. I loved this solitary job—plodding along in bare feet in the cool, freshly turned earth, the trace chains clanking, the mules blowing softly, birds crying in distant fields, an occasional rabbit hopping away. And finally I was assigned to drive the orphanage Allis-Chalmers tractor and Dodge truck, off-road and in the fields—the final and most sought-after badges of big boydom.

Another "big boy" job was hauling coal. Every year the orphanage burned nine train-car loads in the boilers of the dormitories, the laundry, and the huge furnace that produced heat and steam for the Vann Building and dining hall. Four of us rode back and forth to the Seaboard rail siding just off Glenwood Avenue a mile from the orphanage in summer. The coal cars had four chutes that when triggered released coal onto the ground, from which we shoveled it with bent backs onto the truck, hauled it back to the campus, and shoveled it through the openings to the coal bins. We worked shirtless and it took a long shower to remove the accumulated grime from our bodies and faces at day's end.

Now that I had become a teenager, I realized that girls seemed to react to what the older, bolder ones said were my good looks, but I had no sense of myself as being anything other than insufficient and uncomfortable. I always sided with the underdog. My two best friends, Little Jeebie Clay and Cootie Roach, were non-athletic, physically underdeveloped, and extremely shy. They thought of themselves as rebels and outsiders, and so did I. Neither of them exhibited any of the tough-guy posturing of my other classmates. That was restful. Besides, both of them read books and we talked about the ones we liked and didn't. We became an inseparable trio.

I wrote a short play about a mad doctor and my fellow misfits performed it with me—to mild response from the audience—on the auditorium stage as a part of the commencement service when I was fifteen. Little Jeebie, Cootie, and I shared an appetite for jokes, off-color and otherwise, and I had committed hundreds of them to memory. We decided to issue a joke anthology and put all of them we knew in notebooks, only to have our literary efforts confiscated—spotted in study hall by the matron—turned in to Old Man Barnes and destroyed. For that transgression, we were assigned a big stump, which took two weekends of our spare time to excavate.

During the school year, we left the farm at 4 P.M., and from 4:30 to 5:30 we practiced sports, football in the fall, basketball in winter, baseball in spring. When you became a big boy, you automatically went out for sports, no matter your athletic ability. Everybody played, though some were woefully maladroit. I was only slightly above average in ability. On Friday afternoons, and infrequently at night, we played surrounding towns—Cary, Zebulon, Apex, Wake Forest, Roxboro, Garner, Clayton, Fuquay Springs, Hillsborough, and Oxford Orphanage, our toughest rival. We consistently defeated these teams, though their pool of players was much larger than ours. We were better conditioned and better disciplined, and, of course, we prided ourselves on being tougher. Coach Smith constantly warned us against smoking, which he said stunted our growth, and against drinking

The Methodist Orphanage Red Raiders football team, 1943. I'm No. 47 on the back row, already over 6 feet tall, but weighing only 137 pounds.

"belly-washers"—soda pop—and made us run hundred-yard wind sprints in full uniform until we almost dropped.

I was slightly over six feet tall, but thin (137 pounds), and since I had no special talent I was consigned to being a middle lineman in football. But I was center—a low-scoring one—on the basketball team, the pitcher on the baseball team—with a moderate fastball, a looping curve, and good control—and a fair hitter.

I began to develop a shy relationship with a dining girl named Jewel Hayes, who was behind me a year in school. She had thick brown hair, lustrous brown eyes, strong, even white teeth, tiny golden hairs on her arms, flawlessly glowing creamy skin, and a ripe mouth. She was on the girls' basketball team whose games preceded ours, and I was excited by her innocent sexiness. She was shy to the extreme, even more than I was. We corresponded mostly by awkward notes, delivered by an intermediary who had gotten us together, Mildred Carney, the one who called me John Payne. One starry winter night Jewel walked with me amid my teammates and our fans back to the campus from the lighted Devereaux Meadow stadium where we had played a football game, and I silently kissed her on the gravel path outside the dining room where she lived. I almost fainted in ecstasy and delirium and walked back to the Cole Building in a concupiscent daze.

Soon after that, at my imploring, she would sometimes sneak out of her room at night, creep down the iron stairs from her second floor room, and meet me by the dining room porch, barefoot and dressed only in her pajamas. I had crept out of my own bed and stealthily lowered myself down a cast iron drainpipe from my second floor dorm in the Cole Building. The feel of her soft body and her breasts against me, my mouth sealed to hers, sent me into rapture. We kissed endlessly—no French kissing—and wordlessly until she became frightened of discovery and left. I never ventured further than kissing. Such a thought did not even occur to me, out

Not much speed and only a roundhouse curveball but good control as a high school baseball pitcher.

of pure innocence and perhaps because of the unconscious fear of being "sent away."

My conversations with Jewel were mundane and almost monosyllabic during the short times we were together. I didn't know how to talk to her about anything real that was going on with me, nor did she with me. She was sweet-natured and compliant and seemed to be somehow reassured by my urgent priapic attention and my insistent kisses. But I had no idea what she truly thought or believed or felt about anything.

Many of the big boys carried rubbers in their wallets, bought at machines for twenty-five cents in filling stations and beer halls—and so did I when I became sixteen, one of those gold aluminum-covered ones called Coin Pack. On every other Saturday afternoon, we older residents got to go downtown to the movies in a group. One day I took Jewel, and as she stood beside me in the movie line, I reached into my pocket, pulled out my worn Coin Pack—which I carried more as a badge of manhood than any real expectation of sex—instead of a fifty-cent piece, slapped it on the cashier's shelf, and grabbed it back in shocked embarrassment when I saw what had happened. Jewel didn't see it, or pretended not to. If anybody's Coin Packs got used, if any girls actually lost their "cherry," I never heard of it. We did hear that there were girls on the outside who would put out, but these speculations were not backed up with any real testimony. In any case, town girls were beyond our reach or even imagination. There were not even any opportunities to meet them.

By the time I was fifteen and shaving with a double-edged Gillette blade and Barbasol shaving cream, many of our boys had gone off to join the service and came back on leave with exotic tales of sophisticated women who not only would enthusiastically put out but would go down on you and do it "dog fashion." Some told of "losing their cherry" and "getting my ashes hauled" at a cat house called "Katie Mae's" on Raleigh Road a mile from the state capitol. Price: Five dollars.

Our ignorance about life in the outer world, and especially about sex, was complete. We adolescent boys, existing as we did in a state of more or less insistent arousal, talked about sex a lot—told a lot of jokes about it—but with zero actual knowledge. Girls and boys never discussed sex with each other, and our adult governors imparted no information at all—except for the dark exhortations from Old Man Barnes about the sin of "thinking impure thoughts" and masturbating. His message boiled down to this: Sex is sinful, dirty, vile, and disgusting—and you should save it for the one you love.

There was a flag hung across the top of the drapes in the auditorium with a star on it for every orphanage boy in the service. The number increased every month. The war was in all the headlines and newsreels and on the radio. Mr. Barnes was reading letters at chapel services from our boys overseas. Food rationing began, though it did not impact our diet since the farm made us almost self-sufficient. The price of aluminum foil doubled, and so did our efforts to find the aluminum inner casings of cigarette packs. The green emblem on Lucky Strikes disappeared, replaced by red, because something in the green paint was necessary for the war effort. "Lucky Strike Green Has Gone To War," ads proclaimed. Inevitably we suffered our share of the casualties. Lieutenant Douglas Tucker, a Navy pilot, was killed on a training mission off the California coast. Marine Lieutenant Roger Garner was killed in combat in Germany. I had watched them play baseball in the annual Easter games between the residents and the old boys. Soon a steady stream of old boys in the service were visiting with stripes on their arms and medals on their chests—some of them Purple Hearts—and in tailored "old salt" Navy uniforms with tight tops and bell bottoms. Nutsy Perry was one of them.

We all wanted to join up. My mother sent me a postcard she had received from her youngest brother, John Elbert Lewis, a prisoner of war. He was a sergeant in the Army, a career soldier who had joined up during the Depression. He was captured with MacArthur's troops on Corregidor, survived the Bataan Death March, and was in a Japanese POW camp, working, as he later told us when he returned weighing ninety pounds, in a coal mine, eating rice with worms in it.

The convoys we saw on U.S. 401 from the orphanage farm increased every day, and the number of trucks in them kept growing—twenty-five, fifty, a hundred. The young soldiers smiled and waved to us as we worked shirtless in the fields. It all seemed romantic and exciting. One week while we were baling hay a truck load of blond young German prisoners, escorted by rifle-bearing GI's, arrived at the farm. "Heil, Hitler," we cried standing in a row at mock attention, pitchforks at our sides, mimicking the Nazi salute, when they got off their truck. They worked alongside us in the twenty-acre field, pitchforking hay onto a two-mule wagon, smiling, smoking, and uttering unknown phrases. We had been primed to hate them but up close we saw that they were boys not much older than we were.

I imagined my future not at all, except that with any luck I might soon be old enough to go fight against Hitler or Hirohito and come back heroic in a smart uniform with medals and have beautiful girls look at me like the girls looked at the soldiers in the movies.

No one above us ever talked to us about the future, about what we might become, or what might be possible. Perhaps this was because the visions and ambitions of our teachers and matrons had been so limited by the Depression and their own experiences. Perhaps it was because the orphanage felt it was discharging its mandate just by harboring poor children and raising them with good Christian values. Perhaps it was just the hard-headed realization that college was not a possibility because there was no money. Consequently, most of the boys who graduated from the orphanage became sales clerks, machinists, salesman, mechanics, cops, bookkeepers, dental and optical technicians, repairmen. Instead of working on the farm, junior and senior boys were allowed to spend their non-school hours learning trades in apprentice jobs down. Later, of course, there was the GI Bill, and college, and many better opportunities became available.

Some of the girls became secretaries, office functionaries, salesladies in stores, nurses—but most married as quickly as possible and began raising families.

I had continued to read prodigiously in the library—*Wuthering Heights, David Copperfield* and *Great Expectations, The Man in the Iron Mask, Cyrano de Bergerac, Heart of Darkness, Leaves of Grass,* and *Walden*—anything I could get my hands on. I was a fast reader, and was becoming, though I did not realize it, a baby autodidact. I was besotted with books.

In my junior year, one of my classmates, John Parker, and I got jobs ushering on Friday and Saturday night at the downtown Wake Theater, for five dollars each a week. And in December, Old Man Barnes got me a job at the post office helping deliver Christmas packages. The postman drove the Parcel Post truck, handed the packages out the back, and I ran them to each front door. On Christmas Eve I got a U.S. government check for thirty dollars for two weeks work. I bought myself a pair of suspenders, a Wings dress shirt, a pair of slick gabardine pants, a bottle of Old Spice, boxes of Whitman Sampler candy for Jewel and Ethel Gray, and a box of filigreed handkerchiefs for my mother. But Christmas was not much of a holiday for us older boys and girls, especially not this year, two years into the war with the numbers of our friends in the service growing and growing.

I was a low-scoring but determined center, No. 7, and the captain of the orphanage basketball team, 1943.

I was beginning now to develop a kind of split personality. I was a favorite of Old Man Barnes and of Coach Fred Smith, too. I apparently came across as bright, earnest, and honest. I was again president of my class and of the student body. Old Man Barnes attended all of our away sporting events, and he often invited me to ride with him in his black Buick. One night coming home he said he thought someday I might make a good Methodist minister. I didn't respond. Little did he know that I was already a closet atheist or that beneath my respectful exterior was beginning to simmer the anger of a revolutionary, perhaps even an anarchist.

Beneath the dining hall was the storage room where all the food was kept. Shorty Jordan, Big Jeebie Clay, and I picked its lock with a screwdriver one night, filled a gallon jar with peanut butter out of a barrel, took two loaves of bread, and liberated three watermelons from the refrigerated locker. To cap off our crime, we climbed the flagpole in front of the Vann Building and ran up a homemade pirate banner. We hauled our bounty into the woods across St. Mary's Street, invited our friends, and had a feast. Lizzie Sanders, the dining room matron, reported the break-in to Mr. Barnes. He was livid. At chapel service he said he would find the criminals responsible and give them a thrashing. He was especially mad about the watermelons. He had been saving them for a trustee dinner, and the thieves had taken the best ones, he said.

Next day he summoned me to his office. I thought we had been discovered, but instead he said that since I was head of the student body, he was appointing me to investigate this crime. I gravely told him I would. Every few days thereafter he would ask me how it was going. I would say I couldn't find out anything. Naturally no one squealed on us, and before long it was all forgotten.

By spring I was finishing my junior year in high school, in which I had completely lost interest. Sitting in these classes seemed silly matched against the patriotic war fervor that engulfed the nation. The newspapers and radio were full of stories about victorious battles in Europe and the Pacific. At the movies, newsreels showed our infantrymen, our sailors, and our pilots in feats of derring-do against the evil Nazis and Japs. The faithful old female teachers seemed to be only dusty avatars of irrelevance. As my seventeenth birthday approached I began imploring my mother to sign papers allowing me to join the Navy. You could freely join at eighteen but parental consent was required for earlier. Unable to dissuade me from my importuning, she appealed to Mr. Barnes in a letter:

> Karl casually asked me the last time I was there if I would be willing for him to join the Navy and I told him he was much too young to join the Navy or even to reliize what a mistake it would be. I pointed out to him as best I could what a great difference there is between the outer world, that he knows so little about, and the orphanage where he has the great advantages that he needs now more than any other time in his life, in Christian training as well as being important that he finish his education. I also talked to him about discipline in [sic] our own minds in the right way when we are young causes one to grow with the years in the right way of living and thinking. I have also told him many times that when and wherever there were rules to follow it was because someone had cared that we should be led the right way and they were to be honored and never resented. I have told him all along that whatever problem he had in mind at any time to talk it over with you and you would understand and advise what was best. I trust

that he will get the idie [sic] of joining the Navy out of his mind and be content in work and studdies [sic] I have written him and I will go to see him and have a heart to heart talk with him and Mr. Barnes I haven't had any money to help with but with my prayers and full coporation [sic] I have and will at all times do my very best.

He replied: "Karl Payne seems to be better satisfied than he was. Please write him encouraging letters and ask him to take advantage of the many opportunities he has here. If he can just get over this age of wanting to do something he shouldn't do, I believe he will settle down and make a man of himself."

But I was not satisfied, and finally the following spring, just as I was finishing my junior year, my mother reluctantly signed the papers and with three of my buddies, Adrian Clewis, Odis Colville, and Parker Stagg, I walked downtown to the post office and joined the Navy. I had just enough self-awareness to know I was leaving what had become my home and my family. But I was going with three friends. And the orphanage would always be there for me to come back to as an old boy. Most importantly, the lure of adventure, of being even a minor part of a noble and romantic cause, was overpowering. So I made my decision with no hesitation and completely without thought of what might be before me in the years ahead. I spent my last Sunday afternoon after signing up with Jewel Hayes in a small sitting room in the new and fancy Burwell Building where she now lived, kissing without interruption, saying nothing. Next morning I went to the Brown Building to say goodbye to Muh Brown. She hugged me and said she would always love me. I went to the Jackson Building and said goodbye to my sister, feeling sad, remembering the pain of our coming to the orphanage, and guilty that I was repeating the abandonment. She seemed especially fragile and vulnerable. I told her I would write to her often and that I would soon be back on leave. Then I went to Old Man Barnes's office. He shook my hand warmly and said he was sorry to see me go, but that he understood my wanting to get in on the war. I had done pretty well, he said. He repeated his hope that after the war I would consider becoming a Methodist minister. I didn't say so, but this was the farthest thought from my mind.

That afternoon I left the orphanage with nothing but the clothes I was wearing and with my friends and a dozen other recruits boarded the Seaboard Air Lines "Silver Meteor" in downtown Raleigh, heading north. The sooty train was jammed, almost entirely with servicemen, and people were standing in the aisles and even in the open gangways between the cars. I stood all the way, ten hours as the train staggered north through the night. It was the first time I had ever been on a train. I didn't like and never had liked the night. As the train moaned and creaked through the darkness out of North Carolina and into Virginia, I thought for some reason of my mother standing by the dirt road with me the first day I went to school. What was I doing joining the Navy, I wondered. I had seen the ocean once, and I definitely did not care for being confined in small places, such as a ship. I had joined impetuously, because my friends had, and now I was headed toward something I would not like but could not evade. We changed trains in Baltimore, and arrived at the Bainbridge Naval Training Station in Maryland in early darkness and went straightaway by gray bus to the induction center, where we got shots, were issued our seabags, ditty bags, and uniforms, had our heads shaved, were issued dog tags, and then were herded to the chow hall. A vast cornucopia was laid out along the chow line: pancakes, waffles, eggs, bacon, corned beef hash, sausage, French toast, orange juice, grapefruit, jams and jellies, coffee. For the first time in my memory, on an ordinary day, I could eat all I wanted. As we finished our meal and went marching awkwardly off to our barracks to begin training, I felt strangely at ease. I was long accustomed to surviving one day at a time, alone in the company of many. I did not think at all of the future, or of the past—only that I was an orphanage boy no longer.

Chapter 5

Kid Reporter

J UNE 1945. I was in the Navy now. All around me fellow
recruits were sounding off about the food, the endless marching with dummy rifles, being homesick, lifeboat training on the
choppy Susquehanna River, jumping from high platforms into a
flaming swimming pool to simulate abandon-ship tactics, don-
ning a mask and entering a gas-filled chamber, pining for girl-
friends and wives, guard duty on Dempsey Dumpster garbage
units, inspections, standing in lines for everything, and the insipid
3.2 percent beer sold in paper cups in the rec hall. But I was comfortable and secure.

I was used to strict regimen, to hard work, to sleeping in a
barracks-like atmosphere, to eating at communal tables, to
engaging in tough-guy banter, and pleased as I could be with all
of the terrific and plentiful food. Truth be told, the Navy was a

lot easier than the orphanage, and more exciting, though the war was winding down. The Germans had surrendered and the Pacific islands were being recaptured from the Japanese one by one.

With little need to prepare us for deployment abroad, the Navy relegated us to mindless chores. Some nights I stood midnight-to-4-A.M. watch in the second-floor library at the recreation hall. There was a portable record player on a small table by a leather sofa, and one night someone had left on it music I had never heard—Gershwin's "Rhapsody in Blue," and beside it Beethoven's Third Symphony, the *Eroica*. I listened to them endlessly, night after night, sitting on the sofa. I had never been exposed to classical music—only crude jokes about opera singers. The Raleigh stations that we listened to in the orphanage, WPTF and WRAL, played Tommy Dorsey, Kay Kyser, Glenn Miller, Ray Anthony, Spike Jones, a lot of country and religious stuff, moony love songs and patriotic war tunes like "Don't Sit Under The Apple Tree" (with anyone else but me), "Remember Pearl Harbor," and "I'll Be Seeing You."

Beethoven tore something inside of me loose. I had not ached deeply with an emotion as long as I could remember and I had not cried since the first week in the orphanage. Beethoven's alternately explosive and sweet chords made me weep on that couch as a great emptiness arose in my chest. But I dared not bring up this amazing music with anyone, for fear of being made fun of as different or as a sissy. My fellow trainees—working-class kids like myself—could talk of nothing but finishing boot camp, getting liberty, getting laid, and getting knee-walking drunk. One said he knew a girl from Lancaster, Pennsylvania, who "fucked like a mink." Another bragged that he knew a girl who "if she had as many stuck out of her as she's had stuck in, she would look like a porcupine." I joined in the laughter and projected a rough worldliness, but in my barricaded heart I yearned for a pure and noble love, something grander than the animal appetites about which we all bragged so much and about which I remained so unfamiliar.

In the Navy library I read *Main Street*, Sinclair Lewis's bitter attack on American middle-class values, and *You Can't Go Home Again*, in which my fellow Tarheel Thomas Wolfe seemed to voice much that I was beginning to feel: "I am not interested in writing what our pot-bellied members of the Rotary and Kiwanis call a 'good show.' I want to know life and understand it and interpret it without fear or favor. This, I feel, is a man's work and worthy of a man' dignity. For life is not made up of sugary, sticky, sickening Edgar A. Guest sentimentality, it is not made up of dishonest optimism. God is NOT always in His Heaven, all is NOT always right with the world. It is not all bad, but it is not all good; it is not all ugly, but it is not all beautiful; it is life, life, life—the only thing that matters. It is savage, cruel, kind, noble, passionate, generous, stupid, ugly, painful, joyous—and it's all these and more, and BY GOD I shall, though they crucify me for it, I will go to the end of the earth to find it and understand it." I felt that Wolfe was writing just for me. There perhaps was a noble life out there somewhere for me, though I knew not where or how to get there.

But these nascent noble thoughts vanished when I got my first weekend pass at the end of the ten-week boot camp. I drew my first regular salary, cashing a United States Treasury check for forty-two dollars at the paymaster's window. I put on my dress whites—which we scrubbed clean with heavy doses of Clorox—and my spit-polished black shoes, set my white cap at a jaunty angle on my returning hair, thickened my newly grown sparse mustache with a burnt matchstick, stuck my Camels into my left sock as was the sailor style, and went off with two new friends by train to Baltimore. We headed straight to Charles Street, which was famous with sailors on shore leave for its burlesque houses.

When we hitchhiked into Baltimore, garish marquees, photos of headlining dancers or "terpsichoreans," and barkers in threadbare top hats and shiny swallow-tailed coats called to us. We walked into a club with tiny tables and a three-drink minimum. I was still a virgin, of course, and I had never had a drink, though I did not announce either of these embarrassing facts. I let my friends order: "Let us have three old-fashioneds," one of them said bravely to the bored waiter. I was still seventeen, legally underage although I was in uniform and thereby a man.

As we got our first drinks a stripper came on stage to a half-hearted salute from the pit orchestra. She was beyond her best stripper years, obviously, sallow-skinned with tired, dyed red hair, and a pale and protuberant stomach with a big nasty appendectomy scar down the right side. The audience was almost all servicemen. They hooted and shouted, "Take it off."

"Please, don't," I muttered, for she and the strippers who followed as we had our second, third, and fourth round of drinks were many things, but not erotic. I felt disgust and shame, and very soon I was nauseous and disoriented from the drinks. Next thing I knew we were out of town on a two-lane highway, attempting to hitchhike back to the base and reeling back and forth from the gravel apron onto the road. Presently a Maryland highway patrolman stopped, threw us into his car, put us under arrest for drunkenness, and took us to a nearby small-town jail, where I promptly threw up on the disgusted turnkey's desk. Into the drunk tank we were thrust and I sat there forlornly sick on a steel cot wondering how I had sunk to this low place. Next morning shore patrolmen came by and extracted us from the drunk tank and escorted us, along with a truckload of other miscreants from other jails, back to Havre de Grace. There were no charges, but I had my first bilious hangover and my first onslaught of drinker's remorse.

Although it was clear from the beginning that the Navy had no real use for those of us who had joined up when we had, we were not getting out right away. The war was over. Men from overseas were coming home and being discharged first—in order of how much time they had served. The discharge processing centers were glutted. I was assigned to be a cook's helper in a chow hall that was feeding 3,000 men every day. I had a bunk in the enlisted men's quarters over the huge kitchen, where I cracked eggs, peeled potatoes, loaded ovens with hams and legs of lamb, and slopped food onto trays in the chow line at serving time.

I made a friend who worked in the chow hall named Bill Roelecke, a seaman second class like myself. He was from Baltimore. He was pale and skinny, with a slightly pockmarked face. A cigarette dangled constantly from the side of his mouth. He was, like me, different—defiant of authority, a loner, a reader of books. He asked me if I had heard of a famous Baltimore journalist named H. L. Mencken, who was, he said, a disturber of the peace—contemptuous of conventional thinking, especially that which occurred south of the Mason-Dixon line. I admitted I had not, and he lent me a book of Mencken's writings, including a famous article, "The Sahara of the Bozart," in which Mencken criticized what he called the South's intellectual vacuity, its culture built on fundamentalist religious faith where "the Book of Revelation has all the authority of military orders in time of war." He lampooned its "stupid" pretensions—for example, Georgia bragging about being the birthplace of Coca-Cola and designing the first combined badge of the United Daughters of the Confederacy.

"Nearly the whole of Europe would be lost in that stupendous region of worn-out farms, shoddy cities and paralyzed cerebrums," he wrote. "For all its size and wealth and all the 'progress' it babbles of, it is almost as sterile, intellectually, artistically, culturally, as the Sahara Desert.... In all that gargantuan paradise of the fourth-rate, there is not a single picture gallery worth going to, or a single orchestra capable of playing the nine symphonies of Beethoven, or a single theater devoted to decent plays, or a single public monument that is worth looking at, or a single workshop devoted to the making of beautiful things."

I was enthralled with Mencken's piercing style and noncon-formist mind. He gave voice, particularly, to my growing doubts about religion, obedience to authority, and conformity. He became my new hero.

Bill Roelecke invited me to Baltimore and took me to see Mencken's house on Hollins Street. He also got me a blind date with a girl who lived a long streetcar ride out beyond the Pimlico racetrack. We went to a movie, and then to her home where we necked and I tried futilely to seduce her—staying past the time when the last streetcar ran, so I had to walk ten miles back to downtown Baltimore and my room at the YMCA, a sanctuary for single servicemen.

In the fall when I got my first seventy-two-hour pass, I hitch-hiked to Wilson to see my mother. People were good about pick-ing up men in uniform, but the trip still took sixteen hours, part of it spent shivering under a cold starry sky in rural Virginia with no civilization in sight, the only sound the crunching of my feet on the macadam rood. I arrived in darkness and woke my mother. There was the cot set up for me in the hallway. Next day I called Lacy Powell in Raleigh. He was one of five boys, two from town and three from the orphanage, me, John Parker, and Otis Colville, who had gotten thrown in jail for climbing through a basement win-dow at the Raleigh City Auditorium to sneak into a Spike Jones concert my last year at the orphanage. This was when I was six-teen, in a rebellious mood, and sneaking off campus at night. A cop caught us and put us into the drunk tank. A furious Old Man

Home on leave at the orphanage, 1945, age seventeen, in my Navy dress blues as a seaman first class. I had still never been on an ocean.

Barnes had to come down and bail us out. Our punishment was to dig up a big stump. But we became minor celebrities, because the *Raleigh News & Observer* wrote an editorial lambasting the police department. Didn't they have anything else to do but put five kids in jail just for trying to sneak into a band concert? Why not spend taxpayer dollars on catching real criminals?

Lacy Powell had a car, a blue 1938 Plymouth sedan, and said he could get me a blind date. So one day I hitchhiked up to Raleigh and met him for a double date. I had been partnered with Helen Gates (not her real name), a pulpy girl with big breasts. She had straight brown hair, a heavily lipsticked mouth, and was wearing a white blouse, a white skirt, and white pumps. She told me that she was two years out of high school, going to beauty college, still living at home, and that her father was a Methodist minister with a small church in a village near Raleigh.

Helen and I rode in the back seat. Lacy drove out into the countryside and parked on a deserted dirt road beside a cornfield. I began to kiss Helen. She opened her mouth and thrust her tongue into mine. Soon I began to feel her breasts. She did not push my hand away, so I put my hand up her dress and when she did nothing I pushed aside her panties and put a finger inside her. She was breathing heavily and my heart was beating so loudly I thought she could hear it. I asked her if she would get out of the car. She opened the door and I followed her into the field and fell with her into the dirt between the rows. I had been carrying one of those gold-colored aluminum-encased rubbers in my wallet for months, and I unwrapped it and put it on and thrust inside her and ejaculated almost immediately. Wordlessly we got up and went back to the car. I felt confused and let down and slightly embarrassed. It was obvious she had done this before, and I was shocked that she did it so casually and without protest. I never saw her again.

While I was on leave I went back to the orphanage campus to see my friends and to show off my uniform. I felt grown-up and proud to be in the Navy. I necked with Jewel Hayes on the sofa, but it was clear to me now that I was not going to be serious about her. We had never spoken much and were not corresponding now that I was away. We had nothing in common except our shared orphanage experience and shared physical and perhaps emotional hunger. Mr. Barnes invited me and three other boys on leave to come to chapel services and be on stage, where he had us photographed under the flag with all the stars representing orphanage boys in the service. I went to see Coach Fred Smith and he raised the possibility that he might be able to get me a sports scholarship at his alma mater, Appalachian State Teachers College, after I got out of the Navy.

The Japanese had formally surrendered to General Douglas MacArthur on the USS *Missouri* on September 2, 1945, but it wasn't until the following August that I was discharged from the Navy. Coach Smith said he definitely could get me and Bill Long—who was an excellent three-sport athlete—those scholarships. Appalachian State was in Boone in the mountains of North Carolina near the Tennessee line. It had been conceived as a church school to train teachers to instruct illiterate mountain children. It had about 800 students. Bill and I reported in late August, a week early, for football practice. It became obvious immediately I was not going to make the team. The other players, mostly returning veterans, were just too big. I still weighed less than 140 pounds and was not a natural athlete, so I was soon dropped and lost my scholarship. As the year went by, I made the B team in basketball and was good enough to pitch batting practice in baseball but not good enough to make the team.

I was getting eighty dollars a month from the GI Bill, the blessed federal gift that allowed the first generation of orphanage boys to have a shot at college, but that wasn't enough, and it was going to run out soon because of the short time I had been in the service. So I took a job washing dishes ("pearl-diving") in the cafeteria. I was sharing a room in Newland Hall with a black-maned Tennessee boy named Ben Honeycutt, and we began making a little extra money selling warm bottled Cokes and sandwiches in the dorm.

I fit right in at college, again because I was used to living in groups, but I was mostly bored in class, just not interested. The teachers were not inspiring, to say the least. The history teacher said, not altogether facetiously, on the first day of class—noting us football players slinking in the rear—that the way to make an "A" in his class was to sit in the first row and laugh at his jokes. He was a defiantly unreconstructed Confederate, and he opened his first lecture with the brusque announcement that "Abraham Lincoln was a son-of-a-bitch." The pale and sour science teacher was phobic about litter—and dispatched his class once a week to pick up paper on the campus. The literature teacher was a handsomely faded Shakespeare buff who came to class smelling of booze. The athletic director's lithe, red-haired wife taught a modern dance class, and he advised athletes to join and get an easy credit. I did, and performed her choreographed pieces in the college auditorium and on road trips as far away as Birmingham, in a leotard along with another football player, much to the hilarity of our friends. I also joined the college chorus and sang the *Messiah* at concerts, once drunk enough on moonshine to fall from the rear rafter bass section.

There was a jukebox in the gym, and a girl named Maxine Hawks took pity on me and taught me to jitterbug, to "Tuxedo Junction," "String of Pearls," and "Chattanooga Choo-Choo," and to slow dance to "Moonlight Serenade," "I'll Be Seeing You," and "Heart of My Heart." I did not have a regular girlfriend, did not seek one, nor did I date.

When summer came I went to Wilson to stay with my mother and began hanging out on the street in front of Wimpy's Pool Parlor and the Esquire Grill with a bunch of guys who were mostly idle veterans, members of what was jokingly called "The 52–20 Club." Veterans could get a government benefit of twenty dollars for fifty-two weeks, so as to readjust to civilian life. I soon got a job painting public school buildings, for fifty cents an hour. My second school year was as uninspiring as the first. I had no idea where college was taking me. For sure I did not want to graduate and be a school teacher. I felt that I was just drifting, killing time. After the spring term ended, I got a summer sixty-cents-an-hour job nailing down tin roofs on a new all-metal tobacco warehouse going up on the edge of Wilson. This was blisteringly hot work, pounding nails to join and fasten the sections of tin and sealing the nail holes with molten tar. A water boy circulated with a bucket, a dipper, and salt tablets, and at the end of the day I was drained and my skin was crusty with dried salty sweat.

After work on those summer evenings, before supper, I sat on the front porch and drank iced tea and read. I maintained a polite and deferential relationship with my mother, but the old discomfort and the urge to get out of her presence remained. Her third husband now dead, she stayed mostly to herself, reading religious tracts in her room and listening to shouting evangelists on the radio. Her only social life consisted of a church-formed friendship with a farm couple who occasionally invited her to an evening at the Moose Club. Sitting on the porch, I soon fell into regular conversation with a gangly young man of about my age named Vernon Morton. He walked by our house every evening on his way home from his job as sports editor of the local paper, the *Wilson Daily Times*. One day he asked me if I had ever thought of being a reporter. I said I hadn't, really, but come to think of it my main heroes had been reporters— Dickens, Twain, Crane, Bierce, Mencken, and Hemingway. Well, he hadn't read much of that, he said, but there was an opening at the *Daily Times* if I was interested, and if I wanted to come in and apply he would set it up.

Next day I skipped work and went in to see the editor and publisher, Herb Brauff, a pink-faced widower who wore gold-rimmed glasses and black suspenders. He had just bought the paper from the widowed Elizabeth Swindell, a granddaughter of the founder, who now served as the paper's advertising manager. He had moved down from Pennsylvania with his daughter, a pale girl with blonde hair who was about my age. I was nervous and earnest. I told him I was two years into college but not very interested in it, that I had done a lot of reading and a little reporting—phoning in sports results to the newspaper when I was in high school, but no real experience, and that I thought I could learn fast. For whatever reason, he offered me a job, at thirty dollars a week. I accepted without hesitation, and went home very excited. My mother was clearly disappointed. She said she wanted me to finish college. But I didn't see the point, not having some specific ambition that a college degree might advance. And I could see right away that being a reporter was something way out of the ordinary, something that I would want to be.

The *Daily Times* was an afternoon paper, with no Sunday edition, of 9,000 circulation in a city of 25,000 population. It dated back to the incorporation of the town 100 years before. It was housed in an ancient one-story brick building between the Johnson Cotton Company and the Wilson County Courthouse. Besides Vernon Morton, the staff consisted of a city editor, a pleasantly rotund little man named Jim Fulghum, an unmarried female society editor, and a female copy editor. I excitedly reported at 7 A.M. on my first day as instructed, and Fulghum went out with me to show me the ropes. He said my basic job would be to collect information for a daily feature called "News Of Public Record." This page included the police and sheriff's department arrests, Municipal and County Court case dispositions, real estate transfers, births, marriage certificates issued, deaths, civil suits filed, traffic accidents as reported by the State Highway Patrol, the State Superior Court docket, and cases filed in the Federal District Court in the Post Office building.

These I scribbled down with the standard newspaper thick lead pencil on sheets of copy paper, scraps cut from the ends of the giant rolls of paper on which the *Daily Times* was printed. I did not know how to use a typewriter, so it took me a long time to type my reporting up on the ancient Royal, using the two-finger "hunt-and-peck" system.

I was also charged with covering crime stories too important to be relegated to the "News of Public Record," the lunch and supper meetings of the Civitan, Rotary, Lions, Jaycees, and Optimist clubs, the Chamber of Commerce, the Junior Chamber of Commerce, the American Legion, VFW, and AMVETS, plus activities of the county farm and home demonstration agents, the health department, the hospitals, the Tobacco Board of Trade, trials in the superior and federal courts and meetings of the City Council and County Board of Commissioners.

One early fall morning, I got a telephone call from the county coroner, Dr. R. F. "Doc" Gouty. He was an osteopath with an office on the eighth floor of the Wachovia Bank building next to the courthouse—a round little man with thick glasses and wavy gray hair who carried a black Gladstone doctor's bag.

"There's been a nigger killing out at Grab Neck if you want to go," he said. I relayed the news to Jim Fulghum, and he said he would go with me since it was my first murder. We piled into the paper's Ford flatbed truck, which was used mainly for hauling rolls of newsprint from the train station, and fell in behind Doc Gouty as he left the courthouse.

We drove out of downtown beyond the Golden Weed Grill and into the rural area. It was an overcast morning with hoarfrost on the ditch-banks. We could see the murder scene as we pulled off the main road and went along a dirt path behind a tin-topped tenant shack and a dead brown cornfield. A couple of sheriff's cars and an ambulance were parked at the edge of a pine woods and the deputies were standing around, smoking cigarettes and waiting for Doc Gouty. His job was to rule on the cause of death.

We got out of the truck and walked over. The victim was a young black woman. Her body lay grotesquely twisted on the ground just where the cornfield ended and the woods began. Her faded flour sack dress was up to her thighs. She was barefoot. There were knife punctures in her chest. Her throat had been cut right through past the windpipe from ear to ear and her head fell loosely to the side. There was a puddle of drying black blood around her head. Flies buzzed about her wounds. A bloody butcher knife lay next to her. Sitting silently on a nearby pine stump was the supposed murderer. He was a black man of slender build with an unremarkable face except for the blood-shot eyes and matted-down hair and a despairing expression. He was barefoot, too, and wore a pair of worn overalls with one gallus over his naked left shoulder. His head was in his hands.

"They was dancing and drinking busthead over to this nigger juke joint and they got to fighting when he danced with this other nigger girl she claimed he was going out with. They commenced drinking and fighting all night and he drug her out here and cut her thoat," said Deputy Claude Lucas. He had graying wavy hair, a beer gut, and a sardonic manner.

I was nauseous and dizzy looking at the body, and for a moment I thought I was going to faint.

"Well, that'll be a lesson to her," I said.

Lucas grinned and turned to the man on the stump. "Tell these gentlemen of the press your name, boy, so they can give you a nice write-up in the paper."

"Leroy, suh," he said.

"Leroy how much?"

"Leroy Hamilton, suh."

"Well, Leroy, you go on now and git in the car. You're taking a ride to the crowbar hotel."

When we got back in the truck Jim Fulghum gave me a hard look and said, "I don't want to ever hear you make another smart-aleck remark like that. She was a human being even if she was colored." I knew he was right. I didn't explain that my flippancy was a cover-up for my nervousness and nausea.

When we got back I wrote up my story and handed it over to Jim to edit. He made a couple of minor changes, added a head, and put it on the copy hook for the composing room. They set the type on a big clacking Mergenthaler linotype in the back shop behind the newsroom. A cylindrical pig of lead hanging from a chain was lowered into a smoking gas-heated pot. The melted lead was formed into lead lines—lines of type—as the operator hit the keys. Then they arranged the sticks of type in a steel frame called a chase, laid in the cuts (the pictures), and then made the semi-circular molds that were locked onto the press. At 3 P.M. a buzzer in the back shop sounded and the big Doss press began rolling. I was waiting excitedly at the press and caught one of the first copies to come off and there, although with no byline, was my first front-page story, one column with a 24-point head and an 18-point deck:

LOVERS' SQUABBLE
ENDS IN DEATH
Wilson Colored Man
Stabs Girl Friend In
Quarrel Last Night

A love affair between a Wilson colored man and his 24-year-old girl friend ended last night in the fatal stabbing of the girl by her lover following a quarrel.

Louise Parker, 894 Oil Mill Alley, was brutally cut to death supposedly by Leroy Hamilton, her 27-year-old boy friend. Hamilton resided at 202 U.S. Highway 301 South.

According to a report this morning by Dr. R. E. Gouty, Wilson County coroner, the colored girl was stabbed in the chest several times, in the back, and finally in the neck. Dr. Gouty said the wound in the neck was the blow that killed the girl....

The style of the *Daily Times* decreed that unmarried black women of whatever age be called "girl." A married "colored" woman after being identified by her whole name, perhaps Elsie Smith, in the first mention, would in succeeding graphs be called "the Smith woman." This avoided the honorifics "Miss" or "Mrs." being applied to colored women. Colored men, of course, were never referred to as "Mr.," not even on the full page that ran every Saturday headlined "News Of The Colored Community," which catalogued the doings of the colored Charles L. Darden High School, church and Sunday School events, marriages, funerals, and social clubs. Darden ran the colored funeral home and a colored insurance agency and was the colored community's most substantial citizen.

Had it been a story involving whites, the accused would not have been described as the victim's "lover." This term implied a sexual relationship. Whites, it was becoming clearer and clearer to me, had a winking and patronizing attitude about black relationships. "They don't bother to get married. They just jump over a broom," was a common white expression.

Not infrequently in the Municipal Court, unmarried white men and women who lived together in the white trash neighborhood next to the tobacco warehouse section of town would be hauled in on misdemeanor charges of "bedding and cohabiting." This carried a twenty-five dollar fine, plus court costs, and sixty days in jail, but the jail time was usually suspended with a warning to go and sin no more. No respectable white people, of course, lived together, or "shacked up," as the saying went. Such would have been the instant ruination of the woman's reputation and the branding of the man as a playboy of questionable marital reliability.

No such charges were ever brought against colored people, as it was assumed that colored people were just slightly elevated animals, so what could you expect? Among the proofs cited that they were of a sub-order was an alleged peculiarly pungent body odor. What's more, it was a "known fact" that there was no use hitting them over the head with a blackjack. Their skulls were so abnormally thick that they were impervious to these blows. And they were perpetually in heat.

No photograph accompanied my story of the murder. The *Daily Times* did not run pictures of colored crime or accidents.

Wilson and the surrounding county was half white and half colored. The town squatted in the sweltering heart of the table-flat and sandy North Carolina coastal plain, throughout which tobacco was the main cash crop. In the center of town, in front of a marble courthouse with six fluted Doric columns, two magnolia trees, and a Confederate statue, were "White" and "Colored" water fountains. A banner stretched across the intersection of Nash Street and Goldsboro Street proclaimed Wilson to be the "World's Largest Bright Leaf Tobacco Market." Wilson had once been a cotton town, but a popular ditty from the mid-1800s summarized the transition:

> *Cotton was once king*
> *And produced Carolina's cracker.*
> *But now we have a better thing,*
> *The glorious bright tobaccer.*

The tobacco market opened in late August and farmers came in with their pickup trucks loaded with the year's harvest, bringing their families to celebrate this high point of their year. An average yield was 2,000 pounds an acre. As I was learning in my role as a reporter, tobacco was selling that year for an average of one dollar sixty cents a pound, and about one million pounds were sold through the Wilson market. By early fall the warehouse floors were loaded with piles of golden leaf set out in straight lines. Singsong auctioneers moved chanting along the rows, followed by buyers from Liggett & Myers, P. Lorillard, Brown & Williamson, and the American Tobacco Co. A sweet peppery smell infused the whole town. When the farmers got their checks they went shopping—for a new pickup, school clothes for their children, a new Sunday dress for the wife—and ended the day with a barbecue dinner at Godwin's on Tarboro Street or at Parker's out on U.S. 301. This tradition of selling, shopping, and eating barbecue went back almost to the time of Wilson's founding.

In 1849 Wilson's board of commissioners had passed, among

other laws, one decreeing that "no free Negro or slave shall be permitted to be abroad after 9 o'clock at night after ringing of the curfew bell, penalty not to exceed 30 lashes." A century later when I went to work at the *Daily Times* this and other harsh laws were still on the books, though not enforced, but complete segregation prevailed the way it always had. Growing up in the insulated and all-white atmosphere of the orphanage I had not noticed or thought much about race. Life there had been simple and clear. Authority figures told you what to do, and you did it, always by the same rules. They treated everybody the same way, insofar as was observable, and seemed to behave themselves in private the same way they did in public. There were black people in the Navy. I had seen them in uniform. But they were not on my base. They trained I knew not where and served on ships only as cook's helpers.

But now, as I went about my beat as a kid reporter, beginning to observe and question, I saw a different, long-established order of things, one that was complicated and nuanced. Any visitor could understand quickly that there were two different worlds, one for whites, one for colored. These were clear to the naked eye, sometimes even labeled. It was the unspoken and occasionally subtle rules that were harder to learn.

The old train depot, the faded brick six-story Cherry Hotel alongside it, and the tracks of the Atlantic Coast Line railroad separated these black and white worlds. West through the white business district with its three banks at the main intersection, the Hudson-Belk and J.C. Penney department stores, Bissette's Drugs, the post office, the courthouse, Wimpy's Pool Parlor, and the Wilson Theater, Nash Street extended out to block after block of stately old two-story antebellum homes shaded by giant pin oaks that made a canopy over the street. Here lived the old white families—the Cozarts, Andersons, Aycocks, Pittmans, Ruffins, Herrings, Kenans, Walstons, Reddings, Hackneys, Barneses, Boykins, Dews, Raineses, Wainwrights—many with "III's" after their names. Many were absentee owners of rich tobacco farms tended by white and colored tenants on "halves," meaning the owners got half the net profit off the labor of the tenants, or were owners of the dozen sprawling old brick tobacco warehouses that were the economic backbone of the town. Many were the town's leading doctors, lawyers, and business owners. The men played golf and the women played bridge at the Wilson Country Club. They clung together at the Elks Club, in the Christian, Lutheran, Episcopal, and Methodist churches near the center of town, and they vacationed together at their beach houses in Morehead City on the Carolina coast, sent their daughters off to Peace, Goucher, Bryn Mawr, St. Mary's, and Meredith and their sons to Duke, Carolina, and Wake Forest. After college, the children came home and married each other and settled into the family businesses and began the cycle all over again.

The men bought their blue blazers, gray trousers, conservative Hickey-Freeman and Botany 500 suits, repp ties, wing-tipped cordovans, and tasseled loafers at Oettinger's, and the women their hats at Miss Molly's, their proper shoes and modest dresses at Barshay's and Park Avenue. They got their engagement rings, wedding silver, and silver baby cups and spoons for showers at Churchwell's on Nash Street and their furniture at Quinn's, had their wedding pictures taken by Raines and Cox Photographers, kept their money in the Planter's and Wachovia banks. They sent their dead to the Thomas-Yelverton Funeral Home to prepare them for burial in Maplewood Cemetery—where the woman who designed the Confederate stars and bars was buried—beside the municipal power plant.

The men went home for "dinner" at noon each day, and their wives entertained at suppers once a week. They rarely ate out, and when they did it was at Parker's Barbecue, the Golden Weed, or the Silver Slipper Supper Club out past radio station WGTM (World's Greatest Tobacco Market) on U.S. 301 North—where the custom was to bring your whiskey in a brown paper bag and order a bucket of ice and a Coke or 7-Up as mixers. Alcohol was never openly served to guests in people's homes. The men would go into the kitchen or onto the back porch or patio for a drink or perhaps two of "bourbon and branch water." Explicit drunkenness was frowned upon. A Southern gentleman knew how to hold his liquor. The liquor came from the state-run ABC Store on Tarboro Street and the beer from licensed places that advertised "packaged goods," the euphemism for Schlitz, Blatz, Budweiser, and Miller High Life. Wine was never served. That was something exotic, to be had in "Paris, France" or "It-lee" on a rare vacation—always a tour—by the moneyed class.

They supported the sports teams at Charles L. Coon High School, went with their friends to their Wake Forest, Carolina, or Duke alma mater football games in the fall, and occasionally attended the baseball games of the Class D Coastal Plains League team at Fleming Stadium, the Wilson Tobs (Tobacconists). They went to the club on Saturday night and to church on Sunday morning. Most of the conversation centered around their golf games, college football, the state of the tobacco "bidness," their children's engagements, marriages, and graduations, their trips to Morehead City or New York, the occasional divorces, and the suicides, of which there were a lot, I observed, for such a small town.

In late summer during the tobacco season the single young men and women from the better families got engraved invitations from the Carolina Cotillion Club to an annual event in nearby Rocky Mount called the "June German," a formal dance, the men in tuxes and the ladies in evening gowns with orchid corsages, held in a tobacco warehouse, with entertainment by the likes of Kay Kyser, Jimmy Dorsey, Tex Benecke, or Perry Como. The June German was generally attended by about 2,000 people from all around the eastern part of the state and it went on from 10 P.M. until 5 A.M. Getting invited to the June German meant that you had arrived in society or that, by virtue of your family lineage, you were there already.

If you were one of these privileged few, your name did not get into the *Wilson Daily Times* when you were charged with drunken or reckless driving or other non-spectacular crimes. After awhile I knew all these names, and I knew they would be eliminated from the court docket that I typed up and turned in for inclusion in the "News Of Public Record" feature. But I stubbornly included the well-known ones anyhow, knowing full well that there would be a phone call and that Mrs. Swindell would march to the back shop and take them out. Neither was the cause of death made explicit in the paper when members of the well-known families killed themselves. The obituary would say "Allie Fleming, 55, prominent tobacconist and owner of the Wilson TBS, was found dead [a true case, and no relation to my impecunious family] last night at his residence on Nash Street." Everybody understood that "found dead" was a euphemism for suicide.

The reasoning for this politesse was that the *Daily Times* was supposed to present a "positive" view of Wilson. The editor, Mr. Brauff, being a stranger to the Wilson culture and of a quiet and reserved nature, remained more or less aloof in his office, writing editorials and generally letting the reporting staff go its own way. But Mrs. Swindell aggressively intervened in the editorial process to protect the interests of the business community and her friends. She was a tall and exceedingly thin woman who wore heavy red lipstick on her pursed and disapproving mouth and a lot of face powder beneath her reddish, permanent wave hair-do. Behind her back, the linotype operators and pressmen in the back shop, and the editorial staff, too, called her "Olive Oyl," after Popeye's skinny girlfriend.

In the middle of my first smothering summer in Wilson, when the tobacco market opened, she gave me my first lecture regarding her inflexible view of the paper's "supportive" role. Revivals were a summertime tradition at rural churches. These usually featured visiting fire-and-brimstone evangelists who made their living by passing baskets and urging worshippers to support their "ministries." These nomadic evangelists gave part of their proceeds to local pastors who would shill for them from their own pulpits. But I was soon to learn there was a more entrepreneurial brand of evangelist, flamboyant characters who operated on their own independent of established churches—and who came to places like Wilson when the tobacco market was in session and the town was full of farmers with new money in their pockets.

Such a one was the Rev. Joe Green, to whom I was introduced by Mrs. Swindell one day when he came to the paper to place an ad. He had Brilliantined dark wavy hair and small black eyes under heavy brows and wore a powder blue suit with a vest and a loud red tie. He was driving a pink Cadillac with a trailer hitch on it. He was also advertising several times a day on WGTM, exhorting sinners to find salvation by coming to his week-long revival meetings in a big tent on Goldsboro Street just beyond the Wainwright's Warehouse.

Mrs. Swindell said I should go to the first night's services and write a story. Green had set up his faded canvas tent on a grassy lot with naked light bulbs hanging from its wooden pole supports, the flaps open at the sides. Twenty rows of folding wooden chairs were set up, and as the seats filled with sweating farmers and their wives fanning themselves and swatting mosquitoes, he began roaring hoarsely from a portable pulpit on a little wooden raised stage. "Glory be to Jay-suss. Blessed be his nay-aim. Praise be to Gaa-odd. Hallelujah. Thank you, Jay-suss, thank you."

Mopping his brow with a handkerchief, he spouted furious warnings of fiery furnaces and eternal suffering for the unsaved and whispered raspy appeals to surrender to the glory of Jay-suss Christ. But the part of his exhortation that really caught my attention came near the end when he said that "special offerings" were required if he were to carry on his ministry and continue to do the Lord's work.

"My wife who is my partner in this ministry is going to pass the baskets amongst you now," he said, "and I don't want to hear the rude jangle of little coins. I want to hear the quiet rustle of dollar bills, blessed by the name of Jay-suss."

I thought of Sinclair Lewis's Elmer Gantry, that I had come upon a minor version of him in our midst. When I wrote my story, I included the rustling dollar bills quote. Soon after the paper rolled off the press, Mrs. Swindell was at my desk, her mouth turned down. The Rev. Green had called, very upset. He had denounced me as a heathen on his radio show and threatened to pull his ad from the paper. She was disappointed in me, she said. She had thought I was such a nice young man. Obviously I was a mocker and a sinner. I was an outsider in Wilson, too, and did not know its customs and traditions. But I was not to write any more negative things, the mission of the *Wilson Daily Times* being a supportive and positive one.

This was my introduction to a journalistic truism—the business and editorial sides of all newspapers had different agendas, and there was constant tension between them. Olive Oyl was in business to make money first and foremost and did not want anything printed that would anger advertisers or threaten her position as an eminent citizen and leader. The editorial side wanted just to print the news without favoritism to anyone. Mr. Brauff was the buffer against her interfering, and most of the time we thought he did a pretty good job, despite his unassertive manner.

In the summer in Wilson you could see heat waves rising from the tin roofs of the warehouses, and the pavement was so hot your shoe heels stuck in the asphalt on the streets. The humidity hovered at 85 percent, the temperature at ninety-five, smothering the town in a wet and hot blanket that sapped the energy and made every movement a punishment. There was no breeze, and it didn't completely cool off until four o'clock in the morning. The old sun-baked brick buildings seemed to sag. People plodded along the streets as if sleepwalking, their sweat-drenched shirts and dresses stuck to their backs. They took refuge in their air-conditioned offices—those who had them—or in Bissette's and Morrison's drug stores and the Monticello Restaurant.

Writhing and sweating on my hallway cot at night, I would wet a towel in the bathroom, lie on my back, and spread it over my nude body in an attempt to cool down. This only worked for a few minutes because the towel would get hot, and then I would get up and wet it again. There was no light in the hallway, nor any outlet to rig up a lamp, so I couldn't read. Sometimes I got up and sat on the front porch in a rocking chair, but the mosquitoes were numerous and fierce.

"Every time you kill one, a thousand come to the funeral," Jim Fulghum said.

Even before the heat arrived I hadn't been sleeping. It was the first time in many years I was going to bed in a non-communal setting. So I had laid awake hour after hour on the cot, tense and frightened. My heart jumped at every creaking noise the house made as it contracted, releasing the day's blistering heat. I fanta-sized about assailants coming in with knives and attacking me—not bothering to think of what kind of criminal would be so desperate as to invade a thirty-dollar-a-month tin-roofed shack. Sometime before dawn I would finally fall asleep.

My work day began at 7 A. M. and officially ended at 3:30 P.M. when the presses rolled. But I was the general assignment reporter, and if anything was going on at night, I was obliged to cover it. I often rode the highways with the local State Highway Patrol officer or the town cops, covered night civic meetings of various sorts, or hung out with my friends at the Esquire Grill and Wimpy's Pool Parlor and had an occasional date.

My mother had taken a job clerking at Blackwell's News Stand next to the Wilson Theater for fifteen dollars a week, selling popcorn, candy, soda pop, chewing gum, magazines, and paperback books. At home she complained constantly about her miserable life, how she hadn't had any opportunities, how she had never had a house of her own or any of the "finer things" of life. She suffered from "the low blood," feeling tired all the time, and often took to her bed with what she called a "sick headache." She would lie on her back with a wet handkerchief over her forehead. She was, in her words, "about the most unfortunate person who ever lived." I was formally solicitous, but all I felt was a knot in my stomach and an urge to run away. Instead, I would walk sometimes down to the little store called the Millhouse and buy her a bladder of her favorite snuff, Sweet Railroad Mills. She dipped snuff constantly—had since her childhood—spitting the juice into a Dixie Cup she always kept handy.

I sometimes impatiently asked her why she didn't now do something to improve herself: learn to type and take shorthand, go to bookkeeping school, get a job clerking in a bank, become a nursing assistant, do secretarial work, go to night school. I would pay for it, I told her. But she always had an excuse, self-pitying lamentations delivered in her cracked and high-pitched voice: It was too late in life. She was too run down. She could hardly keep a bite down (in actuality, she was a sneakily prodigious eater). She didn't have enough education. She had suffered too many bad breaks.

I was covertly embarrassed and angry that she was working as a menial at a newsstand. It added to the shame and insecurity I felt about being an orphanage boy, poor and without education or class. Though I was developing a contempt and cynicism for the upper classes—their blue blazers and country clubs, their old-fashioneds and martinis, their buttoned-down shirts and cordovan shoes, their seeming pursuit of money as an end in itself, their perceived hypocrisy—I was secretly envious of them, too—of their restrained good manners, their sense of ease, their tastefully understated clothes, their stately old homes, and the III's after their names. I began to buy clothes that I hoped looked like theirs. I learned to tie a Windsor knot, to not wear socks lighter than my pants—or that were too short and showed your ankles—and to quit putting grease in my hair.

Through my involuntary membership in the town's civic clubs I got to be friends with a few of the young bachelors from the good families who were starting out on their careers. Occasionally I got invited to, and self-consciously attended, dances and picnics at the country club. I also was asked to an unofficial Jaycee "smoker" at the Silver Slipper dining and dancing club out on the highway toward Rocky Mount, where someone had somehow acquired and now showed on a sheet draped on a wall a scratchy black-and-white pornographic film featuring a foursome of pale and unappetizing men and women unenthusiastically copulating on a blanket beside a river. I stood at the back, embarrassed.

I also was invited into a bachelor's poker game at the graceful old family home of a corpulently affable young man named Giles Winstead, who was rapidly spending away a coal company he had inherited from his recently deceased parents. When his closet got full of dirty shirts, he simply threw them away and went back to Oettinger's and bought new ones. But the five-dollar limit in the poker game was too much for me, although I had gotten a five-dollar-a-week raise, so I only played a couple of times.

I had good manners, thanks to the orphanage. I stood up when a lady or an older person entered a room. I said "Yes, Sir" and "No, Ma'am." I said "Please" and "Thank You." I opened doors for ladies and let them go in first. I held the chairs for them and let them sit down first. I kept my elbows off the dinner table, chewed with my mouth shut, kept my free hand in my lap, used my napkin, didn't reach for food, didn't take the last serving, didn't talk with my mouth full, and profusely—and genuinely—thanked the cook for the meal. Still, the upper-class world of Wilson on whose fringes I stood was built on familiarity and background, and it did not admit outsiders easily, especially not those below the salt.

In that world, nothing changed, and nobody wanted anything to change, especially regarding the long-settled posture between the races.

All of the good families had a "colored girl." In the mornings on my reportorial rounds, I would see the white ladies from out on Nash Street drive across the tracks to fetch their "girls." They put them in the back seat of their Buicks, Oldsmobiles, and Pontiacs, like an unconscious parody of a limousine service. It was not socially acceptable to ride alongside a colored person. Colored male factotums, of course, got to their jobs on their own. No white woman would ride alone in a car with a colored man. The "colored boy" mowed the grass, raked the leaves, moved the trash cans, washed the cars, and did other chores around the house—and came to the back door with hat in hand for his pay. These servitors were paid as little as five dollars a week, but the whites justified the low wages by allowing them to have what were called "totin' privileges," meaning they could take home leftover food after supper.

Along about this time the faint and faraway rumblings of school desegregation were beginning to be heard, reported by the *Daily Times* through Associated Press stories datelined Washington, D.C. The NAACP had just filed a lawsuit on behalf of black children in Topeka, Kansas, called *Brown v. Board of Education*, challenging the "separate but equal" school doctrine that had been established by the Supreme Court in 1896, meaning it was OK to have separate black and white schools as long as they were equal.

But that was in some distant Yankee place, and the white people of Wilson did not in the late 1940s feel seriously threatened. If the subject came up, the lady of the house would inevitably say, "Well, I talked to our colored girl, and she said they want to keep their own schools. They don't like the idea of mixing."

And if someone had accused the old families out on Nash Street and Raleigh Road of being racist, an accusation that would not have occurred to anyone, at least not anyone white, the old families would have been genuinely astonished and offended. They would have said that they treated "our colored people" extremely well. They would cite examples of having paid for funeral and hospital expenses, of donating cast-off clothes and used furniture, of sending bags of food at Christmas, of continuing to employ and pay their aged factotums beyond their capacity to work with full vigor.

They expressed toward their maids, cooks, and yard men, especially the old "aunties" and "uncles" in long service, a protective and custodial affection. Colored people, after all, were essentially naïve, ignorant, and childlike—docile as long as they were not drunk. As long as they stayed in their place, they could count on being taken care of by their white benefactors.

What the colored people across the tracks may actually have felt about segregation in general and separate schools specifically no one in the white world knew. It was simply assumed that what they said to the white people was true—that they were content with the status quo. The pillars of the black community, the ministers and school teachers and the owners of the few colored businesses allowed to exist because whites wanted nothing to do with them—such as restaurants, beauty parlors, barber shops, funeral homes, pool halls, and juke joints patronized entirely by colored people—did not publicly protest or resist. There seemed to be among them a seeming general air of good-natured acceptance. When one of them excelled, or died, it was said that "he was a credit to his race," suggesting that ordinary blackness was a debit somehow.

The colored community was a close-packed warren of gray unpainted shotgun shacks rented from white landlords on dirt alleys across the railroad tracks. Its only paved roads were Nash Street, becoming Highway 41 going east into the country towards the coast, and U.S. 301 going north and south, the principal highway from New York to Miami. Its inhabitants were for the most part menials of every sort, field hands on the surrounding tobacco farms, manual laborers for the city and county maintenance departments, and unskilled workers in the tobacco warehouses and wholesale packing houses.

Few white people ventured into "niggertown." Even as a reporter I had only rare occasion to go beyond the tracks, except to report on a crime. I was at first confused and even a little hurt that I was given such a cool reception. Where might I find so-and-so? Don't know, suh. Will so-and-so be back soon? Don't know, thank you, suh. But I gradually understood the reason for the guardedness: The arrival of a white man could mean nothing good. He was either "the law," a bill collector, or someone selling

something—usually life or burial insurance. I wanted to say to
them that I was different, I wasn't an exploiter, I understood what
it felt like to be an underdog, I sympathized with their plight. But
I said nothing. I had no experience being personal and emotionally honest with anyone, white or black, and anyway, anything I
said might sound phony or patronizing.

Many poor whites also lived below the radar screen. One winter day when I'd been at the paper maybe four months, I was
driving on U.S. 64 about ten miles out of Wilson, on the way
back from a tobacco barn fire, and I passed a small group of
white men in overalls carrying picket signs in front of the
entrance to a commercial stone quarry. I stopped to see what it
was all about. The men said they were striking for better wages
and living conditions. They were living in a clump of shacks
behind the quarry, some with wives and children. Next day I
came back carrying the cumbersome *Daily Times* 4 x 5 Speed
Graphic camera, ready to interview the strikers and management.
The *Daily Times* did not have a staff photographer. Its reporters
were responsible for taking their own pictures, and I soon learned
to take pretty good ones and develop and print them in the dark-
room behind the newsroom. The strikers told me they were making fifty cents an hour for jackhammering and shoveling the
granite from the quarry, with no benefits of any kind. Out of
these wages they were being charged thirty dollars a month for
living in the company shacks, wretched tarpaper-roofed affairs of
pine-board walls you could see through. The tenants had covered
the inside walls with newspapers and chunks of cardboard to
keep the wind out. There was no electricity or plumbing, just a
common well into which a bucket was lowered and a common
two-hole backhouse. The people, skinny, ill-clad, ill-housed, ill-
fed, and despairing, reminded me of the white Alabama tenant
families poignantly written about by James Agee and pho-

tographed by Walker Evans in the gut-wrenching Depression book *Let Us Now Praise Famous Men.*

The quarry owners, the foreman told me after I had taken my pictures and interviewed the families, were in Raleigh, and I had better get off the property. I was very moved by these poor whites, but I wrote just a simple, straight factual story about the strike, and Jim Fulghum, the city editor, agreed with me that it was so unusual as to warrant a byline and a couple of pictures of the squalid houses and ragged children on the front page. This was my first byline.

I was pleased and proud. I was standing by for a copy of the paper when the bell rang and the presses rolled. There was my story. It was entirely objective and unbiased, but still I felt pleased that I had shed light on an injustice and that Jim and I had slipped one past Mrs. Swindell. As far as I could tell, she rarely actually read the paper—except when some member of the town's elite called to complain. She was interested in the business, social, and civic aspects of the operation, especially the highly profitable annual "Tobacco Edition," which was designed purely as an advertising special full of puff pieces, and had no discernable interest in hard news as such. What did she know of or care about poverty and suffering? She had inherited wealth and lived in an elegant old two-story brick home with magnolias and dogwoods in the yard out on Nash Street. She symbolized for me the greedy hardness of the grasping rich.

I was going home every afternoon after work and reading on the front porch while Aunt Belle or my mother cooked supper. My mother prided herself, as she should have, on her cooking— chicken fried crisp and golden in lard in a cast-iron skillet, tender collard greens seasoned with ham hocks, fresh corn carefully shaved off the cob and simmered with rendered fatback, fresh snap beans or field peas seasoned with a little onion and fatback, fried okra and green tomatoes, hot buttermilk biscuits slathered with butter or skillet-baked cornbread—all of it topped off by her special pineapple upside-down cake or sweet potato pie. This was simple Southern country cooking, unadulterated by any spices, and the love of it would stay with me my whole life. These meals were our happiest times together. At nights, after dinner, I hung out with a half-dozen single young men, most car-less like myself, who gathered each evening in front of the Esquire Grill or Wimpy's Pool Parlor. The Esquire Grill was, like most of the Wilson restaurants—the New York Café, the Golden Weed, the Manhattan Cafe, the Monticello Cafe, Dick's Hot Dogs—owned by a Greek. Charlie Noulis was an affable bachelor in his late twenties. He served up spaghetti, beef stew, pork chops, and meat loaf and did a fair business, not least because he had a beer license. In the group that hung around in front of his place were a couple more Greek guys whose fathers ran restaurants, a Syrian whose father ran a used furniture store, one Jew who clerked in a dry goods store, an auto mechanic, an air-conditioning installer and repairmen, a draftsman for the State Highway Department, and the owner of a small print shop.

Charlie Noulis closed the Esquire Grill at nine. After hours, Charlie often invited us in to play poker, drink, tell dirty jokes, speculate about which girls would put out or which one would go down on you, or who was under no circumstances screwable. There was a woman named Elsie Dawson who reputedly would not put out but who would give you a "hand job" with Johnson's Baby Oil. There was a woman at Western Union who would go down on you if she had a few drinks. There was a woman who clerked for a lawyer who would do it on the floor after work—while her husband was at WGTM giving the farm news.

There was endless bragging, and a lot of lying, about seducing women:

"You getting much?"

"Man, I get more accidental than you do on purpose."

What little "screwing" actually did occur took place in the back seats of automobiles. A joke oft told was that when a newly married guy said to his bride, "Let's make love," she ran out and got in the car. The philandering rich men of Wilson, though, could afford love nests in tree-veiled country cabins they called "fish camps" out on Silver Lake.

Most nights we would chip in and buy a fifth of Jim Beam or Old Hickory at the ABC store on Tarboro Street. It cost $3.25 a bottle. The accustomed drinking style was to pour bourbon into a partly emptied Coke or Pepsi bottle and pass it around. "Let's get drunk and be somebody" was the cry.

I wasn't drinking every night. Some nights I had nothing at all, other times just a beer. But I began to notice that when I drank whiskey, I usually got drunk—and threw up until I had what were called the dry heaves, expelling black bile and then nothing.

But what was wrong with drinking? All of my writing and reporting heroes were serious drinkers, and proud of it. Only prudes and spineless captives of organized religion were teetotalers, and I was defiantly not one of them. I was a newspaperman, and newspapermen were above all that. They were idealistic, even anarchical, always skeptical and cynical about power and money. That was me; that's who I was becoming: a hard-drinking, authority-questioning reporter. I had been at the paper two years. It had been a difficult immersion. I was still lonely and felt like a fish out of water in town and at home with my mother and her insistent neediness. And I was still reading everything I could get my hands on. There was not a bookstore as such in Wilson, but there was a newsstand next to the Cherry Hotel that sold a few out-of-town newspapers, paperbacks, and hard-backed Modern Library books. These cost $1.25 apiece, and I was soon buying two or three a week and devouring them—*Madame Bovary*, *Crime and Punishment*, *Darkness at Noon*, *Native Son*, *Moby-Dick* (again), *The Memoirs of Casanova*, *The Brothers Karamazov*, *Leaves of Grass*, *In the Midst of Life*—and everything I could get my hands on of Hemingway, Fitzgerald, Faulkner, John O'Hara, Robert Benchley, Dorothy Parker, James T. Farrell, Dickens, Twain, O'Henry, Henry Miller, Theodore Dreiser, D. H. Lawrence—even Nietzsche and Emerson—and on and on.

I read without guidance or pattern, one writer and one book after another. This was a solitary pursuit. No one that I knew was reading serious books or serious journalism, or books of any kind for that matter—not my drinking buddies nor the upper class Wilson people who evidenced little interest in the outside world. What little of it that they talked about—"24 War Criminals Hanged In Munich" or "Death On Gallows Ordered For Tojo"— they got from the *Daily Times*, or perhaps the *Raleigh News & Observer*. The *New York Times* might as well have been printed in Moscow.

I did not associate myself with the writers whom I idolized in any real sense. They were mythic figures who might as well have been on some other planet. Nor did I think I could or should become a writer. My talent, if I had any at all, seemed puny and sophomoric. But reading made me see the world around me in a new way. That was especially true with the journalists I read— Mencken, Bierce, Ring Lardner, Ida Tarbell, George Orwell, Damon Runyon, and Lincoln Steffens, who had become famous for exposing corruption in politics and big city government. He wrote a series of articles called "The Shame Of The Cities" that detailed how machine politics and clever politicians siphoned off public money and scuttled public good. Teddy Roosevelt said Steffens spent his time riding through sewers in a glass-bottomed boat and coined for him the term "muckraker."

And that's what I began to daydream I might do—report the truth as I saw it, be as fair as I had been taught in the orphanage, and to think of my career as a reporter as a calling. I was still pretty naïve but learning fast.

Chapter 6

My First Bad Cop

THE WILSON Police Department was quartered in an alley on the ground floor of the two-story municipal building on Goldsboro Street, a half block from the *Daily Times* office and across the street from the courthouse. It was by far the city's newest downtown building and the only one with an art deco facade.

This was usually the first place I stopped on my beat every morning. I looked at the police blotter to see if there had been any interesting arrests. Then I walked back to see if anybody was in jail and ask the desk sergeant if anything was going on either with his colleagues or with the Highway Patrol or Sheriff's Department, all of whom were hooked up by radio. Usually there wasn't, except perhaps for an automobile accident. These were frequent on the narrow macadam roads that ran out from Wilson in all directions, and they usually involved people drinking. Among the first deaths I had seen as a reporter occurred when I went out with the coroner one afternoon to the Tarboro Highway where two men walking down the highway had been decapitated by a board sticking out from a lumber truck. Their heads had rolled into the shallow, muddy ditch off the shoulder of the road. I had brought along the paper's camera but the scene was obviously too gruesome to put in the paper, so I returned to the patrol car as an excuse to walk away and hide my nausea.

I learned from the highway patrolmen I rode with to always walk left, facing traffic, and how to quickly turn a car around on a narrow highway by pulling to the right shoulder, reversing while turning the steering wheel all the way to the left, and then turning right—all one simple maneuver.

Sometimes at the police station I would chat with the police chief, Albert Privette. He was a tall man of fifty with an amused eye, huge feet ("A good under-standing," he said with a twinkle) and a soft manner who viewed his fellow citizens' transgressions with a kindly sufferance. He often hung around after supper or stood in front of the police station on the street and talked to passersby, and thereby in his quiet style kept up with what was going on. There was not much that he did not know about, at least on the surface.

But the chief's knowledge pretty much ended at the edge of "niggertown," into which he rarely ventured. The job of following what was happening across the tracks fell mainly to Detective Ray Hartis. He was a concrete block of a man, five feet, eleven inches and 200 pounds, with a large head covered with bristly graying hair. He had thick eyebrows, cold gray eyes, red cheeks, and a large pickle of a nose lined with tiny red tributaries—marks of the hard drinker that he was. He was about forty, married but childless, a longtime cop who carried a .38 Smith and Wesson pistol on his hip and a blackjack in his rear right pocket. He invariably wore a tan Stetson hat and was a natty dresser, adorned usually in a Hickey-Freeman suit, a Hathaway shirt, and Johnson and Murphy shoes—all of which he got at discount prices at Oettinger's.

He was a loner with the harsh and unapproachable manner of a bitter and disappointed man, disdainful of and not well liked by his fellow cops. For some reason, though, Ray took a liking to me and began inviting me to ride with him on his nightly rounds. I concluded that perhaps this was because he was essentially a lonely man. There was a sad quality about him. Perhaps he liked me because I was the only person who would listen without judgment or comment to his bitter indictments of his fellow man. Maybe my abject innocence appealed to him. For my part, I was drawn to him in some way I did not quite understand. Maybe I identified with his sadness, or maybe I was seeking a father figure. Undoubtedly, I was fascinated by his knowledge of the dark underside of the city—the demimonde—his cynical view of the "goddamned hypocrites" and his willingness to show this world to me.

My night classes ensued in the early evenings. I would be hanging around the police station and Ray Hartis would stop off, get a nickel Coke from the coin machine, and say, "Come on, kid. Let's go out amongst 'em." He drove an unmarked city-owned green and white Pontiac with a small antenna on the trunk.

As we cruised around after dark, we'd occasionally pass a black Buick on an unlit street with the indistinguishable figure of a man inside. The first time I saw it, he identified the driver as a member of a distinguished Wilson manufacturing family that dated from Civil War days. "Goes to the Country Club on Saturday afternoon, the Episcopal Church on Sunday and sucks dicks weeknights—when he can find one." He was Wilson's only known queer, Ray said, and his assignations were with other queers who came over from Rocky Mount, Goldsboro, Tarboro, or Greenville. As far as Ray knew, there were no muff divers (lesbians) in Wilson, although he was not sure about a couple of single women from good families who were built like brick shithouses and had low voices and a lot of hair on their arms.

Soon after I started riding with him, Ray began taking me around to the town's two twenty-dollar whorehouses, run by two veteran madams named Betty Powell and Mattie Paul. The whorehouses were situated in what Ray called "white trash heaven," a few streets of small faded houses with busted cars and chained-up dogs in the yards whose residents were often in Municipal Court on charges of disorderly conduct, public drunkenness, or "bedding and cohabiting." Powell's and Paul's sexual emporia had operated for at least thirty years, Ray said, situated in similar two-story wood houses near each other just behind the tobacco warehouse district. He said that both Betty and Mattie had started out as young whores and eventually saved enough to buy out their retiring madams.

Their big business was during the sultry late summer and fall tobacco market season, when the auctioneers and buyers and other migratory tobacco men were in town, along with the farmers with their pockets full of cash from selling their crops. The warehouse people traveled an annual circuit around Carolina, Tennessee, and Kentucky tobacco towns. In Wilson they always stayed at the Cherry Hotel, ate at Parker's and Godwin's barbecue places, played poker at the Elks and Moose clubs, and drank and "carried on" at the bordellos. The general clientele of the whorehouses, though, were the local regulars, Ray said contemptuously, who were solid members of upper- and middle-class Wilson families, married to women encased in girdles, with their frozen hair and repressed urges. When we pulled up to these places, Ray would identify the clients' cars in the rain-dimpled dirt yards and invariably say with a bitter grin, "They're in there, all the upright pillars of Wilson. They worship bought pussy on weeknights and God on Sunday, the goddamn hypocrites."

We'd always go up the back steps to the kitchens, so as not to make contact with and potentially embarrass the men Ray called "the whore-hoppers." Both of the whorehouses had black maids on duty, to change the sheets after each transaction and to serve drinks and snacks to the clients. When we arrived, the maids would inform Betty or Mattie that Ray was in the kitchen. Shortly the madams would come in, attired in their bathrobes and bedroom slippers, both in their forties, pale with dull eyes and hard, down-turned mouths, and offer us a drink. I declined, but Ray always accepted—bourbon and 7-Up. He would want to know from Betty or Mattie if any strangers were in town or if anyone was throwing money around. There was never any suggestion of the madams being arrested. They were Ray's informers, and thus were immune from arrest. During these visits, I stayed silently in the background, feeling awkward and naïve—slightly revulsed but slightly titillated, too.

Ray was perfectly aware of my shy innocence, and took a perverse pleasure in teasing me, through Betty Powell. We'd be standing around her kitchen, Ray having his bourbon and me hanging back, and he'd say to Betty, "Maybe you'd like the kid here to give you a nice write-up in the *Daily Times*. I betcha he'd do that in exchange for getting his ashes hauled with one of your fine young virgins. How about it, kid, wanna get your knob polished?"

"Thanks but no thanks, Ray," I said, my face warm with embarrassment as Betty gave me a sour, uninterested glance.

Some nights Ray would drive me out West Nash Street to Silver Lake beyond the city limits where he said that several leading citizens, including the sheriff, maintained "fish camps" on dirt paths deep in the pine woods beside the water. He took bitter delight in pointing out the alleged phoniness and two-faced hypocrisy of Wilson's leading citizens—his masters. But I, despite my own nascent cynicism (teetering between naïveté and worldliness), could see that Wilson was no worse or better than a hundred towns just like it, that it had kind and decent people, flawed people, some downright rascals, and a few, like Ray himself, deeply troubled and angry people. So I listened and watched without judgment, hungrily drinking it all in. This was life.

"There's a lot more fuckin' than fishing goes on around those cabins," Ray said. "Stud poker, too. That's the sheriff's cabin over there. And there's Doctor Putnam's, and his car—probably he's in there giving mouth to mouth to Doris the waitress." Doris was a faded blonde who worked at the Esquire Grill.

Then we'd cruise back through town and across the Atlantic Coast Line tracks into the little colored business district, only two blocks long. Ray would slow the car down to a crawl, and as we went along, silence would fall over the little knots of black men laughing and talking on the street. They'd bow and scrape servilely and say, "Evenin', Mistuh Hottis. How you this evening, Mistuh Hottis?"

He responded with a stony imperious nod and continued to drive slowly along. This was designed to let his menacing presence be felt. At the end of those two blocks, he turned and drove again slowly crisscrossing the dirt alleys lined with shotgun shacks and finally would stop in the side yard of what looked like just another shack. But this one was special. It was the home of a colored bootlegger, who in return for being Ray's informer, was allowed to sell bonded booze. The one state-owned and operated ABC (Alcohol Beverage Control) store closed at 6 P.M., and of course there were no bars. Ray's informer came out to the car, a black pudgy man in an old felt hat and baggy pants with galluses, bringing a fifth of Canadian Club wrapped in a paper bag, which he handed to Ray without comment. This was a regular business transaction and of course Ray never handed over any money.

"What's happening, Abraham?"

"Well, sah, Mistuh Ray, ain't nuthin' commencing that ain't the usual," he said. When there was, such as someone having an uncommon amount of money, he would report this to Ray, allowing Ray to keep a handle on the petty thefts and break-ins that occasionally occurred. Ray was keenly alert to anything going on that even slightly skewed the somnolent norm of niggertown.

One sultry night as we cruised the alleys, Ray suddenly stopped the car in front of a shotgun shack and got out.

"Where you going, Ray?" I asked

"I heard this son-of-a-bitch is a member of the N-Double-Fuckin'-A-C-P," he said. This was after the NAACP had gone to the Supreme Court in *Brown v. Board of Education*, news of which had been in the *Daily Times* and on network radio.

I got out of the car and followed him as he went up onto the front porch. He opened the door without knocking and strode into the front room. It was lit by a single bulb hanging by a cord from the ceiling and it contained a faded sofa, a rocking chair, and a plain pine chest of drawers. A cheaply framed picture of Jesus and an insurance company calendar hung on unpainted wooden walls. Ray approached the chest and began opening the drawers and throwing stuff onto the floor.

"What you looking for, Ray?" I asked.

"The son-of-a-bitch's N-Double-A-C-P card," Ray said. Suddenly a gray-haired old black man appeared out of the back room rubbing his eyes and pulling on a pair of overalls over his thin bare shoulders.

"Whatcha doin', Mistuh Hottis? You got a search warrant?" he said.

Ray turned, his face all red, lunged at the black man and slapped him hard across the cheek. Down the old man went on his back to the floor and Ray said, "That's one side of my goddamned search warrant. You wanna see the other one?"

The old man said nothing. Ray glared menacingly at him and walked out, me following. We got in the car and Ray drove slowly off, as if nothing had happened. It was quiet in the car for a long time. Finally I said, "What did you do that for, Ray? He's just an old man."

"You don't know a goddamned thing, do you? You don't know that you have to keep these niggers in their place. Give 'em an inch and they'll take a mile. You don't know them like I do. You can't let 'em get ideas in their heads. You can't let 'em talk back to you. There ain't nothing that pisses me off like an impudent nigger."

Impudence in his view meant having the impertinency to question in even the slightest way anything he said or did, to be what he called an "uppity nigger." Craven silence, or a bowing and scraping "Yas-sah" or "No-sah," were the only appropriate responses to a white man, especially a cop.

Ray prided himself on a vast knowledge of what he considered to be the many peculiarities of niggers and discoursed on them often in a wryly amused manner. There were, for example, the "blue-gum niggers." These according to him were unusually coal-black specimens from somewhere in Africa's darkest interior whose bite was lethally poisonous. Then there were the "bullet-headed niggers," who he said were quick to fight when drunk, usually with straight razors, were dumber than chickens, and everyone knew that chickens were creatures stupid enough to stick their heads up in a rain and drown themselves. And there were the "rock-headed niggers," a special category particularly hard to control, with heads so hard they were totally impervious to blackjack blows.

All niggers were in Ray's mind congenitally ignorant, with the exception of light-skinned "high yellers" who had some white blood in them, and childlike and almost impossible to educate beyond the rudiments. They were by nature undisturbedly happy with no ambition other than to have a good time, which they did no matter what. "If you was a nigger on just one Saturday night," he said, "you'd never want to be white again."

Ray said all nigger men had huge "dicks like donkeys" and were sexually insatiable—always in heat, and especially lustful after white women, though only rarely did one have the nerve to do anything about it. Nigger women were almost as highly sexed as nigger men, Ray said, and therefore were prized as rutting mates by some white men who wanted to "change their luck." This naturally had to be done in secrecy. Ray told me about a prominent married white doctor with two daughters away at fancy private colleges who had a nigger mistress. She would wait for him on a dark corner in niggertown and he would pick her up, make her crouch down and hide in the rear floorboards of his car and drive her out to his cabin and "get a piece of black poontang."

Black males invariably fought each other with knives and razors, he said, and would cut each other "from asshole to appetite." There was a rare nigger shooting with a shotgun or a .22. Few of them could afford guns, else the whole nigger population would be declining, and that would be fine with him. Niggers attacking whites was virtually unheard of, and their violence toward each other usually took place on Saturday nights in the summer. Hot weather accentuated, he said, the animalness of niggers. They were apes really, he said, only recently come down out of the trees, and they all reeked of a special nigger odor, which was hard to wash off if you got any on you. I was shocked by these casual assertions but too timid to challenge them, pitiless and extreme though they were. It had not escaped my scant observation, for one thing, that all but a few of Wilson's black people lived in shacks with no tubs or showers, and some had no plumbing at all, so that a full bath was impossible, and of course they had no money for white-used niceties such as Mum and Old Spice.

Ray usually weighed in on the subject of niggers after we finished our cruise of niggertown. He drove us out to the Silver Slipper carrying his free bottle of whiskey. The elfin, bowing proprietor, "Chinese Louie," would bring out a 7-Up, glasses, and a paper bucket of ice. Ray downed his half-dozen drinks quickly, and then chewed the ice.

Ray could tell I was uncomfortable during his racial dissertations, because I never said anything. But he liked to shock me.

"Don't worry about it, kid," he said. "You got a lot to learn. You don't know niggers like I do. They're different. They're like a damned mule. Only learn when you hit 'em, and then they can't learn much."

After the incident with the NAACP card, I cut back on my riding with Ray Hartis, acceding only when it was awkward to refuse him. He made me too uncomfortable—and a little frightened. What's more, I did not want to be a witness to—and to be inadvertently complicit in—the more serious violence of which I knew he was capable. He had bragged to me that he had killed two niggers. Whether this was true I did not know, but understood it to be possible. Also I began to be otherwise occupied as I got to know Wilson. I began to pitch for a semi-pro baseball team that played in small towns around the county on Saturday afternoons for whatever money—usually five dollars or less per player a game—that came with the passing of a hat. I pitched city league softball, helped coach Little League football, and played center on a city league basketball team at the National Guard Armory. One night we played against a barnstorming all-girls team called the All American Redheads, and the one I was paired off against boldly asked me if I would take her out after the game. I borrowed Wiley Lane's car and drove her out to the country club and parked on a fairway where she kissed me hungrily, unzipped my pants, and sat on my lap. Her legs were as hard as mine.

On my reporting rounds I had begun to meet and then date local girls. The well-schooled, country club daughters of the venerable families seemed far beyond my reach, limiting the pool of my possible dating choices to mostly teachers, secretaries, bank and sales clerks, telephone operators, and nurses.

These young women lived either with their parents, in boarding houses, or with roommates in apartments. Without transportation, there was nothing to do on dates but walk to a movie. And there weren't many more options even if you had a car: perhaps drive out to Parker's for barbecue, go to see the Wilson Tobs baseball team, go to the local drive-in theater. If it was a very special occasion, with a more adventurous date, you might go to dinner and dancing at the Silver Slipper—with your bottle of booze in a brown paper bag.

Even if the girl had a room of her own, it would be a miracle to be allowed into it. The landlady, or the parent, would certainly be watching. Therefore physical contact was confined to nervous necking in their living rooms or on their front porches. With any nice girl the chances of actual sex were minimal. Girls were frightened of getting a reputation for being an easy lay. That would not only make them the butt of cruel jokes but would also reduce their chances of getting married. Men were desperate to have sex, to be sure, but they wanted their brides to be virgins.

This of course put all single women in a terrible position. Aside from damage to their reputations, what was most inhibiting for women was the terrifying prospect of unmarried pregnancy. Having a child out of wedlock mean certain ruination. Having an abortion was a shameful act—in the unlikely chance one could find someone to perform one—sure to mortally tarnish a reputation.

In my second summer on the *Daily Times*, when I was twenty-two, I met and began to date and have sex with a twenty-nine-year-old divorcee named Bobbie Davis. She was secretary to a dentist who had an office on the fourth floor of the Branch Bank & Trust Co. building next to the courthouse. She and her five-year-old daughter lived with her mother in a four-room, second-floor apartment on Bragg Street a dozen blocks from my house. Bobbie was tall and slim with highly rouged cheekbones, a hungry thin mouth, small pointed breasts, straight black hair, and long pale freckled legs.

We had absolutely nothing in common beyond a mutual hunger for sex. I was shocked that she liked it with such unashamed boldness. I would walk to her place, we would stroll downtown to a movie, and upon our return make love standing in the stairwell, she one step above me, with one leg around my waist. Occasionally her mother would go out of town, and we had the bed and could be naked, she rocking beneath me with hip-thrusting lust. I knew nothing about the art of love—beyond what I had read in *Tropic of Cancer* and *The Autobiography of Frank Harris*. She accepted my hurried ineptitude without comment and was aggressive and eager to start over after each time.

She was having sex with other guys, too. I knew this because they said so. Standing in front of the Esquire Grill, they joked that she was a punchboard, a canvasback, a ceiling inspector. But the knowledge that she was sleeping with others only increased my desire for her. I did not admit to my cronies that I was screwing her, out of some innate sense that it wasn't right. Besides, I had heard that guys who talked about it weren't doing it; it was the quiet ones who were "getting it all."

Bobbie had a sister-in-law named Sue Anne who lived nearby. She was married to Bobbie's brother John, an Army captain stationed in Germany. There were also two other brothers who lived in the nearby village of Elm City. Sue Anne was a provocative beauty—flaming red hair, green eyes, freckled milky skin, and thrusting breasts invariably housed in V-necked Betty Grable sweaters. She was secretary to the president of a local bank and was audaciously flirtatious despite being married.

One night I got a ride with Jimmy Ellis and his girlfriend in his father's blue Cadillac convertible and took Bobbie to a BYOB (Bring Your Own Bottle) party in a neighborhood of modest GI tract houses near the baseball stadium—home of a balding and married clothing salesman named Eddie Murphy. Eddie had a stack of records and had moved the furniture out of his living room to make room for dancing. Midway through the evening, with everybody pretty tight and noisy, the door opened and to my shock in walked Ray Hartis and Sue Anne. There was a momentary stunned silence. Everybody knew Ray was married, and everybody knew Sue Anne had a husband in Germany.

But Ray acted as if things were perfectly normal and Sue Anne was completely unabashed. He went to the makeshift bar set up on a folding card table, took a pint of Four Roses out of his hip pocket, poured drinks for himself and Sue Anne, and began dancing with her. He was reeling and raucous, truly knee-walking drunk.

"Ain't she the cat's ass," he yelled, hugging her around the waist from behind. "Come on, redhead, show the folks your prize-winning knockers."

She laughed and gave him a coquettish look.

"No, I mean it. A prize-winning set of headlights like these don't come along often. Break 'em out!" he said.

"OK, hold my drink, honey," she said, and teasingly pulled the sweater up over a pink bra with lace on it. Her freckled white breasts bulged, and she quickly pulled her sweater down. Everybody was embarrassed. Bobbie looked away from me, her mouth turned down, and soon said, "Let's go."

I didn't see Ray for a while after that. But I heard a lot about him, because it was the talk of the other cops around the station that he was taking Sue Anne out at night, and so he wasn't around the police station very much. I thought it was amazing that he could be so brazen. But he had demonstrated that he could do pretty much as he pleased. He knew a lot of dark secrets about the powerful people of Wilson, and this was one way of sticking his thumb in their eyes: "You may not like what I'm doing but you can't do a damned thing about it." I thought I knew what else he was thinking, which was, well, maybe he was two-timing his wife but at least he wasn't a goddamned hypocrite like all those respectable citizens out on Nash Street. He didn't pretend to be anything other than what he was.

I filed him in the back of my mind and went about my own pursuits. Soon, despite the fact I was giving my mother ten dollars a week—a third of my gross salary—I had saved enough money to buy my first car. I paid my lawyer friend Wiley Lane $300 for a four-door faded gray 1936 Lafayette made of what seemed to be battleship steel. It gulped oil and belched black smoke from its exhaust. It had a baseball-sized hole in the floorboards on the passenger side. This was an uncomfortable defect in winter, especially when I parked with girls in the woods on cold nights with the windows rolled up and the motor running to keep warm— risking asphyxiation. I named the car the Gray Goose, and it was my liberation. I was able to take dates to the woods and out to Silver Lake to park on paths amid the fragrant pine needles beneath big buttery moons. Thus equipped, I could date more women, and soon was going out with five of them—but still with minimal sexual success. I had no sense of myself as being good-looking, or appealing in any particular way. But girls called me handsome and Mrs. Swindell warned me that I had better apply myself because I couldn't get by on my looks alone in the newspaper business.

I had no idea what to say to girls, beyond monosyllabic entreaties, nor did I have any concept of dating that might lead to marriage and a family, or even to going steady. I had grown up so isolated among boys, amid male vulgarity, braggadocio, and roughness where the only bridge between the genders was sexual, so far as I knew. People were married, to be sure, but did true love really exist? Love seemed to flourish only in books and movies. There was more convenience, resignation, and even desperation than excitement or romance in the marriages I saw. And I had amusedly noted Ambrose Bierce's mordant definition in *The Devil's Dictionary*:

> Marriage: The state or condition of a community consisting of a master, a mistress and two slaves, making in all, two.

Of course, people around me in Wilson were getting married all the time. The upper class brides' pictures were constantly in the *Daily Times*, with descriptions of the church weddings and what the brides were wearing and who the bridesmaids were and what they were wearing, and the grooms with their best men and ushers, all dressed in tails for receptions at the Country Club. Social life droned on in a perfectly predictable pattern. It was all in the Saturday edition *Daily Times* Social Calendar every week:

civic club meetings, dinner and bridge parties honoring "the bride elect," choir rehearsals, wedding rehearsals, and baby showers.

Summer rolled on with its smothering heat, violent thunderstorms, cicadas growling in the big oak trees, luminescent moons, and the air thick and pungent with the sweet peppery smell of cured tobacco. I bought a blue seersucker suit for twenty-eight dollars, a couple of repp ties, button-down dress shirts, some argyle socks, and a pair of Allen Edmunds cordovan loafers. I also commissioned Clyde Batts, the pale tailor with a basement shop in the alley beside the courthouse, to make me, for sixty dollars—two weeks' gross salary—a tan double-breasted gabardine suit that I intended to wear to the upcoming big dance that was the centerpiece of the annual Wilson Tobacco Festival. This year Tex Benecke was playing at the Wainwright's Warehouse, admission $3.50. I bought a pint of Old Hickory and went with two of my bachelor friends, Jimmy Nellis, who drove his father's Cadillac convertible, and George Sakas, whose father ran a restaurant, in hopes of picking up girls, which seemed promising for once, since there was a beauticians' convention in town.

As Benecke and his sweating band sailed into his signature song, "Chattanooga Choo-Choo," George and I sidled up to a couple of women, somewhat older than we were, surely from out of town, and began jitterbugging with them across the wooden floor. The women were beautician friends from the nearby town of Greenville. They had some drinks with us—Old Hickory mixed in a Coke and the bottle passed around—and agreed to go out with us after the dance. We piled into Jimmy's convertible at midnight and drove out to Godwin's, a beer joint out on 301 South. The women said they were staying at the Cherry Hotel and would be glad to have George and me come to their room later, a wild stroke of good fortune, we thought. I had never been in a hotel room with a woman, and the promise of easy sex was almost too exciting to contemplate. Now, how could we get rid of Jimmy, who had gone to the bathroom? He had the car, and we were riding with him. After conspiring with the women, we came up with a plan: Jimmy would drop me and George off at our houses and then drop the women off at the hotel. Then George and I would walk to the hotel and join them. I lingered in front of my house a minute, and then rushed the six blocks to the hotel and went up to the room and joined the women. We waited for half an hour, and then George's date discreetly went into the bathroom and closed the door saying she had some hose to wash. I got on the bed, quite drunk. My date was quickly willing to remove her clothes and let me make love to her. It was over in a hurry, and I dressed and went home, threw up in the bushes next to the house, and went to bed. George had never appeared at the hotel.

I lurched to work next morning at seven with a nauseous, throbbing hangover, and had been sitting immobile at my desk only a few minutes when George phoned. He was irate and agitated. "What the hell happened to you?" I asked. He had forgotten the hotel room number, he said, and had spent an hour running up and down the hotel halls calling my name. Why hadn't I answered? I hadn't heard him, I said. He was plenty mad. We agreed to meet at Jimmy's father's drugstore at mid-morning for note comparing and a coffee restorative. When we walked in, Jimmy was there behind the counter, an exultant smile on his face.

"You guys sure missed out," he said. "After I dropped you off I went to the hotel and fucked them both."

"No kidding," I said, giving George a knowing wink. We couldn't call Jimmy on his story, though, for it would have revealed our treachery.

My mother never said a word about my drinking, though obviously she was aware of my staying out late with my pals, reeling onto the porch and through the house, and sometimes loudly

heaving into the toilet. We didn't, in fact, talk much about anything. I did consistently have Sunday dinner with her and Aunt
Belle and my sister at the oil-covered table in the kitchen. My sister did not drink at all. She had by then graduated from high
school at the orphanage and been admitted to the Carolina General Hospital Nursing School in Wilson and was living in a dormitory with other nursing students.

In the early fall of my first year as a reporter, I began to hear
about an incident, at first just whispered about by the town's
elite, that was to shake little Wilson to its core. It was a sexual
crime against a white women committed by a black man. Nothing, not even murder, could have been more shocking and unset-
tling to the white community.

What happened was that in the early morning hours of September 2, 1948, the wife of Jimmie Barnes had called the police
and asked them to come quickly to her home, which was an
apartment in a house at 204 Park Avenue, located in a quiet,
upper-middle-class neighborhood near downtown. When the
police arrived, they found her in a distraught and frightened state.
She said her husband was out of town, in Washington, D.C., on
business (he was a lawyer), and she had gone to sleep in their
antique bed. At 2 A.M. she was awakened by the touch of a hand
on her shoulder. She said she immediately jumped from the bed
but the intruder, a colored man, grabbed both her wrists and told
her to be quiet.

"Who are you?" she asked.

"Never mind who I am," he said.

"How did you get in here?"

"That's all right. I got in here. You get back on the bed."

"What do you want?" she asked.

The exact words of the next exchange were not to be made
public, but they would prove critical in the case. The ensuing

court documents said that "he wanted to commit an act which would have, had it been accomplished, constituted a crime against nature."

"I want you to leave me alone and leave here right now," she said.

"You just get back on the bed. This won't take long," he said.

When she refused he grabbed her again and began twisting her wrists. She shouted "Sarah! Sarah!" at the top of her voice. Mrs. Sarah Mayo was her resident landlady. At this, Mrs. Barnes said, the intruder leapt head-first out the window he had entered through and fled, and she called the police. When they examined the window they saw that the screen had been cut, and they found a couple of Treet single-edged razor blades on the sill.

Mrs. Barnes said she did not know her assailant. He was colored, of medium build and height, and appeared to be about thirty years old. There was whiskey on his breath, his eyes appeared bloodshot, and he spoke with a slur, she said.

Sgt. A. J. Hayes was the police fingerprint man, a black-haired, taciturn, former door-rattling beat cop who had recently graduated from the FBI's fingerprint school. When he arrived he found clear prints on the windowsill and on the razor blades, but who they belonged to nobody knew, at least right then. Early that morning there came a report of a wrecked and abandoned Chevrolet automobile a dozen blocks from the Barnes apartment. It had run off the road and was stuck on the tracks of the Norfolk & Southern Railroad. On the front floorboards police found a wrapping from a Treet razor blade. They quickly traced ownership of the car to a colored man named Austin Reid, and by that afternoon they were at his house. He said he had loaned the car to his son, Allen, the previous night, September 1, "to go to the show." Allen Reid had not been seen since.

When the cops looked for Allen Reid in their files, there he was. He had been arrested several times and had served jail time on Peeping Tom charges. And the Peeping Tom incidents had taken place in the same white neighborhood where Mrs. Barnes lived. His fingerprints matched the ones found on the Park Avenue windowsill. He had been, quite clearly, either very stupid or very drunk to leave such a clear trail to his identity.

A warrant was quickly issued for his arrest stating that "Allen T. Reid, on or about the 2nd. of September, 1948, at and in the county aforesaid, did unlawfully, willfully and feloniously violate Sec. 4232 of the consolidated statues by breaking and entering the home of Mrs. Jimmie Barnes with the intent to commit rape, and while the house was being occupied, and while Mrs. Barnes was asleep, and did assault and threaten the life of Mrs. Jimmie Barnes."

I saw the warrant when I went on my beat that morning, got the details, bit by bit, from lawyer contacts and friends around the courthouse, and from a couple of friendly cops, and wrote my story. The Reid case quickly became the talk of the town. Any crime of violence by a black against a white was rare, and a sexual crime against a white woman by a black was virtually unheard of and was an extremely serious affront. The chief asked me to keep it quiet and called Jim Fulghum with the same request. "If you put it in the paper Reid will know we are looking for him," he said. That seemed totally senseless to me. Of course Reid would already be aware the cops were looking for him. In any case, not a word about the case got into the paper just yet. Meantime, detectives Ray Hartis and his sometime partner, Claude Fulghum (no relation to my colleague Jim Fulghum), a friendly, plodding man about Ray's age who never had much to say about anything, began their efforts to bring Reid in.

Ray kept me posted, off the record, about what was going on. He and Fulghum started getting tips, including some from Ray's black bootlegger informers, and soon they found out that Reid had fled to Richmond, Virginia, and was working at a restaurant under an assumed name. When he wrote home for money the cops intercepted the letter at the post office. He had included a return address. They informed Richmond police, who arrested him without resistance. Hartis and Fulghum drove to Richmond and picked him up. On the way back, Reid told Hartis and Fulghum a fantastical tale: on the night he borrowed his father's car, he was kidnapped by two men who robbed him, forced him to wreck the car, carried him to Richmond, and kept him under close guard the entire time he was there.

Once back in Wilson, Reid waived his right to a preliminary hearing in Recorder's Court, which was where I first saw him. He was of completely undistinguished features, medium dark, of average height and weight, a person you would never look at twice. Unshaven, wearing old brogans without socks beneath a pair of worn overalls and a bleached-out denim shirt, he looked defeated and confused. He was ordered bound over and held without bail for Superior Court, and that court quickly indicted him, saying:

Allen T. Reid . . . did enter the dwelling house of one Mrs. James Barnes . . . and feloniously and burglariously did break and enter, with the felonious intent against the said Mrs. James Barnes then and there feloniously, forcibly and against her will to ravish and carnally know her.

Reid didn't have a lawyer, so the court assigned one, George Tatum, a broken-down old drunk of a lawyer who hung around the courthouse every day in hopes of picking up assignments. He had droopy bloodshot eyes like a bloodhound and a red W. C. Fields nose. He invariably, even in winter, wore a seedy seersucker suit and a faded red tie.

The trial opened December 6, Judge W. H. S. Burgwyn presiding. Burgwyn was from nearby New Bern, member of a "good" Eastern Carolina family, gray-haired and gray-browed. He was in black robes behind a raised mahogany bench. Two jury boxes flanked him, with the prosecutor and defense arrayed before him at polished oak tables with a wooden railing separating them from a packed audience. The prosecuter was George Fountain from nearby Rocky Mount, a slender young lawyer in a crisp white shirt, blue suit, and striped tie. It was a big courtroom with high ceilings from which wood-bladed fans slowly stirred the hot, still, stifling air.

The charges against Reid had been distilled to simply first-degree burglary with intent to commit rape. There was no need to add on the issue of "a crime against nature" (which could have been sodomy or "going down on" a woman), because first-degree burglary—entering by force an occupied home at night—was by itself a capital offense. This meant that if convicted Reid would get the gas chamber. First-degree burglary was derived from the old English common law that a man's home was his castle, but its Southern permutation had a unmistakable racial twist—meant to be the sternest possible warning to a black person with the audacity to contemplate entering uninvited a white person's house, especially with intent to violate a white woman.

It seemed pretty clear to me that if Reid had climbed through a black woman's window and did what he did, he certainly would not be on trial for his life. Probably he would not be on trial at all. But though it had been fifteen years since anyone from Wilson County had been sent off to Raleigh to be executed, it looked for sure like Reid, given his offense against a prominent white woman, didn't have much of a chance.

Just as all the participants were seated and the trial was about to begin, there was a strange occurrence. All heads in the courtroom turned as two colored men wearing suits and ties—an unusual sight just by itself in Wilson—entered and approached the bar, carrying briefcases. They did not sit but stood behind the rail as everyone in the courtroom gaped in astonishment. They identified themselves to the judge as attorneys, C. J. Gates from Durham and Herman L. Taylor from Raleigh. They said they had been engaged by the NAACP to defend Reid. (The NAACP was then beginning to challenge the legality of all-white juries in the South.) They immediately moved for a continuance, on the grounds they had not had time enough to prepare a defense. Judge Burgwn tersely responded that Reid already had counsel "competent to prepare any defense which the defendant might have," and accordingly denied the motion. But the NAACP lawyers stayed and my front-page single-column story that afternoon would be headlined "Colored Lawyers To Defend Reid."

Reid's case was my first capital punishment trial, the most important story I had covered. I felt like I was in way over my head. I didn't understand the nuances of the criminal legal system at all and struggled through the early proceedings, with the help of Jim Fulghum, to keep up and get it right.

This being a capital case, a special bloc of sixty-five jurors had been selected from which twelve would be chosen, and Gates and Taylor moved immediately that day for a mistrial on the grounds, theretofore unheard of in Wilson, that in this case and "systematically and continuously over a long period of years, Negroes have been excluded from juries solely on account of their race." Burgwyn abruptly refused this motion as well, and jury selection was promptly completed.

The investigating detectives told their stories, without challenge from the defense, and two State Bureau of Investigation fingerprint experts verified that fingerprints on the window were Reid's. Judge Burgwyn nodded off with his head on one hand and awoke with a jerk several times. He spent his evenings at the Elks Club when he was in Wilson, and it was no secret that he liked his bourbon and branch water.

On the second day of the trial the judge cleared the courtroom, the distinguished gentleman from the *Daily Times* included, so Mrs. Barnes could tell her story. A lady of her refinement was not to be forced to testify in public on such an issue. She was on the stand for less than thirty minutes and was spared, I heard later, from having to repeat Reid's allegedly salacious demand. She did not look at Reid, and he looked at the floor. After that, the state quickly rested its case. Reid's lawyer Tatum, slumped bored in his chair, did not put up any witnesses, nor did he call Reid to the stand. The NAACP lawyers did not attempt to question her.

The next morning, Friday, the prosecution briefly summed up the evidence—the cut screen, the razor blades, the fingerprints, Mrs. Barnes's testimony—for the jury. Tatum did not get up to address the jury at all. Gates spoke for himself and Taylor and said there was no denying that Reid entered Mrs. Barnes's window, but said that since he entered with the intent to commit "a crime against nature," and not rape, and since he had been unsuccessful in any case, he could not be legally found guilty of first-degree burglary with intent to commit rape. The jury was not impressed and took just forty-four minutes to come back with a guilty verdict on those charges. The jury could have found Reid guilty of second-degree burglary, which would have spared his life, but I learned later this had not been considered. Reid looked forlornly at the colored lawyers as the jury foreman read the verdict, but they did not look back at him.

The courtroom was packed next morning and Reid stared bleakly down at the table as Burgwyn took a sip of water and read the sentence in a somber voice:

Now therefore in compliance with the law, the judgment of the court is that the defendant, Allen Reid, be taken hence by Sheriff J. W. Thompson, and by him delivered into the custody of the Warden of the Penitentiary of North Carolina in the City of Raleigh, to be by said warden detained until the 28th of January, 1949, and shall deliver Allen Reid to a place prepared for execution, and there cause the said Allen Reid to inhale lethal gas of sufficient quantity to cause death, and the administration of such lethal gas must be continued until said Allen Reid is dead.

There was a momentary hush. No one looked at Reid. It was as if he was already dead. Taylor and Gates immediately announced notice of appeal, and began putting papers into their briefcases. Judge Burgwyn said, "Duly noted," banged his gavel, and said, "This court is adjourned."

I sat numbly. Burgwyn's flatly delivered words stuck like a weight in my mind. I tried to take notes and watched Reid's back as he docilely followed a deputy sheriff out of the emptying courtroom. I turned and looked at his parents. Their shoulders sagged and their heads hung down. The NAACP lawyers stopped for a moment to shake his parents' hands and then they walked out. The judge came down off the bench and went quickly back to his chambers. Prosecutor Fountain stood quietly gathering his papers. As I walked up to the court clerk's desk to write down the exact wording of the sentence, I saw in my mind's eye Reid strapped down in the gas chamber, struggling to hold his breath as the mechanical arm dropped the fatal cyanide pellet into the bucket.

I went out and down the back stairs of the courthouse, across the alley, and in the back way through the *Daily Times* pressroom, where Claude, the adult "colored boy" who melted the used lead back into pigs, stood silently working. I kept my head down as I passed, too embarrassed to look him in the eye.

My front-page one-column story (no byline) was headlined, "Reid Is Given Death Sentence For Burglary."

Down in the body of the story I wrote: "Reid remained calm all through the trial, and was unemotionally cool when the death sentence was passed."

After work I trudged home, ate supper quickly, walked out to Maplewood Cemetery, and sat under a cedar tree with a knot in my stomach and my head in turmoil. Then I walked up to the Esquire Grill. The guys were out in front as usual, hanging on the parking meters.

"I heard the nigger got the gas chamber," said George Sakas. "You know what they say: The only good nigger is a dead nigger."

"That's dead Indian, George, and you're a mean prick," I said.

"Hell's the matter with you?" he said. "You turning into some kind of nigger lover?"

I felt a surge of rage but I turned and walked quickly away. He was a stupid bigot, and a waste of my time. I spent the weekend depressed, quiet, and alone, reading and brooding. I had not thought much about the death penalty before. Now I had seen a real human being, sitting a few feet from me, who had done a bad thing for sure with who knew what in his heart. He had caused a woman to feel mortally threatened in the sanctity of her home. But did he deserve the dreaded days that would tick agonizingly by, until he would be dragged along by guards, wanting to cry out for help that would not, could not come, and then the awful gasping end in the gas chamber?

On Monday, Reid went off to the state prison in Raleigh to await execution. Appeals by the NAACP lawyers went forward. The State Supreme Court turned them down, one by one. The

colored lawyers had failed to prove, the court said, that Wilson
County had systematically and disproportionally kept blacks off
juries over a long period, citing that one colored person was on
the grand jury that indicted Reid and that another four "of that
race" were on the special bloc of 135 chosen for the trial. (This
may have been technically true, but they were not present in the
courtroom when the jury was picked). The court said:

> while the bill of indictment charges the defendant with bur-
> glarious entry with the felonious intent to ravish and carnally
> know Mrs. James Barnes, forcibly and against her will, the
> evidence [the defense claims] tends to show only an intent to
> commit a crime against nature. The conduct of the defendant
> in breaking and entering the bedroom of the prosecutrix in
> the nighttime, and under the circumstances disclosed by the
> evidence, indicates the extent to which he was willing to go to
> accomplish his purpose. He may have preferred and intended
> to commit a crime against nature, or his statement in that
> respect may have been indicative of his actual intent. We
> think the evidence was sufficient to carry the case to the jury
> under the allegations contained in the bill on indictment, and
> it was for the jury to determine, under all the circumstances,
> whether or not the defendant had the ulterior criminal intent
> to commit the felony charged in the bill of indictment.

Accordingly, the Supreme Court found no error, and a final
judgment so saying was signed by the chief justice, Sam J. Ervin
Jr., later to become a U.S. senator and a major figure in the
Watergate case.

As the date of Reid's execution neared, the Wilson County
Superior Court was again in session with Judge W. H. S. Burgwyn
presiding. On the eve of Reid's execution date, the judge had a

call from Mrs. Barnes, I heard from Ray Hartis. Her conscience was bothering her, she said. She had been terribly frightened by Reid, and certainly he was guilty of first-degree burglary, she said. But she thought killing him was too extreme a penalty, even though she believed in capital punishment. So she pleaded with Judge Burgwyn to see what he could do. The judge immediately telephoned Governor Kerr Scott and told him of his conversation with Mrs. Barnes, said he agreed with her, and asked him to commute the sentence.

On the night before his scheduled execution, Reid confessed for the first time, to the prison warden, that he was guilty. The warden relayed this confession to the governor. The governor telephoned the judge back and said since Reid had confessed, he would not commute the sentence.

So Reid went to the gas chamber in Raleigh almost a year to the day after he was convicted. I had been invited by Jim Fulghum to attend as the reporter who'd covered his trial. But I thought this would be unbearable, and didn't go. No one from his family was there. Two other black men were executed the same day. The story was on the front page of the *Daily Times*, though without the details of Mrs. Barnes's attempted intervention, along with stories about Hitler's car being on display in front of the courthouse, sponsored by the Lions Club, and movie star Ava Gardner coming to Wilson from her birthplace in nearby Smithfield to shop at Hudson-Belk. I read the *Daily Times* story on Reid with a leaden heart: "It required 15 minutes for the gas to kill Reid. The warden said that he and the other two men had made peace with the Lord and were ready to die."

Reid's eleventh-hour confession, his apparent attempt to get right with God, may have cost him his life.

I had read the story of his death instead of writing it because I was not covering crime and the courts or the tobacco market anymore. I had just become sports editor, a promotion that brought with it another five-dollar-a-week raise, to forty-five dollars, and a daily column, "Fleming's Trimmings," which was adorned by a head shot of me in a striped sports jacket and a polka-dot bow tie. I began covering the doings of the Charles L. Coon High School Cyclones, the Wilson Tobs (short for Tobacconists) baseball team, Wilson's entry in the Class D Coastal Plains League, and the local Atlantic Christian College. The Tobs played at night in a rickety unpainted wooden stadium on the edge of town. Absent much other group entertainment, baseball was a big deal, and the Tobs drew an average of 3,000 to their games—including Ray Hartis, whom I would spot occasionally and wave to as I sat in the tiny press box behind home plate keeping a box score and taking notes. I telephoned the box scores in after every game to the Associated Press in Raleigh, for one dollar a game.

Where this sportswriting job was taking me I did not know, nor did I think about it much. One day in front of the police station, I stopped to chat with Chief Privette and he said he thought I would be a good cop and he would give me a job if I wanted one. But I wanted no part of that kind of life. I by now loved reporters, and reporting, and writing, although the hope to have a much larger career as a reporter, or a writer, never occurred to me. I did the best I could day after day on the job and hoped that I was learning to write a good clear sentence.

Meantime, my dalliance with Bobbie the divorcee had cooled and I quit going out with her as summer rolled around again. From one of the guys who I hung out with on the street I heard that Ray Hartis was still going out with Bobbie's sister-in-law. The word was that Bobbie's two brothers who lived in the nearby village of Elm City had warned him to keep away from Sue Anne or else. This was not to be taken lightly.

Soon I heard a detailed and gruesome story about Ray. One

hot night he staggered half-drunk and cursing into the police station, his face twisted with pain and his clothes torn and dirty. His customary Stetson hat was not on his sweaty head. Fingerprint man A. J. Hayes was at the station, working on a case, and Ray lurched past the desk sergeant into Hayes's office.

"What's the matter, Ray?" he asked.

"Two niggers surprised me and got aholt of me," he said. "I'm in bad shape. The black son-of-a-bitches tried to chop my balls out." He pulled down his bloody pants and boxer shorts to reveal a nasty patchwork of bruises, cuts, and puncture wounds on his thighs, penis, and testicles. His scrotum was grotesquely swollen and purple. He was breathing heavily and grimacing.

"Goddamned big niggers got me down," he said.

"Who were they?" Hayes ask.

"Damned if I know," he said.

Hayes got him into his car and rushed him around to Carolina General Hospital. He was treated in the emergency room and then stashed in a room under an assumed name. Hayes did not believe his account of what happened.

"Ray knows every nigger in Wilson and he would have had the whole police department out looking for them if niggers had really done it," he said.

Nobody took Ray's account of what happened seriously. There had to be some other explanation, and soon Ray offered one. What really happened, he said, was that his girlfriend, not the married redhead, but another one, attacked him. No one had heard about this girlfriend, and his claim didn't make much sense anyway. How could any woman this side of an amazon get the 225-pound Ray down on his back and render him defenseless, like a flipped-over turtle? Ray offered no more details.

But soon there began to be murmurs and open talk around town of another, darker story. This was that Bobbie's two brothers from Elm City had finally had enough of Ray's messing with their brother's wife, even after their warning, and gave him his comeuppance. They confronted him one night as he was leaving the Silver Slipper after a bout of solitary drinking. They obviously had been stalking him. They forced him at gunpoint into a nearby cornfield, threatened to kill him, ordered him to the dirt, and while one held the gun on him the other one methodically worked him over with an ice pick—where it counted. They left him in the field, and he made his way back to his car and drove into town and to the police station.

The brothers soon let it be known about town exactly what had happened. They had warned him, by God, and he hadn't listened. I did not call up or go see Bobbie Doris to verify what happened.

It would have been hard to find many people in Wilson who said they were sorry for what had happened to Ray. There wasn't anyone who didn't know him or his brutish reputation. He had done the dirty work of keeping the niggers in line. They had wanted him to do it, and they hadn't wanted to know any of the unpleasant details. And that he had done it well hadn't won him any friends.

He was universally feared and disliked across the tracks, of course, though no one would have openly dared to say so. But he was feared out on Nash Street and Raleigh Road, too. He knew the dark secrets of the ruling families, and they knew that he knew—about their mistresses, their drunken binges, their secret love nests, and their furtive visits to the whorehouses. Thus he had had power over them and thus down deep they must have hated him, I thought. But now he was, literally and figuratively, impotent.

So with the exception of a few cops who had a grudging respect for him, most everybody thought Ray got what he had coming to him—a kind of justifiable Old Testament revenge, not only fitting because of his own violent behavior, but also appropriate because he violated the prevailing moral code about marriage. You might covet another man's wife, but you had to take the consequences if you got caught acting on it. In fact, if a husband caught another man "on the nest" it was more or less OK to kill him, and it was common-law practice not to prosecute such killings. Consequently, there was no move to prosecute Ray's supposed attackers, nor did Ray move against them.

For myself, I began to see that violence begets violence, and in Wilson it lay just below the surface ready to explode, like the weather.

I had no reason to seek Ray out, and I didn't. But I did feel a little sorry for him. Despite his cynicism, racism, and brutality, something about his isolation had touched me. I had learned a lot riding around with him. Much of it was ugly, but I was a better reporter because of him—more skeptical, more questioning, and more armed to see beneath the surface of things.

Ray lingered for awhile in Wilson, his reputation shot, but finally took a job policing in a smaller town near the coast. His wife did not go with him when he left. I lost contact with him entirely, but he was lodged ineluctably in my consciousness. I did not know it then, but he was the pitiless prototype of countless bigoted cops and sheriffs I would encounter across the segregated South in the years ahead.

Meantime, the redhead with the prize-winning knockers who was at the heart of Ray's downfall was divorced by her husband when he came home from Germany, and she, too, left town, for parts unknown.

Not long after that I read in *Editor & Publisher* that the *Morning Herald* in Durham, North Carolina, seventy miles west, home of Duke University, the American Tobacco Co., and many cotton mills, was looking for a sportswriter. It was a morning paper, six times as big as the *Daily Times*. I went for an interview and was hired on the spot, for sixty-five dollars a week. I went back and sold my old car for $200 and packed my clothes into a suitcase and my favorite books in a paper box.

I went by the Carolina General Hospital and said goodbye to my sister. I went back to the house on Pine Street, hugged my mother, said goodbye, and left her crying on the front porch. She had said many times that she hoped we would stay together when I became a man and get the little white house with the picket fence around it and chickens and a vegetable garden. But I wanted to get away from her. And I yearned for something else away from there, something better, something nobler and grander, though I did not know what it was or where I could find it.

I walked down to the depot, got on a Trailways bus, and took a seat near the back. There were just a few people on the bus. There was a colored man in an old hat and blue coat sitting in the back row eating what looked like a pork chop sandwich. It was a sullen winter day as we went out Highway 64 towards Raleigh, past the tobacco barns, country churches, crossroads filling stations and stores, and dried cornfields and sagebrush. I changed to another bus in downtown Raleigh. It went slowly out Hillsborough Street beyond the marble capitol and turned right at the Esso station where we used to gas up the orphanage farm truck. It went on out Glenwood Avenue by the Pine State Creamery and the Seaboard side yard where we used to load coal, and on out beyond Jordan's Drug Store and finally by Fred Fletcher's house and the entrance to the orphanage. Up the hill beside the now-paved road going up to the Vann Building were a dozen orphanage boys in black wool jackets and knickers raking leaves into rows in the grove in the gray afternoon.

Chapter 7

A Turn for the Worse

F OR THE FIRST TIME in my life I was alone. I had moved into a small dingy ten-dollar-a-week room with an iron cot and a gray metal cabinet at the musty old Durham YMCA. Down the hall was a communal bath. One of the other young residents spotted me as a newcomer and warned me to look out: two queers lived there.

The *Herald* was housed in a gray two-story concrete building on Market Street in downtown Durham. The newsroom was one big open space on the second floor over the business offices. The sports department was two desks in the corner next to the composing room. The hours in my new job were unlike anything I had experienced: 2 until 11 P.M., and that made my life even more lonely. I felt mildly depressed for the first time since the first months in the orphanage.

The *Herald*, circulation 60,000, was staffed by a half-dozen talented young reporters, most of them yearning to write novels some day. They were serious reporters, and all graduates of the University of North Carolina, Duke, and Wake Forest. I was just a sportswriter and had not finished college. But they tolerated me, and after we put the paper to bed, we usually went across the street to the Washington Duke Hotel, chipped in for a twenty-dollar room, and stayed until near dawn drinking, playing poker, and talking about literature. I felt self-conscious that they were talking about great books, and perhaps writing them, and that they were reporting on politics and capital punishment, while here I was writing about the mundane world of sports—although some of my heroes, Damon Runyon, Ring Lardner, and Red Smith, had been sportswriters. But I was well-read enough to hold my own in these conversations, and already enough of a drinker and cynic to happily engage in the dismissing of people not fortunate enough to be in the newspaper business.

With the fall, football came, a miserable period for me. The sports editor, my boss, was Jack Horner, a stocky man with thinning brown hair and a mirthless laugh. He wrote a column called "Horner's Corner," and that is about all he did. His deputies—I was the new one—fled serially after a few months. To my chagrin, I had not checked him out before I took the job. I was too lacking in self-confidence to do that. And I had had no experience making intelligent moves on my own behalf, nor any mentor to advise me, nor any clue as to how to ask the right questions about a job.

Horner left all of the prodigious work of actually producing the sports section to me: the laying out of the pages, the selection and cropping of the photos, the caption writing, the editing and sizing of the stories, the writing of the headlines, the checking of the page proofs, and, of course, writing the stories that I was responsible for. During the week this was a manageable task, but the *Herald* had an enormous Sunday sports section, eight pages usually with only a few ads on them. So on many fall Saturdays I would have to go to one of the Big Four (Duke, Carolina, North Carolina State, Wake Forest) stadiums, take notes on the game, come back, and write a main story and a sidebar—and then do all of the laying out, editing, and head-writing for all of the stories— about forty columns on eight pages, including thirty-five long stories, twenty short ones, a half-dozen photos with cutlines, and columns of statistics and scores. The pressure to get it all done, all by myself, and meet the 11 P.M. deadline was enormous, beyond my capacity really, and occasionally I made a mistake, got a score wrong, or got the wrong head on a story. This would send Horner into a tirade. Why couldn't I pay attention? What kind of stupid bastard was I anyway? These rebukes usually took place in front of my colleagues, leaving me humiliated—igniting my buried old anxieties about not being good enough and man enough, the fear and anger that being bullied by my stepfather, by the boys who had abused me, and by Fatty Clark in the orphanage had produced. I was at a loss as to how to respond to him. I knew I wasn't supposed to make mistakes. They were unforgivable in the newspaper business.

I did not have the wit to ask for a transfer to the city side where I could go back to being a general assignment reporter or the confidence to simply quit. So I soldiered on. I had been at this job only a few months when I got a call from Bill Jackson, a Charles Laughton lookalike whom I'd gotten to know when he was a radio announcer in Wilson and I was writing sports for the *Daily Times*. He was now at a Greensboro station fifty miles west of Durham and he had a woman he wanted me to meet. Her name was Sandra Sisk and she worked at his station. He arranged a blind date. It went fine. I drove to Greensboro and took her out to the Plantation Supper Club, out on Highway 70, where you

As a still relatively innocent sports writer on the Durham Morning Herald *when I was twenty-five, in 1952, with no one to turn to for guidance.*

brought whiskey in a brown paper bag, sat in leather booths, paid a five-dollar cover charge, and bought Coke or 7-Up to mix. The club had a small band, playing forties music, and Sandy was a good if restrained dancer. I didn't like dancing much, but recognized it as necessary for success with women. I liked her. She seemed to like me, if in a careful way. She had that thing I thought I lacked: class. She was a graduate of the University of North Carolina, a pretty, dark-haired woman slightly younger than I was. She had high cheekbones, brown eyes, a good figure, and she moved with a delicate grace. She was well-spoken, "well-bred," and intelligent and seemed a person of principle and good values. As I got to know her on further dates, it was clear she was not passionate about books and words and writers and reporting and the world of politics and conflict, but that did not seem critical to me. That was my world. She seemed more interested in family and friends and home, and I was at a time when that had begun to be appealing.

I had saved enough money to buy a tan 1949 Chevy coupe for $750, and I began commuting to Greensboro every other weekend to see her. The other weekend I was commuting to Winston-Salem, forty miles west of Greensboro, to see a nurse I had regularly dated when we were in Wilson. I had made no friends outside of work in Durham, and weekends at the YMCA were lonely and depressing.

I had dated Sandy for four months, and slowly our relationship took on a more serious tone. She was clearly ready to get married and have children. I said that was what I yearned for, a home and children. Whether I was in love with her I had no idea, although I did not say so to her. I had no concept of what being in love felt like, except abstractly, based on what I had read in books and seen in movies. I was not swept away, but maybe that kind of overpowering love was something just a few people, rarely, felt.

What I did know deep down was that I yearned for the security and comfort of a family, and according to all custom it was high time, perhaps past time, that I should start one. Nearly all of my orphanage contemporaries were married—most to orphanage sweethearts—and had children or were on the way to having them. It was the 1950s, a time of renewed hope for a better life for people all across the country. New cars and new refrigerators and freezers and TV sets were rolling off the assembly lines. New and better jobs were just over the horizon. Because of lingering memories of World War II and forced separations and fear—and before that the Depression—there was much focus on home and family and security. I was now twenty-five, and I concluded that what I had with Sandy was as good as it was going to get—and perhaps she did too, though neither of us said so. Maybe this was in fact love. I didn't know. I told her I loved her and said we should get married, and she agreed.

I went up to Asheville, far west of Durham in the mountains, to talk to Sandy's father, Charles Sisk—to ask his permission, which was still the recognized custom. He and his wife, Frances, lived in an old two-story wooden house a mile from the drug store he owned. He was a handsome man with a great shock of gray hair and a finely chiseled face. He led me into the kitchen and pulled down a fifth of Jack Daniels from a cabinet and poured us both a drink. He sat solemn and silent, pushing his glass back and forth on the table, as I awkwardly told him we wanted to get married. He was noncommittal. He said Sandy should talk to her mother, who was a tiny woman with pock-marked skin, deep-set gray eyes, and a high-strung manner. She, it turned out, was totally opposed to our marriage. She told Sandy I reminded her too much of her husband—too strong-willed and maybe a bad drinker, too. Besides, I had a weak chin.

Nonetheless, we were married in the ivy-covered First

Methodist Church of Asheville on June 5, 1952. It was an unusually hot ninety-five-degree day. I'd had four shots of Old Hickory
with my best man, my old childhood orphanage friend Russell
"Little Jeebie" Clay, and the sweat rolled down my legs as the
ceremony ensued. Sandy wore a white ballerina-length dress with
a veil and white jacket. We drove further west to Fontana Lake
for the honeymoon. Fontana was a modest resort of cabins left
over from construction of a TVA dam that had created a huge
lake. There we met and became instant friends with a couple
from Atlanta, a rotund school photographer named Malcolm
Newell and his blonde wife, Irene, and we drove a twisting road
down into Tennessee to buy a case of beer. Even beer was illegal
in that Baptist-dominated corner of North Carolina. We stayed a
week and vowed to our new friends, our first married friends,
that we would see them in Atlanta in five years. I had signed on to
do a Sunday feature article for the *Herald* about honeymooning
in Fontana. Adorned by three photos, it appeared the next week,
and earned me an extra fifty dollars in my little tan pay envelope.

My new wife and I moved into an eighty-five-dollar-a-month
one-bedroom apartment near Duke University and I resumed my
job under the harsh rule of Jack Horner. I began to have stomach
trouble and the doctor I went to said I had an incipient ulcer and
that I'd better do something about dealing with the tension I was
working under—other than getting drunk in order to sleep.
Things didn't get any better, and in August, when my wife and I
were vacationing with her parents in Asheville, I went by the local
morning paper, the *Asheville Citizen*, to see if they had an opening. They did, and I signed on for their sports department for
eighty dollars a week. We moved to Asheville in September.

It became apparent right away that this was a bad move—
except for getting me out from under the heel of Jack Horner.
Whereas in Durham I had been sitting in big press boxes among

Square-dancing with my first wife, Sandy, on our honeymoon at Fontana Lake, North Carolina, in June 1952.

famous sportswriters eating country ham biscuits and watching
some of the nation's top college teams in action, now I was relegated to running up and down the sidelines with a clipboard in
hand on Friday nights reporting on the high school games of tiny
little schools like Swannanoa and Leicester (pronounced *Lee-
CESTER*). Plus that, the sports editor, a puffy-faced man of sixty
or so named Red Miller, was a drunk who frequently didn't show
up for work at all. One of the other two sports writers was a
drunk, too, as well as were several others on the city-side staff.
Asheville appeared to be the last stop on the way down for these
men. Plus that, I didn't like the town, though it was surrounded
by lush rolling mountains and cold sparkling streams. It had none
of the earthy vitality of Wilson or even Durham.

Asheville was the westernmost town of any size (65,000 population) in North Carolina. It had been made infamous by the exco-
riating novels of native son Thomas Wolfe. O. Henry (William
Sydney Porter) was buried there. Zelda Fitzgerald had died in a
sanitarium fire there. And one of the Vanderbilt boys had built a
$50 million mansion there in the 1920s, when Asheville was hav-
ing its glory days with rich people following this Vanderbilt down
from the North to build big homes and play on his golf course.
When I moved there it was mostly a tourist town, but extremely
hard to get to, a nine-and-a-half-hour automobile trip over tortu-
ously twisted roads from Raleigh, for example, so the tourist
industry did not thrive. Asheville attracted a fair number of
"snowbirds," retired Northern people who lived in Florida in winter and Asheville and surrounding communities in summer, who
played golf and supported a little theater group and occasional visiting concert groups who performed in a downtown auditorium
built by the WPA during the Depression.

But Asheville seemed to me a dark, joyless, insular place,
much like Wolfe had described it in *Look Homeward, Angel*, its

residents evidencing little interest in the outside world and not much excitement about the one they were in. There was a listless, dead feeling about the town, the only attitude a sullen and almost sulky one, as if its people had never gotten over the insults Wolfe had visited upon them. There was, of course, an actual stone angel—Wolfe's angel—perched atop an obelisk in nearby Hendersonville, carved by Wolfe's stonecutter father. But Wolfe remained a hated figure in Asheville, though his scorching portraits of its citizens had been written in the 1930s. His surviving sister, Mabel, still lived in the old Wolfe home just off Pack Square in downtown Asheville, and she hung around the newspaper constantly. She was exactly as Wolfe had described her in his fiction, a coarse, self-involved, grasping, publicity-seeking woman who laid in wait for people who came to worship at the Wolfe altar or who came to the newspaper to look up articles and to inquire about people to interview. She was eager to give interviews—to get her name in the paper and to set the record straight about the unfair things Wolfe had written about his family.

Wolfe had mercilessly described the huge bond issues floated by crooked local pols—and the graft skimmed off—to build water and sewer lines way out into the uninhabited county during the boom years of the 1920s. When I arrived, those lines were still in place on miles and miles of empty land, complete with roadside fire hydrants. Little development had taken place—mostly because of Asheville's physical isolation.

A rayon manufacturing plant on the western outskirts and a stinking pulp mill fifteen miles west—both of which fouled the beautiful French Broad River that ran through Asheville—were the city's only industries. Beyond that lay a vast mountainous sparsely inhabited expanse of twenty-four counties populated by fiercely anti-government Baptists who lived in unpainted wood houses clinging to the sides of hills, a Cherokee Indian reserva-

tion, and a few tourist havens, such as Flat Rock, where the poet
Carl Sandburg lived in a graceful old house built as a summer
retreat by the treasurer of the Confederacy. Not a legal drink was
to be had anywhere between Asheville and the Tennessee and
South Carolina borders. Bootleggers—that is, illegal sellers of
"bonded" whiskey and beer, and manufacturers of moonshine—
flourished, one result being that the sheriff of Buncombe County,
Asheville's seat, was a wealthy man who had a 2,000-acre ranch
near evangelist Billy Graham's home at Montreat. The sheriffs of
surrounding counties were also, owing to payoffs from the flour-
ishing bootlegging business, the most powerful and well-off political figures in the region.

The *Citizen* and its afternoon sister, the *Times*, were don't-
make-waves papers that followed the Chamber of Commerce
line, dutifully publishing an annual "Industrial Edition" con-
cocted entirely for the purpose of extracting a few more dollars
from advertisers. Reporters were called on to write puff pieces
about the industries that bought ads, but were discouraged from
anything approaching investigative journalism—such as exploring what wheels might have been greased to allow the paper mill
to spoil the air and to poison the French Broad River—or the
venality of its local politicians. There were a few bright young
reporters on the paper, and a sad and elegant old gentleman
named Sloan Coleman, a nephew of O. Henry, who befriended
me and even said I should get away from there as quickly as I
could. I remained idealistic about newspapers and being a
reporter and thus was disillusioned and disappointed in the same
way I had been with the Wilson *Daily Times*. One of my most
prized and most read possessions was a book called *A Treasury of
Great Reporting*. It was a compendium of brilliant reporting
from a 1699 article on a London almshouse for madmen to an
1859 London *Times* articles on the charge of the Light Brigade, a

New York Herald article on a Savannah slave auction to a 1906 Jack London piece on the San Francisco earthquake, an 1925 H. L. Mencken article on a holy roller meeting in the hills above the courthouse where John Scopes was on trial for teaching evolution to a 1946 piece by Rebecca West on the Nuremburg trials, and so on through great reporting history. I fantasized about being a reporter like that, but I was far from that kind of reporting and the kind of newspapers that encouraged it. But even average newspapers, such as the one I was working on, were supposed to be above the ordinary corruption that sullied other enterprises, I believed. Newspapers had a public trust, a duty above simply coining money. On the other hand, who was I to judge? What had I done to warrant being superior?

Sandy and I had agreed before we got married that we wanted four children. Not having had a father, or a mother for that matter, something deep in me yearned for a family. Part of me was frozen over, but I knew I could love my children unreservedly. I would see in them myself as a child, and I would protect them against cruelty, loneliness, and hurt. Sandy became pregnant right after we married, and on May 24, 1955, she had our first son at Asheville Memorial Hospital while I sat nervously in the waiting room. We named him Charles, after her father. I was enchanted to have a son, but he was not a happy baby. He cried constantly, obviously in some kind of pain that we could not figure out. The worst part for us was the frustration of his being in pain and our not being able to do anything about it. We read Dr. Spock to try to figure out what was wrong. Finally a doctor decided Charles was allergic to whole milk, and when we switched him to buttermilk, he got rosy and happy, and I could pay attention to my job again and to the town we were in.

Two years later, on May 6, 1957, we had another son. We named him David after my father. Like his brother, he was blonde

Though I kept up a smiling facade, I was unhappy in my reporting job on the Asheville Citizen *in 1954.*

and rosy-skinned. If I did not know much about being a father, I knew a lot about being a boy and I exulted in them as they grew out of babyhood. I would teach them what I knew, about defending themselves, about the boyhood games I had learned, about climbing trees, wading in creeks, wallowing in the dirt, looking at cloud shapes, foraging for berries and apples, playing ball, reading *Tom Sawyer* and *Call of the Wild*, knowing the difference between a robin and a mockingbird, sucking the sweet juice out of honeysuckle blooms, and loving good food and music. I resolved to let them roam free, and invent their own games, as I had as a boy, but to be home at a certain time, where lunch and dinner would be on the table at a prescribed hour. I remembered my mother's bell, calling me home to our shack on Mauls Swamp, and Muh Brown's bell, summoning her charges back to the Brown Building at the orphanage. And God help anybody who ever laid a hand on them or bullied them in any way.

Meantime, my father-in-law had sponsored me to become a member of the Lodge 1401, Benevolent and Protective Order of Elks, otherwise known as the Asheville Elks Club. It was a square two-story stone and concrete building three blocks from the *Citizen*, with a set of antlers over its front door. It was all male and, of course, all white. Each member had a small assigned locker in which he could keep his private stock of liquor, purchased at the local ABC store. No drinks were sold in public places anywhere in that part of the world. The club served mainly as a refuge for imbibing and playing poker, but the Elks had their rituals. At eleven each night, the lights dimmed, a gong sounded, members raised their arms in the form of elk antlers, and recited, "To our absent brothers." In the poker games that ran all day every day from opening at 11 A.M. to closing at 1 A.M., players collectively said, "To our absent dollars."

These regular poker games were full of Runyonesque characters. The most colorful one was a mean old man who had once run whiskey and stolen furs for Al Capone. He was about eighty-five with angry, red, chicken-like eyes, stained gray hair, and fierce eyebrows like those of the labor leader John L. Lewis. No one seemed to know his real name. Everybody in this poker game addressed him simply as Mr. Mac.

The game was two-dollar limit, six-card stud, tense affairs for me to be in as I was then earning eighty dollars a week, and a fifty-dollar loss in a game, easily possible, would have been serious. The dozen regular players were mostly retired men of one sort or another, including one of the original U.S. mail pilots, who had a steel plate in his head from flying his plane into Stone Mountain in Georgia; a veteran who'd gotten a leg shot off in World War II; the Asheville city clerk and his brother, a retired butcher; a jewelry store owner; and the local Orkin man. They were mostly good, careful players. I was a novice.

But Mr. Mac was the toughest bird in the game. He had spent World War II going from one defense construction site to another—such as Aiken, South Carolina, where they were building an A-bomb plant—posing in hard hat and overalls as a worker and fleecing the unsuspecting in nightly poker games at motels. He was a grim, taciturn old guy, dressed every day in the same frayed twill suit, blotchy red tie with a diamond stickpin in it, and florid gold cufflinks.

My work hours were from 1 to 11 P.M., and I usually dropped by the club and played until it closed at 1 A.M. I did pretty well, considering my relative inexperience—well enough to buy a new Hathaway shirt and a Hickey-Freeman suit—but one night I was complaining about a bad run of cards when Mr. Mac gave me a sour glare and said, "Listen, son, let me tell you something about poker. Sometimes you sit down to play and you can't win a hand. Eleven o'clock, 1 A.M., and you haven't won a single hand;

3 A.M., 5 A.M., all night long, and not one goddamned winner. But, then, along about daybreak, things take a turn for the worse."

That's how I felt like my reporting life was going at this time. I had gotten myself in a bad professional situation, was miserable, and thus was drinking way too much and spending too many hours at the poker table. And sure enough, things then took a turn for the worse.

One day the publisher, a beetle-browed former correspondent for the Associated Press named Bob Bunnelle, announced by memo that the paper had been sold and the new owners had ordered a 25 percent reduction in staff, meaning the junior member of every department had to go. That meant me, among others.

I was shocked and alarmed. Here in my face was potential great humiliation, perhaps with people laughing at me—my profoundest fear. And there would be real consequences, too. My wife and I had, for $8,000, bought and, with our two small sons, moved into a small white bungalow at 101 Mitchell Avenue in west Asheville, near her parents' home. She was a full-time mom, so our sole income was my salary and whatever modest sums I was earning writing freelance pieces. We were frugal, though I had gotten a bank loan and bought for $1,800 my first new car, a blue and white 1957 Ford Fairlane with a stick shift. For recreation we did the free things. We took the boys on summer weekend picnics high up on the beautiful Blue Ridge Parkway in the Great Smoky Mountains National Park, went sledding in winter on nearby hills (Asheville was at 3,000-feet elevation and there was a lot of winter snow), went swimming in a motel pool run by some friends of my wife's parents, and worked in the vegetable garden I started on a vacant lot next to our house. In the summer when I got a vacation we made the long trek by car to visit my mother in Wilson to let her spend time with her grandchildren. We stayed a night at the Wilsonian Motel and then took her with us for a week at Wrightsville Beach on the Carolina coast. By now my Aunt Belle had died and my mother had moved into a fifty-dollar-a-month second-floor apartment next to the fire station. I was sending her money every month, as was my sister, who had taken a job as a nurse in nearby Smithfield. It was a strain to send her money. I did so out of guilt and, I supposed, honor—a sense that a good son was obligated to take care of his mother. The financial pressure was constant.

Upon receiving Bunnelle's dire bulletin about my impending dismissal, I rushed into his office protesting, "This is a helluva way to run a railroad," that I had hoped this was a paper run on merit and not seniority. He listened sympathetically and told me to go take a desk in the city room and be a general assignment reporter until I could find another job. I immediately set about to prove I could earn my way—and discovered again how much I truly liked being a reporter, the daily challenge of learning new things and reducing disparate and sometimes very technical information to clear, simple language.

Madison County adjoined Asheville's Buncombe County to the south. Its county seat, Marshall, a shadowed little town of 2,000 in a ravine beside the French Broad River, was thirty miles south of Asheville and involved a drive over a narrow mountain road so crooked that the trip was an hour and a half going and one hour coming, the "going" lane being on the outside of most of the mountain hairpin turns. Soon after I left the sports department, I was sent over to Marshall to cover a murder trial. The courthouse was an old wooden building with two big potbellied wood stoves in a small courtroom with unpainted wooden benches. The defendants were two lean, dark-haired bootleggers who had walked across the state border from Flag Pond, Tennessee, and built a still in the Madison County woods. An old retired couple who lived within smelling distance of the still turned them in to the feds. They were arrested and their still chopped down. One Sunday morning after that they appeared at the old couple's house, called the old man out into the yard, and proceeded to stomp him to death. When the old lady came out to protest, they held her down on a log and cut her throat.

Although they had admitted all this to the sheriff, the bootleggers had pleaded not guilty. Instead of being repentant they were indignant. In the mountain culture with its emphasis on independence and minding your own business, killing someone for revealing a whiskey still's existence was considered justifiable homicide—like catching someone "on the nest" with your wife. The evidence against the men was undeniable, and the verdict came back guilty. But they got only twenty years each. Since I was an outsider still ignorant of backwoods mountain customs, this seemed unjust to me, but the sheriff, a small, sallow-faced man named E. Y. Ponder, explained the unwritten rules to me and further said—and I so quoted him in my story—that they would have gotten off completely except that they were from Tennessee.

The Ponder family had for many years ruled Madison County. They were Republicans. After the November 1956 election following the summer murder trial, I was assigned to cover a federal vote fraud trial in which the Madison County Democratic Party charged that the local Republicans, headed by Sheriff Ponder, had stolen the election—that they had thrown thrown into the river ballot boxes from Democrat precincts and stuffed boxes with the names of dead people and of live ones who had long since moved to Chicago. Plus that, the Democrat chairman testified in the trial, held in the Asheville federal building, when he approached a polling place to observe—which was his legal right—Sheriff Ponder pulled a gun on him and drove him off.

Federal judges, I learned as I spent time as a reporter, have enormous power in their courtrooms, far beyond that of state court judges, and this judge was a staunch Republican. Therefore, the jury, strongly guided by the judge, came back with a verdict of not guilty. After court adjourned, I went up to Sheriff Ponder and asked him if he had actually pulled a gun on the Democrat. "I did," he laughed, "And when I pulled it on him, he pissed in his pants." That didn't make it into my story. The managing editor said it was off the record, though it wasn't.

Soon I was back in Madison County again. This time, it was to cover a debate in the local Baptist church over whether to use religious literature from the Southern Baptist Convention, the very conservative Baptist governing body but still too liberal for the church's deacons, who believed that the only book necessary for salvation was the Bible. The debate got so fiery that the deacons literally pulled their newly arrived minister from the pulpit and beat him up.

Mountaineers, I thus learned, took their religion as strongly as they did their sense of freedom from government control. Traveling evangelists ranging from snake handlers to holy rollers did brisk summertime business in the rural "hollers," and when Billy Graham held a rally before 700 people in the Asheville Municipal Auditorium, it warranted the presence of a reporter—and a front-page story. Graham was a fiery, charismatic speaker and I found myself furiously taking notes trying to keep up with his staccato pace—all the while thinking I had to record every sentence, because this was obviously great stuff. But when I rushed back to my typewriter it was as if I had taken notes in invisible ink. I couldn't find a lead or a single quote that made sense on paper. It was all sound and fury and no substance. My story said he had spoken to a record crowd but it contained few direct quotes.

A little later, on November 7, 1958, I went down to Montreat to interview Graham on the occasion of his fortieth birthday. He had startling laser-like blue eyes and bushy blonde eyebrows over high cheekbones and a strong chin—a blonde Rasputin, I thought. I made the front page with his response when I asked him about public school integration. North Carolina was then trying to figure out how to deal with the 1954 Supreme Court order to integrate schools with "all deliberate speed." So what was the great herald of Jesus thinking on this issue? Graham said he was against the court's ordering "forced mixing" of the races. The races had gotten along well to now, he said. It would be better to go slow and let the states work things out voluntarily. Otherwise, there would be bad feelings, a white backlash. The South moved at its own pace and would work things out when the time was right, which would be better than having the federal government try to dictate such a drastic change in custom. This was the first time Graham had taken a public position on integration, or on any racial issue. Perhaps no reporter had asked him before. But his answer was big enough news to make the *Citizen*'s front page with my byline and to get prominent play in other North Carolina papers when it went out over the AP wire. I got a complimentary handwritten note from Bob Bunnelle, raising my hope that maybe I was a pretty good reporter after all.

Unlike in Eastern Carolina with its huge black population, in the mountains, school integration wasn't much of an issue, for there were only a few black people there, maids and male servitors for the well-off retirees who lived in the Biltmore Estates and laborers at the great old stone Grove Park Inn nearby. There was a black cook named George at the Elks Club—he prepared a great beef stew every Wednesday, which was meeting night—but I saw black people rarely. Clay County, far to the west, had no black citizens whatever, but had a law that said any black person in the county had to be out by sundown.

After my reporting life improved, and my children grew into little boys, I cut down on my poker playing and drinking at the

Elks Club, but only after I'd had one bad incident. There was a man named Bob Scott in the game, a traveling salesman with arms so big he had to slit the sleeves of his short-sleeved shirts to get his biceps in. He was an abusive, hectoring presence. One night he was verbally bullying a small and timid Jewish man in the game—a night I'd had too much to drink—and I said, "Why don't you leave him alone?"

"What the hell are you going to do about it?," he said.

"Come out here with me," I said, gesturing toward the bar area. He followed me out, and I turned and punched him as hard as I could in the face. He didn't even flinch. When I swung again, he grabbed my arm and jerked. Off came my Bulova wristwatch and the sleeve of my new Hathaway shirt and down I went against the wall. The blood spurted from my head. It took fourteen stitches to sew up the gash. My wife was angry at my drunkenness and recklessness (although she was used to alcoholics, for her father was one, now more or less sober, and her mother was a pill addict). Later, I cockily told the men in the poker game I'd probably have to give up fighting because I could no longer stand the loss of blood.

In my second year as a general assignment reporter, I got an interview with a man I truly revered, the great working-class poet Carl Sandburg. He'd said, "I won't take my religion from any man who never works except with his mouth," and I admired that. He had bought and was living in a plain two-story home—built by Andrew Memminger, the secretary of the Confederacy—on thirty acres of pastureland in Flat Rock, thirty miles west of Asheville. I went over to interview him on the occasion of his eightieth birthday on January 6, 1958. His wife, Helga, the sister of the great photographer Edward Steichen, raised dairy goats, and she shoved a glass of goat milk into my hand as I nervously sat down in the book-filled living room to interview the great man. Dressed in a denim shirt and canvas pants, the famous shock of white hair falling over his face, he put his right foot on a brick, played the guitar, sang a few folk songs for me, and then uttered a great and obviously carefully thought-out quote when we got around to his birthday:

> I will die at an age divisible by eleven. It is inevitable. It is written in the book of fate. I had two great grandfathers and a grandfather who died in years divisible by eleven. If I don't die at eighty-eight I will go on to ninety-nine. It was easy to pass through seventy-seven for an old crapshooter, for that is an age divisible by both seven and eleven. I'll keep producing. I'll probably die propped up in bed trying to write a poem about a man who prayed to God to live to an age divisible by eleven.

Mr. Jim, the slight ancient old telegrapher in the green eye-shade who manned our AP wire machines, tapped out my story and it went chattering out over the AP wires and ended up in *Newsweek* the following week, much to my satisfaction, for it was the first time anything of mine had gotten into a national publication. (Sandburg's prediction didn't come true. He died at Flat Rock on July 22, 1967, at age eighty-nine.)

The pull of my orphanage memories was powerful, and I had been going back there at least every other year for the Easter reunion ever since I left. This Easter, fourteen years after I had run off to join the Navy, I drove down to Raleigh and went straight to the old campus. The old road up the hill from Glenwood Avenue was still there, but Old Man Barnes's house at the bottom of the hill was gone and so were all of the old orphanage buildings. The land had been sold off to a developer and the Brown, Page, and Cole Buildings where I had lived, the Vann Building where I had gone to school and to morning chapel services, and the cavernous dining hall where I had eaten corn flakes and peanut butter and government surplus prunes had all been scraped away, replaced by rows of condominiums. The Methodist Children's Home now operated by placing children in foster care. I was suddenly angry. Why had they done this? For pure commerce? Surely there was still a need for this orphanage. And they had destroyed my history, just like that. The Borden Building had been preserved, as part of the deal, as a historical monument and the grove in front of the Vann Building was now a city park. I got out of my car and walked down under the budding oaks. The dogwood and azaleas were in bloom and the three giant pecan trees which we used to pick clean before the nuts were dry were leafing out.

As always happened when I went back, a great wave of sadness swept over me and a thousand memories rushed in. I remembered everything, every detail, every tree, every spot in the creek where I caught tadpoles and crawfish, every rock thrown at a squirrel in a hickory nut tree, the musty smell of the classrooms, the smell of the disinfectant with which we scrubbed the floors, the Bon Ami with which we cleaned the toilets, Muh Brown's soft voice, Old Man Barnes swaying back and forth on his heels as he warned us against the beckoning evils of sex and drink, the feel of Jewel Hayes's soft body against me in the chill moonlight outside the dining room. The orphanage as I knew it was no more. The reunion was now held in a Hilton Hotel west of Raleigh, near where I once delivered Christmas packages for the post office and where as a boy I roamed for wild plums and blackberries. Three hundred or so of the "old" boys and girls had come. There was a Sunday morning church service with a choir cobbled together from alumni who had once sung in the orphanage choir. When they began singing the old Methodist hymn "He Is Risen," I choked back tears.

At night we all sat around and recalled stories from the past. I recounted once again how I had vowed to kill my nemesis Fatty Clark if I ever got big enough. I talked about how he had beaten and bullied me. In the group was a pudgy man with thinning hair named Colin Maultsby. He had been the object of much teasing when we were in our early teens. Then he had fashioned a cape out of a blue piece of cloth and ran around the basement proclaiming he was Captain Marvel—after a comic book character—and pretending he could fly. As I was talking about Fatty Clark bullying me, he suddenly said, "You did the same thing to me."

"What?" I said.

"You picked on me all the time. You made my life as miserable as you say Fatty Clark did yours."

"What did I do?"

"One day you and Bobby Brown picked me up and put me in a filthy garbage can side of the hog pen and tried to push the lid down on me. And one day you pushed me off the back of the truck. And you put an apple on my brother Dickie's head and threatened to play William Tell with him. You didn't hit me, but you humiliated me. And I wanted to kill you.

"After I came back from being in the Army in Korea I was up in Asheville visiting some relatives and I went by the paper where I knew you were working with every intention of killing you. I was going to choke you to death. But when I looked through the sports department window, you looked a lot smaller, and you didn't look like the same Karl at all. You didn't look as mean. So I said to hell with it and just left."

I was shocked. I had been a bully, too, according to him, the very thing I so hated, the very thing I prided myself on not being. I had no memory of doing this, but certainly it had to be true. I was ashamed. How could I have been capable of this? I wondered if he had hated me as much as I had hated Fatty Clark. I wondered if his being bullied had had as much effect on his life as it had on mine. But we did not have this discussion. I told him I was sorry. That was all. Our gathering broke up, and we went our separate ways. By the time he saw me in Asheville I was wearing a crew cut but weighed 150 pounds and obviously didn't look very tough. And didn't feel tough, either. I was still just a confused kid trying to find a place for himself in a daunting world I knew little about.

A few weeks after that I was working as state editor one Sunday on the July 4 weekend when I got a call from one of our stringers. A swinging bridge over the Oconaluftee River on the Cherokee Indian Reservation had broken, dumping dozens of tourists into the water. Two of them were dead. I was on the phone collecting information and writing for the next several hours, updating our stories and adding to the bulletins that went out over our AP wire. For the first time, I felt the great adrenaline rush, the totally focused, calm, and accurate speed with which one could write under great pressure that I had heard veteran reporters talk about. Maybe at last I was a real reporter after all. It took several hours and a bottle of Jim Beam shared with the men in the composing room to calm down from the adrenaline rush.

I loved the heat, pressure, and excitement of the composing room, the clatter of the linotype machines, the smell of the burning lead, and the salty cynicism of the back-room veterans. When I stood in as state editor on Sundays, I designed the pages, edited the wire copy, took stories over the phone from several stringers—mostly obits—wrote the heads, and went back to the composing room to stand at the ready when stories in type needed to be cut or moved. I learned to read type upside down and backwards, and in so doing felt like a real newspaperman.

Right after the bridge collapse, the publisher came into the newsroom and told me I could have a job on the *Citizen* as long as I wanted to stay. But then came a break that was to change my life.

I was doing some freelancing on the side, and one day a call came in from the editor of the *Atlanta Journal-Constitution Sunday Magazine* looking for someone to do a profile on a Methodist preacher named Charles Allen, who was pastor of Atlanta's biggest Methodist Church. He was vacationing with his family at Lake Junaluska, a Methodist summer retreat near Sandburg's home. I dutifully wrote a long piece highlighted, at least in my mind, by my description of him showing me with great pride a diamond ring, which he said cost $9,000, given him by his congregation.

Upon receiving my article the editor of the magazine called and told me that if I was interested in a job there I should send him clips of some of my other work. These went to the hands of Gene Patterson, the editor of the *Constitution*, and he shortly called and offered me a job on the magazine, at $102.50 a week. After conferring with my wife I immediately accepted. I had languished in Asheville for five long years and was eager to get out. I'd never even seen the *Atlanta Journal-Constitution Magazine*, except for the issue they sent me with my article in it. I just figured that being a part of the well-respected *Atlanta Constitution*, it had to be better than where I was. Besides, Atlanta was a big city, a definite step up for me, and I was excited to go. Asheville wasn't the end of the world, but you could see it from there, as some said.

We sold our house in Asheville for what we had paid for it, and I left my family with my wife's parents and drove down to Atlanta to find us a new home. What lay ahead I did not know. I did know I was leaving North Carolina probably forever. The orphanage, my mother, and the intense experiences of my first newspaper job in Wilson would always be a part of me. I knew that. But I wanted no more of the past, except for bittersweet memories of it. I felt a small ache of sadness thinking of this, but I was voracious for new life, in whatever form it might come.

Chapter 8

Into the Racial Fray

I HAD LIVED among and around Negroes all of my life, but it was not until I was thirty-four years old that I had my first man-to-man conversation with a black person, one equal professional talking to another. That happened in early 1961 right after I had gone to work for *Newsweek* magazine in its Atlanta bureau. I felt almost miraculously lucky to have gotten this job, and I plunged into it anxiously determined to get off on the right foot.

Among other things, this meant cultivating contacts in the young but expanding civil rights movement and aggressively checking in with them on a regular basis for possible stories. I was powerfully drawn to this story, more than to any other, right from the start. It was the underdogs against the bullies, and I immediately and strongly identified with the underdogs. Plus that, I could see right away that the civil rights story was going to be an epic and long-running one, and I wanted to be in on it as much as possible.

Jim Forman, then, was a contact I needed to cultivate. He was the executive secretary of the Atlanta-headquartered Student Nonviolent Coordinating Committee. SNCC (or Snick, as it was called), was an aggressive activist group less than a year old, having been formed by Negro college students in Raleigh, North Carolina. They had gotten a lot of attention staging successful sit-ins at segregated department store lunch counters in Greensboro, North Carolina, the first such in the Confederate South.

I drove down to see Forman at SNCC's tiny cluttered office in an old, two-story brick building on Auburn Avenue, the main business street of Atlanta's sprawling Negro section. He was a year younger than I was—the old-timer, in fact, in SNCC, which consisted almost entirely of college students. He was a brooding, glowering concrete block of a man with prematurely graying hair and tiny ears. He smoked a pipe, and rarely smiled. He was, I had learned, a Korean War veteran, a graduate of Roosevelt University, and a former reporter for a prominent black newspaper, the *Chicago Defender*.

Forman greeted me with a dismissive sigh, as if to say that if I thought I was a good person because I had expressed interest in SNCC—which few publications and no TV at all had at that time— then he was there to set me straight. The white media had a lot of Negro blood on its hands, he said by way of greeting, and I, as its agent, was definitely a part of the problem and not the solution.

"How many Negroes work for *Newsweek*?" he asked.

I had to admit there were none that I knew of.

"What's your background, Karl?" he asked.

"I grew up in a Methodist Church orphanage, was in the Navy a while, went to college a couple of years, and worked on four Southern newspapers before coming to *Newsweek*."

"Have you ever worked anywhere where there were any Negro reporters?" he asked, puffing his pipe and eyeing me coolly.

"Not a one," I said, knowing he knew the answer before he asked the question. After all, this was the South.

"The whole mass media establishment is racist per se," he said wearily. "There is just no way you white reporters can understand the depth of racism in this country."

I wanted to tell him that at least I knew, because of my own past, what it felt like to be an underdog, but I realized it would sound like a silly and unseemly defense. Also, it was undeniably true that the newspapers I had worked on were racist. I thought of how the *Wilson Daily Times* covered Alan Reid, the Negro man in Wilson sent to the gas chamber for climbing through a white woman's window and saying something lewd to her with perhaps an intent to rape her. I also thought of Ray Hartis and the Negroes bowing and scraping in fear of him, and how he had slapped that old black man across the face for politely questioning his presence in his home. I thought of the papers I had worked on, where the only Negro employee face I ever saw was Claude, the "boy" who swept up the pressroom at the *Wilson Daily Times*. I thought, in fact, of all the newspapers and magazines I read and television news I watched—all of it run by white people for white people. Oh, Forman was right all right. The media were as racist as any other part of the society. And maybe I should have done more to change them—to not, for example, work for a paper that was racist. But that would have meant not working for any of them, including the Northern ones that I knew anything about. I didn't think of myself as racist. Not at all. I thought I was fair-minded. If I had a prejudice, it was against racist whites. But I didn't challenge Forman's assertions nor did I share my personal beliefs with him. That would not have been professional. So I kept my mouth shut and let him continue.

I did not like his aggressive personal accusations, but I liked this manner better than the bowing and scraping subservience or the studied evasiveness and coolness with which Negroes had theretofore responded to me. The Negro's customarily practiced obsequiousness always made me cringe with embarrassment, and their careful evasiveness always made me feel soiled somehow. At least Forman was honest. So I admired him for that. He held nothing back. He could be just as abrasive and confrontational as I was turning out to be.

My own confrontational tendencies had, in fact, expressed themselves at a SNCC demonstration a few months earlier. The leadership had corralled students from the five Negro colleges in Atlanta to stage sit-ins at segregated facilities, including the Heart of Atlanta Motel. I wasn't on assignment—this wasn't a big enough story—but I went anyway. About fifty kids, led by Forman, had occupied the motel restaurant. The management responded by locking the doors and turning off the air-conditioning. Everybody milled around not knowing what to do next as the temperature rose. I began to feel a little claustrophobic, and angry. So I got the manager on the house phone, identified myself, and said, "You've locked us in here and if there was a fire we would be trapped. That's against the law. So if someone doesn't unlock the door in five minutes. I'm going to kick it in." The door was promptly unlocked.

Atlanta was the most sophisticated and progressive city in the South at this time, but still totally segregated 100 years after it was burned by Union General William T. Sherman during its *Gone with the Wind* days. The "Athens of the South," Atlanta called itself, but it was best known as the birthplace of Coca-Cola, Georgia Tech's football teams, and golfer Bobby Jones and for its beautiful "flower of the South" women and its graceful old mansions set back from dogwood-dotted wide lawns on

Peachtree Street. Its metropolitan area had grown to one million, and a new system of expressways and an enlarged international airport helped its go-getters attract a rapid new influx of Northern capital and business. It impressed me as bursting with energy and vitality compared to Asheville or the sleep-walking pace of Eastern Carolina. And it was changing rapidly on the racial front. After a few minor dust-ups in the form of sit-ins and picketing at the city's biggest department store, Rich's, a popular downtown delicatessen named Loeb's, and the Heart of Atlanta, the city's business leaders shrewdly decided to yield gracefully to what seemed the inevitable. They adopted and widely advertised a new slogan, "Atlanta: The City Too Busy to Hate" and quietly began integrating all public facilities. Atlanta's mayor, Bill Hartsfield, declared, "We've accepted what is world opinion. We're not consumed with hatred of each other. We are free to use our talents and energies to grow and attract industry."

Not everybody was accepting of what was going on. The Ku Klux Klan was staging rallies in protest, but being held in close check by the Atlanta police, while a flamboyantly racist restaurateur named Lester Maddox, who ran a chain of fried chicken joints called The Pickrick, was passing out pickaxe handles on the corner of Peachtree and Luckie Streets in the heart of downtown.

"Just in case some of you Communists, Socialists, and other integrationists have any doubt, The Pickrick will never be integrated," he said.

At the same time most places in the South were frantically hardening their lines of defense against any form of integration. The well-organized and well-funded segregationists had the view that the civil rights movement was a monolithic organization under the direction of Martin Luther King Jr., who himself was under the direction of the Communist Party. But, in fact, it wasn't a united front. First there was King's Southern Christian Leadership Conference (SCLC), also headquartered in Atlanta. Then there was the Congress of Racial Equality (CORE), founded in Chicago in 1942, which had sponsored the Freedom Rides and started chapters in the South. There was also the National Association for the Advancement of Colored People (NAACP), which had branches all over the South and a regional headquarters in Atlanta. And finally there was SNCC. All these groups were struggling to define and lay claim to a piece of the civil rights turf. And there were, as might have been expected, disputes, jealousies, power struggles, and personality clashes. At the conservative end of this spectrum was the NAACP, which had long practiced a go-slow, legalistic approach, and at the other end were the firebrands of CORE and SNCC, who espoused and practiced more confrontational and provocative methods. In the middle was King and the SCLC, still trying to find an aggressive role for itself while retaining its Christian, nonviolent philosophy. King was the only civil rights leader who had any real public recognition at that point. It was apparent that big showdowns were coming, and I had a dawning and happy realization that I was in exactly the right place at exactly the right time to see and be a part of this historical drama.

In the job I had just left at the *Atlanta Journal-Constitution Sunday Magazine*—the one that had brought me to Atlanta in the first place—I had had absolutely nothing to do with the civil rights movement or any other serious stories. Its mandate was "soft features," most of which seemed to have a mathematical or superlative underpinning: the tallest tree, the biggest watermelon, the oldest Confederate veteran, the longest river, the heaviest hog, the most productive cow, the most decorated hero.

Riding around with a staff photographer, I did stories on a young Georgia woman who'd become Miss America, a Georgia man who'd won a Medal of Honor in World War II as a combat medic despite being a conscientious objector, a skin-diving champion, and a prize-winning bass fisherman. I was happy to be in Atlanta, working in a larger arena, but I was not being intellectually challenged, and I was soon bored. Assigned to do a piece on amateur pilots, I took lessons in a Piper Super Cub at the Peachtree-DeKalb airport near our house and got my private license. I was scheduled to take the flying part of the test on New Year's Day, 1959. The weather report the day before predicted clear, calm conditions, so I invited over two of my flying buddies, barbecued a two-inch thick steak, and we got very drunk on Old Hickory. I awoke next morning to a radiant blue sky and one of the worst hangovers I'd ever had. I downed an Alka-Seltzer and two aspirin and somehow managed to fly the turbulent 100 miles down to Columbus and pass the test with a Federal Aviation Agency inspector in the back seat.

And I learned to scuba dive when I was assigned to accompany four Atlanta men who'd rented a converted PT boat in Miami and went on an island-hopping diving vacation in the Bahamas. I was beginning to have a glimpse that I went after my vocation and my avocations—cooking, flying, poker, drinking—passionately and excessively. I often cited Oscar Wilde's dictum "Anything worth doing is worth overdoing."

I had transferred my Elks membership to the Elks Club in Decatur on the edge of Atlanta and went out there every couple of weeks to eat dinner, drink, and play poker. I invariably got drunk and after one such night I went out in the morning with my usual hangover to find the front end of my Ford smashed in. I had no idea what had happened. That afternoon I went to the Decatur police department and asked the desk sergeant if there had been any unreported accidents the night before. My car was damaged and I had been too drunk to know what happened.

"What kind of car do you drive?" he asked.

"A blue and white 1957 Ford," I said.

He excused himself and came back a moment later and shook blue and white paint flecks from a small brown envelope.

"You mowed down a traffic sign and a fire hydrant," he said. "Do you know how much a fire hydrant costs? $700."

I must have turned pale. He laughed and said, "OK, since you were so honest, get the hell out of here."

I definitely did not drink like a gentleman. That a man could "hold his liquor" was a Southern badge of pride. That wasn't me. I drank with a defiant pride in not being a Southern gentleman. I was a poor boy, and a newspaper reporter—like Hemingway and Ring Lardner and Dorothy Parker—and damned proud of it.

Ironically, it was another reporter's excessive drinking that led to my becoming a part-time worker for *Newsweek*—a "stringer." *Newsweek*'s regular Atlanta stringer was Bill Hammack, another writer on the *Journal-Constitution* magazine who sat at the desk next to mine. He was a hard drinker, which showed in his bespectacled watery eyes and on his red face. On many days he was afflicted with horrendous hangovers, and he began to turn his *Newsweek* assignments over to me. They usually consisted of making a dozen or so phone calls, rounding up information on this or that subject, typing up the results and walking them over to the nearby *Newsweek* office. I got between twenty-five dollars and fifty dollars per assignment, depending on its difficulty. Bill and I often lamented our low wages and agreed that if we could ever make just $9,000 a year, we would be satisfied.

The *Newsweek* bureau chief was a flamboyantly verbal Atlanta native named Bill Emerson, with thinning hair, protruding eyes, and a booming voice. He gave me my stringer assignments, and I sometimes sat at his elbow and listened in awe at how much he was able to get out of people, interviewing them on the phone. He was fascinated with every detail of his interviewee's life, and I learned from him how flattered people were just to be listened to with avid intensity. I'd been on the Sunday magazine for a year when suddenly Emerson was promoted to "back of the book" editor in New York, creating a vacancy in the Atlanta bureau. I immediately put my hat in the ring. There were many applicants, for jobs on the two major newsmagazines represented the very top of the heap in journalism, along with the *New York Times*. I submitted a batch of clippings from my past work to Emerson and waited anxiously, for more than a month. He was interviewing other applicants. Finally I went to Emerson and brashly said, "You might as well go ahead and hire me, because you are not going to find anyone better." A day later he called and said I had the job—at $9,000 a year.

I excitedly called Sandy and told her we could start looking for a bigger house. This was fortunate, for she was pregnant with our third child, and he was born three weeks later, on Oct. 14, 1960. We named him Russell, after my best friend from the orphanage and my best man at our wedding, Russell Clay. We lived what would be a typical 1950s family life, mom at home with the kids, dad long hours at work, home for dinner—and, in my case, often off to carouse with buddies after the kids were in bed. I assumed Sandy was happy. We didn't talk about things like that—or much of anything except our kids, my mother and her parents, and our friends. She never complained about my long hours at the magazine, though she did sometimes complain when I came home late and drunk.

The *Newsweek* bureau was in a plain two-room suite on the ninth floor of the Citizens & Southern Bank Building on Marietta Street just off Peachtree. My new boss was Joseph B. (Joe) Cumming Jr., a poetry-loving graduate of Sewannee and spawn of an old Augusta family He was my age, with wispy blonde hair, a full mouth, and an infectious laugh. He and his wife, Emily, had four children and constituted a kind of Southern Von Trapp family. They all played musical instruments—Joe, the saxophone.

I plunged eagerly into my *Newsweek* work. It was a very different style from that of newspapers. Instead of writing completed stories, the *Newsweek* correspondent was supposed to over-report, that is, send in "files" rich with detail, description, and quotes, and a New York writer—perhaps with input from other bureaus—would distill it all down into a short, crisp finished story. Plus that, our job was to come up with story ideas, and every Sunday afternoon we went to the office with all the Southern papers we could round up and combed them for raw material and that night wired off a list of suggestions. It turned out I was pretty good at this and could see, for example, that the annual Mule Day celebration at Benson, North Carolina, could be turned into a lifestyle feature about the vanishing role of the once indispensable mule—a stubborn creature that had been such a part of my early life—in rural America.

Newsweek was then running a poor second to the well-established, more conservative, more Establishment Republican-oriented *Time*. *Newsweek* wasn't as well written, wasn't as sharp, and it didn't look as good. But—as luck would have it for me—*Newsweek* was beginning to come on strong, mainly because of its instant understanding and embrace of the civil rights story. This happened because *Newsweek* was under new young leadership. Kay Graham's *Washington Post* had bought *Newsweek* in 1960 when Ben Bradlee, *Newsweek*'s adventurous young Washington bureau chief, told Kay Graham's entrepreneur husband, Phil, that *Newsweek* was an untapped resource. Graham promoted Harvard-educated Osborn Elliott, then the *Newsweek* business editor, to editor in chief, and Elliott quickly assembled a team of extremely talented and bold young editors. Fortunately for *Newsweek*'s rapid growth and prestige, *Time* seemed stuck in the fifties. Its pieces were in the ivory tower, thumb-sucker style—produced by New York writers who used what their reporters sent in to support conservative points of view already set in stone. *Newsweek* was immediately more fresh and bold and willing to see that great social change was in the making. Accordingly (to use a favorite *Newsweek* word), *Newsweek* rapidly gained reputation and circulation, and by the time I got there had seventy-five correspondents working in twenty-four foreign and domestic bureaus. I thought it was the best possible place to be a reporter. I was learning a lot, and quickly.

One of the best short journalism lessons I ever had came when, early in my *Newsweek* career, I was sent to New Orleans to write a story about the annual convention of the American Newspaper Publishers Association. There would be debate and discussion about the growing controversy around the media's role in covering the civil rights movement. Was there too much attention being paid to the growing protests, or too little?

Midweek while I was there I got a call from Bill Emerson in New York. Part of his new turf was the religion section of *Newsweek*. He said he knew I was in New Orleans covering a different story, but he needed a minor bit of help from me on a piece that our New Orleans stringer had sent in. It contained the basic facts about an incident in which the Catholic archbishop of New Orleans, Joseph Rummel—who had ordered parochial schools to be integrated—had been confronted by a group of angry parishioners, headed by a woman named Una Gaillot, on the lawn outside his manse.

"I need just two questions answered," Bill said. "Number one, what does the archbishop's house look like? Is it wood, stone, brick, two-story, or what? Is it Victorian with ivy on the walls? What kind of day was it? Was it balmy and sunny or overcast and muggy? Was it hot? What does the archbishop look like? Is he old and bespectacled, or what? How did he walk when he came out of the house? Did he stride angrily? Or did he walk haltingly, leaning on a cane? What is the walkway like? Is it brick, concrete, gravel or dirt? What do the grounds look like? Are there oak trees, magnolias, jasmine and roses? What was happening on the street outside the grounds? Was an angry crowd assembled, or was it business as usual with people oblivious to the drama going on inside? What were Mrs. Gaillot and her friends wearing? Did they have on their Sunday best, or just casual clothes? What happened just as the archbishop approached the women? Was he stern and silent? Or did he rebuke Mrs. Gaillot? What did she say, exactly?

"And, question number two . . . "

I hurried out to the archbishop's home, interviewed his secretary, looked over the grounds and house, got Mrs. Gaillot on the phone, and quickly pieced together the information and forwarded it to New York.

When the story appeared next week, here were its first two paragraphs:

"It was a cloudless, languid spring morning last week when Archbishop Joseph Francis Rummel emerged from his two-story, red-brick residence in uptown New Orleans and unknowingly moved toward a uniquely dramatic confrontation. Dressed in a long, black cassock topped by a velvet-lined cape, carrying a black cane in his left hand, the 85-year-old prelate walked haltingly toward a statue of Our Lady of Fatima. There, fifteen neatly-dressed ladies, on an annual pilgrimage to the shrine, awaited his greeting.

"The gray-haired archbishop had just finished welcoming the group when Mrs. Una Gaillot, excommunicated by Rummel the day before for her attempts to block desegregation of the area's Catholic schools, came stalking past fifteen pickets who were protesting the desegregation outside the archbishop's garden.

Marching onto the lawn, Mrs. Gaillot threw herself down in front of him...."

My 1,500 words had been distilled into 250 that put the reader right there, in what *Newsweek* called a "scene-setter." That experience helped my reporting and writing immensely, and soon I felt like I could keep up with the fast pace and high demands at *Newsweek*. I began to get complimentary notes from Oz Elliott and from the fast-talking, gum-popping, brilliant Gordon Manning, the managing editor, famous for sending "Gordograms" to field reporters peppering them with questions.

Looking at the end of six months like I was a keeper, I was invited to go to New York with my wife to visit the *Newsweek* mother ship and meet the people with whom I had been working. I was excited but nervous, and so was my wife. It would be her first trip to New York and my second, the first having been a weekend I'd spent hanging around Times Square on leave from the Navy fifteen years earlier. Despite my "Gordograms" and the approbation of my bosses, I still felt very much the outsider when I came face to face with them, maladroit among the much more worldly and sophisticated New Yorkers.

That was especially true of Oz Elliott and Fritz Beebe, *Newsweek*'s publisher, who took Sandy and me to dinner the first night we were there. We went to a Szechwan restaurant. Both Oz and Fritz were urbane with an ease of manner, grace, and poise that bespoke blue blood and old money. Oz had a refined patrician nose and wore gold cufflinks and a tiepin that looked as if they had been in his family for 500 years. The Ivy League white-shoe lawyer Beebe wore a perfectly fitted gray suit with a vest, a striped shirt, and elegantly quiet tie. With my ill-fitted suit and crew cut and my rough manner I felt like a true bumpkin although they, along with their wives, could not have been less aloof or more engagingly kind.

I felt much more at ease when I got to the *Newsweek* office at 444 Madison Avenue and met the writers, most of whom were former newspaper reporters. One of them I especially sparked to was a droll and cynical native Mississippian named Frank Trippett, an adroit writer in the national affairs section. The first day he came to work, so the minor legend about him went, he got in the elevator with Oz Elliott and on the way up Oz extended his hand and said, "Oz Elliott."

"Ah's Trippett," said Frank.

Frank was, like me, a prodigious drinker and a profane talker, and he joined Sandy and me for a night of boozy revelry at the Oak Bar in the Waldorf-Astoria where *Newsweek* had stashed us. It was stunning to me that two years earlier I had been languishing on a mediocre newspaper in the remote town of Asheville, North Carolina, and now I was at the famous Waldorf—eating in fancy restaurants, going to the "theatah" (*Cat on a Hot Tin Roof, Will Success Spoil Rock Hunter?*), working with some of the country's finest journalists, visiting the Metropolitan Museum, and in general—to use the Southern vernacular—riding the gravy train with biscuit wheels. I had come a long way for sure from Mauls Swamp and the Methodist Orphanage.

Right after that, with my hefty pay boost, Sandy and I moved out of the small, $12,000 GI tract house in Northeast Atlanta that we'd bought when we moved to Atlanta, and we bought for $18,000 a Victorian home on a big lot in an old neighborhood called Ansley Park. It had four bedrooms, leaded glass windows, and parquet floors and was a half block from a capacious park and two blocks from the governor's mansion. We began making neighborhood friends who had children, and the kids ran freely in the park in perfect safety. It was all white, of course.

Meantime, I had sought out and become friends with Vernon Jordan, the field director of the NAACP's Southern regional office.

Jordan was twenty-six years old, the son of an Atlanta woman who had raised and educated him by operating a catering service for white clients. He was a strikingly handsome, newly minted lawyer, six foot, three inches tall and 200 pounds, with a rich basso of a voice, an incandescent smile, a booming laugh, and the regal poise of an African prince. I thought of him as the potent nightmare of every emasculated white Southern male—and there were thousands of them—who fearfully believed that what "they" really wanted was not equal access and treatment but "our wimmin." I liked Jordan enormously. He seemed entirely comfortable with who and where he was, the perfect man for me to take to lunch at Herren's on Luckie Street just off Peachtree. Herren's was the favorite lunching spot for Atlanta's business elite, a place of dark wood and leather and quiet tradition and certainly, for me, there was some pleasure in tweaking the white establishment. It was a first for Jordan—his first meal in a white Southern restaurant—and a first for the downtown white businessmen sitting there in their dark suits, button-down shirts, and repp ties who looked up, taken aback, as we walked in, and who then tried mightily and politely to ignore our presence. We ordered London broil, Herren's signature lunch offering, and made laughing conversation as if we had done this a hundred times before.

We had not, of course, nor had anyone much in the South. In the few places that were desegregating—eating places, hotels, transportation, and other public facilities, mainly in Atlanta and Nashville—both whites and blacks were struggling to adjust to their new footings with each other, and it was awkward. I was no different, despite my pleasure in being a rebel. In addition to Vernon Jordan, I had also made friends with Samuel Du Bois Cook, a light-skinned and freckled academic who was head of the political science department at Atlanta University, and I invited him and his wife, Sylvia, to a Saturday night dinner.

Sam accepted my invitation, but called a day later and asked if I'd do him a favor. He said a Negro friend of his had recently gone to a white neighborhood for dinner and a resident saw him walking toward his host's house and called the police. He was stopped and harassed and searched and questioned. What was he doing in a white neighborhood at night? So would I call the police and let them know I had Negro guests coming for dinner? I did. I knew the Atlanta police's PR man, so I called him, and he said he would take care of it. I was finding out that police were only as good—or bad—as their bosses—the white power structure. It was only when they had the tacit or real approval—and sometimes active encouragement—from political and business leaders that cops, or even ordinary racists and Klansmen, behaved brutally toward Negroes.

I'd invited three white couples from our neighborhood, two other newspapermen and their wives, plus a doctor and his wife I knew to be liberal on the race issue. I was cooking a lot by then, as well as flying sailplanes, playing poker at the Decatur Elks Club, playing golf, and spending as much time as possible with my sons—and I would have loved to prepare one of my favorite Southern meals: my mother's Southern-fried chicken, fried okra and green tomatoes, greens cooked with ham hocks, and buttermilk biscuits. But I feared that would be playing to a racist cliché. So I made beef bourguignon instead.

Usually a Saturday night with our friends was a long night of heavy drinking, smoking cigarettes—everybody smoked—raucous jokes, and perhaps a marital fight. One recent boozy night at a neighbor's house a wife had slapped her husband at the dinner table. But this was a polite and slightly stiff evening. Nobody dared have too much to drink. The risk of saying something improper was too great. Everybody struggled to be friendly, but not excessively so, which would have come across as patronizing.

Everybody tried to be racially liberal and large-minded, but not condescendingly so. We were all, white and black, feeling our way in foreign waters. Integration, of course, could not be discussed. Nor sex. Nor Southern politics, except for Governor Lester Maddox, who everybody could agree was a buffoon and an idiot. Nor books or writers. Suppose someone brought up one that our guests had not read? The conversation stayed on safe and mostly inane topics. The recent, unseasonably heavy hailstorm was good for ten minutes. Atlanta's festering traffic problems kept everybody going for ten. The Russians and the Cold War were safe, especially the recent Cuban missile crisis and how frightened everybody had been. I told how I had sent Sandy and the kids up to Asheville to spend the weekend with her family. The way food and gas prices kept going up was a cause for collective concern. Those speed traps in South Georgia that caught unsuspecting Northern tourists on the way to Florida were a disgrace. And wasn't *Bonanza* a great TV show? Time for dessert and coffee mercifully came and then the evening ended with everybody departing all at once. My wife and I were relieved it was over and grateful it had gone pretty well. It hadn't been much fun, but it was a right thing to do.

We then had Vernon Jordan and his wife over a couple of times, and then we were invited to his house, an awkward event like ours until Vernon put on some records and his black friends unrestrainedly let go while my wife and I stiffly did the boogie-woogie. The Negroes we invited, and who invited us, were much more at ease than the whites. Both Jordan and Cook had been to college up North and were used to mixing socially with whites. Indeed, Vernon had had a white college roommate at DePauw University. But this was all new territory for white people with zero experience meeting Negroes on an equal or social footing.

Word apparently soon got around in Atlanta's journalistic circles that I had had Negroes to my home. The editor of the *Atlanta Constitution* was Ralph McGill, a Tennessee-born liberal who'd won the Pulitzer Prize in 1959 for his editorials condemning white violence against blacks. He was famous up North for being a liberal Southern editor, and infamous among Southern segregationists—especially Georgia politicians—for advocating racial change. Among them, his name was "Rastus McGill." Graying with bushy brows, a gravel voice, and an avuncular manner, he was a good drinking companion and a great storyteller. He telephoned me one day at my *Newsweek* office. He wanted to have some Negroes to his home for dinner. He had not done that before. How did you go about it? Who should he invite? Would I help? I suggested Sam Cook and Sylvia, and McGill invited them along with my friend Claude Sitton, Atlanta bureau chief of the *New York Times*, and his wife, Eva. McGill had a graceful white old Southern home set back from a huge lawn in the Piedmont Park section. He was, Cook reported to me later, a charming, witty, and sophisticated host, though he got up from time to time to look nervously out the front window.

I then mailed Cook a bumper sticker that read "Be A Man. Join The Klan."

I was not in any way, despite hosting dinner parties and inviting Negroes, a social sophisticate. I'd acquired the requisite Eastern uniforms of success—a couple of Brooks Brothers suits, cordovan shoes, Talbot regimental ties, and button-down shirts. But I was still ill at ease and somewhat divided—wanting to belong to the easeful class and at the same time cynical about and contemptuous of what I perceived to be their snobbery, their privileged upbringing, private schools, and Ivy League education—and, in many cases, their unearned income. I still hadn't been around very much. I rented a tux to go to the first formal gathering my wife and I were invited to, a charity fundraiser at the

Dinkier Plaza Hotel in downtown Atlanta featuring Douglas Fairbanks Jr. as the main attraction. Friends had given us free tickets. We were seated at long banquet tables with white table cloths. Wine, which I hardly ever drank, was served. The appetizer was an artichoke and I was sawing away on it with a knife and fork when I looked around to see others picking off the leaves and dipping them in butter. I wanted to crawl under the table, but instead got very drunk.

In many ways I was still an orphanage boy. I believed I had a special stamp on me, one that made me different, perhaps irretrievably so. I was blunt talking and quick tongued, impatient with people who seemed inauthentic, especially politicians and clerics, or those who went along with the accepted Southern platitudes about segregation. I was smoking two packs of unfiltered Camels a day and a lot of cigars and had become a hard if not habitual drinker. I didn't drink every night, never drank during working hours nor let it interfere with my work, but I had finally begun to be aware of the fact that when I drank, I drank too much.

One Sunday night after an afternoon of flying—I flew an eight-dollar-an-hour rental Piper Cub with a tail wheel—I went with my flying pals Charlie Hurt and Mac Sale out to an illegal gambling joint across the Chattahoochie River in Cobb County. It was a permanent brick one-story building back from the main road, obviously protected by paid-off law enforcement, with slot machines, craps, and blackjack tables. The drinks were free, and I had a lot of them. I didn't gamble much but we stayed a long time and the next thing I knew I awoke lying in a hayfield on my back, covered with dew and with the morning sun on my face. My suit coat was missing. I heard cars and lurched unsteadily toward the sound, which turned out to be a freeway. I started hitchhiking. Shortly a man picked me up and I sat there sick and dazed as he drove until he asked me where I was going. Atlanta, I said. "You're going in the wrong direction," he said. I got out, crossed over, got a ride into town, went straight to work. I called my wife to let her know I was OK and to apologize.

I was lucky enough to have an appetite for hard work, a good eye for detail, and an ear for a great quote. I got my first great ones for *Newsweek* from the Ku Klux Klan. Every year the Klan had a rally and traditional cross-burning at the foot of Stone Mountain near Atlanta. For the 1961 rally, which was on a warm night in July, I dressed in jeans and a plaid work shirt, drove out and parked on a dirt road from where I could see the already lit cross. I took out my Pentax camera, crept close, and took several shots lying down in the weeds. I sneaked back and put my camera in the car and then walked into the rally as if I was just another interested spectator. For some reason I was not afraid, perhaps because I believed that I could talk my way out of anything and that I could play the good ol' boy routine with the best cross-burner among them. The crowd was a mixture of 300 men in Klan robes and work clothes. The cross was about thirty feet high and was guttering in air heavy with the smell of burning oil. Several old geezers stood near me, expressing disapproval to each other. These young Klansmen, they said, had no respect for honored ways.

"They don't know how to burn a real good ol' cross like we did in the old days when we cut down a young pine tree and made a cross that gave off a natural light and good ol' turpentiny smell," one of them said.

"These lazy young Klansmen," he said, "they don't have no respect for tradition, just get iron pipes, tie rags to 'em with wire and soak 'em with oil and make a nasty smelling-fire that leaves a mess afterwards."

The main rally speaker was Bobby Shelton, the Imperial Wiz-

I warily hid in the weeds to photograph this Ku Klux Klan rally, my first one, at Stone Mountain, Georgia, in 1961.

ard of the Klan. He was a pinch-faced worker at a Goodyear tire factory in Tuscaloosa, Alabama. Shelton had his name in the paper a lot and tried to pass himself off as being just an ordinary reasonable white man concerned about adulterating white blood by "mixing" the races. So I figured I was at least reasonably safe and went up and introduced myself to him and to Calvin Craig, a stolid machinist from Waycross, Georgia, who was Grand Dragon of the Georgia Klan. There weren't any other reporters around, at far as I could tell.

Shelton was not a fiery speaker, was boring in fact, but he had the Klan patter down just right: Race mixing was not only against Southern tradition, it was against God's plan. All true Southerners were obliged to defend their women and children against the evil plans of the Jews and the Catholics who were behind these new efforts to adulterate pure white blood. The Klan was the only organization not too spineless to resist mixing of the races with whatever force it took. The Klan was misunderstood. It was for honor and integrity of the races as God had planned them. Most of the politicians had sold out, and outside agitators from the North could only be resisted by the uncompromising principles and brave men of the Klan and the wives who supported them. "The Klan," he shouted, "must protect the chastity of white womanhood from the creeping black cloud. We don't want no violence, but we ain't gonna let the nigger spit in our face either."

I dutifully took notes on all this, with my notebook in plain view. I was nervous to be sure, but introducing myself to Shelton and Craig had apparently guaranteed my safety. I stuck around after the rally. Shelton said he and Craig were having several more rallies across Georgia in the next few days, and invited me to come along. I eagerly accepted, wanting to know more about this much-feared and secret organization—which, by the way,

had been getting unfavorable publicity because of recent bombings of Negro homes in Birmingham that they supposedly had
carried out.

Shelton and Craig were traveling together, changing in and
out of their Klan regalia at stops where rallies had been arranged.
The final one was on a Sunday afternoon at a dirt automobile
racetrack on the outskirts of Augusta. It was attended by about
200 men, women, and children. Afterwards Shelton invited me to
go to dinner with them. We went to a place serving all the fried
catfish you could eat for a dollar fifty. Neither of them drank. I
had a Schlitz. Over dinner they got philosophical. Craig especially
wanted to make it clear he wasn't a racist. He was fair-minded. It
was just that blacks and whites were not supposed to mix
socially. "I ain't against niggers improving themselves. They
ought to be able to get jobs," he said.

"Now wait a minute, Calvin," said Shelton. "Before we start
giving niggers jobs, they have to start improving their own status
quo."

Naturally that quote appeared in my *Newsweek* story, along
with my photograph of the burning Stone Mountain iron, rag,
and oil cross. It was funny in a sick sort of way, for those few
words told a lot about the quality of leadership the Klan
attracted. At the same time that the Klan was a motley collection
of ignorant buffoons, it was also a night-riding terrorist organization that operated in dark, robed secrecy to brutalize black people
who dared to speak out against "their own status quo." Georgia
had the sorry distinction of being behind only Mississippi in the
number of lynching of Negroes carried out by the Klan and other
racists. "Judge Lynch got that nigger," was a common joke. Even
as late as the early 1960s the Klan still operated with the tacit and
frequently open approval, and indeed encouragement, of the
white power structure and law enforcement people—who, in fact,

were often active members. There was not on record, insofar as I could find out, a single recorded incident of a Klan member being convicted in the South of a crime against a black person.

Some time later, on a tip from Calvin Craig about another KKK rally, I followed in my Ford as a motorcade of about twenty-five cars formed up outside Roswell, Georgia. The lead car was an old Cadillac decorated with a cross of light bulbs attached to the front bumper, powered by a wire from the cigarette lighter. All the cars flew Confederate flags. I was driving in the rear. Suddenly a car raced past me with two Negro men in it. As they drew alongside the lead car, the one on the passenger side reached out with a pistol and began firing. I could hear the pop, pop, pop of the gun. The car raced on and the motorcade ground to a stop and everybody ran to the front. The driver of the lead KKK car got out, a heavyset, balding man in a white short-sleeved shirt. He was holding his left eye. One of the bullets had just nicked him. His fat wife, her hair tied up in polka-dot bows, ran crying to him. Blood trickled from his eye.

"Goddamned sorry-assed niggers. If they think they can stop us they've got another think coming," he said.

"Let's git after 'em," somebody shouted. But they didn't pursue them.

My account of this incident ran in *Newsweek* the next week, along with a photograph I took of the fat wife comforting her wounded Klan husband.

I learned from Jim Forman that the Georgia Klan was most active south of Atlanta in a six-county rural area centered on Albany, a city of about 60,000 that was evenly divided in racial makeup but completely segregated. Albany had been a slave-trading center during the plantation era and Negroes still outnumbered whites five to one at the turn of the century. Now Albany was a regional center of commerce, home of a Negro college, and two small military bases. SNCC operatives had been working the rural country around it for many months trying with no success at all to get Negroes registered to vote. Mainly because of intimidation, fewer than 5 percent of Negroes were registered to vote in the half-dozen counties around Albany, most of which had black majorities. Five churches in the countryside around Albany that had allowed the SNCC workers to hold voter registration rallies in them were burned, with no intercession at all by law enforcement. One sheriff laughingly claimed that lightning had struck one of the churches.

Homes of Negroes in Terrell County—"Terrible Terrell" is what the SNCC kids called it—where white civil rights workers from the North were staying were sprayed with bullets. Several people were wounded. Sheriff Z. T. (Zeke) Matthews told my friend Claude Sitton that the shootings—and perhaps the church burnings, too—came about as a result of black and whites living together. "It's unusual for white folks to go down there living with niggers, pretty unusual. The better niggers are upset about it, too," he said.

Discouraged at their lack of success in the rural areas, the SNCC workers decided to try to gain a strong beachhead in Albany, where Negroes were more affluent, more established, and better educated, where white businesses might be vulnerable to pressure from boycotts and sit-ins, and where the cops allegedly were less brutal. The kids were able to get the various Negro civic and church groups amalgamated into one group called the Albany Movement—All-BENNY Move-MENT is the way Negroes pronounced it. A handsome Negro osteopath named Dr. William G. Anderson was elected president and a program of "direct action" was laid out.

After the 1960 Freedom Rides through the South in which young black and white activists were brutally beaten and jailed when they had ridden "mixed" on buses, the Interstate Commerce Commission ruled that all public transportation facilities be integrated, effective November 1, 1961. Immediately after that date, Forman and two other SNCC operatives went to Jake's Restaurant in the fly-ridden Trailways bus terminal in Albany to test the new law. They were promptly arrested, as were dozens who followed. When other protesters tried to integrate other public facilities, they were jailed on charges of trespassing, loitering, unlawful assembly, and parading without a permit. These trumped-up charges would be adopted by cops all over the South in coming demonstrations. The mayor and his city council closed the bus lines, libraries, parks, and swimming pools. Merchants shut their lunch counters and within two weeks Chief Laurie Pritchett had arrested and jailed 750, filling his jail, the National Guard Armory, and the jails of five surrounding counties. But the arrests were done politely and with no violence. Pritchett was quite unusual for a Southern cop. He was intelligent, well-educated, and smart about satisfying the urgings of his racist bosses but at the same time not engaging in or allowing the kind of brutality that would attract network television cameras. His firm but correct mass arrests provoked almost no violence—and little attention outside of the *New York Times* and *Newsweek*. He had made it clear to the Klan and others eager to beat up demonstrators that they were not welcome in Albany. A few Negro youths threw stones at cops as they were arresting demonstrators, prompting Pritchett to say to Sitton and me, "Did you see them nonviolent rocks?"

When fourteen Negro youths arrived to enroll at Albany High School, they were greeted by a sign at the building entrance that said "No Niggers—Please." They left, and there was scant confrontation. Due to methods like these, there was no television coverage of any Albany events and no concession whatever from Albany's white power structure.

One afternoon Chief Pritchett asked Claude and me to have a drink with him. We went into a yeasty, darkened beer parlor next to the police station. Sitton and I ordered a beer. Pritchett ordered buttermilk. That was an odd thing to drink in a bar, I said.

"There are three things I like to do," he said. "Drink buttermilk, put niggers in jail, and kick reporters' asses."

"Well, what do you know—an honest cop," I said. He laughed.

It was clear he had invited us in order to pick our brains. After all, we were loyal white Southerners, presumably on the same side he was on—namely the white side. But we didn't tell him anything. We knew he would be especially interested in the fact that the Albany Movement and the SNCC kids were debating whether to invite Martin Luther King Jr. down to give their drives a spark. But, in fact, we never shared anything we knew, even with local reporters. Often the local reporters were unreconstructed racists themselves, representing racist papers, and some were snitches for the cops. They would be let into the mass meetings Negroes were holding and report what they saw and heard to the police. We had overheard them so doing.

That weekend, I went home to Atlanta. *Newsweek* had decided not to do anything on Albany that week. This happened often. *Newsweek* didn't mind spending money to send me and its other correspondents somewhere, and then not doing a story. There was a lot of competition for not much space in the magazine. Except for the *New York Times*, which was not competitive with *Newsweek*, there was virtually no national coverage of "The Movement."

Forman had gone back to Atlanta from Albany, too, to rethink SNCC's position. On Monday I went down to the SNCC office to see him. He was vehemently against inviting King to Albany. The Albany Movement, he and other SNCC thinkers believed, should develop its own indigenous leaders and not get seduced into a "messiah" mindset in which some great outside leader like King would rescue the movement. Forman and others in SNCC also disagreed with King's belief that "redemptive suffering" on the part of Negroes would awaken white America's conscience. They were against King's embrace of Gandhi's philosophy of passive resistance. Actual power, especially at the polling place, was what Negroes needed to capture their own destiny, not waiting for white America to relent and "give" them something. Finally, though, Forman was outvoted, and it was decided to call in King and his Southern Christian Leadership Conference. King's presence might provoke more national media attention, which might persuade the local white leadership to make some concessions.

In early February, I packed my suitcase again, rented a Hertz car, drove back down to Albany, and checked into the Holiday Inn. I was unpacking when the phone rang. "Hello, Karl. This is Chief Pritchett. What brings you to our town? Is something special going on?"

"Oh, I don't know. I'm just checking a few things out," I said.

He caught me completely by surprise. Obviously he had a deal with someone at the Holiday Inn to tip him off when outside reporters checked in. I had registered my business affiliation as *Newsweek* magazine. It would be the last time I would ever do that in the South. I left that line on the form blank from then on. But as green as I was, I was smart enough to give the chief an evasive answer and not to play the role of inadvertent police informant.

Albany was my first big civil rights assignment, and I was nervous. Claude Sitton showed up and so did my counterpart from *Time* magazine's Atlanta bureau. The movement's plan was to hold large nightly "mass meetings" in the Mt. Zion and Shiloh Baptist churches and have King inspire Albany's Negroes to march en masse downtown every morning to protest unequal treatment. The first night more than 1,000 Negroes packed themselves into the little brick Mt. Zion Baptist Church to hear King speak. A huge overflow crowd gathered outside, unable to get in. There were even people in trees. I was ushered in my Brooks Brothers suit to a hard pine front-row pew. I watched the Negroes come in, the men dressed in their shiny blue Sunday suits, boiled white shirts, and ties, the women in their best dresses and hats. The had nickels, dimes, and quarters tied into the corners of handkerchiefs to give to the movement.

This night, I later learned, was the first time in the civil rights struggle that freedom songs were used as a warm-up act for speakers. A luminous young Negro woman named Bernice Reagan led the small church choir behind the pulpit. Dark-skinned, with a deep, rich, pained and poignant voice, perspiration coursing down her face, she thrust back her head and sang, "Over my head, I see freedom in the air, over my head I see freedom in the air, over my head I see freedom in the air." Swaying from side to side, the audience joined in the refrain, "Free-dom, Free-dom."

And then with the crowd locking hands and joining in, she led what was becoming the anthem of the civil rights movement: "We shall overcome, we shall overcome, we shall overcome, some day, some day. Deep in my heart, I do believe, we shall overcome, some day."

It was powerful stuff. It was plain to see in the depth of the feeling that swept the jammed, overly warm room that "some day" had been but a wistful fantasy for Negroes, but now it was beckoning just over the horizon. It was odd for me to be feeling emotion in a church, because for a long time, since I had left the orphanage, in fact, I had been increasingly bitter and angry about God and his varied earthly emissaries. And the civil rights move-

ment to which I had become a front-row witness to played a large
role in this increasing anger at the church. All across the Deep
South, especially since the Freedom Rides, civil rights workers
and Negroes who heeded their calls to action were being beaten,
jailed, castrated—yes, castrated—and killed. The dominant white
Methodist and Baptist churches, and their numerous Southern
off-shoots, stayed all but silent. A few preachers had spoken out,
and most of them were forced from their churches. I wanted no
part of this kind of religion. But here in this simple little church in
Albany, something powerful was pulling me back to childhood
and the small country churches where I had sat among poor
white people as they sang songs of hope and listened to promises
of a better life. And I felt something else, too: a sudden strong
recognition of how much I identified with these people and their
yearnings and how much I actually envied them and the pure
fight they were in.

The church had been the only gathering place whites had
allowed Negroes to have since slavery days. And they could
preach, pray, and sing in peace as long as they worshipped a
white God who had deliberately separated the races and meant to
keep it that way—God, the supreme segregationist. But now
came the SNCC troublemakers, no respecters of religion, heathen
college students who were, in fact, trying to use the churches to
upset the voting patterns that kept Negroes powerless, and
behind them came Martin Luther King, using the churches to
preach a new and revolutionary gospel.

When King rose to call them to action in his cadenced but
urgent voice I could feel hope rise in the room. It was the first
time I had heard him speak and his voice rolled through the
church like a mighty organ. He was not a classical orator. He was
a preacher, and he preached in a language Negroes had practiced
since slavery: rhythmic, stirring, steeped in the Bible and the

promise of hope. And he had a message they could accept within the context of their religion. Passive mass resistance, he said, was not a surrender. It was a dynamic tactic, militant in nature, in the best Christian tradition. Its exercise, in the form of hundreds of well-dressed and well-mannered Negroes marching on City Hall, would create a moral crisis that would reveal to the nation the true nature of segregation. The hand of the racists would be forced, and the conscience of America would be roused. Immense pressure would be put on the politicians to make changes in the laws and on local merchants and white leaders to give Negroes their real freedom. "Amen." "That's right." "You tell it," the crowd answered back as he spoke. I had heard black preachers before, but never one with the depth of moral suasion I heard in Martin Luther King's voice that night.

Next morning, at ten o'clock, answering his call, 250 Negroes lined up in columns of four with King and his deputy, the Rev. Ralph Abernathy, in front and prepared to march to City Hall.

"We are marching to freedom," King told them.

I was standing beside Vernon Jordan as the march formed up. "Bullshit, they ain't marching to freedom. They're going to jail," he said with a wry smile, knowing full well that his organization—specifically, the NAACP Legal Defense Fund—would have to bail them out. Jordan was ever the realist. And he was right. King and Abernathy and all who followed them were quickly arrested for "parading without a permit" and jailed. Nightly "mass meetings" and daily marches followed until at week's end more than 400 Negroes were behind bars. I attended every mass meeting, every press conference, every march, every confrontation. Meantime, I had been going sixteen hours a day and I had still not seen the *Time* reporter all week. Where was he? What was he up to? Was he getting a story I wasn't? I was worried as I sat down Thursday night in my room in the Holiday Inn to put on paper everything I had taken notes on all week. I had a small green Lettera 22 portable typewriter, and it took me five hours, using my two-fingered hunt-and-peck system—tearing up pages and starting over—to finish my twelve-page report. I carried it down to Western Union next to the Tramways bus station and sent it off "Night Press Rate Collect" to the national affairs section of *Newsweek*.

There was another march next morning. And there, suddenly, was the *Time* correspondent. Where had he been all week? In his room at the Holiday Inn reading poetry, he said. What he sent in to New York, if anything, didn't really matter, he said, because New York would write it any way it wanted to. I was grateful that *Newsweek* wasn't like that. At my urging, in fact, on Saturday just before the magazine was locked up, someone from New York would call and read me the story I had reported on over the phone to make sure it was accurate. I was much relieved to hear that my *Time* counterpart had been reading poetry, but when I got back to the motel I had a disturbing call from New York.

Joe Carter, the *Newsweek* national affairs editor, was a grizzled old former *Herald Tribune* reporter who kept a bottle of Jim Beam in his right-hand desk drawer and sometimes didn't come back to work after lunch. My copy had gone to his desk.

"I looked over your stuff, Karl," he said in a world-weary voice. "The facts are interesting, but what does it all add up to? What does it all mean?"

I was getting another good lesson in how to be reporter for *Newsweek*. This was different from the "Five W's—Who, What, When, Where, Why"—rules that guided newspaper reporters. *Newsweek*'s ambition was to not only report the facts but also to crystallize them into an accurate big picture. What did the facts add up to? I was called upon to exercise some mature judgment, to say what it all meant.

What it meant was that Albany was a failure for King. He had roused Albany's Negroes, but he had not succeeded in rousing the conscience of America. There being no violence, so despite the mass marches and mass jailing, few network television cameras came, nor did newspaper reporters pour in. And though hundreds upon hundreds had been jailed, huge energy expended, and big money paid out in fines and bail money, Albany's city fathers had not budged an inch. At one point it appeared there had been a public relations triumph. King and Ralph Abernathy had gotten themselves arrested and opted to spend forty-five days in jail rather than pay fines of $278 each. New York's Governor Nelson Rockefeller urged U.S. Attorney General Bobby Kennedy to "take immediate action to insure the physical safety" of King, and President John F. Kennedy himself asked for a full report. But suddenly King and Abernathy were released. Chief Pritchett announced that an anonymous "well-dressed Negro man" had appeared and paid the fines, and King and Abernathy were more or less kicked out of jail—against their will.

"This is the first time that I'm out of jail and not happy to be out," King said.

"Now they don't have a martyr," crowed Albany Mayor Asa Kelley.

The 3,000 words I had sent in, with 500 more filed after my conversation with Joe Carter, were finally distilled down to 300. The story began:

> The worst thing that happened to the Rev. Martin Luther King last week was getting out of jail.

Whether an anonymous bail payer actually existed was not known. It was all very suspicious. But Pritchett and Albany's city fathers had played it smart. The Albany Movement, finally, ran out of steam, its participants and its funds exhausted. King had picked the wrong town and the wrong police chief adversary to make his first big play. That was the sum of *Newsweek*'s final story. I had learned a good lesson covering that story—to try to say what it all added up to. And King had learned a lesson, too. He would not make the Albany mistake again.

As a kind of bonus for my Albany reporting, I soon received notes from both Chief Pritchett and from the NAACP's Ruby Hurley congratulating me on my objectivity. I was passionately committed to justice for Negroes, but I was proud to be considered fair and objective in my work. I typed up distillations of those notes and put them on two sides of a card, and used them to good effect in coming events when people on both sides were reluctant to talk to me.

It was clear that I would be using this card a lot, that the civil rights war was expanding on several fronts and I would be there, living on the road, calling home at night to talk to my wife and boys, going home on Fridays after the magazine closed—unless there was a crisis—to get a change of clothes and get back in touch with my family. We packed a lot into those weekends—playing, cooking, going to lakes and all-you-can-eat fried chicken and catfish joints—and when I left on Monday, to go back to the front, as it were, I always felt sad to be leaving but lucky to feel engaged in both places—work and home.

Week by eventful week, I was becoming more deeply immersed in an often violent racial struggle that would for the next few years consume all of my passion and energy and keep submerged the demons of shame, self-doubt, and anger that lurked beneath my tough-guy exterior. I had no time to think about myself or my problems, nor any inclination to do so. I made a duty call to my mother every week but, except for that, long stretches would go by when I didn't think of her at all, or of my feelings of being different and not good enough or tough enough to cut the mustard. There was a festering contradiction between who I truly was and who I was trying to prove to the world that I was, but I had no inkling that a day of reckoning would come about this. For the next stretch of time my personal doubts and confusions would be obscured, and appropriately so, by my involvement in the fight of black people to win their basic constitutional rights.

Many of the skirmishes in this enlarging war would be physically unsafe, but for me there was an emotional safety in the charged routine of my life as a reporter on this beat. It was oddly reminiscent of my life of discipline and routine in the orphanage. I flew from battleground to battleground, rented a car, checked into a motel, got up early each day, got cleaned up and dressed, had breakfast, went from person to place interviewing and observing, had a fast lunch, rushed back to work, had dinner (with a few bourbons tossed down), transcribed my notes, collapsed into bed, then rose next day and the next, doing it all over again until the end of the week when I wrote and "filed" my story to New York. This non-stop examination of outward events demanded my full, focused attention and suppressed any self-examination I might have otherwise done—a mixed blessing, as it would later turn out.

Chapter 9

A Brave or Crazy Man

THE FIRST TIME I saw James Meredith, on September 20, 1962, I thought, "This guy must be crazy." He was standing, flanked by two officials of the U.S. government, in the registrar's office of the University of Mississippi, trying to become the first Negro in history to attend school there. Meredith was five feet, six inches tall, weighed 130 pounds, and had long girlish eyelashes, setting off doe-like eyes, and a delicate little ebony face. He was meticulously dressed in a brown suit, white shirt, and red tie and carried a brown leather briefcase. He was as still as a stone, even though the governor of Mississippi himself, backed by armed men, was there to deny him enrollment.

Meredith had decided, all on his own, without the backing of any organization or court order, to become the first Negro to get into Ole Miss, the most prideful, powerful, and stubbornly defended remaining bastion of segregation in the United States. So he was either very crazy—or very brave. Reason came down on the former probability, because the first Negro to try to get into Ole Miss two years earlier was immediately clapped into the state insane asylum and then run out of the state, and the second, who tried to get into Mississippi State, was sent to Parchman State Penitentiary for seven years on a trumped-up charge of "receiving stolen goods:" five sacks of chicken feed valued at less than twenty-five dollars.

Meredith was a married twenty-nine-year-old Air Force veteran with a three-year-old son. He was the seventh of fourteen children of a proud farmer who had saved enough money as a tenant to buy an eighty-four-acre farm near the small town of Kosciusko, Mississippi—the first Negro in history to own a farm in Attala County. Meredith's mother worked in the local Negro school cafeteria. His parents were proud enough to believe that the lowest thing a Negro woman could do was work in a white woman's kitchen and take care of her children. "Death is preferred to indignity," Cap Meredith told his children. As a boy, Meredith walked four miles to school every day and watched the school bus come by driving white children to their segregated school. By the time he was out of high school, Meredith had decided, he later told me, that he had a "divine mission" to crack the system of "white supremacy" so that other Negroes would be emboldened to follow. He very early believed that he was possessed of "superhuman powers." He said he joined the Air Force to further his education and to save money for this mission. After nine years, including service in Japan, he left the Air Force and entered the Jackson State College for Negroes.

He had already decided it was his constitutional right to go to Ole Miss, and the day after JFK was inaugurated as president, January 20, 1961, Meredith wrote to the Ole Miss registrar asking for an application. The registrar sent him the blank form with a letter saying, "We are very pleased to know of your interest in becoming a member of our student body."

Meredith filled this out and returned it, asking to be registered for the upcoming February semester, along with a ten-dollar room deposit, and now saying in a cover letter that "I am an American—Mississippi—Negro citizen." Four days later he got a telegram from the registrar saying that "for your information and guidance it has been found necessary to discontinue consideration of all applications for admission or registration for the second semester which were received after Jan. 15. We must advise you not to appear for registration."

Meredith then went to see Medgar Evers, head of the Mississippi NAACP, who referred him to Constance Baker Motley, the lawyer who headed the NAACP's Legal Defense and Education Fund in New York. She filed suit in federal court demanding Meredith's admission. Thus began a long dance by Mississippi to delay, avoid, confuse, or defeat federal law suits filed by the NAACP on Meredith's behalf.

On June 25, 1962, in New Orleans, the Fifth Circuit Court of Appeals ordered Meredith admitted, and on September 3—after another round of feints and delays on the part of Governor Ross Barnett and the Mississippi legislature—the judges declared Barnett and the trustees in contempt of court. On September 13 Barnett, citing the Tenth Amendment's provision that "powers not specifically delegated to the Federal government are reserved to the several states," declared he was "interposing" himself between Mississippi and the federal government, because of "this unwarranted, illegal and arbitrary usurpation of power."

He then made a statewide radio and television address and declared that the Meredith threat "is our greatest crisis since the War Between the States." He vowed that "no school in Mississippi will be integrated while I am your governor." He threatened to close all state schools, including Ole Miss, rather than give in to federal authority, and he called on all state officials to go to jail rather than submit. "If there be any official who is not prepared to suffer imprisonment for this righteous cause, I ask him now to submit his resignation.... The day of expediency has past. We must either submit to the unlawful dictates of the Federal Government or stand up like men and tell them 'Never!'"

Barnett was a tall, ponderous Uriah Heep figure with sagging shoulders and parchment-pale skin. He was thin-lipped with a large sharp nose, thick graying eyebrows, and oiled gray hair. He invariably dressed in a funereal black suit, white shirt, and black tie. A former personal injury lawyer, he had been elected two years earlier by painting the sitting governor, James P. Coleman, as the worst thing you could call a Mississippi politician in this over-heated racial atmosphere—a moderate.

Among knowing journalists, Barnett had a reputation for being somewhat of a buffoon. He once addressed a lunch of B'nai B'rith members in Jackson as "you fine Christian gentleman," and he had walked into the spinning propeller of his campaign plane and injured a shoulder. During the Kennedy–Nixon presidential debates in 1960 there was a headline-making exchange about what the U.S. posture should be over China threatening the islands of Matsui and Quemoy to intimidate Taiwan. Barnett's PR man thought the governor should weigh in.

"What do you think we should do about Matsui and Quemoy?" he asked Barnett.

"I guess we can find a place for them over in the Fish and Game Commission," the governor said.

His clownish reputation aside, Barnett was a venomous and dedicated segregationist. He once said that "God made niggers black because they are so mean and evil."

In 1954, following the Supreme Court's *Brown v. Board of Education* ruling that separate schools were not equal, Mississippi was the birthplace of the White Citizens Council, whose purpose was to "promote the advantages of segregation and the dangers of integration." A kind of middle-class KKK, the Citizens Council quickly grew to 250 chapters across the South and 60,000 dues-paying members. Barnett was a dedicated member, and his chief adviser on matters racial was the man who founded the Citizens Council, William J. (Mustache Bill) Simmons of Greenwood, Mississippi.

In mid-September, Barnett pressured Ole Miss's trustees, who were beginning to waver under the federal judiciary's threat of contempt fines and possible jail for not registering Meredith, into ceding their authority and appointing him special registrar. He told a cheering state legislature on September 17 that "I'm going to keep the faith in order that we may preserve the great Christian ideals and principles that our forefathers handed down to us."

It was clear that white Mississippi's resistance—and the resistance of other Southern states—was not about the classroom. It was about the bedroom. And its obsession about "racial purity" was not that at all. It was, I had come to believe, the white Southern male's profound fear of the black man's alleged animal-like sexual potency. All through the white Southern male culture, dating to my own childhood and well back surely, were strewn jokes about the size of the Negro penis—and his insatiable sexual appetite. I had heard dozens of these jokes—and to my later chagrin, had told them myself.

The walls of school segregation had by now been breached in every other Southern state where Negroes had applied. Transportation services, lunch counters, and hotels had been integrated in many places, pursuant to new federal laws, but Mississippi had not budged one inch. When the Freedom Riders arrived in Jackson, after being beaten in Alabama and then promised protection in Mississippi, they were promptly jailed. When a group of black students from Jackson State and the private Tougaloo College attempted to sit in at Jackson five-and-dime stores in 1960, they were beaten, showered with catsup while cops looked on—and then arrested and jailed.

Mississippi was last in everything else—per capita income, education, economic growth, life expectancy, infant mortality, and poverty—but it was first in the lynching, beating, burning, bombing, and jailing of the rare impudent Negro who dared to challenge the system. It was also first in organized, state-funded opposition to integration.

Many blacks who could get out did so by taking the train from Memphis to the North, Chicago particularly, was the way out for thousands of Negroes seeking better work and more rights. And Memphis was the way in, too, for those returning or coming to the brutal segregated life of Mississippi. Negroes had a joke about it: When a Chicago Negro minister got the call to go preach in Mississippi he fell to his knees and asked God if he would go with him.

"Well, I'll go as far as Memphis," God said.

Soon after the *Brown v. Board of Education* ruling, the state of Mississippi formed and funded a "Sovereignty Commission" to spy on civil right organizations, intimidate white integration sympathizers (if any could be found), and to work with sheriffs and cops to collect and spread information on "outside agitators" and Mississippi Negroes who joined the NAACP or otherwise strayed beyond their assigned roles. Whatever was required would be done to protect "our Southern way of life."

No place represented the romanticized, glorious white history of Mississippi, its misty-eyed nostalgia and defiant pride, like its beloved Ole Miss. Not for nothing were Ole Miss's sports teams nicknamed "Rebels." Thus the whole force and weight of Mississippi, its real power as well as its stubborn pride, were arrayed to prevent Meredith from fulfilling his "divine mission." That included Mississippi's press. Mississippi had a half-dozen small newspapers that tried to behave responsibly, calling on the state in editorials to follow the rule of law in the Meredith case. Their editors were threatened. Their advertisers deserted them and circulation plummeted. At the height of the fever, Hodding Carter III, editor of the *Greenville Delta Democrat*, and his father and brother barricaded themselves in their house with guns. Carter had merely written an editorial calling for law and order. But most of Mississippi's newspapers were blatantly racist, the worst being the virulent *Jackson Clarion-Ledger*, which ran a regular racist cartoon on its front page.

Now, here to challenge all of it and all of them, on a crisp fall afternoon in Oxford, home of the recently buried William Faulkner, stood the tiny, almost effete-looking James Meredith, about as unlikely a candidate for this seeming suicide mission as could be imagined. Alone at first in his quixotic quest, he now had a powerfully ally, the United States government, whose will would be expressed through the Fifth Circuit Court of Appeals in New Orleans and through three improbable figures: the attorney general, Bobby Kennedy; the head of his civil rights division, a slight, pale, and soft-spoken man named Burke Marshall; and Marshall's chief deputy, a blue-eyed, square-jawed, six-foot, two-inch Irish Republican from Wisconsin, John Doar.

On that day, Meredith was flanked on one side by the lanky and laconic Doar and on the other by John J. P. McShane, a ruddy-faced Irishman from New York who was chief deputy U.S. marshal. They had accompanied Meredith to Oxford on a Cessna 220 from New Orleans, where the Fifth Circuit had made its final ruling, and were armed with the court order mandating his admission. I stood behind him with Claude Sitton, a guy from AP, and several reporters from Mississippi newspapers.

I had walked across the Illinois Central Railroad overpass leading onto the campus and through what was called the Grove, a 500-yard long oval of oaks and elms at the entrance of which was a huge statue of a Confederate soldier. The oval was ringed by old brick classroom buildings and at its head was the Lyceum (locally pronounced Li-SEE-um), the white-columned pink brick administration building put up when Ole Miss was started 114 years earlier. A large crowd of students had been waiting since mid-morning. Some of them tried to pull down the American flag from the pole in front of the Lyceum before student leaders stopped them. At 4 P.M. seventy-five State Highway patrolmen with pistols on their sides arrived in a motorcade and cleared a path in the crowd, and at 4:30 Meredith rolled onto the campus in a green-and-white Plymouth, tailed by another carload of marshals. The crowd booed loudly, and several students yelled, "Go home, nigger."

As we entered the Center for Continuation Studies Building through a rear door, there awaited Barnett, seated in a chair, a grim-faced retinue of aides and Highway Patrolman behind him. He then read a proclamation saying, "You, James H. Meredith, are hereby refused admission as a student at the University of Mississippi." As he spoke, he looked not at Meredith but at Doar and McShane. Nothing more was said and the men left, knowing—as Barnett himself knew—that they would be back. As Burke Marshall had made plainly clear before the Fifth Circuit, "There is no question that the order of this court is going to be carried out. There is no question but that the executive branch of the government will use whatever force—physical force if that is required—to enforce the order of the court. Mr. Meredith not only had the right to go in and be registered but he also has the right to remain there as a student."

The day after Meredith's first attempt, the *Meridian Star* editorialized, "Integrationists, according to their own statements, will never be satisfied with token integration. Massive integration will mean future intermarriage. Intermarriage in the South, where we are so evenly divided white and colored, means the end of both races, and the emergence of a tribe of mongrels."

Meredith's second stand took place not in Oxford, but in Jackson on September 25, where he—again with Doar and McShane at his side—decided to try to register directly with the thirteen-man university board of trustees in their office in the gray marble E. J. Woolfolk State Office Building across from the capitol. Word had gotten out that Meredith was coming, and when he arrived in another little green government Plymouth, an angry crowd of 500 whites lined the sidewalk, again yelling, "Go home, nigger" and other epithets. I followed Doar, McShane, and Meredith into the elevator, along with Claude Sitton, and up we went to the tenth floor. At the end of the corridor stood Barnett blocking the trustees' door.

Doar firmly asked him to step aside and let Meredith register pursuant to the final court order.

"I politely refuse," said Barnett.

"And we politely leave," said Doar.

Someone asked Barnett if he would go to jail himself rather than submit to federal authority, as he had ordered other state officials to do.

"Well, I would if I could," he said—another one of his nonsensical utterances.

The next day, September 26, Doar and McShane decided to go back to Oxford with Meredith. They flew into Oxford again from New Orleans, where a large crowd of marshals, local sheriffs and cops, newsmen, and angry citizens awaited at the little airport. A half-mile from the campus, a roadblock had been set up at the intersection of Fifth Street and University Avenue, behind which stood Lieutenant Governor Paul Johnson, a sour-looking man in a snap-brim hat, and fifty heavily armed state highway patrolmen in gas masks. Governor Barnett's plane had been turned back because of bad weather, and it was left to Johnson to refuse the federal force once again. A crowd of 2,500, including many students, had gathered at the roadblock. Two hundred police and sheriff's deputies carrying clubs surrounded the campus.

Violence was definitely in the air. Johnson, obviously alarmed at the situation, took a bullhorn from a highway patrolman and said, "I plead with you to return to the campus. We have a tense situation and it is dangerous for you to be here. Someone could easily be killed, and it could be an innocent party. If you want to have the nigger in Ole Miss, just stay where you are."

I was standing directly behind Meredith, who was dressed as usual in a suit, tie, and white shirt and was carrying his ever-present briefcase. He stood as calm and expressionless as if he were waiting in line to get into a movie theater. McShane tried to hand Johnson papers ordering Meredith's admission; Johnson just let them fall to the ground.

"Governor, we need to go to the campus now and register Mr. Meredith," McShane said.

Johnson then took Barnett's proclamation from his pocket and read it. It cited the Tenth Amendment, which says that powers not specifically delegated to the federal government are reserved to the states, and it said in part that "I do hereby proclaim that the operation of the public schools, universities and colleges of the State of Mississippi is vested in the duly elected and appointed officials to uphold and enforces the laws duly and legally enacted by the Legislature of the State of Mississippi, regardless of this unwarranted, illegal and arbitrary usurpation of powers; and to interpose the State Sovereignty and themselves between the people of the State and any body politic seeking to usurp such power." McShane's face turned redder, and he then moved up and tried to physically push Johnson aside. The highway patrolmen gathered around the lieutenant governor pushed back. It was a tense moment, until McShane finally said, "Let's go," and the federal party left, driving north to the Millington Air Force Base near Memphis, Tennessee.

The next day, Thursday, September 27, the Meredith party drove at high speed toward Oxford from Memphis, this time with a force of fifty marshals carrying guns and tear gas. A government plane was overhead maintaining contact with Bobby Kennedy in Washington. At Oxford another huge angry crowd awaited. With the threat of violence clearly high, Kennedy ordered the Meredith party to turn back again.

During a Friday conversation with Bobby Kennedy, Barnett, having run out of wiggle room, finally accepted the inevitable. He agreed that Meredith would be allowed to slip onto the campus quietly on Sunday and be registered Monday morning. Barnett told Kennedy that it would be better to bring Meredith in on Sunday, since it would be relatively quiet on campus. During the conversation, he pleaded with Kennedy to order the federal marshals to pull a gun on him at Oxford, to force him to stand aside for the television cameras and save just a little of his face. "I've got to have a show of force," he said. Kennedy coolly told him no. At midnight Saturday, President Kennedy federalized the Mississippi National Guard and sent regular Army troops to wait in Memphis.

I was running back and forth between Jackson and Oxford as the story shifted, a three-hour drive each way, which only added to my fatigue and tension. In Oxford, I was staying at the rundown, one-story, brick Ole Miss Motel on a slope at the edge of town. It was run by a tall, belligerent segregationist named R. J.

(Rusty) Nail. He didn't say so straight out, but based on a few hints, Sitton and I assumed he was a proud member of the Klan. He did say that though he was accepting the business of Yankee reporters, this would not be a healthy place for people like us to be when the forces ready to act against Meredith and the hated Kennedys began to have their say. When the moment of truth arrived, he said, they would be arriving from all over the South, armed and ready. Meantime, he said, he had whiskey for sale, and I bought a fifth of Old Hickory.

As usual I asked for a room near the front adjoining Sitton's. We were somewhat dismayed to see that the windows were not big enough to escape through. I noticed immediately a sour smell which I knew to be a sign that the air-conditioning filter had not been changed in a long time. I had occasional asthma and the bitter air affected my breathing and my sleep—adding again to my escalating tense weariness.

I got up groggy Sunday morning, September 30, and walked into the downtown area with Claude. There were a lot of cars and pickup trucks with Tennessee, Louisiana, Alabama, Georgia, and even Texas plates parked around town. By the time I had country ham, eggs, grits, buttermilk biscuits, and three cups of strong coffee in Faulkner's booth at the Mansion Inn and walked across the overpass in the cool fall morning under a blue sky and onto the campus, a crowd was already forming. Word had obviously gotten out that Meredith was coming that day—a word no doubt deliberately leaked by Barnett and/or his Citizens Council advisers. The resistance fighters arriving were rough-looking Snopesian characters, many with angry faces and sagging bellies, in a variety of work clothes. They definitely were not students, and I wondered with Claude how many pistols, shotguns, and rifles were in the cars and pick-ups we had seen on the streets. They had been summoned to duty by no less an authority than the governor of Mississippi himself—through his defiant state-ments—and so here they were massing, ready to repel the "nig-ger" and his infidel protectors.

By this time, keen to provide all of the detail that a *Newsweek* story demanded, I was carrying two small Audubon books that included the illustrated names of the birds, trees, and flowers of the South, and I had noted as I arrived in Oxford that the luxuri-ant oaks and maples in the countryside were beginning to turn and sage was beginning to color in the fields. I didn't know exactly when Meredith was coming, but coming he was. The final showdown was at hand.

Two hundred booing spectators were waiting as a small gov-ernment plane carrying James Meredith and Justice Department officials landed at the tiny Oxford airport that afternoon and headed down Highway 6 toward the campus. Roadside fields glowed yellow with goldenrod. On a nearby hill a small boy stood waving a Confederate flag. More than 300 U.S. marshals had already entered the campus in cars and Army trucks and set up a command post in the Lyceum. Meredith was rushed onto the campus and ushered quietly into a sparsely furnished two-room suite on the second floor of the Baxter Hall dormitory. There were cots set up for eight marshals who would provide him round-the-clock protection.

An historic event imminent, with mass violence almost cer-tain, *Newsweek* had geared up for a cover story. My Atlanta bureau colleague Joe Cumming would come in to help with the reporting, and Peter Goldman, the national affairs writer usually assigned to boil down my civil rights files, would fly down from New York to get the feel and look of the place. Goldman was a sensitive and felicitous writer who always distilled my long and sometimes disconnected reports into clear and poetical prose. He was originally from St. Louis but, with his slight figure, pale face, unruly light hair, and nasal voice, he looked and sounded like a prototypical New Yorker—not the kind of instantly recognizable Yankee, frankly, I wanted to have by my side when the rednecks erupted. After lunch I got into my Hertz car and drove the seventy-five miles over to Memphis to pick him up. I brought him up to date on the two-hour drive back.

We could see a huge mob surging back and forth but moving toward the Lyceum as we drove across the railroad overpass onto the campus. A two-deep wall of marshals had formed in the driveway in front of the Lyceum's white columns. Rocks and bottles were flying and the marshals, wearing gas masks, helmets, and orange vests with pockets for tear gas canisters, were rapidly firing tear gas shells into the crowd. Maddened screams and taunts rent the air.

"Welcome to Mississippi, Peter," I said.

I parked the car beside some bushes, got out, and told Peter to follow me. "If anybody comes up to us, let me do the talking," I said. It was clear as I ran that we were not going to be able to get into the Lyceum where the marshals and Justice operatives had set up their command post and where the Justice officials were on the phone with Bobby Kennedy in Washington. There were too many rocks and bottles flying and too much tear gas.

I led Peter as we ran weaving through the crowd and we ducked into the Science Building across the grove and into what appeared to be a lab classroom. We crouched beneath windows through which we could see the wild mob rampaging in front of us and hear the angry shouts:

"Kill the nigger!"

"Down with the goddamned Kennedys!"

"Hooray for Ole Ross."

Nightfall had come and by now the mob numbered 2,500. Peter and I could see little puffs of tear gas wafting through the trees as the maddened rabble let loose its fury. The sickly sweet smell of the tear gas filled the air, stinging our eyes. The rioters seemed immune to its effects as they rushed forward hurling rocks, bottles, pieces of concrete, and steel rods—anything that could be found or torn loose.

"You goddamned Communists," one screamed.

"You nigger lovers go to hell," yelled another.

Three neatly dressed young men walked into the room where we kneeled looking out the windows. I took them to be students. They seemed to know their way around.

"Anybody in here with you?" one of them asked.

"Naw. Just us chickens," I said in my most elongated Southern drawl. They harvested several bottles of some kind of liquids, and quietly left. Probably acid to throw at the marshals, I told Peter.

Outside, the badly outnumbered and outgunned marshals were fighting for their lives. They crouched now behind their cars as bullets, projectiles, and glass rained around them. We could hear gunshots through the melee. At 9 P.M. we saw a tall wild-eyed man in a Stetson hat mount the Confederate statue at the top of the grove and encourage the rioters. This was retired Army General Edwin Walker, who had been recently called back from Germany by President Kennedy for making incendiary remarks that increased East–West tensions. Five years before this night, he had commanded troops sent to Little Rock by Eisenhower.

"This time I am on the right side," he shouted. "Don't let up now," he exhorted the mob from his perch. "You may lose this battle but you will have to be heard. You must be prepared for possible death. If you are not, go home now."

The Mississippi state troopers, whose protective service Barnett had promised, had retreated to their cars behind the Lyceum and did nothing to stop the violence. Some of them sneeringly referred to the marshals as "Kennedy's Coon Clan." Then I watched stunned and angry as they drove in a slow line—I counted sixty-eight cars in all—past our window and out of the campus, leaving the marshals on their own. The front entrance to the campus was now unguarded, and more rioters poured in, armed with .22 squirrel guns, high-powered rifles, shotguns, knives, clubs, and blackjacks.

"Give us the nigger and we'll quit," one of the rioters shouted at the marshals.

During a lull in the battle I signaled Peter to follow me. I was going to make a run for the Lyceum. We dashed across the grove, now profusely littered with empty tear gas shells, rocks, and bottles, onto the porch of the Lyceum and into the building. The lobby was jammed with marshals, Justice officials, and a few reporters. Associated Press reporter Bill Grider lay on the floor bleeding. He had gone outside and been hit in the back by a shotgun.

At 9:30 P.M., an old red fire truck commandeered by the rioters rumbled across the Grove with students and outsiders arrayed behind it in a charge that broke past the marshals' line and hit a tree. The driver was rescued by the rioters, sobbing, and then came a bulldozer, stolen from a nearby construction site, but it also hit a tree.

"What we need is a machine gun," one of the rioters cried. Another, armed with a shotgun, fired on a squad of marshals on the right flank of their line, hitting Marshal Gene Same of Indiana in the neck. He bled almost to death before a local doctor could be convoyed through the mob to treat him.

At 10 P.M., Deputy Attorney General Nick Katzenbach, who had accompanied Meredith to the campus, called Kennedy and said, "For God's sake, we need those troops." They arrived on campus soon, a hometown National Guard cavalry troop commanded by blue-eyed Captain Murry Falkner, William Faulkner's nephew. (The nephew's branch of the family spelled their name without the "u.") Shortly after, as the riot wore on, his wrist was cracked by a brick. Just before midnight, Barnett, urged by his Citizens Council advisers, went on statewide radio again and said, "I call on all Mississippians to keep the faith and courage. We will never surrender."

The besieged Lyceum looked like a scene out of *Gone with the Wind*. Wounded and wearied marshals lay everywhere on the bloodied floor, smoking cigarettes, drinking coffee, and eating franks and sauerkraut brought in through the mob. Snipers among the rabble had opened fire from buildings at the top of the grove. Right after 1 A.M., a border patrolman staggered in, shot in the leg.

I opened the front door of the Lyceum and went out onto the porch for a better view of the battle. Suddenly I heard successive splatting noises right behind me. I looked over my right shoulder and saw four bullet holes stitched into the white wood column behind me, six inches from my head. I went back inside and angrily announced, "If I was James Meredith, I wouldn't go to school with these people." (That quote appeared next week in *Time* magazine, attributed to a marshal.)

The marshals were about to run out of tear gas when a red truck pulled up with a new supply. Marshals had had to club a Mississippi state cop to get it through. By now the rioters were hurling Molotov cocktails—Coke and Pepsi bottles filled with gasoline. We were told that Meredith, meanwhile, had retired at 10 P.M., guarded by forty marshals, and that all was quiet where he was secured. At 2:30, the marshals were running dangerously low on tear gas again. McShane, who was in charge of them, called Washington for permission to return fire with sidearms, but Bobby Kennedy said no.

Now the rioters began setting cars on fire. Using huge stones, they also set up roadblocks at the campus entrance and when rescue trucks tried to go around them they were bombarded with a hail of rocks, bottles, and Molotov cocktails. The state troopers who had left the battlefield lounged outside the gate, watching and doing nothing.

At 4 A.M., 162 Army jeeps and trucks loaded with soldiers arrived to reinforce the marshals. They took up positions in front of the Lyceum, M-14 rifles at their sides. Shortly after 5 A.M. they formed a solid line with the marshals and moved forward through the Grove, driving the remaining 200 or so rioters from the campus and across the overpass. As the first rays of sun rose pink across the littered Grove, the horn of one of the burning cars gave off a ghostly wail and beyond the entrance came the chant "Two, four, six, eight, we don't want to integrate."

I walked bleary-eyed and sick with revulsion off the campus at 6. A.M., still running on pure adrenaline. I suddenly realized that though I should probably have been scared, I wasn't. I was too angry, and too pumped up. As I came off the campus and reached the corner of Lamar Street and University Avenue, I saw a crowd gathered, screaming and pitching bottles at jeeploads of soldiers hurrying to the campus. State patrolmen leaned languidly against their cars. A platoon of military police soon arrived, to be greeted by missiles and a fifty-five-gallon oil drum tossed onto a windshield from a balcony. There were a few Negroes among the MP's.

"Why'd they have to send the niggers in here?" growled one protester. Soon the troops were firing live ammunition over the rioters' heads into the trees, and they were dispersed. The National Guardsmen led thirty captives onto the campus and into the Lyceum. The prize catch was General Walker, his arrest ordered by Katzenbach. He was spotted near the town square, unshaven and haggard but still wearing his Stetson. "I appear," he said ruefully after being questioned in the Lyceum, "to be taken in custody." He was charged with insurrection, held on $500,000 bail, and later in the week sent to Springfield, Missouri, for psychiatric examination.

I lurched back to the Ole Miss Motel, and stopped at the front office to see if I had any phone messages.

"So, they forced the little nigger in, did they?" asked Rusty Nail.

"Yep, he's an Ole Miss Rebel now," I said.

"He won't last long," Nail said.

I showered, shaved, changed clothes, and headed back toward the campus. I hadn't eaten for twenty-four hours but I wasn't hungry. The downtown mob had been dispersed and driven off. As I crossed the overpass, a slack-bellied Mississippi highway patrolman whom I had gotten to know slightly was leaning against the guardrail, smoking a cigar.

"Where you going, Mister *Newsweek*?"

"Over to the Ly-See-um," I drawled. "Meredith is holding a press conference."

"If that ain't the goddamndest thing I ever heard of," he said with disgust, "a nigger holding a press conference."

Meredith entered the Lyceum under heavy guard at 7:30 A.M., wearing a blue-gray suit and carrying his briefcase. He looked as if he had dressed for a business meeting, and his impassive face revealed not the slightest emotion. Actually he looked fresh and rested, while everybody else looked exhausted and frazzled. The school registrar silently handed him a form, which he signed without speaking. Moments later he walked across the campus to his first class (Colonial American history) in a knot of marshals.

"The blood is on your hands, nigger bastard," a white student screamed at him.

I was told that not a soul spoke to him in his class as he took notes in a looseleaf binder with marshals stationed outside the door. A one-sentence notice was tacked onto the Lyceum entrance. "Pursuant to the mandate of the federal courts, the orders for the registration of Meredith have been followed."

At mid-morning, Meredith sat behind a fold-up card table in the lobby of the Lyceum to meet the large press assemblage, dressed impeccably in the same suit, briefcase at his side. He said he had slept fitfully through the night, that he could hear the uproar, and gunshots, but was unaware of the full ferocity of the riot. And was he pleased?

"No," he said with a tight little smile. "This is not a happy occasion."

By Tuesday there were 14,000 Army troops bivouacked in tents on a hillside behind the campus. In New York, Gordon Manning had put researchers to work on Mississippi and came up with a startling fact, which was the lead in our cover story:

In the fall of 1862, Gen. U.S. Grant had driven deep into Mississippi. By December Grant's federal troops had reached the young and prosperous town of Oxford. They billeted on the 14-year-old campus of the University of Mississippi—then almost deserted by the exodus of students to the Confederate Army. Grant's troops settled in at Oxford until Christmas Day; their boots echoed in the town square, and their wounded lay ... in the University's Lyceum building. Almost exactly 100 years after Grant's invasion, the tramp of federal boots was heard once again in the streets of the tiny college town.

School attendance was still off from the accustomed 5,000 to 1,200 two days after the riot when Nick Katzenbach, the balding deputy attorney general, who had accompanied Meredith on campus, announced the federal casualties from the all-night rampage: 168 marshals, more than a third of the total force, were injured, twenty-nine with gunshot wounds. A half-dozen had acid burns. Two hundred soldiers were hurt.

I had already been informed that Monday, after daylight came and the smoke cleared in the Grove, passersby found the body of red-headed Agence France-Presse reporter Paul Guihard in a clump of bushes. He had been shot in the back. There was one other death: a white Oxford repairman who, standing at the perimeter of the riot, was hit in the head, probably by a stray bullet.

Downtown, the federalized Mississippi National Guard ringed the courthouse, and anger still ran high. Oxford was under military lockdown. Guardsmen and Army troops set up roadblocks and searched the trunks of cars for weapons. Next to the courthouse I saw what I thought was an ironic sight: Oxford native Captain Murry Falkner standing there with a grim look on his clean face, holding a gun on his fellow townsmen, some of them undoubtedly his childhood schoolmates and family acquaintances.

Peter Goldman flew back to New York on Tuesday, and most of the visiting media departed, too. The *New York Times*, meanwhile, had sent a feature writer down to write sidebars. A day after he arrived, Rusty Nail called Sitton into his office and said, "You'd better get that guy the hell out of here. He must be crazy." He had asked Nail to fix him up with one of the Negro maids—an act of pure insanity in Mississippi in 1962. Claude had him back on a plane to New York that afternoon. I stayed around doing more interviews and on Thursday drove back to Jackson and checked back into the Sun 'N' Sand motel. Jackson's Western Union, where I filed my copy to New York, stayed open all night. I had two drinks, went out to Le Fleur's on the edge of town for some crawfish bisque, came back and sat down facing my Lettera

22 portable sick with fatigue and tension. I had filled two entire notebooks with hastily scribbled facts, observations, and quotes, and the stomach-grinding task at hand was to discard the unimportant and render the rest into comprehensible English. I sat there until daybreak, smoking Camels and drinking coffee, wrote twenty pages of double-spaced copy, and drove them down to the Western Union on Capitol Street. Peter Goldman would put it all together Friday and the magazine would be assembled and sent to the printer Saturday night.

Then I drove back to Ole Miss. By the weekend Meredith was safe enough to walk to class accompanied by just two marshals, one in front, one behind. Soldiers, though, were still camped in tents on a hill behind his dorm. On the way to the library Friday, a coed shouted as he passed: "Why doesn't somebody kill him?"

That week, John F. Kennedy made a nationwide address to explain why he had sent the troops. "Americans are free to disagree with the law, but not to disobey it," he said, " for we are a government of laws, and not of men. And no man, however prominent or powerful, and no mob, however unruly or contentious, is entitled to defy a court of law."

This was the first riot I had seen and been in the middle of. And as I flew home for the weekend Saturday, carrying in my suitcase three of the still-pungent tear gas shells I had picked up in the Grove, I couldn't get it out of my mind—the tear gas, the bullets, Meredith's impassive face, the roiling mob, the marshals, Mississippi state cops driving sixty-eight cars off the campus. As it progressed the riot seemed to develop the energy of a cyclone, sweeping up everybody in its path and turning them into maddened animals. I had seen some bad things up to then in my native South, but nothing approaching this. I for some reason remembered seeing *The Birth of a Nation* when I was a small boy (my Aunt Belle took me, the first movie I ever saw), and the frightening sight of a Klan mob pulling a black man from a jail and lynching him. A mob, obviously, was capable of doing things an individual wouldn't do, although there were on Mississippi's sorry record plenty of savage individual murders and lynchings. I was ashamed as well as angry. These were my fellow Southerners. We came from the same gene pool—Irish and Scotch and English—and most of us from the same impoverished past. But I had identified not with them, but with Meredith, the black interloper.

When I got back to Ole Miss the next week, Meredith was able to get to class alone. The hottest steam seemed to have gone out of the white students. I had made friends with an Ole Miss history professor named Jim Silver, a craggy-faced transplanted Yankee who had been in Oxford for twenty-five years. He was the first person in either the faculty or the student body to befriend Meredith. He invited him to dinner at his two-story home on the campus one night and included me and Claude Sitton. Silver and I drank a lot of bourbon. Claude was with drinking as he was with everything: prudent. Meredith said he sometimes had a drink but he declined one now. "I have to keep my head clear at all times," he said. Meredith was cool and composed, almost monosyllabic in conversation. He said he didn't care what the white students did or said. "I don't waste any time thinking about them," he said. "I have too much studying to do."

Next day, I walked across the campus with him to the cafeteria. There were a few shouts and taunts. "Go home, nigger" was the favorite. There was a popping sound, like gunfire, behind us. Meredith didn't flinch. He just kept walking, his eyes straight ahead. Someone had exploded a cherry bomb on the sidewalk behind us. "That happens all the time," he said.

I asked him if he had made any friends on campus. He looked at me with a tight smile. "Haven't you noticed that they don't like me?" he said.

We went through the food line and he served himself the makings of a ham sandwich and got an iced tea. We sat at a table by ourselves. The white students ringed us several tables away, looking at us and whispering. He said he knew some of the students were sympathetic to him but that the few who had spoken to him had been ostracized by their schoolmates.

"You must have nerves of steel," I said.

"They don't bother me. They do what they do. I do what I have to do. I don't have time to get involved in what they are doing or thinking."

Then he explained to me his "divine responsibility to change the status of my people." He had had, he told me, a "master plan" since high school and was on a "divine mission" to see that no one trampled on his pride or on that of the "multitudes" who would follow his lead.

"Are you a good student?"

"About average, but I have to work hard to keep up."

"What are you planning to do after you graduate?"

"I don't know. I may stay here and go to law school. Or I may not stay at all, since my mission is accomplished," he said with his funny little laugh. Two months later I telephoned him on a Friday from Atlanta.

"Meredith here," he answered. He didn't like using his first name, or being called by it. He signed his letters "J. H. Meredith." I'd come to like Meredith, I realized, his quirky humor and certainly his personal bravery. I identified with him, too, since I also was an outsider who liked personal discipline, but didn't like authority, didn't like anybody telling me I couldn't do something. I didn't, however, think I'd have the nerve to do what he was doing. Again I thought he was either the bravest, or craziest, person I'd ever known. It was probably some of both. In any case, for whatever reason, he seemed to open up to me in a way he hadn't with other reporters. So I told him I'd like to come down and see how he was doing.

"Listen, I'm flying into Memphis and renting a car and getting to the campus about two o'clock. Where will I find you?" I said.

"Heh, heh, heh," he laughed his funny little laugh. "You'll see me. I'm not very hard to spot on this campus."

Meredith had by then brought his wife's automobile to the campus: an almost new white Thunderbird. He himself owned a blue Cadillac. This inflamed the white students even more. "Niggers" were supposed to drive old Chevies and Fords, not Thunderbirds and Cadillacs. Meredith, of course, had every right to have a fancy car and bring it to the campus, but I couldn't help asking him if in doing so he was being deliberately provocative, sticking his thumb in the eyes of the white students again.

"Heh, heh, heh. Actually I'm thinking of selling it and getting me a big black Lincoln Continental, just like Chancellor Williams," he said slyly. My admiration for him went up. He was totally fearless.

He said he was much encouraged by the mail he was getting: 200 letters a week from all over the country, most of them from sympathetic white people. He said his family was feeling a lot of pressure in Kosciusko, though. Their house had been shot into. Teachers in the local Negro school were told they would be fired if they were seen in Meredith's company when he visited his family.

One night that week Hal Holbrook brought his Mark Twain monologue to the school auditorium. Jim Silver arranged for tickets for himself, me, Claude Sitton, and Meredith. I sat beside Meredith as Holbrook, dressed in a white suit and smoking a cigar, acted Twain's speeches and writing, including a passage about Huck and Nigger Jim—a subtle condemnation of racism.

Many applauded Holbrook's performance, but as usual Meredith was silent and noncommittal.

Jim Silver wrote a long essay soon after the riot called "Mississippi: The Closed Society," which he presented in my old haunt of Asheville at a Historical Society convention. In it, he vividly described how Mississippians, including even its business and political elite, barricaded themselves behind their wounded pride, held delusions about their victimization by hostile outsiders, and absolutely did not believe themselves bound by the federal laws that the rest of the country peacefully followed.

The smell of the tear gas stayed in my nose and the maddened screams of the hate-filled mob played in my heads for weeks after I got back home to Atlanta. The anger lingered too. I was not so much angry at the rabble as at Mississippi's political, social, and religious leaders. The rabble were, well, the rabble—ignorant and struggling white folks. But the leaders, the members of what in Mississippi passed for the intellectually elite, most of the clergy and the press, knew better. And they had, either by their active encouragement, as in the case of the governor and the Citizens Council, or by their silent abdication of responsibility, actually licensed and encouraged the rioters. They had done their state a great disservice, and Mississippi would pay that price and carry that stigma for many years to come.

But as I thought about it more, I also realized that the Meredith crisis represented a singular bright moment in our country's history. The whole force of the United States—physical, legal, and moral—had been brought to bear to protect the constitutional right of one tiny black man. And that was something extraordinary to witness, and to be proud of as a citizen.

Chapter 10

Distress in the Delta

THE ELECTRICITY of impending violence was in the air at mid-morning on March 27, 1963, when Claude Sitton and I pulled up in front of the courthouse in the small Delta town of Greenwood, Mississippi. After Old Miss, I had been to several racial flashpoints in Alabama and Mississippi, places like Selma and Itta Bena, but Greenwood was shaping up as the next big battleground. Five hundred angry whites were massed on the lawn and the street around the LeFlore County Courthouse entrance waiting for a SNCC-led protest of 150 Negroes, all dressed in their Sunday best. They had been recruited and tutored by SNCC leaders Jim Forman and local field commander, Bob Moses, to go to the courthouse and try to register to vote. This day, they were actually protesting the firing of shotguns into the home of a Negro paperhanger, Dewey Green, who was himself active in the SNCC registration drive. Though it was only March, it was a steamy day. The acrid odor of pesticides sprayed onto the vast surrounding cotton fields permeated the air. The marchers were apprehensive, and with good reason. The Green shooting was the fifth such incident in three months. And just three days before, night-riding racists had burned down the SNCC office in Greenwood.

A sagging town of 23,000 on the banks of the Yazoo River, Greenwood was situated on the eastern edge of the vast, fertile, triangular Delta that ran as flat as a tabletop 200 miles between the Mississippi and Yazoo rivers from Vicksburg all the way to Memphis, a land of endless cotton and soybean fields, pastures and swamp stands of hardwood trees. Within the Delta's reaches, in eighteen counties, lived a half-million, mainly poor, voting-age Negroes, mostly cotton workers. Fewer than 5 percent were registered to vote. In five of thirteen counties that were more than 50 percent Negro, not a single one was registered. Another three counties each had one registered Negro voter, but none had actually voted. There were 5,000 Negro adults in Amite County, near the Louisiana line, but only one was registered, and no one knew who he was. In Greenwood itself, 95 percent of the whites eligible to vote were registered. But white intimidation was such that of 13,000 Negroes eligible to vote, only 600 had tried to register since SNCC came to town, and only 100 had made it.

SNCC's tiny cadre of guerrilla fighters was having a tough time making any headway. Their field general, Bob Moses, was a man so modest and soft-spoken that you had to lean forward to hear him speak. He was deeply committed to nonviolence. One of three children of a poor New York family, he was so intellectually gifted that he was awarded scholarships and eventually got a masters in philosophy from Harvard. He read Bertrand Russell, and Camus and Sartre in the original French. He connected with

SNCC during its formative months in 1960 and in 1961 quit his job as a math teacher at Horace Mann High School in New York and went to the Delta all by himself to establish a SNCC voter registration beachhead. He began wearing overalls and a white T-shirt—these would become the official SNCC uniform—to identify with working people. When he spoke at meetings, he did so from a seat in the audience, shunning the podium. He strongly believed local Negroes should develop their own leaders and control their own destiny.

A month earlier, Moses and two other SNCC operatives, Randolph Blackwell and Jimmy Travis, had been shot at as they drove away from the Greenwood SNCC office at 9:30 at night—their car sprayed with bullets from a passing Buick containing three white men in sunglasses. Travis, who was driving, was seriously wounded. There were no convictions, of course, in either this incident or the burning of their office, and Greenwood's mayor, Charles Sampson, an active Citizens Council member, said the arson and shooting were publicity stunts to provoke sympathy in the Northern media and to stir up more local Negro support.

Then in late February, a black business whose owner had tried to register to vote was firebombed, and when SNCC worker Sam Block suggested it was white retaliation, he was arrested and jailed on a charge of "uttering a public statement calculated to provoke a breach of the peace."

"Where you from, boy?" Sheriff John Ed Cothran challenged him in jail.

"I'm a native Mississippian," Block said.

"Yeah, but where are you from? I know all the niggers and their mammies around here?"

"Do you know any colored people?" Block asked.

The sheriff answered that by spitting in Block's face and then allowing him to be beaten up by a crowd of onlookers.

In nearby Clarksdale, a bomb shattered the drugstore owned by Aaron Henry, who was active in the NAACP and in the vote drive. Sheriff Marshall Hopkins ascribed the blast to a bolt of lightning.

The previous fall, LeFlore County's board of supervisors voted to cut off distribution of federally supplied surplus milk, rice, beans, and flour to the poor, who were overwhelmingly Negro, as obvious revenge against the voter drives. "LeFlore Stops The Moochers," the racist *Jackson Clarion-Ledger* exulted in its headline. Poverty and hunger were widespread. Many families ate only hoecake and syrup made from sugar and water. There was no milk at all. One night Claude and I went out to a shotgun shack to visit a fifty-seven-year-old Negro who took home ten dollars a week as a repairman in a plantation workshop to feed his wife and eleven children. They had just eaten a dinner of cornbread and potatoes and there was no milk for the children. But he said his main wish was to have "rights—freedom to speak, to have a voice. Not be condemned or nothing like that. You know, we don't have no voice out here."

White landowners had their own reprisal tactic for people like that. They kicked off their farms Negro families who had lived there for three generations—just for trying to get the right to vote. In addition to physical and economic intimidation, the state used an old law, the poll tax, which had been invented after Reconstruction to disenfranchise freed slaves. The poll tax was a fee required to vote. Most Negroes were too poor to pay it. For those who could afford it, Holmes County Sheriff Andrew Smith had an answer: He simply refused to allow Negroes to pay their poll tax. He vowed "no nigger will ever be allowed to vote as long as I am sheriff." In Mississippi, sheriffs were the tax collectors as well as the law enforcers—the chief protectors of the segregated system.

And Mississippi had in 1954, after *Brown v. Board of Education*, adopted a twenty-one-page law—aimed at blacks—requiring citizens to be able to read, write, and interpret any amendment to the U.S. Constitution, or any one of 285 paragraphs of the state constitution, in order to register to vote. This had to be done in the presence of the country registrar, whose power was supreme. Some counties posed impossible questions to Negro registrants, and joked about them: How many bubbles are there in a cake of soap? Who was the first president? What size shoes did he wear?

Such treatment was premised on the widely held belief, expressed by Mississippi's most revered white supremacist, James K. Vardeman, governor in the early 1900s, that "the Negro is a lying, lustful animal which no conceivable amount of training can transform into a useful citizen. Education would be a positive unkindness to him. Why squander money on his education when the only effect is to spoil a field hand and make an insolent cook?"

The other adored Mississippi icon of segregation was Theodore Bilbo, who served twice as governor and beginning in 1916 three terms as U.S. senator, a member of Klan No. 40 of Poplarville. He said that "the nigger is only 150 years removed from the jungles of Africa" and that "teaching a nigger to read and write is just ruining a good cotton-picker." Those who opposed his threat to filibuster in the Senate against repeal of the poll tax, he said, were mainly "New York Jew kikes that are fraternizing and socializing with the Negroes for selfish and political reasons." Negro voting, he said, was a step toward producing "a motley melee of miscegenated mongrels." He endorsed a plan to "repatriate" 12 million Negroes back to Africa.

Brain-washing the white population and intimidating economically or through violence the black population had been spectacularly successful. Led by Moses, SNCC had been trying to get Negroes registered to vote in the vast Mississippi Delta for more than two years. And now, here they were again, their small protest march—headed by Moses and Forman, who had come down from Atlanta to try to help—heading straight for the courthouse and the tense white mob just as Claude and I alighted from our Hertz car. I was as usual carrying my .35 Pentax camera, and I put it around my neck. I took pictures on civil rights stories because it was impossible to get local photographers to do so for *Newsweek*. They either hated *Newsweek* and other outside publications, or they were afraid they would be fired for shooting pictures for me. Besides, *Newsweek* paid me twenty-five dollars extra for any photograph of mine they printed, and there had already been quite a few.

White tempers had been rising for three days since this round of marches to the courthouse began. Sensing danger and being the prudent though fearless person he was, Claude had said, "Better leave the camera in the car, Karl."

"I gotta get some pictures," was my answer. Claude followed me and almost immediately as we moved forward, we were surrounded by a clot of whites muttering threats. One of them, a stubbled, red-faced man in a tan work shirt and dirty brogans, stepped in front of me.

"We could use that goddamned camera strap to hang you with. You better git out of Greenwood," he yelled in my face.

"Our grandfathers killed two-month-old Indian babies to take this country, and now they want us to give it away to the niggers," somebody said to Claude.

I turned and whispered to Claude, "I think I'll put the camera back in the car."

"Good idea," he said dryly.

By the time I returned, the Greenwood cops, armed with shotguns, had turned their one snarling police dog onto the marchers and were otherwise shoving them back into the street from the sidewalk. Moses had told friends he had a neurotic fear of dogs, but he didn't back off as a dog lunged at him and tore his trousers. The cops arrested and jailed both Moses and Forman on charges of disorderly conduct. I watched and took notes, but the local white officials could have cared less what the national press thought or wrote. As far as was known, nobody in Greenwood read *Newsweek* or the *New York Times*. Their paper was the local *Commonwealth*, which mostly refused to print anything at all about the demonstrations, and the virulently racist *Jackson Clarion-Ledger* and its sister paper, the *Daily News*, where the story about Greenwood was headlined "Agitators Spoil Another Quiet Little Town."

Next day, Forman, Moses, and the six other SNCC staff members who'd been arrested were handed maximum sentences of four months in jail and $200 fines. In the tiny smothering municipal courtroom I caught Forman's defiant eye as he sat in the witness chair, broken glasses in one hand and a bottle of Maalox in the other, as he testily defended his right to walk downtown. He gave me what I took to be an "I told you so" look of cynical resignation. He was unapologetic and defiant on the stand and said he had been roughed up in jail. He and Moses refused bail and said they would serve their sentences.

Supporting them was the dapper, fast-talking comedian from New York, Dick Gregory. Though he was a national celebrity, he had left the big money of the comedy circuit and network TV appearances to go South and lend aid and comfort to the movement. He had been attracted to the civil rights movement by the Freedom Rides and particularly admired and supported Bob Moses. Gregory wore a pointed goatee, sunglasses, a white shirt, a Countess Mara tie, and an tailored Italian suit, and adopted a mocking manner with local police.

The day of the sentencing, a couple of FBI agents were present filming as he led nineteen Negroes to the courthouse to register. When a cop moved and grabbed Gregory's arm, the police commissioner, B. A. (Buff) Hammond, moved in and said, "Wait a minute, wait a minute." He whispered something to the cop and Gregory was released.

"You're nothing but a bunch of dirty dogs," Gregory taunted.

"Look at those cops," he said loudly, pointing to a group of Greenwood police who were pushing the black registrants back. "They're a bunch of illiterates who couldn't even pass the test themselves."

Then he said to Hammond, "I don't know what you're getting so worked up about. You probably got more nigger blood in you than I have."

The local Negroes standing nearby listened to him frightened and astonished, knowing that such "uppity" talk by one of them would have meant a brutal beating or perhaps even a lynching. Standing two feet away, I cringed. I had never heard a Negro talk so brazenly to a cop in the South before, certainly not in Mississippi, and I was sure Gregory would pay an immediate painful price. Hammond's face flushed red, but he turned and walked away. Later I was told by a local businessman that the Citizen's Council had ordered cops to leave Gregory alone, fearing bad national publicity. Gregory's presence had drawn more national media than just the usual *Newsweek* and *New York Times*.

The night before, Gregory had spoken at a mass meeting in nearby Clarksdale, during which a tear gas canister was thrown into the crowded Baptist church. Some people started to run out. "I don't know what you're running for. I don't know why you're afraid to die, because you haven't got a damned thing to live for," he had said.

But Gregory didn't live in Mississippi, where there was plenty to be afraid of if you were black, or even white and on the wrong side of the system. In general, I felt safer in crowds than alone. I believed I could bluff and brazen myself out of danger in a crowd. I could talk and look just as tough as the bigots did. Except for the suit, clean-shaven cheeks, and evidence of a recent bath, I looked more or less like one of them—a crew-cut, 210-pound, belligerent, profane, reckless, cigar-smoking, hard-drinking, drawling redneck. I could talk the cracker talk and walk the plowboy walk—since I had actually plowed mules as a boy. I might read Dostoevsky and Conrad alone in my motel room, but I could tell dirty jokes—I knew hundreds of them—and use bucolic Southernisms, like "useless as socks on a rooster" and "happy as a dog with two dicks" with the best of the good ol' boys. I could sip martinis from long-stemmed crystal and eat caviar and soufflés in the Palm Court at the Plaza—and I could gulp Schlitz out of an icy bottle and eat pickled pigs' feet in a backroads beer joint with a naked woman on a calendar on the wall. I could exalt at the glory of Stravinsky and Beethoven—and hum along with the country ballads of Patsy Cline and Hank Williams. I could revel in the recorded speeches of Churchill and Roosevelt—and be fascinated by the incessant braying of pecker-wood radio evangelists shouting "Glory be to Jay-suss." I could play tennis in Wimbledon whites on clay courts—and pitch horse-shoes barefoot and barechested behind a cow barn. I could play contract bridge—and seven-card stud poker with the deuces wild. I could talk about my opposition to capital punishment and to hunting—and invite someone into an alley behind a bar to settle an argument with fists.

This was a complicated posture, of course, that I had carefully cultivated since coming out of the orphanage determined not to be perceived as weak, dependent, as a sissy, or as giving a good goddamn what anybody thought. I was an autodidactic, authority-hating, boss-pleasing, spit-in-your eye nonconformist—in a Brooks Brothers suit.

To most of those extents, I was the polar opposite of my traveling companion and friend, Claude Sitton. We were a kind of odd couple of journalism, together all the time covering stories, but very different, though we had similar backgrounds. Our publications were not competitive. We liked each other and shared common values. But mostly we traveled together for reasons of safety.

Claude was my age, of medium height with thin graying hair, always impeccably dressed, his spare clothes neatly arranged in an aluminum suitcase, and his papers and notes as neatly stacked as a corporate secretary's. My room looked always like a tornado had hit it. Claude had been on the civil rights beat since Little Rock in 1957. He was a fearless and tough reporter, but he operated as unobtrusively and carefully as possible. He'd had shatterproof glass installed in his spectacles, this after he'd been threatened and after a colleague of ours, Simmons Fentress, the *Time* Atlanta bureau chief, was thrown though a plate glass window during a violent sit-in we covered in McComb, Mississippi. Claude refused to sit with his back to the front door in Southern restaurants. When I teased him about being excessively cautious, he said, "Just prudent, Fleming, prudent."

My confrontational and even sometimes reckless behavior, my willingness to go toe-to-toe with local cops, sheriffs, and the rabble who menaced us often made him uncomfortable. Sometimes he moved away from me and pretended he didn't know me. He was tough-minded and relentless, but remained the very model of *New York Times* decorum, circumspection, and professional detachment. He watched his weight and had at most two drinks—and none if we were in a tense place. I ate prodigiously and drank with excessive defiance. He smoked moderately. I smoked three packs of unfiltered Camels a day. He cursed selectively. I did so relentlessly.

His prudence was well-founded, because being a reporter in those places at this time was dangerous. It was not by any means as perilous as being a SNCC operative, or a Negro citizen challenging the system in any way, but there was still every reason to be cautious. After all, Paul Guihard of Agence France-Presse, had been shot in the back and killed at Ole Miss, and another had been wounded by shotgun fire. I myself had been shot at, hit, shoved, threatened, tailed, chased, spied on, informed on, and had my phone tapped. Claude had had doses of the same. I imagined it felt almost like being behind enemy lines in some hostile, warring country. Who could you trust? Who could you turn to if you got in real trouble? Who would come to your aid if you were dragged out of your motel room in the middle of the night? Who would care if you were waylaid and killed in your car on a dark country road?

The local cops were at the least totally unsympathetic and at the most in league with the KKK and the other violent actors. They believed—and I had not run into an exception—that there had been no race problem in the South at all, that "their niggers" had been content with their lot until Northern "outside agitators" and the "Yankee Jew-Communist press" began stirring them up. And they reserved special hostility for reporters like Claude and me. It was understandable, if contemptible, that New York "Jew" reporters and other agents of the Communist-controlled Northern press were agitating the "niggers." But Southerners like me and Claude were worse. We knew better. We were traitors, and we were looked upon with uncomprehending hatred.

We didn't even trust the FBI. The FBI was sometimes around but the agents always merely observed and perhaps photographed incidents. They never took action. Its agents were mostly Southern, presumably conservative, as most cops were, and sympathetic to the white Southern cause. In front of the courthouse in Greenwood, I overheard an FBI agent apologizing to the local sheriffs for being there at a voter registration incident. Just following orders, he said.

Acutely sensitive to all this, we had developed over months of traveling together some rules of self-protection. We always stayed in adjoining rooms in motels, preferably chain motels like Holiday Inn whose owners likely were not members of the Klan. We always insisted on rooms on the front side, as close to the manager's office as possible, and in a well-lighted spot. This lessened the risk of being dragged out of our rooms in the dark of night with God knows what horrific result. We spurned rooms with windows through which guns might be fired or dynamite tossed.

When possible, we avoided motel or hotel phones, for fear they were tapped, and instead used pay phones and made collect calls. And if anyone walked up, or by, we stopped talking. Claude was on the phone from his room one night in a small Mississippi town dictating his story to the *Times* in New York (that was its system), when a voice came on the line and said, "You nigger-loving son-of-a-bitch."

We did not tell cops anything about what we were doing or who we were seeing, not only because we didn't want to be sucked into the role of informers but also because we feared they would pass on information to people who might do us harm. We were often photographed by obvious undercover cops, and we assumed these pictures were passed along to other police in other towns—or to the Citizens Council and the Mississippi Sovereignty Commission, perhaps even to the Klan. It was known that the Sovereignty Commission compiled and disseminated a list of individuals and organizations threatening the segregated order, and we assumed we were on it.

We alternated renting cars, rode together when possible, and shared the driving. Claude frequently drove while I typed with my Lettera portable on my lap, and vice versa. We were extremely careful not to violate any traffic laws—hard for me, because I liked to drive fast. We kept a close eye on the rear-view mirror. We were sometimes followed by pickup trucks with whiplash citizens band antennas and rifles on racks behind the driver's seat. We assumed the Citizens Council, Klan, and cop network knew where we were at all times. One day we were having lunch at the Blue Bell restaurant in McComb, just driving through on the way to some other hot spot, when the police chief walked in and wanted to know what we reporters were doing in town.

We always wore suits and button-down shirts, repp ties and cordovan shoes, and drove bland American rental cars, the same look that the FBI agents had—who also always traveled in pairs—so it was a kind of inadvertent camouflage. At least it struck me that way.

We tried not to be out in rural places on back roads at night, and if we were, to go to and from our destination, if possible, with other cars carrying perhaps Justice officials, other reporters, or civil rights workers. If we went to a mass meeting in a rural church, we made sure to leave with a crowd. Both of us avoided, absolutely, going anywhere alone at night—out, say, to an interview "in the country."

I never got quite as drunk as I wanted to, not drunk enough to be arrested or to do something truly foolish, such as drive drunk, which I had done many times on my home turf. Nor did I consider—as a friend ignorant of Mississippi reality suggested—carrying a gun. That would have been suicide. There was a good possibility I would have been shot dead by a cop, or somebody not a cop, who would claim self-defense, and no questions would be asked. Was such thinking paranoid? Maybe. But maybe not.

As the saying went, even paranoids have real enemies. For sure we outside reporters had them, and there was nothing much to inhibit them from doing anything they wanted to do and getting away with it.

I was existing then in a constant state of tension, biliousness, and fatigue, working twelve to sixteen hours a day, every day, and running mostly on raw adrenaline and nervous exhaustion. I was getting no exercise, no recreation, no time simply to calm down and be quiet. I slept fitfully, ate irregularly and badly, smoked too many cigarettes, had too much coffee, and drank when I could. The result was that I felt ragged and edgy all the time—but alive as I had never been before. *Newsweek* had promised I could be home with my family at least every other weekend, but sometimes, such as during this prolonged siege of Greenwood, that was simply not possible. I phoned home every night—when I could get to a phone—but did not share with my wife the realities of the danger I felt myself in. She was worried, though, because she read the papers and watched television, saw the violence, knew I was in the middle of it—and sometimes, she told me, cried with her women friends in Ansley Park.

The night after the long tense day when Dick Gregory taunted the Greenwood police, Claude and I went back to the Travel Inn, had a couple of drinks, ate dinner, and fell exhausted into bed. I was sleeping my usual just-below-the-surface sleep when there came a loud pounding on my door. I leaped up and looked at the clock. It was 4 A.M. Claude immediately came flying through the door that joined our rooms in his boxer shorts and T-shirt, his hair disheveled.

The pounding went on, louder and insistent. I stood momentarily frozen by my bed, fearing the worst—that someone had come to drag us from our rooms.

"Let me in, let me in!" I heard a female voice shouting.

"Don't open the door! Don't open the door!" Claude yelled.

"Are you crazy. I'm not about to open the goddamned door," I said.

The pounding went on, and after what seemed like thirty minutes, I pulled a chair over to the narrow overhead rectangular window by the door, stood up on it and looked out. There stood a barefoot young Negro woman in a loose dress pounding away and yelling, "Let me in, please, let me in."

I stayed quietly at the window, watching her, and watching Claude. I put my forefinger up to my mouth, signaling him to stay quiet. We said not a word, but I knew we were thinking the same thing, for we had talked about it many times. Suppose this was a plant by the cops, a woman sent to our room to entrap us. This kind of scenario was one of the things we feared. We would be arrested, with her in our room, and perhaps charged with rape. It would make a nice headline in the *Jackson Clarion-Ledger*: "Yankee Newsmen Charged With Raping Negro Woman." We'd be jailed, and knowing what we knew about Mississippi judges and juries, likely convicted.

Finally the woman quit pounding and yelling and walked off into the cotton field beside our motel.

"It's probably just some drunk woman or somebody crazy," I said to Claude.

"Jesus, I hope so. I thought we'd had it," said Claude.

"So did I," I said.

Next day and the rest of that week, it was clear that the Greenwood and Delta voter registration movement was bogging down, with little success achieved, few Negroes registered, the SNNC workers exhausted physically and emotionally, their funds running low. Moses, Forman, and the others arrested and convicted were released from jail, under pressure from the Justice Department, on April 4. The deal, announced by John Doar, was that if the local cops would drop the charges against Forman, Moses, and the others—and let them out of jail—the Justice Department, in turn, would drop charges against the locals for interfering with voter registration, providing they would agree not to do it anymore.

After the Greenwood incidents, Claude and I thought further about what else we could do to protect ourselves. We knew that one thing that gave us away as reporters was our notebooks, big secretarial pads that were always in plain sight. A smaller one that fit into and could be hidden away in our pants and suit jacket pockets might be an improvement. That might increase the odds that we would be mistaken for FBI agents, not much of an edge because we believed 90 percent of people who might imperil us knew who we were even before we got to wherever we were going. But even a tiny edge would help. So we measured and came up with a four-by-eight inch model, and called the Richmond stationery wholesaler we used and ordered a gross. They arrived in Atlanta ten days later—a big square package wrapped in butcher paper. They were simply the old secretarial notebooks with the sides and bottoms cut off to our specifications, the end and side pieces included in the package. We began carrying them immediately. (But the very first time we used them, which was in Jackson at a demonstration protesting the murder of Medgar Evers, a crowd of whites spotted us and one yelled, "There them nigger-loving reporters. Git 'em!") Other reporters we ran into on the civil rights beat, impressed by how handy they were, wanted to know where we got them, and they began ordering them, too.

After Greenwood, I had a breather with my family. We went up to Asheville for a week, swam, picnicked in the mountains, pitched horseshoes and baseballs, and played hide-and-seek in my in-laws' backyard. I played gin rummy and drank Jack Daniels with my father-in-law under his carport and went with him on a

Wednesday to revisit the Elks Club and play poker. The terror of the game, mean old Mr. Mac, had died, but the rest were still there, sitting at the same table playing the same six-card stud game with the lights dimming at eleven o'clock and the players chanting "to our absent dollars" when the gong sounded. I thought about what a miraculous and fortunate change had come in my life. I thought about the embittered Mr. Mac and his gloomy prediction about things going bad and then suddenly taking a turn for the worse and how lucky I was that things had suddenly taken a huge turn for the better in my life. I was thirty-five and, tough as the times were, had come so far so quickly from those dark, unhappy days in Asheville. Right now, I was getting good cards, and I hoped I would continue to be able to play them well. I had a lot to be grateful for.

Chapter 11

Bombs, Bullets, and Tears

B Y 1963 I had seen a lot of cops in action on the Southern civil rights beat—a few good ones and a lot of bad ones— but I never saw any cop like Birmingham's public safety commissioner, Eugene V. "Bull" Connor. He was in a class all by himself, a twisted caricature of the quintessential dumb and vicious redneck cop. When I saw him in action I didn't know whether to laugh in derision or cry in shame.

Rumpled and pudgy, Connor was a jug-eared, raspy-voiced, one-eyed (he'd lost the sight of the other in a childhood accident) ex-baseball announcer chosen by Birmingham's ruling business elite, its so-called Big Mules, to maintain total segregation at any cost. He had close ties to the Klan and had ignored or been complicit in so many racial bombings in that city that one Negro section of it was known as Dynamite Hill.

I first encountered him when I went to his office in early 1963 to get his response to what I had heard would be a Justice Department effort to try to get him to be more conciliatory and less violent toward Birmingham Negroes who were boycotting, picketing, and marching against total segregation. He wore a wrinkled blue polyester suit, an old pork-pie hat—even though we were in his disorderly downtown office—and a loud red tie that ended about where his big belly began.

"I ain't talking to them FBI. But they can interview my German shepherd po-lice dawgs if they want to," he cackled. He'd acquired the trained dogs as another anti-integration tool, though he had not yet used them.

I learned that when Fred Shuttlesworth, the tall, skinny, and impassioned local Negro preacher leading Negro protests, was beaten by whites during a demonstration—while cops idly looked on—and was being loaded into an ambulance, Connor sneered: "Too bad it ain't a hearse instead of a ambulance." I also was aware that Connor held back his cops to give a white mob time to beat Freedom Riders bloody when their bus hit Birmingham on Mother's Day, May 14, 1961.

"Ole Bull" was always good for a laugh among the elite at the Mountain Brook Club, as when he said, after breaking up an interracial conference, "We ain't gonna segregate no niggers and whites together in this town." But though the Big Mules laughed at him behind his back, he served their purpose, which was to keep Birmingham's Negroes in line with whatever brute force it took.

In the previous decade, there had been fifty recorded bombings of Negro homes, business, and churches in Birmingham—all, of course, unsolved. Steel-making Birmingham, population 340,000, lay at the southern end of the Appalachian mountains and was rich in iron ore, coal, and limestone. Its two dominant corporations, Tennessee Coal and Iron and United States Steel, had since the 1930s ruthlessly used the Klan to intimidate and kill union sympathizers with dynamite, and the Klan's use of bombs against aspirant Negroes was an outgrowth of that.

Fred Shuttlesworth had for seven years staged many unsuccessful demonstrations against Birmingham's rigidly segregated stores, restaurants, and public facilities. To keep Birmingham's public facilities—sixty-eight public parks, thirty-eight swimming pools, and four golf courses—all white, the three-man City Commission, at Connor's behest, simply closed them. And the city's merchants refused to budge an inch, maintaining all-white sales forces, lunch counters, and even separate dressing rooms.

Martin Luther King Jr. called Birmingham "the meanest segregated town in America," and when, in February 1963, Shuttlesworth invited King to come down from Atlanta and help, King accepted. Among other reasons for going to Birmingham, King badly needed a clear victory. He had been catapulted from obscurity as the twenty-six-year-old pastor of Montgomery's Dexter Avenue Baptist Church to quick national fame by leading the 1955 Montgomery bus boycott. After moving back to his native Atlanta in 1957 to form the Southern Christian Leadership Conference, he had become the favorite of Northern liberals and media because of his non-threatening manner and message and his spellbinding oratorical skills. He was much in demand as a speaker and raised a lot of money.

But by early 1963, things were not going well. The previous year he had suffered a big defeat in Albany, Georgia, at the hands of a sophisticated police chief who put all demonstrators in jail politely, with the result that nothing changed. SCLC was floundering without a clear mandate or defined goal and lacked an identifiable piece of the civil rights turf. J. Edgar Hoover was leaking stories to the press about King's dalliance with a white woman and his close association with a New York adviser who had been a Communist. The well-funded Citizens Council was widely distributing a large photographic poster, and putting up billboards, that showed King attending a leftist conference at the Highlander Folk School in Monteagle, Tennessee, entitled "Martin Luther King At Communist Training School." Some younger and more aggressive members of SNCC and CORE gossiped to some of us reporters that King was too effete and too chicken to go to tough places as they had, where he might get hurt or killed.

So King and his SCLC lieutenants, James Bevel, Andy Young, and Wyatt Tee Walker, all young Negro ministers, were well aware that they needed a new adversary—and no Hollywood casting director could have picked a better one than the loud-mouthed, strutting Bull Connor. Given his track record, they believed it wouldn't take much to provoke Ole Bull into violence. And they knew that though it might be sad, it was true about the civil rights movement that violence, and only violence, attracted much national media attention, especially television.

King and his staff moved into the two-story, stucco Gaston Motel just off Birmingham's Kelly Ingram Park in early February and began organizing mass protest marches into Birmingham's white business district. I hadn't had a personal interview with King since Albany, but Birmingham was now shaping up as a showdown, so I called Walker, who was the gatekeeper, and asked for one. It was quickly granted. King by then knew me and presumably trusted me. Besides, publicity in the national media like *Newsweek* was just what SCLC was hoping for.

I found King sitting in shirtsleeves on his bed in his small second-floor room at the Gaston. There was no place to sit but on the bed with him. He was, as usual, quiet, open, and accommodating. He insisted he would stay in Birmingham until Connor's true violent self—expressive of the real character of Birmingham's segregationist system—was revealed. Recruiting for demonstrations and marches had begun to fall off, even though King was there, and Wyatt Tee Walker had announced that high school students would now be used in marches. I asked King if he felt any conscious pangs about using children. He said he did, but that they were old enough to make the sacrifices their parents were making, and that this was a noble cause they would forever be proud of having fought for.

On April 10, King announced he himself was going to march and go to jail. The city instantly responded with a legal injunction prohibiting King and 135 named others from further sit-ins or marches. A deputy rushed the injunction to the Gaston after midnight where King and his lieutenants, and several of us reporters, were hanging out. Shuttlesworth angrily announced to the press that they would not obey the injunction. King called the injunction "unjust, undemocratic and unconstitutional" and said "I am prepared to go to jail and stay as long as necessary.... Too many people are depending on me. I have no choice. I have to march." It was an electric moment, for it was clear that now all the previous months of marches and failed attempts at negotiation were over, that the battle of Birmingham was moving into a new and more dangerous stage.

Violence seemed to loom, too, because Connor's police dogs had been brought to the scene a week before when King's brother, A.D., and another local minister led a forty-person march through the park. A young Negro spectator swung at one of the dogs with a knife, and a dog lunged at another man, setting off a minor melee.

King and his top lieutenant, the Reverend Ralph Abernathy, emerged from Zion Hill Baptist Church shortly before 3 P.M. on Good Friday, April 12, at the head of a column of fifty protesters, and headed toward white downtown along Fifth Avenue alongside Kelly Ingram Park. Connor and his heavily armed cops, backed up by balding, melon-bellied "Colonel" Al Lingo, head of the Alabama State Highway Patrol, and 100 shotgun-toting state troopers—whom Connor had invited as backup—were waiting. I thought suddenly of the Light Brigade marching into the Valley of Death.

As the cops approached to arrest them at Connor's order, King and Abernathy knelt on the ground, and as cameras snapped pictures, they were hauled up and shoved into a paddy wagon along with the other marchers. Connor put King in solitary confinement and refused to let him see a lawyer.

But the march had its desired effect: The picture of King being pushed into the police van ran on the front page of the *New York Times* and in papers all over the world the next day and in magazines including mine the next week. There was more national publicity when JFK himself called King's wife, Coretta, to inquire about King's safety and when King wrote a long letter from jail justifying defiance of the court order against marching. Excerpts were widely published, the most controversial being his statement "I have almost reached the regrettable conclusion that the Negro's greatest stumbling block toward freedom is not The Citizens Council or the Ku Klux Klan but the white moderate who... is more devoted to 'order' than to justice, who says 'I agree with the goal you seek but I cannot agree with your methods of direct action.'"

In the days that followed, King's lieutenants had increasing trouble rounding up recruits for demonstrations, and after King and Abernathy posted $300 bonds and left jail April 20, the movement began to falter, and the media began to leave.

That included both Claude Sitton and me. We moved on in early May to cover the next brushfire, the next battleground. It was always this way; things quieted in one place, on one front, and heated up on the next. What looked like a big story now was a CORE-sponsored march from Chattanooga, Tennessee, to Jackson, Mississippi, to finish a march begun by a white Baltimore postman who'd set out on the same route, carrying a sandwich board that said "Eat At Joe's Both Black And White." He was shot in the back on April 24 just over the Alabama line. Claude and I rented a station wagon and bought two sleeping bags. Crowds of whites lined Highway 11 as we walked along. They shouted epithets and threw rocks and eggs at the fifty or so marchers—and reporters. A motorcade of fifty cars bearing white, anti-integration protesters tailed us. An Alabama Highway Patrol spotter plane lazed overhead. Claude and I took turns walking and going back for the station wagon. Near the village of Rising Fawn, a white man jumped out of his car and rushed at me as I walked on the highway shoulder right behind the marchers. He shoved me hard into the low steel guardrail, opening a two-inch cut on my left shin. He yelled, "Kill the white men first," and disappeared among his cohorts.

My cut leg was hurting badly when, late in the afternoon of May 2, after two nights, we reached the Alabama line, where Colonel Al Lingo was waiting. Lingo yelled over a portable loudspeaker for the marchers to disperse, and when they didn't, his men charged. The marchers dropped prone to the ground. The troopers moved in and jabbed them repeatedly in the genitals with three-foot-long electric cattle prods. Then the marchers were dragged up and thrown into police trucks. Lingo told us half-dozen reporters they were being taken to jail on charges of breach of the peace.

The same day Lingo arrested the marchers at the Alabama line, King and the SCLC finally got the response from Bull Connor they had hoped for. Urged on by Jim Bevel, Andy Young, and Wyatt Tee Walker, King's people had continued marching and

Connor had continued arresting them. Now came the clarifying event: Pictures that would finally stun—and horrify—the nation. A column of 1,500 protesters, mostly students, moved from the Sixteenth Street Baptist Church through Kelly Ingram Park toward Connor and his waiting cops and a phalanx of firemen and fire trucks. (As public safety commissioner Connor was also in charge of the fire department.) Suddenly, ragtag Negro kids—not in the march—started to yell and pelt the police with rocks and pop bottles. Connor ordered firehoses and dogs into action—against the wishes, by the way, of the fire chief and many of his more reasonable officers.

Network television and still cameras recorded dozens of Negroes, including children and old people, slammed against walls and to the ground by the cannon-like force of the water, their shirts and blouses peeled off, and the police dogs lunging, biting, and tearing clothes. It was the lead national television story, and was on newspaper front pages worldwide. And Charles Moore's dramatic photographs in *Life* magazine the next week erased what might have been any lingering national doubt that what King had been saying about the cruelty of Birmingham and Southern segregation was true.

As a reporter, I was disappointed to have missed this moment, for it was a seminal one—the pay-off for what I later realized added up to being the first truly staged media event of the civil rights movement. I had made the choice to leave Birmingham and follow the Moore march. It was a good story, but I missed out on a bigger one—the first such I had missed.

On Thursday, May 7, after months of negotiating, the white power structure of Birmingham caved in and agreed to Negro demands—in return for an immediate end to demonstrations. Fitting rooms would be desegregated. White and colored signs would be removed from restrooms and water fountains. Lunch

counters would be desegregated. One Negro salesperson would
be hired by each of the leading stores. King and Shuttlesworth
announced the settlement at a press conference in the Gaston
courtyard Friday afternoon. King said his work was done in
Birmingham and he was going home to Atlanta.

I'd made one good white friend in Birmingham, a Rabelaisian,
garrulous, and bibulous liberal lawyer named Charles (Chuck)
Morgan Jr., one of a small group of younger Birmingham leaders
who openly defied the Big Mules and urged conciliation with the
Negro community. He had helped draft King's settlement statement to the media Friday, and Saturday night he invited me,
Claude Sitton, and the *Time* reporter on hand, Dudley Morris, to
go to dinner with him at a fancy restaurant out in the fashionable
section of Mountain Brook, where the Big Mules lived. We'd had
several drinks and were into steaks when Morgan got a call. The
Gaston Motel had just been bombed. We raced to the nearest car,
which turned out to be Dudley Morris's, and headed down. Morris was an irritatingly slow driver, a New York Ivy Leaguer with
fine manners. We could hear shouts, sirens, and the crash of rocks
and bottles as we turned onto Sixth at the edge of Kelly Ingram.
A riot was raging. Cars were ablaze. Negroes were racing everywhere, throwing rocks, shouting, breaking windshields, chasing
whites. Suddenly a fire truck appeared behind us, and Morris
pulled over as a shower of rocks and bottles rained our way.
"Don't stop. Drive, you crazy son of a bitch," I yelled at him.
"You're gonna get us killed."

We made our way toward the Gaston and parked. There was
a huge pile of debris right under the corner suite King had occupied and where daily meetings had gone on for more than a
month. It was clearly an assassination attempt on King's life. But
King had gone back to Atlanta and the person who had taken
over his room luckily was not there, so the huge bomb hurt no

one. Nearby a little earlier, a bomb had been hurled at the home of King's brother, A. D. The front door was blown back into the kitchen and the walls heavily damaged. A. D. King and his wife were in bed but got out of the house uninjured.

Twenty-five hundred angry Negroes were surging in all directions, shouting, "Kill the cops," "Kill the Klan," "Bomb Bull Connor's house." Cops were running after them and clubbing all they could catch. One cop was knifed, several were hit with rocks and bottles. A small crowd was singing "We Shall Overcome," trying to calm the angry crowd, but to no avail. A fire started in a white-owned grocery store spread to two Negro houses. Bull Connor's specially equipped armored car, his "tank," drove around firing tear gas, to no effect. Soon an entire block was on fire.

I ran to a pay phone on Fifth Street across from the park to call my New York office and see if it was too late to update the magazine. While I was talking, three shouting Negroes rocked the booth back and forth with me in it, turning it over. They ran away, and I clambered up and stumbled off.

At 2 A.M., after several hours of rioting, Colonel Lingo and 100 troopers appeared in their cars, brandishing shotguns and rifles out of their windows, followed by Selma's Sheriff Jim Clark and 100 of his appointed armed posse men on horseback. Clark, a virulent racist, had volunteered his force, and Connor accepted. Lingo got out of his car brandishing a shotgun, backed up by bodyguards carrying Thompson machine guns. Police Chief Jamie Moore pleaded with Lingo to "put that shotgun away. You're going to start a race war." Lingo ignored him. Clark and his people charged the courtyard, flailing at Negroes standing around.

I had ridden with Lingo around Birmingham one night during demonstrations in the weeks before and had quoted him in a story. Spotting me now, Lingo came over and got right in my face.

I smelled whiskey on his breath. He poked his shotgun into my stomach and said, "I could blow your sorry ass away."

"What the hell for?" I asked.

"You made me sound like an ignorant redneck. You quoted me in that damn magazine saying 'ain't' and I ain't ever said 'ain't' in my life," he yelled. I turned and walked away, worrying that he was crazy enough, or drunk enough, to shoot me in the back.

I thought of what my friend Claude had said when someone asked him how we reporters stopped ourselves from expressing bias against demonstrably bad people such as Lingo and Clark. "There would never be any need to twist the facts, even if you wanted to. All you have to do is quote them," Claude replied. And he was right. The simple facts of this on-going story laid out calmly with no adornment, and the simple stenographic recording of what the whites with power in their hands actually said, was worse than anything we reporters might make up, or distort.

State troopers were clubbing Negroes with their gun butts, including the wife of Wyatt Tee Walker, who went to the hospital with a gash on her head. Lingo ordered the troopers to march the assembled dozen press people at gunpoint into the courtyard of the Gaston. And we stayed there until daybreak, shielded from seeing the rest of the violence. It was mid-morning Sunday, Mother's Day, before the riot—the first race riot since whites rioted at Oxford over James Meredith—was brought under control.

The settlement with the Birmingham white power structure had been a big victory for King and his tactics of nonviolent confrontation. But the ensuing violence, specifically the violence of the Negro response to the post-settlement bombings, signaled something else of significance: the end of passive acceptance of white violence by Southern Negroes. I wondered to myself why it had taken so long. I had been in awe of the Southern Negro's seemingly patient acceptance of white brutality and the use of only nonviolent tactics against it. But I hadn't been fully aware of the universal and justified fear under which they lived, especially in the small rural towns where sheriffs ruled with brutal fists. Nor had I fully understood what a restraining role the Negro churches played. They had preached the same nonviolent doctrine that King had taken from Gandhi and used as a powerful weapon. But urban Birmingham was very different from the small rural towns of Mississippi, Georgia, and Alabama. Birmingham was teeming with young black men not affiliated with or influenced by the church, who scoffed at the NAACP and their elders' go-slow attitudes. It was they who had fueled the riots—a harbinger not then noticed of the black uprisings that would roll across urban America soon enough, beginning with Watts later in 1965.

Watching all this—here in Birmingham as earlier in Greenwood and Albany and standing beside James Meredith those days at Ole Miss—my own feelings about what constituted bravery had undergone a dramatic change. I'd been brought up to believe that only a coward and a sissy didn't hit back when hit. "Yellowbelly" was what you were called if you backed away. But what I had seen King and his followers and all the SNCC and CORE kids do, that is, keep nonviolently moving forward in the face of threats and beatings, and even death, I now believed, took a lot more courage than fighting. It was clear that King and these kids were the bravest people I had ever seen. I was in awe of them for that, especially King, and I envied the moral purity of their struggle. This new belief, however, did not quell my rage at what I saw whites doing to blacks, nor lessen what I realized was my own angry and sometimes belligerent intolerance toward intolerance.

I thought about this as I thought about my four sons and what kind of role model for them I should be and what I should teach them about when to fight and when not to. I was feeling my way as a father, acting out of instinct and my own experience as a fatherless child. I had had to leave a newborn baby, my fourth son, Mark, in Atlanta, to go to Birmingham, and I couldn't help but think of him and my other sons and what I would and should tell them about how to live their lives. I was pretty clear on a few things. One was that I would teach them to stand up for what was honest, right, and honorable, no matter what. Another was not to be afraid to stand alone when standing up for what they believed in—that the popular way was not always the right way. But I found I was unable to tell them to turn the other cheek when they were hit. I told them never to start a fight, but when hit, to hit back, harder. My own lingering anger at being bullied, and my shame at sometimes not fighting back, was too strong to put into practice King's policy of Christian nonviolence.

As for Christianity in general, I remained skeptical of and cynical about religion, in part because of my own childhood experiences and because most of the white churches had remained silent in the face of so much obvious injustice. There were ministers, to be sure, who stood for what was right and suffered for it, but most chose to be popular rather than principled. My wife's family was not religious. Her father, in fact, was bitter at his own sternly Christian and physically abusive father, and neither he nor her mother ever went to church, as far as I knew. So we decided to keep our children away from organized religion, to let them know they could lead moral and principled lives without having religion crammed down their throats, as it had been crammed down mine. They would be free to examine all forms of belief, or nonbelief, and make a choice for themselves.

A month after Birmingham I was in Tuscaloosa to watch Alabama's Governor George Wallace fulfill his promise to "Stand in the Schoolhouse Door" to prevent the Communist-inspired

Kennedy government from forcing the integration of the nation's only remaining segregated state university system, the University of Alabama—mediocre in every way except for its Bear Bryant–coached football powerhouse, the Crimson Tide.

I'd first met Wallace not long after he delivered on his vow to "out-nigger" the opposition to become governor of Alabama and said, in his inaugural speech—setting the tone for a violent year to come—"I draw a line in the dust and toss the gauntlet before the feet of tyranny. And I say, segregation now, segregation tomorrow, segregation forever." But when I walked into his Montgomery office in mid-1964, segregation was not on his mind. Dressed in a double-breasted gabardine suit, his hair slicked back, chewing an unlit cigar in a way that made him look like a bantam rooster Edward G. Robinson, Wallace was fuming not about the national media but at the main local newspaper, the *Montgomery Advertiser,* which was accusing him of corruption.

"Oh, come on, governor," I said, "you know you enjoy a fight like this."

He laughed and said, "Yeah I do, but in this particular case I'm like the guy who was fucking a skunk: I've enjoyed about all of this I can stand."

Wallace liked this kind of rough humor. He once allowed a photographer colleague of mine, Flip Schutze of *Life* magazine, to ride with him. Going down the road one day he asked Schultze if he wanted to see something unusual. Sure, said Flip. "Stop the car and let me out," Wallace said to his state highway patrol driver, "and I'll kick the shit out of this nigger kid walking down the road." Flip said no thanks.

Now Wallace was going to have his carefully orchestrated national moment. Unlike Ole Miss's tragedy, however, this one was shaping up as farce—an event arranged only to advance Wallace's presidential ambitions. Whereas Ross Barnett went on television and summoned the rabble to Ole Miss to repel the invaders, Wallace went on statewide television and urged everybody to stay home—and quietly passed word to the Klan through Bull Connor and Al Lingo to stay out of the way and let him have his moment on the national stage.

In terms of publicity, Wallace was having some success. He'd come back to Alabama from an appearance on *Meet the Press* to find 500 reporters encamped in Tuscaloosa at the Stafford Hotel—along with a sizable force of U.S. marshals plus Deputy Attorney General Nick Katzenbach and his staff. Klan Imperial Wizard Bobby Shelton, in a suit and tie, was holding forth in the Stafford lobby to any reporter who would talk to him. He had previously promised a huge riot for this moment, but now said the Klan would behave.

On the broiling morning of June 11, the entrance to the red-brick and white-columned Foster Auditorium on the campus of the University of Alabama resembled a movie set. A white line was painted across the sidewalk in front of the double doors where Wallace's skinny lectern was set up. Another line was painted three feet forward. This was to be Wallace's "line in the dust" that he dared the government to cross. I stood sweating with the rest of the media horde in the near 100-degree sun when at 11 A.M. the oily-haired Wallace stepped through the doors, wearing a lavaliere mike with his script in hand, and took up his position behind the podium. Nearly 200 state troopers lined the sidewalk, which Katzenbach and the two prospective students, Vivian Malone and James Hood, would walk along. A hundred other troopers blocked entrances to the campus.

Wallace was waiting behind his podium when Katzenbach drove up in a white government Plymouth. Malone and Hood remained in the car. Katzenbach glanced down at the line on the sidewalk and immediately crossed it, handed Wallace the government order, and asked him to stand aside. Wallace then read his lengthy statement, asserting that "I stand here today as governor of this sovereign state and refuse to willingly submit to illegal usurpation of power by the central government."

"Governor, I am not interested in a show," Katzenbach coldly responded. "I don't know what the purpose of this show is. I am interested in the orders of these courts being enforced. These students will remain on this campus. They will register today. They will go to class tomorrow."

Wallace still refused to move, and then Katzenbach radioed Brigadier General Henry Graham, whose Alabama national guard division had been federalized by President Kennedy, and Graham arrived at two o'clock with three troop carriers filled with Guardsmen armed with M-1 rifles and told Wallace it was his "sad duty" to ask him to stand aside. Wallace denounced what he called a federal "military dictatorship" and said he was returning to Montgomery to continue his noble fight. Within five minutes, Malone and Hood were brought in and registered, the "show" was over, and the parched gentlemen of the press returned to the hotel for some beers. There had never been any thought on our part that violence would occur, but we had all come, and Wallace's purpose had been served.

After this, I went back to my room, showered, had a nap and then dinner with some reporter friends. Afterwards, we all repaired to the bar to watch President Kennedy respond to Wallace's grandstanding:

> We preach freedom around the world, and we mean it. And we cherish our freedom here at home. But are we to say to the world, and much more importantly to each other, this is the land of the free, except for Negroes; that we have no second class citizens, except for the Negroes; that we have no caste

system, no ghettoes, no master race, except with respect to Negroes. . . . This is one country. It has become one country because all of us and all those who came here had an equal chance to develop their talents. We cannot say to 10 percent of the population that you can't have that right; that your children can't have the chance to develop whatever talents they have; that the only way they are going to get their rights is to go into the streets and demonstrate. I think we owe them, and we owe ourselves, a better country than that.

The assembled gentlemen of the press (there were no women reporters here; indeed, I had seen not a single one during my entire time covering civil rights) agreed that though Kennedy was a cool political animal who had first extended his hand to King for pure political reasons, this was a morally courageous speech. We remained in the hotel bar and I was chatting with John Doar and Ed Guthman, the Pulitzer Prize–winning reporter cum Justice Department PR man whom I had gotten to know at Ole Miss, when Doar was called to the phone. He came back a minute later, pale and almost in tears.

"Medgar Evers has been killed in Jackson. Someone shot him in the back," he said.

I immediately raced upstairs to my room and began to pack my stuff. Then I called the Tuscaloosa airport and lined up the one rental plane available, a Piper Tri-Pacer, a plane I had flown a lot. I called Claude's room and woke him up. (He was not a late-night reveler like me.) I told him what had happened and asked him if he wanted to fly with me. He hesitated a moment. He knew I had a license. I reassured him that I had accumulated almost 400 hours of flying time, a lot of it at night. I hadn't told him that more than once I'd gone out at night fairly loaded and flown the Super Cub I rented from Peachtree-DeKalb airport over to Atlanta's big commercial airport, got in traffic, and landed and took off with the big jets—just for the hell of it. Finally Claude said yes. We hurried out to the Tuscaloosa airport and left our rental cars. I bought a map and plotted a course to Jackson, filed a flight plan, and we got in the plane and I taxied out to the end of the one 3,000-foot lighted runway. When I did the usual full-throttle engine run-up routine, however, it didn't check out properly, so I turned the plane around and went back. We then chartered a piloted plane and flew to Jackson.

Flying down, I thought about the many times I had seen Evers in action. He was another of these outwardly calm and polite but incredibly brave black warriors. I had known him since the Meredith days. At the time of his death he was thirty-seven years old. He was calm-mannered and clean-featured with close-cropped hair and a thin mustache. He was the son of a Mississippi sawmill worker. He walked twelve miles to school when he was a kid, and at twelve years old he saw the body of a family friend whom whites had beaten to death for "sassing" a white woman. These whites left the friend's bloody clothes on a fence for a year as a warning to other potentially "uppity" Negroes. Evers was in combat in France and Germany in World War II, came home, finished college, and was doing well selling insurance when, after a white mob turned him and his brother Charlie away when they tried to vote, he became active in the NAACP. In that job, he had been beaten, and his life had been threatened so many times—and his house firebombed—that he and his wife had trained their children to drop to the floor at the sound of any unusual outside noises.

Claude and I arrived in Jackson about eight o'clock Wednesday morning and drove directly out to Evers's suburban house at 2332 Guynes Street. He had been shot in the back as he got out of his powder-blue 1962 Oldsmobile under his carport and was headed into the house, carrying an armload of "Jim Crow Must Go" T-shirts. He made it almost to the door before collapsing and dying. There was still a large pool of dried blood on the concrete. There were a lot of Jackson cops around, plus FBI agents, and local Negroes were coming into the house to comfort Myrlie Evers and her three small children, who had run out of the house screaming, "Daddy, get up!" when he was shot. A neighbor had run over with a mattress and cradled Evers in it, trying to stop the bleeding, as Evers murmured, "Let me go. Let me go." I walked across the street, where FBI agents had roped off a small wooded area. They had found a .30-06 high-powered rifle with a new telescopic sight suspended on bushes in the honeysuckle thicket 150 feet across the street. I quickly interviewed the Jackson police chief, who was at the scene. He was confident an outsider had done it, perhaps a Negro bent on making Mississippi look bad. The FBI people as usual would not say much, except that the rifle would be shipped off to the crime lab for testing.

In the months leading up to his death, Medgar Evers had been leading marches, boycotts, sit-ins, prayer vigils, voter registration drives, and picketing in Jackson. The city had responded by beating and arresting demonstrators and housing them in a makeshift fence stockade at the fairgrounds designed to hold 10,000 people. To add to the humiliation, officials forced temporarily deputized Negro policemen to make the arrests. The Panglossian mayor, Allen Thompson, a staunch member of the Citizens Council, called Jackson "the nearest thing to heaven on earth" and claimed he had done nothing but good for Jackson's Negroes— including building them their own golf course. He had talked the City Council into buying a big armored troop-carrying vehicle, which was quickly dubbed "Thompson's Tank" and he was laughed at after a tear-gas canister accidentally exploded inside it, sending twelve choking cops toppling into the street.

But Jackson's uniformed upholders of the law were no Keystone Kops. At noon the day after Evers was killed, 200 young Negroes in their Sunday best, including many children, set off from the Pearl Street African Methodist Episcopal (A.M.E.) Church on a march downtown to protest the killing. They walked silently and slowly in columns of two, each carrying an American flag. Halted by a roadblock leading into downtown, they turned right onto a dirt side street. The temperature was nearing 100. I walked up onto a porch to watch as the marchers approached a point where police cars had raced ahead of them and set up another blockade. The deputy police chief, a sullen man named J. L. Ray, confronted the marchers and ordered them to disperse. When they didn't, he ordered them arrested. The charge: parading without a permit. Cops and deputies then waded in, snatching flags from the marchers' hands and throwing them to the ground.

Several marchers broke free and ran up onto porches, including the one from where I watched, where they jeered the cops and chanted "Freedom! Freedom!" The cops went wielding their nightsticks after them. Some were clubbed to the ground. Others were choked with the nightsticks. Right next to me, John Salter, a white professor at Jackson's Tougaloo Southern Christian College, a long-time civil rights activist, was clubbed over the head and dragged off the porch. As he lay bleeding, a cop yelled, "Here he is, here he is," and another cop moved in and repeatedly hit him until he lay bleeding and unconscious on the ground. Eighty-two people were arrested. When I got back to my room at the Sun 'N' Sand Motel, I went into the bathroom and threw up, sickened and deeply angered by what I had seen. For many months to come, I would hear the thud of police clubs on heads, and see the flags being ripped from the hands of children in the middle of the night as I tossed fitfully in bed.

Evers's death was, of course, big national news, he being the first prominent civil rights leader to be assassinated. Well-known leaders from JFK on down sent their condolences as Evers's body lay in state at the Collins Funeral Home on Farish Street the day after he was killed. Governor Ross Barnett issued a terse statement saying that "apparently, this was a dastardly act."

Evers's funeral was held Saturday, June 15, in the Masonic Temple on Lynch Street at the regular church hour, 11 A.M. He lay in a flag-draped casket at the front, dressed in a blue suit, a white shirt, and red tie with his Masonic apron around his waist. The hall was packed, including all the major civil rights leaders like King, and 5,000 more stood in the sweltering street outside. We reporters were sequestered in a kind of press box behind the podium, on the same side where Myrlie Evers sat in a black dress and a black veil with her three children, quietly crying as the NAACP's Roy Wilkins, the Urban League's Whitney Young, and U.N. ambassador Ralph Bunche extolled Evers and denounced the Mississippi system.

"The killer must have felt that he had, if not an immunity, then certainly a protection for whatever he chose to do, no matter how dastardly it might be," Wilkins said.

A silent protest procession of 5,000, fronted by the national leaders, then made its way downtown. As this huge procession disbanded peacefully, I went with John Doar to have lunch at a small cafe on Capitol Street. We were finishing ham sandwiches when we began to hear shouts. We left our suit jackets in our seats and rushed out to see 250 cops, deputies, and highway patrolman massed where Farish Street ran into Capitol. Fifty yards in front of them, about 100 young Negroes roiled in the street, throwing rocks and bottles at the cops and shouting, "We want the killer! We want the killer!"

The cops were pointing their pistols, rifles, and shotguns at the crowd and were holding police dogs back. As Doar rushed between the cops and the young Negro crowd, with me close on his heel, I heard Colonel T. B. Birdsong, the head of the State Patrol, say, "One more goddamned rock and we're opening fire."

His shirtsleeves pushed up to his elbows, Doar strode like Gary Cooper in *High Noon* between the two forces, held up his arms in front of the shouting Negroes, and loudly said, "I'm John Doar from the United States Department of Justice. Everybody who knows me knows whose side I am on. But this is not the way to do it. If you continue to throw rocks and bottles, a lot of people are going to be killed, and it is not going to be these police. I don't think you want your mothers and fathers to have to go to your funeral. So, please, let's break this up and go quietly and continue this fight in some other way."

Slowly, reluctantly, the Negro kids quieted down and began to disperse. I walked back toward where the cops were arrayed in the middle of the street. Birdsong walked over and muttered to me and a CBS network crew who were standing there helplessly, their sound line cut by a cop.

"Goddamned Martin Luther Coon started all this," Birdsong said.

"One of these days this country will be grateful to have King," I said, meaning I thought his nonviolent approach would not hold for long, a demonstration of which we had just seen in the first mass violent response by blacks in Mississippi.

"Did King say the country would be grateful?" Birdsong asked.

"No, I did," I said. He glared at me and walked away.

There was no question that this incident had been a second away from a massacre. I had been taking notes in my reporter's notebook and as I glanced down at them I noticed the lettering was about an inch high. My adrenaline had been pumping just that much. John Doar, though, had seemed as calm as if he were addressing a judge in court. How he had remained so I did not know. He could have been killed by someone in either camp. It was one of the bravest things I had ever seen.

The search for the killer, meantime, continued. The rabidly racist *Jackson Clarion-Ledger* opined that "a paid (Negro) assassin might have done the job. There are rumors that the man was expendable." JFK ordered J. Edgar Hoover to give the killing top priority. The gun used to kill Evers had been carefully wiped clean of fingerprints, but Jackson police in taking it apart found a clean print on the underside of the telescopic sight mounted on the stock. On June 22, FBI agents drove the ninety miles from Jackson to Greenwood and arrested Byron De La Beckwith, a salesmen for a liquid plant fertilizer company, and charged him with the murder. They had identified his fingerprint on the telescopic sight from Marine Corps records. Beckwith, or "Delay" as he was called, was born in the small Northern California town of Colusa on November 9, 1920, but when his alcoholic, debt-ridden father died when he was five years old, he moved to Greenwood with his mother, whose plantation-owning family went back to before the Civil War. He had lived in Greenwood all of his life, except for a stretch in the Marine Corps in World War II.

"Californian Is Charged With Murder Of Evers" headlined the *Clarion-Ledger* next day. Both Beckwith and his lawyer, Greenwood attorney Hardy Lott, were active and vocal members of the Citizens Council, and Beckwith was a tireless writer of letters to editors denouncing Communists, Jews, and race-mixers. He had written one for the *Greenwood Commonwealth*, dug up by Bill Minor, the fearless and much-threatened Jackson-based reporter for the New Orleans *Times-Picayune*, our *Newsweek* stringer. The letter said, "I believe in segregation just like I believe in God. I shall oppose any person, place or thing that opposes segregation. I shall combat the evils of integration and shall bend every effort to rid the United States of America of the integrationists, whoever and wherever they may be."

Housed in the Hinds County jail in the Jackson courthouse, above the courtroom, Beckwith was treated like a celebrity. A flood of well-wishers brought him steak, fresh gulf shrimp, and rich desserts, and supportive restaurants took turns delivering meals. The Meridian Citizens Council gave him a portable typewriter, and his employer, Delta Liquid Plant Food Company, mimeographed the fundraising letters he ceaselessly typed and sent. He was allowed to freely roam the jail building and was accompanied through the city for haircuts or a lunch by one of his jailers. Beckwith was housed in a private cell away from the other prisoners and his wife, Willie, was allowed in for conjugal visits, this possible because the Greenwood Citizens Council quickly formed a fundraising committee, and donations and fan letters poured in.

When Beckwith, a slight man with slicked-back hair and a fidgety air, was arraigned in July on a state murder charge, he was nattily dressed in a double-breasted blue suit, with a four-pointed handkerchief in the breast pocket, a dotted red tie, and a white shirt. He smiled cockily and waved to fans in the packed courtroom before being led out.

That afternoon I walked over to the capitol building. A set of marble steps led down into a small rotunda below the lobby. In the middle was a statue of the state's favorite segregationist, Senator Theodore Bilbo, flanked by huge color photographs, framed with varicolored light bulbs, of Mississippi's two Miss Americas. Standing there, in this absurd setting, I thought of Faulkner and Eudora Welty and the way their humane voices had not been much heard in their native state. Such voices as theirs, and those of all the decent people of Mississippi, had been silenced or drowned out by the shrill extremists like Bilbo. I remembered a famous Bilbo quote: "The best way to keep a nigger from the polls is to visit him the night before the election."

Bilbo's heirs had visited Evers in the night, and he had been silenced, but as Roy Wilkins said at his funeral, "In life he was a constant threat to the system that murdered him.... In the manner of his death he was a victor over that system. The bullet that tore away his life tore away at the system and helped signal its end."

I went home to Atlanta and took my family down to Wrightsville Beach in North Carolina after we stopped in Wilson to gather up my mother. We stayed in a faded old two-story beachfront hotel that served glorious family-style meals at communal tables—huge bowls of fresh corn, beans, tomatoes, okra, and squash, biscuits and cornbread, fresh fried fish and shrimp, fried chicken and country ham, all of the Southern food I so loved. I took the boys out to a rock jetty and taught them how to catch crabs on the end of a string with a piece of fatback tied to it. We played in the surf and tossed balls on the beach and built huge sand castles and turned red and then brown and happily lay under the sun coated with salt and sand. I temporarily forgot all about the hatred and bloodshed I had seen that year, and the tension and anger subsided.

My mother didn't like going onto the beach. Neither did my wife, much. They stayed on the hotel verandah in rocking chairs or walked to shops in the village. My mother was now sixty-four years old, still ramrod straight, still working at the popcorn stand in Wilson, her very small salary complemented by money I sent her every month. I called her once a week, but never talked to her about my work. She evidenced not the slightest interest in what I was doing or what was going on in these turbulent days across the South. She didn't read the paper or listen to the news. I had my usual hard time making conversation with her. It was confined to the boys—her grandchildren—or food, or her talking about our past, especially that last happy summer on the edge of the swamp in Vanceboro where we raised and canned all those Mason jars of vegetables before the worst event of her life—my going to the orphanage. This was not one of my favorite topics of conversation.

The summer for me was relatively quiet, though I always kept the radio and television on at home, and late Sunday morning, September 15, there was a bulletin that the Sixteenth Street Baptist Church in Birmingham, gathering point for so many of King's demonstrations, had been bombed and four little girls were dead. I packed and caught a plane immediately and drove my rental car back to the familiar church at mid-afternoon. People were milling around, many of them crying. There was a gaping hole and a pile of brick rubble beside the concrete stairs leading up into the main hall of the church. A shoebox of dynamite, with a timer on it, had been secreted there and the smell of cordite was still in the air. The bomb had gone off next to a Sunday school class and the bathrooms.

I went through the hole in the wall and into the bombed-out Sunday school room. Pieces of paper were mixed among the dust, fabric (dresses had been blown off some of the girls), and broken bricks. I picked up a Sunday school program for that day, with an outline of girl on the cover, her hands folded in a prayerful attitude. The face had been colored black with a crayon.

"Dirty rotten no-good sons-of-bitches," I said out loud. There was no doubt who had done it, and no faith, as I went about interviewing Negroes, that the Klan would be brought to justice. There had been more than fifty bombings in Negro Birmingham in the 1950s and 1960s and not a single person had been indicted.

Outside the church, a Negro man, eyes wild, repeatedly screamed, "Let me at the bastards. I'll kill them. I'll kill them." A Negro woman standing in the glass and rubble outside the church shrieked, "In church! My God, you're not even safe in church." The neighborhood erupted again, as it had after the dogs and fire-hoses and the bombing of King's motel. Many threw rocks and bottles at police cars and fire trucks as they arrived, sirens blaring. White kids waving Confederate flags faced off with a crowd of Negro kids on a side street away from the church. They taunted each other and threw rocks until the police arrived and dispersed the Negro kids. The violence continued on past afternoon and into the night. Governor George Wallace responded by sending in Al Lingo and a company of his tough state troopers. "Sending in Lingo was like spitting in our face," said one Negro.

Bobby Kennedy dispatched Burke Marshall to Birmingham, who found a city almost paralyzed with fear. The Negro community put armed vigilantes on the street to protect themselves and their homes. The police were preoccupied elsewhere—protecting the whites. Negro children attending newly desegregated schools couldn't get police protection. Burke Marshall dispatched a half dozen U.S. marshals.

Since the bombing took place on Sunday, I had plenty of time to gather information for next week's story. I decided to go to each of the four families of the slain little girls and trace their Sunday mornings until the time they were killed. I had always felt awkward as a reporter approaching people in such moments of extreme loss, but had discovered that they seemed to get some kind of relief from talking about what happened. Their families did want to talk and I knew that getting the minute details describing their children's getting ready for Sunday school that morning would humanize them more and make for a powerful "scene-setter" for our story. When my words were distilled into the finished story in New York, they produced some moving paragraphs:

> Because his wife was ailing, Claude A. Wesley, 54, gray-haired principal of a Negro school, oversaw the Sunday morning routine for his daughter, a bright-eyed bubbly 14-year-old named Cynthia. Together they did the dishes after a breakfast of bacon, eggs, and coffee before she got into her Sunday best—a ruffled white dress. Cynthia draped a red sweater over her shoulders and quickly fed her cocker spaniel, Toots. Then she was ready.
>
> After pausing under the sugar-berry trees before their brick-front home to wave good-bye to Mrs. Wesley, father and daughter climbed into the family's black Mercury and drove to the 16th Street Baptist Church.
>
> Wesley let Cynthia out at the curb and gently shooed her into the buff brick church. "You go on in, honey," he said. "I'm going to get some gas and I'll be back in a minute."
>
> At 9:22, Claude Wesley stood by his car at a service station two blocks away, watching the attendant fill the tank. Suddenly, Sunday blew up. Rocks and glass rattled through the trees. Wesley heard screams and broke into a run toward the church. Someone had dynamited the Sunday school. Outside the church, Claude Wesley had been walking around and around looking for Cynthia. Someone finally suggested that Claude Wesley should go to the hospital. There he met his slender wife and they were taken to the room where the dead girls lay covered. "They asked me if my daughter was wearing a ring," the father said. "I said yes, she was, and they pulled her little hand out and there the ring was."

I sat on a back row on Thursday when King preached at the funeral for the girls, their bodies arrayed in caskets in front of the pulpit. Except for a few reporters and Justice Department officials, the pews were filled with Negroes—the girls' parents in the front row—and I could hear muffled sobbing as King spoke. It was always strange in situations like this, sitting there taking notes as a detached observer, while feeling a host of other things at the same time: rage, pain, frustration, impotence—and shame for the cruelty of my fellow white Southerners.

"They have something to say to us in their death," King said. "They have something to say to every minister of the gospel who has remained silent behind the safe security of stained glass windows. They have something to say to every politician who has fed his constituents the stale bread of hatred and the spoiled meat of racism. They have something to say to a federal government that has compromised with the undemocratic practices of Southern Dixiecrats and the blatant hypocrisy of right-wing northern Republicans. They have something to say to every Negro who passively accepts the evil system of segregation and stands on the sidelines in the midst of a mighty struggle for justice. They say to each of us, black and white, that we must substitute courage for caution. They say to us that we must be concerned not merely about who murdered them, but about the system, the way of life, and the philosophy which produced the murderers."

It had taken many hours of careful reporting and what might have seemed insensitive questioning to gather the facts that went into the words I sat up late Thursday night typing and carrying to Western Union. But I felt good about it. A powerfully evocative story that simply laid out in exacting detail the events of the day—and the background of the city—would best express my sadness and rage at what had happened and would be the best epitaph *Newsweek* could write for the four little girls. I felt I had learned my early lessons at *Newsweek* well, and that at last I was a good enough reporter to do a story like this at least partial justice.

My confidence grew, as well, when *Newsweek*'s chief of correspondents, Jim Cannon, called and asked me if I would come down to West Palm Beach in Florida to stand in as the weekend White House reporter covering John Kennedy. There would be no heavy lifting. Kennedy was just going to the family compound and I could spend most of the weekend on the beach or in the bar playing poker. I was immensely flattered and went on down Friday afternoon. And on Saturday I saw Kennedy for the first and only time. I got in the press bus and followed as his entourage went out to the Travis Air Force Base. I watched him emerge from his armored car, brush back his hair in that familiar style, and take a seat with his staff and a bunch of generals in a makeshift set of stands set up like a football arena. We were there to see a mock Strategic Air Command alert, and I watched Kennedy as twenty B-15 bombers lumbered down the runway all at once in an earth-shattering, smoke-filled roar and disappeared into the air. Soon after that, Kennedy was gone.

On November 22, I was at the University of Miami—a party school nicknamed "Sunshine U."—doing a piece. I was walking across the campus toward the administration office when kids suddenly began racing in all directions, crying, and shouting that Kennedy was dead. I turned around immediately and flew home. Atlanta was silent, the streets practically empty. I went home to Ansley Park and watched on television as the body arrived in Washington and scenes from Dallas were played over and over. It felt like the whole nation was paralyzed with shock and grief. I called in to New York and asked if I could help out in Dallas. The answer was yes and I flew to Dallas on Friday. *Newsweek* had taken several rooms in the downtown Hilton Hotel.

Once in Dallas, I walked over to Dealy Plaza and looked up at the red-brick School Book Depository window from which Lee Harvey Oswald had fired his shots. Cops and FBI agents were everywhere and people were still aimlessly milling around, crying. I picked up a nine-by-twelve-inch poster from the ground whose headline, beneath front-on and profile photos of Kennedy, said "WANTED FOR TREASON." It was a seven-point John Birch Society screed accusing Kennedy of treasonous acts, mostly of being pro-Communist and anti-Christian, and it had been handed out all through the Dallas streets the day he was shot. Dallas' temper felt not much different from Jackson or Birmingham. The accents were roughly the same, and there was a huge amount of anger in the air of the same right-wing, anti-Communist fervor.

On Sunday, I was in *Newsweek*'s suite in the middle of a story conference with about a dozen of my colleagues—Oz Elliot presiding—and we were watching on television as Oswald was led out of the city jail and Jack Ruby stepped forward and shot him. We momentarily sat in stunned silence and then we did immediately what newspeople do: decided who was going to do what.

I was assigned to dig up some background on Ruby and discovered, through contacts provided by our excellent Dallas stringer, Hugh Aynesworth, that Ruby was a kind of joke around town—a low-grade, no-class crook with a long petty crime rap sheet who ran a strip joint and loved to hang around with cops. There was no evidence he had any attachment to the Mafia—the local cops howled at that notion, Ruby being such an absurd figure—or that he had any other motive other than the one he stated, that he loved the Kennedys and wanted to protect Jackie from having to testify at a trial.

I was also assigned to dig into Oswald's Dallas life, which led me to Ruth Payne. The wife of a Bell Helicopter engineer, she had befriended Marina Oswald at the Dallas Russian club (Marina was Russian) and taken her in when Marina, tired of Oswald's abusive behavior and lack of ambition, left her husband. I drove out to Payne's house in suburban Dallas with Jack Langguth, a very smart and affable *New York Times* reporter I had met in Mississippi the previous year. Again, the *Times* and *Newsweek* were not competing, so I did not feel compromised teaming up with him. Mrs. Payne was a tall, big-boned woman, black-haired with an open face, and she warmly asked us in and talked openly about Oswald and Marina.

Mrs. Payne told us that Lee had come there the night before the shooting from his room in Dallas and begged Marina first to come back to him and then to sleep with him that night. Marina refused on both counts, and Oswald slept on the couch. Mrs. Payne was aware he had put stuff away in her garage overnight, including a long burlap-wrapped bag, but was not up early enough the next morning to see Oswald depart.

I caught a sense right away of an Oswald who was sexually insecure and jealous of the relationship between his wife and Ruth Payne and that that rage and insecurity could have helped drive him into a murderous rage at Kennedy, the very epitome of attractive American male virility. This always remained my gut feeling, reaffirmed a few days later when I met Oswald's mother, who was coarse, grasping, insensitive, and self-involved. She had lost no time selling his personal possessions after the shooting and was immediately available for all interviews—at a price—and talked about Oswald as if he was an object rather than a person, an object that she knew very little about—except that, as she said, it was sweet to its mother.

Langguth and I met Mrs. Oswald at the Dallas airport one night as she arrived from Boston where she had been giving radio interviews, again for a price. She was a short, potato-faced woman in a baggy print dress with a narrow mouth and a self-pitying air, though not, it was clear, torn with grief over her dead son. We had no intention of paying her, but when she said she was hungry, we went to an airport dining room, where she immediately asked if she could have some champagne. A couple of bottles later, between her talking about what a burden this whole affair had been for her and how she was sure her Lee was innocent, she said she had no way of getting home to Fort Worth, which was twenty miles from Dallas, and it was too late anyway and she was tired and could we get her a room. Jack and I were in adjoining rooms with twin beds at the Baker Hotel, so, perhaps influenced by too much champagne, we did something unorthodox: We offered her one of the rooms for the night, which she immediately accepted. We bought her a breakfast in the hotel coffee shop the next morning and dropped her off at the Dallas bus station.

I came away from her—as from the interview with Ruth Payne—with the deep sense that Oswald, a disappointed runt of a man with a twisted, gnome-like face, had been driven by personal demons and not by political motive. The thought that an unstable loser like Oswald had been hired as a killer in some grand Mafia or Communist or CIA or FBI scheme seemed absurd—a killer who had allowed himself to be captured sitting in a movie theater. Wouldn't his handlers, if indeed there were any, have gotten him immediately out of town—or killed him before had had a chance to open his mouth? The conspiracy theories, which blossomed immediately, seemed totally farfetched, certainly to the hard-nosed established reporters I worked with who covered the story, just as later those theories didn't impress the Warren Commission which was set up to investigate them.

Dallas was different than my civil rights beat. It was highly competitive—it was swarming with reporters—but it wasn't dangerous and there wasn't that constant tension. And by this point, I had complete confidence in my ability as a reporter. I'd earned my stripes. My instincts were good. I had become a good interviewer, mostly because I had a great curiosity about everything and everybody, and people picked that up. I knew the questions to ask and I was a good listener. I sucked up everything, observing detail and surroundings and what was left unsaid. Sometimes I'd come away from a seemingly peripheral interview with a whole notebook filled up.

A few weeks after Dallas, I got a call from Jim Cannon, *Newsweek*'s chief of correspondents. Since Lyndon B. Johnson was now president and since the space center near Houston was becoming a bigger and bigger story, *Newsweek* had decided to open a bureau in Houston. The magazine would like me to move and be the bureau chief. I had an immediate negative reaction. I liked Atlanta and I would be leaving the civil rights story I was so deeply attached to. But Cannon said he had talked it over with Oz Elliott and I could keep that story and cover as much of it as I wanted to. There would be a substantial raise, to $18,000, he said, and I would be my own boss with my own territory. And he thought it would be good for my future at *Newsweek*. How could I refuse? Everything that had happened to me at *Newsweek* had been good. I had no desire whatever to go to New York and climb the editorial ladder. In fact, that idea was repellent to me. I was a reporter pure and simple. I talked it over with my wife. She was not initially enthusiastic either. She would be farther removed from her family in Asheville and her friends in Atlanta. But she wanted what was best for me, so she agreed, and I called Jim Cannon and took the job.

I flew out to Houston and found a house in an old—old for Houston anyway—neighborhood near Rice University, a two-story, four-bedroom home with a big back yard on a quiet street. We decided to rent this time instead of buy—out of some instinct that said I would not be here, or want to be here, long. I went back home and bought a 1962 Chevrolet station wagon and during the Christmas school break drove my family to Houston.

The profane, cigar-smoking, bourbon-drinking tough guy Karl and his four sons, Houston, 1964. I loved being a father.

The Dallas trial of Jack Ruby in March 1964 was my first media circus. The circus was haphazardly presided over by Judge Joe B. Brown, a buffoonish former justice of the peace who chewed tobacco and read comic books on the bench, and Ruby's attorney, a flamboyant personal injury lawyer from San Francisco named Melvin Belli.

Belli came to court on opening day wearing a green velvet suit and carrying a purple velvet briefcase. He spoke in an arch falsetto voice, and his defense was that Ruby suffered from something he called "psychomotor epilepsy," which he told the jury rendered Ruby incapable of rational thought. As the jury was composed of leather-faced Texas guys with pale half moons on their brows from where their hats had been, it was the immediate consensus of the press corps that Ruby was doomed from the moment we saw and heard this exotic creature Belli from the Sodom and Gomorrah that was San Francisco. This was underscored when somebody heard one of the Texas good ol' boys who packed the second-floor courtroom say to another one, "Heh, Bobby Joe, did you get your psychomotor started this morning?"

Belli—it was pronounced "BELL-eye" but the local boys called him "Belly"—usually held court for those of us in the press in the courtroom after lunch, which I took daily with other reporters at a Dallas barbecue palace called The Cattleman's. During one such session, in which Belli was asserting medical proof that Ruby didn't know what he was doing when he shot Oswald, Judge Brown walked in. When no one paid the slightest attention to his entrance, he loudly yelled, "Fire! Fire!"

Conspiracy theorists hung about the courthouse in large numbers, tying Ruby to the Mafia or to a Communist network or to the theories already attached to Oswald, but no one in the press took any of this seriously. Ruby was just a cheap, show-off local stripjoint owner who loved hanging out with the Dallas cops, despite having been arrested by them eight times for everything from carrying a concealed weapon, to selling booze after hours at his Carousel Club, to allowing lewd dancing, to simple assault. I didn't talk to a single reporter there—and there were some hard-boiled ones like Homer Bigart of the *New York Times*, Dorothy Kilgallen of the *New York Journal-American,* and Bob Considine of the International News Service—who didn't believe Ruby when he said he shot Oswald to spare Jackie Kennedy from having to testify at a trial. He had told plenty of people he loved the Kennedys, mostly for their class. The morning he shot Oswald, he had been at Western Union sending a money order to one of his strippers and just happened to walk over to the police station because of the excitement, arriving at the exact moment police were bringing Oswald out to transfer him to another jail. He pulled out the pistol he always carried to protect his money and shot him.

At the Dallas Press Club, where the press from around the world repaired every night to drink and gossip about the case, Ruby was a more or less ridiculous and pathetic figure, a nut case actually. When he was found guilty and sentenced to death by Judge Brown on March 24, 1964, standing pale and, I thought, uncomprehending beside Belli, a murmur of sympathy went through the crowd. There was everything sad and tawdry about Ruby and about the trial. I didn't think anyone walked away feeling exultant that an evil criminal, or the tool of some sinister conspiracy, had gotten what he deserved.

Chapter 12

The Philadelphia Story

THE FINAL MASSIVE activist assault on Mississippi was coming and I didn't want to miss it. So on Sunday, June 24, 1964, I said goodbye again to my wife and four sons, boarded a Delta DC-3 with a week's supply of clothes, my Pentax camera, and my Lettera 22 portable typewriter, and flew to Cincinnati. I rented a car and drove north to Oxford, Ohio. There at the small Western College for Women, 200 volunteer college kids, most of whom whites from the Northeast, a few from California and Illinois, were arriving by old Volkswagens, beat-up Fords and Chevies, motorcycles and buses for a week of training to participate in Mississippi Freedom Summer, the nonviolent invasion to finally break down segregation in the most violently intransigent of the South's racist states.

Eighty veteran civil rights workers, almost all of them black and in their early twenties, were there to tutor these kids on the ways of life, and death, in Mississippi. SNCC's Jim Forman warned the trainees right off: "You may be killed. I may be killed. If you recognize that, then the question of whether you're put in jail will become very, very minute."

At that time only three lawyers in the entire state of Mississippi would accept civil rights cases. All were "Negro." One of them was a bent and gray old man named Jess Brown, and he warned the kids about how whites would respond to their arrival: "There's no question they will be looking for you. So if you're riding down the road at 12:30 at night and the police stop you and arrest you, don't get out and argue with the cop and say, 'I know my rights.' There ain't any use standing there trying to teach him constitutional law at twelve o'clock at night. There's no need of resisting. Go to jail, and wait for your lawyer."

And there were unnerving requirements: Each volunteer had to come up with $500 bail money, list a next of kin, and sit for a photo with an ID number across the chest to be released upon arrest, injury, or death. There were instructions on how to protect yourself when beaten: Curl up in a fetal position, hands over your head, and try to protect your vital organs as much as possible. Look out for cars with no license tags, they were warned, and don't stand in front of lighted windows. Get to know the back roads and the location of safe houses. And do not even think about interracial dating.

The aggressive guerrilla campaign that had been waged in Mississippi by a handful of young black activists for three years had produced depressingly low results. Ole Miss had been integrated, by one person, but only with massive federal force and a riot that cost two lives and hundreds of injuries. There had been a few attempts to integrate lunch counters and other public facilities with sit-ins, the only result being bloodied heads and arrests of the victims. Not a single high school or elementary school in Mississippi was integrated—ten years after the Supreme Court ruled that segregation be ended "with all deliberate speed." Despite dozens of intense campaigns to register Negroes to vote, considerably more of them had been bombed, beaten, jailed, and otherwise harassed than had gained the right to cast a ballot. Of the 500,000 Negroes of voting age in the Delta, fewer than 25,000 were registered.

Mississippi, then, remained, despite the best efforts of COFO (the Council of Federated Organizations, including SNCC, CORE, and the NAACP) and dozens of federal lawsuits, the most rigidly segregated state in the country—and the most adamantly determined to stay that way at whatever the costs. Power remained completely in the hands of a white elite that carefully selected, licensed, and cheered on cops and sheriffs willing to deal with anyone who dared to challenge the system.

What was needed, the young black guerrilla fighters decided, was something dramatically different: a massive, D-Day-like non-violent summer invasion of 1,000 volunteers whose force even Mississippi could not resist. The volunteers in Ohio would be the first wave.

I had just come back from a boozy dinner on the third night of the training and entered the gym, where classes were still under way, when Forman asked me if I would play a Mississippi sheriff with a trainee "outside agitator" in custody in a rural Mississippi town. I was well-qualified for this role, for I had seen Southern sheriffs and cops in action against black people since my first days as a reporter. I looked the part, too, except perhaps a bit too clean-cut in my suit and button-down shirt. I was thirty-six years old, six foot one, 210 pounds, crew cut, profane, gruff, and feisty.

I was clearly crossing the line here taking part in one of their exercises. But I felt it was OK because I had demonstrated my toughness and objectivity and sense of fairness. I had by this time a close working relationship with all of the black CORE and SNCC workers who had been risking their lives in the South—and who were now on hand to show these white kids how to help Negroes register to vote, learn to read and write, how to apply for previously unobtainable jobs, how to participate in sit-ins at segregated lunch counters—and how to do all this without getting maimed or killed. At the same time, I showed no favoritism in my work. My heroes remained hard-drinking, tough-minded reporters—Mark Twain, Ambrose Bierce, Ernest Hemingway, and H. L. Mencken. So I took a fierce pride in being a hardboiled and objective reporter—and, indeed, in the fact that I had written things that the black kids of SNCC and CORE had not liked at all—such as the fact that some of them sarcastically referred to Martin Luther King as "De Lawd" and derided him as being afraid to operate in Mississippi.

So I felt qualified to play a redneck sheriff without being compromised. When I said yes, Forman brought forth a pale, skinny white kid and stood him in front of me as my victim as the white college kid recruits made a circle around us.

"On your knees, boy," I said.

"What?"

"You mean 'What, sir,' don't you, boy?" And I said again, "On your goddamned knees."

He hesitated, then kneeled down and I continued, my voice rising.

"Are you a goddamned Jew?"

"Well, I'm Jewish, yes, sir."

"I thought so. All of your nigger-loving Northern agitators are Jews. And how much did the goddamned Communists pay you to come down here and stir up our niggers?"

"Nothing, sir. I'm a volunteer."

"Well, you've just volunteered for me to beat the shit out of you or kill your sorry ass right here in this jail cell and throw you in the river and nobody would ever find your skinny ass, did you know that?"

"No, sir."

"Well, you better skeedaddle your ass out of here by sundown today and hurry back up there with your nigger-loving Yankee friends or you're dead meat. Your soul may belong to the Communists and the niggers but your ass belongs to me."

He retreated, pale and shaken. Forman came over to me with a sly grin and said, "Karl, you were a little too convincing."

I didn't reply, and walked away. In truth I was shaken up, stunned at how the anger that made my portrayal so real had come up in me so quickly. To be sure I was exhausted and on edge from the previous long days and nights on the civil rights beat. For a long time I had been running on too little sleep, too much fear, too much booze, too much coffee, too many irregular bad meals, and a pervasive sense of shame and rage—all barely concealed behind a facade of brash cynicism and raw humor—at what I saw white cops, sheriffs, and redneck riffraff doing to black people.

Still, how had I so easily slipped into that role? I came to understand what a part anger played in all this and that these white racists were angry about a lot of things that didn't have to do with black people at all—poverty, ignorance, impotence, fear, shame. Here was my own anger so easily exposed, the long-ago bullied kid turned into a bully himself. I had carried that always, it was down there, and when presented with even a play victim, I had been able to personify the very kind of person I hated. I knew I never would behave that way in real life, but it was unnerving nevertheless. I realized that in using that word "boy" in my mock tirade, I had touched on something that went to the heart of male racism. It had to do with the white males' fear of black males as potent, sexual threats. They couldn't stand the idea of black men as men. They needed to diminish them by calling them boy. Until the word came out of my own mouth, even though I was talking to a white kid, I hadn't quite realized the full fear-filled import behind its everyday use.

In the weeks leading up to the training school, there had been a lot of agonizing debate among the veteran young black soldiers about recruiting white kids for the summer—which I had reported on in my *Newsweek* stories. One faction, led by Stokely Carmichael, the cocky young SNCC worker who had earlier founded the Black Panther Party in Alabama and who came up with the term "black power," wanted whites kicked out of the fight altogether. This faction believed this should be a pure black revolution. Further, they thought—and with some justification— that whites tended to take over whenever they got involved. More practical hands, like Forman, and the jowly, sonorous-voiced Jim Farmer, the chairman of CORE, argued that the white kids were needed because they had the education and the skills to do the necessary work, because they were affluent enough to spare the time, and because their mere presence would provoke more media attention to the summer invasion.

At the same time there was a mixed feeling of concern, guilt, and calculation—expressed to me by the black kids and by Bob Moses, in particular—as the white volunteers settled in for their week's boot camp in Ohio. Could these woefully guileless white college kids be taught enough to protect themselves against almost certain arrest or physical attack? Would they be, inevitably, lambs led to slaughter? And if that happened, would or should it be on everybody's conscience? And if so, why so? Were white lives any more valuable than black lives? The cold truth, viewed in calculating military terms, was that white lives indeed would be viewed as vastly more valuable, at least to the national media and to the white political powers in Washington.

I filed my story of the training sessions to *Newsweek* by Western Union Thursday night and mailed in my photographs. I flew down to Jackson Sunday morning, checked into the Sun 'N' Sand Motel, and started making calls. Soon John Herbers of the *New York Times* arrived with the *Times*'s David Halberstam, fresh back from Vietnam, who had been assigned to do pieces around the state on what the Mississippi Freedom Summer volunteers were up to. The Harvard-educated Halberstam had started his career on a small newspaper in Mississippi and went to the Nashville *Tennessean* before going to the *Times*—and to Vietnam. Tall, intense, dogged, he was a reporter's reporter and he instantly became my friend.

Claude Sitton had flown down with me from Ohio. When we reached the COFO office in Jackson by phone, we found it in a high state of agitation. Three of the first arrivals in Mississippi from Oxford, Ohio, were already missing. They were Michael (Mickey) Schwerner and Andrew (Andy) Goodman, white kids from New York, and James Chaney, a black kid from Meridian, Miss.

Schwerner and Chaney had been working for the movement in Meridian, a small town of 30,000, 150 miles west of Jackson, for several months, and were already schooled in the nuances and brutalities of the Mississippi system. For that reason, they had left Ohio by station wagons at 3:30 A.M. Saturday, carrying six volunteers, including Goodman, with the intention of not being on the road in Mississippi in a mixed group after dark. They arrived on schedule in Meridian at 5:30 Saturday. Early Sunday, the three men had driven twenty miles over to Longdale, a hamlet in neighboring Neshoba County, to visit the congregation of the black Mount Zion Methodist Church. On the night of June 16, while

Chaney, Goodman, and Schwerner were in Ohio, armed Klansmen had intercepted the church's leaders as they were coming out of a meeting, herded them into a ditch, and beat them. Later that night, they returned and burned down the church. This was in retaliation for the church's leaders allowing it to be used as a freedom school for voter registration classes.

Though the COFO workers were holding out hope, Claude and I had the terrible certainty that we were gathering information about these young men for their obituaries. The slender, bearded Schwerner, twenty-four, was a Cornell graduate, son of a New York Jewish businessman. While at Cornell, he began dating an intense young woman from Mt. Vernon, New York, named Rita Levant. When Mickey enrolled at Columbia's graduate School of Social Work, she transferred to Queens College. After Cornell, Schwerner dropped out of Columbia in June 1962, and took a job as a social worker in a settlement house, right after which he and Rita were married. He and Rita were involved in several civil rights demonstrations in New York in the next months, and after the Sixteenth Street Baptist Church was bombed, they applied to CORE to go South to work. They left New York for Meridian in a VW Beetle in mid-January 1964. They were the first full-time civil rights workers in Mississippi, aside from the NAACP staff people.

The baby-faced, black-haired Goodman, twenty-one, was also a native New Yorker and a Queens College student. He had signed up for the Oxford training after hearing Aaron Henry, the Clarksdale druggist and NAACP activist, and several SNCC activists speak at Queens in April as a part of Freedom Week. Jewish, brought up in a leftist, pacifist household during the 1950s era of Red-baiting McCarthyism, Goodman had immediately seen a role for himself in this battle between good and evil.

Chaney, twenty-one, was one of four children of a Meridian

plasterer whose wife worked for a dollar fifty a day washing, cleaning, ironing, and mending for a white couple. A rebellious teen-ager who thought the NAACP was too conservative, Chaney had been kicked out of junior college as a troublemaker. His parents had by then separated, and Chaney went to work as a trainee union plasterer for his father, but quit when he found out that his father was sending money to his girlfriend instead of to his ex-wife. He was introduced to the Meridian CORE field office director by a girl he had a crush on and went to work there in October 1963. He had deep-set brown eyes and was asthmatic enough to have been turned down for military service.

The Meridian office and the others around the state, anticipating trouble, had established a system to keep tabs on workers going out into the field. Workers were supposed to call in every two hours. Goodman, Schwerner, and Chaney, we were told, hadn't been heard from since they left Meridian to go to the black church early that morning. We telephoned the COFO office again and then again. The kids were now overdue on their scheduled call-in by six hours. Meantime, we had been joined in the vigil by Nick Von Hoffman of the *Chicago Daily News*, on assignment to write a series of feature stories about Freedom Summer. Nick was about the whitest white man I had ever seen—tall, blonde-haired, and blue-eyed with cream-white skin. He had an engaging, sardonic manner and I took to him immediately.

"They're dead," I said to Claude and Nick after the last call.

"What else could it be?" Claude said.

Neshoba County, where the kids had gone, was in northeast Mississippi, population 20,000—15 per cent Choctaw Indian, 15 percent black, and the rest white. It was all piney woods and swamps, an insular place, hostile to outsiders. Most of its blacks and the white families had been there since before the Civil War.

Not part of the cotton-rich alluvial Delta, it was hardscrabble country of hand-to-mouth existence—fertile ground for the Ku Klux Klan. Its county seat, Philadelphia, was notable for being the birthplace of Turner Catledge, managing editor of the *New York Times*, and Chuckin' Chuck Conerly of the New York Giants. Its residents were rueful about the first and boastful about the latter. Philadelphia also hosted the annual Neshoba County Fair, where gubernatorial candidates historically announced for office with stump speeches under a stifling tent.

Claude and I arrived there at 8:30 A.M. Monday, the first reporters on the scene, and went straight to the courthouse. It was a faded brick building with a small dome, at the center of the town square, its scraggly lawn decorated with Confederate statuary, white and colored water fountains, and a few old geezers smoking and chewing tobacco on wooden benches next to the front entrance.

The sheriff's office was just off the small lobby, its door open, and inside behind the counter stood Sheriff Lawrence Rainey and his deputy, Cecil Price, as if they were expecting us. Rainey was a large, menacing man with a big gut. He had a wad of Redman chewing tobacco in his jaw—a plug of it in his tan shirt pocket—and a defiant look. Price was smaller, a pale, pulpy man with a soft and sweaty face. He seemed extremely nervous and furtive, but Rainey, to use a common Southernism, was "as cool as the center seed of a cucumber." Both wore tan Stetson hats, tan shirts and pants, Western boots, and big guns on their hips.

Rainey listened to us impassively, with Price hovering damply in the background, as we explained why we were there. We were reporters with *Newsweek* and the *New York Times*. Three civil rights workers had been missing in the county since Sunday morning. Did they know anything?

"Well, yeah," Rainey said blandly. "Deputy Price here arrested these two Jews and a nigger yesterday afternoon for speeding and we held them in jail for awhile and turned them loose after they paid the fine."

All he knew, he said, was that the station wagon was speeding and that Deputy Price had properly stopped the car. It was the custom around there for a speeder to just be given a ticket and pay the fine later, he acknowledged, but these three were strangers, he said, and it certainly was unusual for "a nigger to be riding in the same car with two white boys," so there were legitimate grounds for being suspicious.

Price admitted the kids had told them they had been over in Longdale at the burned-out church. "I figured they might have something to do with it," he said.

Rainey and Price then escorted us over to the jail a block away where the jailer's wife, Minnie Herring, showed us the log bearing Schwerner's, Goodman's, and Chaney's names and assured us that, yes, they had been turned loose at 10 P.M. after paying the twenty-dollar speeding ticket. She showed us the signed receipt.

"We don't know what happened after that. Probably they went on back up North," Rainey said.

"We were nice to them, and they were nice to us," Price said.

As we left, Claude muttered, "Those kids are definitely dead."

"Yeah, and these sons of bitches are involved up to their necks," I said.

We drove to the edge of town and checked into the dingy old Delphian Court Motel, a one-story rectangle of two dozen or so brick-walled rooms with faded doors on a concrete lot. Then we drove the 35 miles over to Meridian. We found Jim Farmer, the head of CORE, sitting on a bed in a room at the black E. F. Young Hotel, gloomily munching on a chicken sandwich. There had been no further news of Chaney, Goodman, and Schwerner and Farmer and others gathered around now assumed the worst.

They had called the Justice Department in Washington to ask for help and the FBI regional office in Memphis to request that agents be sent to Philadelphia. They didn't expect much from the FBI. But Lyndon Johnson's Justice Department had gone to court in several counties in behalf of black voter registrants in recent months and Justice's John Doar had aggressively mounted several voter and school integration cases in Mississippi.

Volunteers and SNCC and CORE staff members drifted in and out, all of whom I knew, as calls to Washington, New York, Atlanta, and Jackson were made. We told Farmer and the others what Rainey and Price had told us—that Chaney, Goodman, and Schwerner had been arrested and released on the edge of town. The only logical conclusion was that they had been abducted somewhere on the road back to Meridian. And since it was unheard of that kids like these might be held for ransom, the next logical conclusion was that they had been murdered. The further logical assumption was that the Klan was involved in the disappearance. It would have taken more than one person, certainly, to pull off something like this, some coordination of cars, people, and weapons, and it was the well-organized Klan that could do it. The only question was whether either Rainey or Price, or both, had delivered Chaney, Goodman, and Schwerner into their hands.

In Jackson, Governor Paul Johnson, called upon to comment on the disappearances, said, "They could be in Cuba. There are many possibilities, and I'd be a very large fool to try to make a guess." In Washington, Mississippi Senator Jim Eastland joined that chorus: "No one wants to charge that a hoax has been perpetrated because there is too little evidence to show just what did happen. But as time goes on and the search continues and no evidence of a crime is produced, I think the people of America will be justified in considering other alternatives as more valid solutions to the mystery, instead of accepting as more true the accusation of the agitators that a heinous crime has been committed."

Late that afternoon we checked into a Meridian motel, our belongings still in Philadelphia. I called Atlanta and told my wife this was going to be a long one, and that I couldn't foresee when I might get home. I reassured my four sons, one by one, that I would be home soon and that we would go off and do something fun, and then went to dinner at a local place reputed to have good food, a restaurant called Wideman's, fashioned out of old railroad cars with red-checkered tablecloths. I had a steak, always a fairly safe thing to order in an unknown restaurant. When I paid my check, the cashier handed me, as part of my change, a shiny new John F. Kennedy half dollar. They'd just come out and were great conversation pieces and hard to get, at least at home in Atlanta. People were grabbing them up.

"Have you got any more of these?" I asked.

"Oh, I've got three or four rolls of them that we got from the bank," he said. "Nobody around here wants 'em. You can have them all." The Kennedys were despised in Mississippi. It was on the record that many Mississippians cheered when JFK was shot.

Next morning Claude and I set off for Philadelphia again. We went to our rooms at the Delphian, showered and shaved and put on fresh clothes and went back to the courthouse. This time Price was absent but Rainey was in his office, as sullen and defiant as before. He had not learned anything new about the kids, he said, but he had a new explanation for where they might be found: "Everybody around here knows the Communists are behind these Jew agitators coming down here. If they're missing, they hid somewhere trying to stir up a lot of publicity. I'm sure they are somewhere laughing at the commotion they've stirred up. They're probably already in Cuba by now. Why don't you tell the Justice

Department to look there? And I ain't got no more time to waste
on talking about this."

When we went back out into the lobby, our way out of the
courthouse was blocked by a crowd of thirty white men waiting
for us. Their leader, a big-boned, big-bellied man of about fifty in
capacious tan pants and a short-sleeved sports shirt, thrust himself in our faces. His face was crimson with anger, and he immediately launched into a tirade:

"Our goddamned niggers were always happy and not causing
anybody any trouble around here until these outside agitators
started coming down from the North and stirring them up. And
they keep on coming because you goddamned son-of-a-bitch
reporters for the nigger-loving Yankee Jew Communist press give
them publicity. Why don't you son-of-a-bitches mind your own
goddamned bidness wherever you come from? Why do you have
to come down here stirring up trouble? If it weren't for you nigger-loving Jew Communist reporters we wouldn't be having all
this trouble. And don't think we don't know who you are and
where you are staying. You have no idea what trouble you could
be in. So my advice to you is to get your nigger-loving asses out of
this town right now and stay away or you could get goddamned
killed."

When he paused for breath I feebly tried to explain, with my
best cornpone drawl, that Claude and I were just two good ol'
Southern boys, he from Georgia and I from North Carolina, trying to do our jobs. But that seemed only to inflame him and
the others more. Not only was I an agent for the Yankee nigger-
loving Jew-Communist press, I was worse—a traitor to "our precious Southern way of life."

"You ought to know better than to be whoring for the Jews
and Communists up North, so I'm telling you again, you'd better
get your asses out of here," he bellowed.

We edged our way out the back door onto the town square and Claude said, "Come on over here," pointing to a one-story corner business with a sign over the door that said "Turner Hardware." Then I remembered that Claude had told me that Turner Catledge had an uncle who lived in Philadelphia. We walked over there quickly.

A tall, thin man with sparse, sandy hair, a narrow mouth, and eyes behind thick glasses, stood a few feet inside the door.

"Mr. Turner," Claude said, "I'm Claude Sitton of the *New York Times* and this is Karl Fleming from *Newsweek* magazine. And Turner said if we got in any trouble here, you might be able to help us out. You probably have heard about these three civil rights workers who are missing. Our job is to be down here and report on what might have happened to them. We're both Southern boys just doing our jobs. We're not on anybody's side. We're not causing any trouble. But this crowd over there at the courthouse where we went to talk to the sheriff has just threatened to kill us if we don't get out of town."

Turner gazed at Claude blankly, coldly, and said in a flat voice: "Well, I'll tell you this: If those old boys had you two down on the ground kicking the living crap out of you, like a couple of niggers, I wouldn't participate in that, no sir. But on the other hand, if it weren't for you reporters coming down here stirring these niggers up we wouldn't be having these problems. So I wouldn't lift one goddamned finger to help you, and my advice is, do like those boys over at the courthouse said and get the hell out of this town before you get killed."

We walked out and I said, "Well, Claude, it's a good thing you've got some influence in this town or we'd be in big damned trouble."

When we got back to the Delphian and into our rooms, I

noticed a hole in the back wall and someone looking in. There was also someone at the door, peering in through a crack. We went to the front desk to complain to the owner, a rough-looking character with a flushed face and a stained hat on his head. We had, as usual, not signed the register listing our company affiliations. But the manager knew exactly who we were, and when Claude complained about people spying on us he said, "You boys don't like it, why don't you all leave? I would if I were you, anyway, because you could get killed around here."

"That might happen," Claude said. "But if you kill us, there'll be ten more just like us here next week."

When we got back to our rooms I noticed that a muddy car with a Mississippi tag had parked close to us. Its doors were open and four men sat inside, passing around a quart fruit jar of moonshine. There were shotguns visible in both the front and back seats. I decided we'd better find out what they were up to and went out to their car.

"How you boys doin' today," I drawled. They were drinking the moonshine straight, and it was strong-smelling stuff.

They were just lazing away the afternoon, one of them said, just keeping up with what was going on. "What are you boys doing down here? You ain't from around here," the one closest to me said.

"Oh, we're just a couple of good ol' boys from Atlanta who got sent down here to check on these missing kids," I said. I left it open that we might be FBI.

"Them troublemakers ain't around here. They probably went back to New York or Chicago or wherever the Communists sent 'em to. Have a drink with us."

"Sure, why not?" I said. He handed me the fruit jar and I took a slug. It was awful stuff, even by bad busthead standards. I was barely able to hold it down without gagging.

"We ain't causing anybody any trouble. We just got sent down here to do our jobs," I said. "We'll be gone from here soon."

"It's interesting country around here, some good farms and good white people who've been here a long time without anybody disturbing our ways. Maybe you boys would like to take a ride with us out in the country," the driver said.

"No, we gotta go over to the courthouse to see the sheriff," I said, retreating. I went back to the room. Nick had come over. I said, "We gotta get the hell out of here. Those guys are dangerous."

We packed quickly and since Nick's car was closest to the door we got into it and headed out toward Meridian. The car with the four guys fell in behind us. Nick was obviously unused to driving. He was creeping along at about fifty-five, and it was getting dark.

"Drive faster, goddammit," I said.

"I'm driving the speed limit," he said.

"Fuck the speed limit," I screamed. "You're going to get us killed."

"Damn right," Claude yelled from the back.

Nick reluctantly sped up, and soon we reached the county line, whereupon the car behind us slowed and its headlights gradually disappeared.

Next day, Tuesday, came the first break in the case. Midmorning, FBI agents working out of Meridian got a call from the superintendent of the Choctaw Indian Reservation near Philadelphia. He told them that two Indians had found a smoldering car off Highway 21 just out from the crossroads village of Bogue Chitta. They found the totally burned-out car back from the highway on an old logging road thick with blackberry and sweetgum bushes. The agents tried to keep their find secret, but word spread rapidly after they began questioning people who lived in houses on the road. By the time I got there, in late afternoon, the agents were poking around in the snake-infested swamp, and a small crowd had gathered. I took several pictures of the car, one of which appeared along with my *Newsweek* story the next week.

We had decided not to spend the night in Philadelphia, so we drove back to Meridian and checked in at the Summer Project office to see what was going on. Rita Schwerner and Goodman's parents were contacting their senators and congressmen in Washington to demand action, and Jim Farmer was leading a group to Neshoba County next day. Wednesday morning, Forman, John Lewis, one of the early Nashville sit-inners, a Freedom Rider, veteran of dozens of protests, and victim of many beatings and arrests, and Dick Gregory led a motorcade of thirty-five cars toward Philadelphia, where they were stopped by Rainey and other cops. They said they wanted to visit the burned-out church, and the spot where the car was found. No dice, said Rainey.

Meanwhile, the FBI had brought in 100 sailors from the Meridian Naval Air Station in three buses, and they fanned out through the swampy water, some in boats with grappling hooks, at Bogue Chitta, where the car had been found. About fifty local whites watched from a concrete bridge, smirking and making remarks. It was a smothering hot day. I watched from the bridge, took pictures, and listened to the talk.

"I don't know how they're gonna find the Jewboys, but if they want to find the nigger, all they have to do is wave a welfare check over the water and he'll come right up," said one.

"Ain't gonna find anything in that swamp," said a highway patrolman. "Water's too deep. It's too damn hot and they got skeeters in that swamp so big they could stand flatfooted and fuck a turkey."

Rita Schwerner got back to Meridian from Ohio on Wednesday and told reporters at the airport that the disappearances would have gone unnoticed had not two white Northern kids been involved. She was not going to play the role of hapless stricken widow. She was angry, and she issued a set of demands: that federal marshals be sent to Mississippi to protect civil rights workers, that the feds launch an investigation of Mississippi law enforcement's intimidation and attacks on workers, that those hindering voter registration efforts be prosecuted, that Allen Dulles, former CIA boss, and now President Johnson's "personal envoy," go to Meridian and interview Summer Project officials. (LBJ did, in fact, under intense pressure from the Goodman and Schwerner families and from congressmen, send Dulles to Jackson to meet with Governor Paul Johnson.)

The next day, Rita Schwerner, accompanied by Bob Zellner, an Alabama native who in 1961 become SNCC's first white field secretary, and who had been beaten and jailed, drove to Jackson to confront the governor and Dulles. The governor, as it happened, was meeting with George Wallace, in town to make a speech, and was overheard while chatting with reporters to say, in regards to the missing kids, that "Governor Wallace and I are the only ones who know where they are, and we aren't telling." Johnson then shook hands with Zellner, thinking he was a constituent, and Zellner said, "This is Rita Schwerner, and I think it is reprehensible for you to be joking about this situation." They then went to see Dulles, who told Rita that he offered his sympathy, whereupon she said, "I don't want sympathy. I want my husband back."

Next morning there was a pounding on my door at the Delphian Court in Philadephia and I opened it to find Rita and Zellner standing there. Zellner, who I had known since 1961, was pale and shaking. I poured him a shot of bourbon and he downed it. He said they had come looking for FBI agents who were quartered at the Delphian Court. They wanted to report an incident and were looking for protection. They had just come from Longdale, to which they had driven in the dark from Jackson, so as not to attract attention, only to find at daybreak a large number of white men waiting at the burned-out church which her husband, Goodman, and Chaney had visited. Two of the white men had pursued them at high speed in a pickup truck and they had barely gotten away.

I walked them across the courtyard and introduced them to an FBI agent, who told them the Delphia was being watched by local white men in pickup trucks. Suddenly, Sheriff Rainey and a state highway patrol investigator pulled into the lot and Rainey growled at the five-foot, ninety-pound Rita, "What the god-damned hell are you doing here?"

"I'm not leaving until I see Mickey's car," she said. "I'm not leaving until I find out what happened to my husband. I'm going to keep drawing attention here until I find out, and if you don't like it, you'll just have to kill me too."

Rainey turned crimson. He very likely had never been spoken to like this before by anyone, certainly not a woman. He had already arrested and jailed one local woman, member of a respected old Philadelphia merchant family, whose crime was to offer iced tea to FBI agents going door-to-door questioning people. But he restrained himself, under the eye of *Newsweek*, the *New York Times*, and the FBI, and said he'd give them five minutes with the car, which had been stowed in a local body shop. They inspected it briefly, then headed back to Meridian, only to have their car pelted with rocks and bottles at the edge of town and to be pursued into the countryside by pickups and cars.

By this time, the town was crawling with national reporters, most of whom had never been to Mississippi before, and a hundred FBI agents. The reporters were stunned at the hostility they met and by the universal explanation from locals that it was all a hoax—even after the car was found.

The FBI had set up its main shop at the old wooden Benwalt Hotel just off the courthouse. Most of the arriving reporters stayed there, too. One of them, a TV reporter from a New Orleans station, was chased in his TV truck around the courthouse square by a carload of white toughs. He was finally cornered and one of the toughs pulled a knife and threatened to kill him. When he went to the police station to complain, they gave him a ticket for obstructing traffic.

Late Thursday evening I drove back to Jackson, exhausted, angry, and depressed, with all the notes I had taken during the week, plus the film I had shot. There were flights out of Jackson to take the film to New York and Western Union stayed open all night. I went back to a room at the Sun 'N' Sand and sat down at my portable, sick with exhaustion, tension, and apprehension at the long night's work of distilling my notes and making some kind of sense of them. I went to the bathroom and threw up. I finished at 2 A.M., drove to Western Union on Capitol Street, and sent my twenty pages to New York, then drove back and fell into bed. The next day I returned to Philadelphia as the search continued and the glare of national media heightened. *Newsweek* had decided to do a cover on Philadelphia and Mississippi the next week, and sent down my bureau mate from Atlanta, Joe Cumming, and from New York, my pal Frank Trippett, the gifted national affairs section writer, a droll, hard-drinking native of Mississippi. On his way down to the state, Frank called his Aunt Minnie in his native Tupelo to tell her he was coming.

"Don't you go be telling lies about us in Mississippi, Frank," she said.

"I'm gonna do worse than that, Aunt Minnie," he said. "I'm gonna tell the truth."

Over the weekend, the FBI had broadened its search. The main focus was near bridges over rivers and creeks large and small, including the large Pearl River. That's where the body of a young Negro man named Mack Charles Parker had been found in 1957. Jailed on the charge of raping a white woman, he was taken from his cell and shot in the head and his weighted body dumped from a bridge into the Pearl. The discovery of black bodies in rivers was not unusual, and there were several cruel "jokes" that whites told on that subject. One of them went that when a black man was found in the river wrapped in chains, the sheriff said, "Ain't that just like a nigger to steal more chain than he can swim with." Another one was that when a Negro body was found in the Pearl with nine bullet holes in its back, the sheriff said "this is the worst case of suicide I have ever seen."

Under pressure from LBJ, J. Edgar Hoover came down to Jackson and opened an FBI office there, headed by the agent who had led the investigation of the Birmingham church bombing the previous September. Hoover reported back to Johnson that progress was being made, and no amount of manpower or money was to be spared. But in fact, the investigation was quickly in a stalemate; 1,000 people had been interviewed and not one person had said a thing. A combination of fear of Klan retribution and insular hatred of the federal government was the cause of that.

At the end of the second week, I drove back up to Jackson, accompanied by Joe Cumming, to write my story and file it at Western Union. We took adjoining rooms at the Sun 'N' Sand, and he stayed in his room working while I went out to LeFleur's with Claude Sitton. LeFleur's was a Cajun restaurant on the edge of town that attracted Jackson's best white people. The waiters were white-jacketed blacks. The two main walls were covered with huge murals, one depicting happy blacks picking cotton, singing, and eating watermelons in a field, the other showing a typical plantation mansion with its owner in front in a white suit and his wife in a billowing crinoline skirt and, in the foreground, a little black boy pushing a fancily dressed little white girl in a swing on a magnolia tree.

We'd stopped on the way to buy a bottle of bourbon at a bootlegger's house that was well known by the locals. Though Mississippi was officially a dry state, the bootleggers operated openly and paid taxes, which were collected by the sheriff, who got a cut. The Hinds County sheriff was, in fact, at a salary of $80,000, Mississippi's highest-paid public official.

Claude had his usual two drinks, and I had about five, along with crawfish bisque and oysters Bienville and ordered baked Alaska for dessert. I made a small cross out of two matchsticks, stuck it in the flaming cake when it arrived and lit it. People at nearby tables glared at us. Claude shook his head helplessly. I was hopeless.

I was smoking three packs of unfiltered Camels a day by then. Claude was a smoker, too, but as he was in everything else, more moderate. We had both tried to quit many times. That night, perhaps as a way to distract myself from the fatigue and tension, and because I was feeling beaten down, exhausted, and in poor health generally, I issued Claude a challenge: The first one of us who smoked again would have to pay the other one $500. This was a bet with teeth in it, for we were both earning $10,000 a year, I having had one healthy raise. He agreed, and we both quit, on the spot, a decision followed by agonizing weeks of withdrawal for me.

Later that night I went back to the motel. Joe Cumming and I were in my room trying to write our files, both of us worn and frayed from the week's tension. At one point, I was in the bed with the covers pulled over my head and Joe was in the bathroom throwing up. We finally finished at 3 A.M., and I drove our copy to Western Union. Next day, I flew back to Houston and drove my family out to Galveston and the beach.

Meantime, the Neshoba County search for Goodman, Chaney, and Schwerner went on, while in other parts of the state, the toll of bombed and burned churches and the attacks on Freedom Summer volunteers went on. Two other bodies of Negro men were found in a small river eighty miles west of Jackson. Falsely thought by the Klan to be smuggling guns and ammo into Mississippi to aid the agitators, they were beaten to death and their bodies weighted down. In the two months between when the first wave of volunteers hit the state and mid-August, COFO compiled a frightful list of misdeeds against their people: fifty beatings, thirteen churches burned down, fifteen other churches damaged by bombs or fire, four shootings, and ten cars destroyed.

Unable to make any headway otherwise, the FBI used the same bait that had broken the Emmett Till case (the teenaged Till was murdered in Mississippi for allegedly flirting with a white woman): They offered big money, $30,000, for information. Finally a tip came through, and on August 1, they found the bodies, using a giant bulldozer, on a 106-degree day, buried in an earthen farm dam ten miles out from Philadelphia on Highway 21. They had all been shot and the autopsy showed that two guns had been used and that the victims had been savagely beaten.

In the following months, Sheriff Rainey, Deputy Price, and the other Klansmen involved in the killings became big local celebrities, speaking at huge Klan rallies all over the state, including one in Philadelphia where promotional material was handed out at a KKK stand on the courthouse lawn.

The flood of national indignation produced by the Mississippi murders finally gave Congress the political will to pass the Civil Rights Act, which JFK had urged in 1963, and on August 2, the day after the discovery of the bodies, LBJ signed it into law. It banned discrimination in all public facilities, such as restaurants and theaters, provided for equal employment opportunity, and pretty much eliminated literacy tests in voter applications. On August 6 the next year, Johnson would sign into law the Voting Rights Act, which officially did in literacy tests and the poll tax and appointed federal voter examiners.

Buoyed by federal action and by the energy coming out of Mississippi Freedom Summer, COFO leaders formed a break-away political body called the Mississippi Freedom Democratic Party. They held a state convention in Jackson, elected officers, and chose a slate of delegates to go to the 1964 Democratic convention in Atlantic City. This fulfilled the dream of Bob Moses that Mississippi's Negroes would find their own strength and develop their own leaders—and not be masterminded by outsiders like him.

The sixty-eight MFDP delegates and alternatives arrived by bus in Atlantic City on Friday, August 21, with high hopes that their moral cause was strong enough to force the party to give them half of the seats of the regular Mississippi delegation. I had flown into New York from Los Angeles and drove to Atlantic City with Oz Elliott, Jim Cannon, and Peter Goldman. My assignment was to cover the Freedom Democratic Party, and I went with them the next day as they presented their case before the convention's rules committee.

What none of us knew immediately was that MFDP's fate had already been decided. Despite his populist roots and liberal tendencies, LBJ was one tough politician. And, as he often reminded reporters who covered him, he could count. He was looking forward to a punishing campaign against conservative Senator Barry Goldwater, who had opposed the Civil Rights Act and otherwise allied himself with white Southern segregationists. Because of what JFK had done in behalf of Southern Negroes before, and what he had himself done, LBJ figured he had already lost Mississippi and Alabama to the Republican Party. But he thought he might hold onto the rest of the South—unless the convention turned into a nationally televised referendum on civil rights with the MFDP's sympathetic delegates stealing the spotlight. He threatened to hold up Hubert Humphrey's nomination as his vice presidential candidate unless and until Humphrey could get the MFDP to accept a compromise under which they would be seated as "honorary" delegates—in return for a pledge to not seat any segregated delegation at the 1968 convention.

On Friday I went with the MFDP delegates to make their case before the convention's credentials committee. They hadn't as yet heard about Johnson's compromise offer. Because of the drama caused by a group of powerless Mississippi Negroes challenging the Democratic establishment, this event was nationally televised on all three networks. The third witness called was the MFDP's vice chair, round-faced, rich-voiced Mrs. Fannie Lou Hamer of Ruleville, Mississippi. The nation was transfixed when she told how she had been beaten by cops in the Winona, Mississippi, jail until her skin turned blue and the cops got too tired to beat her any more. With tears running down her face, she sobbed "all of this is on account of we want to register, to become first-class citizens. If the Freedom Democratic Party is not seated now, I question America."

Martin Luther King Jr. testified, too, saying of the MFDP delegates that "you cannot imagine the anguish and suffering they have gone through to get to this point."

Telegrams by the thousands poured into the convention supporting the Negro group, and LBJ was forced to offer a new compromise: Two of the MFDP delegates would be officially seated, and the others accepted as "honored guests." Without the MFDP approving this move, the credentials committee voted in favor of it. Moses, Foreman, Fannie Lou Hamer, and the other MFDP members were angry—and hurt. Aaron Henry, the mild-man-

I always tried to be in the middle of things, as with the Mississippi Free-dom Party delegation at the Democratic National Convention, Atlantic City, 1964.

nered chairman whose Clarksdale drugstore had been firebombed for his registration efforts, said, "We did not come to Atlantic City to get the same kind of back-of-the-bus treatment we have gotten in Mississippi."

The compromise was way too little for them, and way too much for the all-white Mississippi delegation. They walked out of the convention and issued a statement saying, "The Mississippi delegation did not leave the Democratic Party. It left us." (Ronald Reagan appropriated this phrase later when he joined the Republican Party.) I joined as the MFDP delegates immediately occupied their seats and refused guards' orders to leave. That night, SNCC and Core organized an all-night protest rally on the boardwalk, and sang "We Shall Overcome" and "This Little Light of Mine" as the media, official delegates, and other spectators looked on. That was the last such rally I ever attended—and the last big peaceful protest rally at which movement songs were sung.

The SNCC and CORE kids and the Mississippi Negroes they had inspired left the convention disillusioned and bitter. All their hard work and risking of their lives had been for naught in the real world of cold-blooded politics. They believed, and with some justification I thought, that they had been betrayed by the very white liberals who gave lip service to supporting them—until the power chips were down.

There was residual bitterness about Philadelphia, too. The thinking of Moses, Forman, and others that national publicity for Mississippi Freedom Summer would be generated only if something bad happened to white kids had proved all too true. Would swarms of FBI agents and reporters have appeared had the three slain kids all been black? There was no doubt as to the answer to that. There was the recognition, certainly, that good things—the Civil Rights Act, for example—sometimes happen for the wrong reasons, but it was, nonetheless, a bitter pill to swallow. That bitterness would grow and soon would become the excuse to kick all white kids out of SNCC, for the birth of the separatist Black Power movement, and for the creation of the urban Black Panther Party, whose members brazenly brandished guns and angrily renounced the nonviolent posture of SNCC, CORE, and Martin Luther King Jr.

Chapter 13

The End of It All

I WAS IN Washington, D.C., on April 4, 1968, working on a big political story for *Newsweek* when I heard that Martin Luther King Jr. had been shot and killed in Memphis. Just days before, on March 31, LBJ had stunned the country by announcing that he would not seek reelection. The Vietnam War was taking him down, we were rushing a cover into print exploring the implications of his stepping aside, and I was making calls in the bureau office at 1750 Pennsylvania office when someone burst in with the news about King.

Somebody turned on a television set. All three networks were interrupting their regular programming with bulletins. There was that photograph of him prone on the balcony of the Lorraine Motel and his associates pointing to where the shot came from. We all sat there looking at the set. There was a kind of stunned silence. I felt all that old sickness—a mix of anger and sadness and impotence—come up in me from the days on the road when I'd seen such cruel things happen to black people. And, of course, this was the worst because of who King was and what he represented. I was the only one in the room who had known him, so I didn't say a word to anybody about what I was feeling.

Then the reporter's instinct kicked in and everybody started to scramble to get on the story. In that way, being a reporter was always a great solace because you didn't have time to sit and grieve and thumb through your own memories. They would be stored away and come back powerfully later. But right now you had to go to work. It was decided that I would stay around and help—and then go to the funeral.

The first thing I did was call my old pal Claude Sitton in New York, where he was now national editor of the *Times*.

"Well, the sons-of-bitches finally got him," I said.

"Yep. Too bad. But we knew it would happen sooner or later," he said. All those years we were with King down South—and around people who hated him—we had talked about his being killed. It had always seemed inevitable. And now, Claude and I agreed it was no doubt the work of some white segregationists eager to have the honor of bagging the ultimate trophy.

The *Newsweek* people scrambled around, but—because it's a weekly—they weren't on a hard deadline and soon the office emptied out. People went home. But I wanted and needed to stay connected to the story, so I walked over to the *Washington Post* building on L Street where everyone would still be in high reportorial gear. I went immediately to Ben Bradlee's office, where reporters were getting assignments and coming in and out with tidbits of news. In the wake of the assassination, black riots were breaking out all over the country, including in Washington. Bradlee asked me if I would help him with something. I'd have done most anything for him anyway, since he had been one of the people who created the atmosphere at *Newsweek* that had been so good for me—and besides, adrenaline flowing, I wanted to get in on the story, so I said, "Sure."

The King obituary that the regular obit guy had written was, he said in his raspy voice, "a pile of crap." Would I rewrite it if he got Nick Von Hoffman to help me? Nick had become disenchanted at the *Chicago Daily News,* where he'd been working when I met him in Mississippi in 1964, and I had been instrumental in getting him to the *Post.* Now we sat side by side at an old Remington in the *Post* newsroom—the first time I'd worked in one in twenty years—and, amid the old familiar clatter of typewriters, we wrote a five-column eulogy based a lot on our personal recollections. We talked back and forth, kicking around stories we remembered, as I did my two-finger, hunt-and-peck typing. I remembered hearing about King's first brush with the harsh rules of segregation. Growing up in Atlanta, where his father was pastor at Ebenezer Baptist Church, King played daily with a white friend until he was six when his friend's mother told him her son was "getting too big to run around playing with niggers." There was another humiliation King told people he never forgot, a white woman cursing him at Rich's Department Store in Atlanta. "You're the nigger that stepped on my foot," she said, just before slapping him in the face. Those quotes had already been in print, and we put them in King's obit.

We noted also that from an early age King seemed to respond to affronts toward him and toward other Negroes not with anger but with a quiet resolve to do something. His first big moment, of course, had come in 1955 in Montgomery, where Rosa Parks refused to go to the back of the bus and young preacher King was drafted to lead a boycott that would bring him to national attention. And his crowning moment came when he went to Stockholm on December 10, 1964, to receive the Nobel Peace Prize. Nick and I put it all in—the highlights and the humiliations.

Newsweek and *Post* publisher Kay Graham had stayed around the paper that night, interested in the developing drama and perhaps nervous about going outside given the bedlam on the streets. It was around 9 P.M. and she was in Bradlee's office when we finished the 1,800-word King obit. I'd met her in New York in my first days at *Newsweek* and had spent time walking on the beach with her at a magazine retreat in the Virgin Islands. I liked her spunk and the forceful if quiet way she had taken over the business of running the *Post* company. After we turned in the obit I asked her if she'd like to go out on the streets and see some of the action. I'd gone out myself several times during the evening. It was far from the worst riot I'd seen. It seemed more like a carnival of looting, and whites were not being attacked—though they were in other cities. I figured we'd be safe. I didn't feel like I was going to be responsible for getting the head of the *Washington Post* Company killed.

She was dressed in a gray business suit and sensible black shoes. She took my arm and broken glass crackled under our feet as we went along Fourteenth Street near the *Post*. Blacks were running everywhere laughing, shouting, and carrying off everything that wasn't nailed down in dozens of stores—many of which were being set ablaze after they'd been looted.

"Take everything you need, baby," we heard a looter exultantly shout from a shattered window. Even children were roaming the streets loading shopping carts with stolen food.

"This is awful, awful," Graham said, but if she was scared she didn't show it.

Washington's outnumbered police were all but helpless. At Fourteenth and G streets, a cop had a looter spread-eagled over the trunk of a car. Several pairs of new shoes were on the trunk beside him.

"They killed my brother! They killed Luther King," he yelled as he was being cuffed.

"Was he stealing shoes when they killed him?" the cop said as he put the handcuffs on him.

"That's a great quote," I said to Kay Graham, and indeed it ended up in our lengthy cover story the next week.

"I've seen enough," she finally said, and we went back to the Post. When we got back to Bradlee's office, we saw Bobby Kennedy on TV, hunched and wan on an Indianapolis street corner where he was speaking at a politically rally. LBJ now out of the picture, he was running for president.

"For those of you who are black—considering the evidence there evidently is that white people were responsible—you can be filled with bitterness, with hatred and a desire for revenge," he said with a bowed head. "We can move in that direction as a country, in great polarization—black people amongst black, white people amongst white, filled with hatred toward one another. Or we can make an effort, as Martin Luther King did, to understand and to comprehend and to replace that violence, that stain of bloodshed that has spread across our land, with an effort to understand with compassion and love. For those of you who are black and are tempted to be filled with hatred, I can only say that I feel in my own heart the same kind of feeling. I had a member of my family killed. . . . But we have to make an effort to understand. Let us dedicate ourselves to that and say a prayer for our country and for our people."

Many blacks across urban America were in no mood for such talk. That night and the next day and night, and the next, violence swept across black America from Oakland, California, to Tallahassee, Florida, Denver, Chicago, Detroit, New York, Boston, Pittsburgh, and Toledo, Ohio—to virtually every large city that had a ghetto.

King's moment, in fact, had passed. So there was a bitter irony in his death coming now, instead of earlier when he'd been such a direct thorn in the side of Southerners. Events in black America since the Watts riots that grew out of a police arrest, which I had covered—and where I had been shocked to hear him mocked to his face by militant young "Blood Brothers," seemed to have surged past him. His message of Christian forgiveness and nonviolent action had been shouted down with cries of "Black Power" and "Get Whitey" as the Black Panthers and the Black Muslims struck new chords among angry young blacks on urban streets. Newspaper and TV pictures of King leading prayerful marches with blacks and whites holding hands and singing "We Shall Overcome" had been replaced with threatening photographs of leather-clad Black Panthers brandishing rifles and daring whites to provoke them.

King had become an old voice and Stokely Carmichael was the new one that appealed to the unschooled, jobless, rootless blacks who roamed the streets of the North filled with pent-up rage, scornful of the churches that nourished their parents—and out of which King had come. Carmichael, in fact, was in Washington the day King was killed. Into the streets he went, wearing wrap-around sunglasses and a black leather jacket, brandishing a pistol, telling black crowds that "when white America killed Dr. King she declared war on us. We have to retaliate for the death of our leaders. Go home and get your guns. When the white man comes he is coming to kill you. I don't want any black blood in the street. So go home and get your gun and come back, 'cause I got me a gun."

King had grown increasingly concerned about Carmichael since the two men had been at a "March Against Fear" staged by James Meredith from the Alabama line to Jackson, Mississippi, in June 1966, during which Meredith was shot and wounded by a white man. But the march continued on without Meredith and when it reached Greenwood, Carmichael and others were arrested for trespassing. Out on bail, at a rally that night, Carmichael angrily shouted: "This is the twenty-seventh time I have been arrested. I ain't going to jail no more. What we're gonna say now is Black Power! Black Power! Black Power!" Out of that moment came the abrupt move for racial separation in the form of the Black Panthers and the rise of Malcolm X and the Black Muslims.

King had always been discreet about the frictions in the movement over philosophy, tactics, and turf. But he made no secret of his objections to Carmichael's open calls for responding to white violence with black violence. Despite what seemed to be hypocrisy and a refusal by the white power structure to address black grievances in the urban North in the mid-1960s, King still believed in integration—the principles he had set down in his "I Have a Dream" speech in Washington.

"The term black power is unfortunate because it gives the impression of black nationalism," King said in an Atlanta interview. "I do not see the solution to our problem in violence. Our movement's adherence to nonviolence has been a major factor in the creation of a moral climate that has made progress possible. This climate may well be dissipated not only by acts of violence but by the threat of it verbalized by those who equate it with militancy."

Carmichael obviously had not been slowed by these cautionary words, nor had other urban black militants. They were made only more bitter by King's own death, and their theme song on ghetto streets was "Burn, Baby, Burn," not "We Shall Overcome." It was Carmichael who had provoked that angry crowd against me that day in Watts in 1966 just before I was hit over the head, stomped, and nearly killed.

I stayed east after the Washington riots, filed my notes to

Newsweek in New York, and went down to Atlanta for the Tuesday funeral at King's old Ebenezer Baptist Church. There were hundreds of people there, black and white, who I knew: scarred survivors of jails and beatings in the hard battles that had been fought, white reporters I had worked alongside who had moved on, as I had, to other places and other stories, lawyers from the Justice Department whom I'd come to admire, and even Stokely Carmichael himself, who had been so critical of King.

There was a section roped off for the press in the church, where I had heard King preach years before. I walked down front to where he was laid out in a black suit, thin black tie, and white shirt with a white handkerchief in the jacket pocket. The casket was lined with ruffled silk. A lighted electric cross was set up behind it. Fifty thousand people had waited outside all night to see him one last time, and they sobbed quietly as they passed the casket. Some patted him on the chest.

I remembered first hearing him speak at a meeting in the little brick Mt. Zion Baptist Church in Albany, Georgia, and how I had been mesmerized by his ability to rouse hope in the hopeless. He was the most powerful speaker I had ever heard. After that, I had heard him do the same thing many times—in Atlanta, in Philadelphia, Mississippi, in Montgomery, in Selma, in Birmingham, Alabama, in Jackson, Mississippi, in Washington, D.C. I remembered a night in another little Baptist church, in Selma in 1962, where he was helping SNCC rally wary Negroes to go up against Sheriff Jim Clark and his mounted posse, who were beating them when they tried to register to vote. The writer James Baldwin preceded King to the pulpit and gave a brilliant intellectual dissertation on the subtleties and cruelties of segregation. But the words had come from Baldwin's head and not his heart, and the audience listened politely but unmoved. Then King stood up and within two minutes had the audience soaring—rocking back and forth, saying

"Tell it!" and "Amen" as a powerful energy rose in the room. And now the mighty organ of King's voice was stilled.

At his funeral service that day there were six presidential aspirants, twenty-three senators, forty-seven congressmen, a Supreme Court justice, and even Jackie Kennedy. I remembered a time when King couldn't get a hearing in Washington, when politicians, from presidents on down, had been scared to receive him for fear of losing white votes. But now—given the rise of black militancy—he had become the unthreatening and reassuring voice and all those leaders were here to pay him homage. The church held 800, and it was so packed with celebrities that even some of King's staff had to stand outside. The three networks beamed the services live to an audience estimated at 120 million. Banks, stores, and the government shut down. Even Las Vegas cut off its gambling for three hours. Inside the church, many wept as Mahalia Jackson sang "Take My Hand, Precious Lord," and then listened quietly as taped excerpts from King's own speeches and sermons rang through the church: "If any of you are around when I have to meet my day, I don't want a long funeral, and if you get somebody to deliver a eulogy, tell them not to talk too long. Tell them not to mention that I have a Nobel Prize. I'd like somebody to mention that day that Martin Luther King Jr. tried to give his life serving others...."

Outside after the service, King's coffin was loaded onto an old mule-drawn oak wagon. It moved slowly away from the church out along Hunter Street toward the South View Cemetery in Atlanta, a great sea of 150,000 black and white mourners walking silently behind it under a broiling sun. I walked slightly ahead of the mahogany coffin, beside the two spavined old Georgia mules, Ada and Betty, listening to their quiet breathing, the clank of their chains, and the crunch of the iron wheels on the pavement.

*I wanted to be close to Martin Luther King one last time (left foreground),
and not talk to anyone, at his funeral in Atlanta, Ga., April 9, 1968.*

Toward the end, King had been ill a lot, with colds and fevers brought on by fatigue and constant demands on his time. "I'm tired of marching," he said at a rally in Chicago in 1967 supporting an SCLC drive for open housing. "I'm tired of the tensions surrounding our days. . . . I'm tired of living every day under the threat of death. . . . I march because I must. I have no martyr complex. I want to live as long as anybody in this building tonight. Sometimes I begin to doubt whether I'm going to make it through."

If death had often been on his mind, close to the end he seemed to have made peace with it.

"I've looked over and I've seen the promised land," he'd told a rally in support of striking sanitation workers in Memphis the night before he was shot. "I may not get there with you, but I want you to know tonight that we as a people will get to the promised land. So I'm happy tonight. I'm not worried about anything. I'm not fearing any man. Mine eyes have seen the glory of the coming of the Lord."

Walking along beside the coffin—quiet, not wanting to talk to anybody—I thought about how deep ran both King's faith and his courage and that they are not given to many men. And it was not given to many reporters to have known—and covered—such a man, one who faced such hatred on such a daily basis. Even that day, that hatred made itself heard. Georgia's segregationist governor, Lester Maddox, who had only reluctantly ordered the flag to be flown at half-staff, was barricaded in the gold-domed capitol under heavy state police guard. A reporter friend of mine told me that Maddox said, as the procession passed, "If they start coming in here, we're gonna stack them up." And one of his aides joked, "Hey, y'all hear they caught the fellow who killed King? They fined him fifteen dollars for killin' coons out of season."

At last the procession entered the cemetery, founded a century

before by black men tired of burying their dead through the back
gate of the municipal cemetery. The blue sky had turned gray but
the dogwood and azalea throbbed white and red as King's old
deputy Ralph Abernathy said, tears falling from his face, "This
cemetery is too small for his spirit." Then King's body was rolled
into the white Georgia marble crypt bearing his name, dates, and
the end of his March on Washington speech half a decade earlier:
"Free at last, free at last. Thank God Almighty, I'm free at last."

I didn't feel like staying around and drinking with my old
buddies, so I flew back to Los Angeles that night, to my family
and my life away from the South. It was going to be a big political year and I had been assigned a slice of it—helping cover
Bobby Kennedy in the spring primaries. He had a huge press con-
tingent following him, including some hard-nosed political
reporters I'd worked with. Kennedy had a reputation for being
ruthless, his brother's hatchet man, who had gone after Jimmy
Hoffa, the Teamster leader, with a vengeance and had approved
the tapping of King's telephone to get dirt on him, specifically
conversations between him and his white girlfriend. So I was surprised to see that many of these "hard-boiled" reporters had
become Kennedy's rapt admirers. They said he had changed since
his brother's death. He had become gentler, taken on an almost
ethereal and fatalistic quality. He had been genuinely moved by
the poverty he saw when he went to Mississippi in 1967, they
said, and had become a true champion of poor people. He seemed
to them now deeply vulnerable, fragile even, deeply sad, and they
pressed almost reverently close to him, fought to be near him as if
sensing some dread event. While armed with my usual skepticism
towards politicians, I saw these qualities in him myself.

Kennedy was touring California with a large entourage, including most of the Kennedy family, in May, getting ready for the June
6 primary, and I was on the press bus that went along. He drew

huge crowds everywhere, especially among working people in California's Central Valley, where the popular Chicano labor leader Cesar Chavez campaigned with him, and in Watts where black leaders had endorsed him. People surged toward him everywhere, arms outstretched, literally pulling the cuffs from his shirts—which he changed three or four times a day. There was something about him that palpably touched a hunger among poor people and minorities, a hunger that King could no longer fill.

Kennedy had been on the road non-stop for two and a half months, through a string of primaries, putting in fourteen-hour days, and was looking exhausted and gaunt. The day before the California primary, he was campaigning in San Francisco on the last northern California swing, a motorcade through Chinatown that would make good television pictures. He was standing in shirtsleeves on the rear seat of a convertible, held up by two staff people, as the motorcade went under the Oriental sign that was the entrance to Chinatown on Grant Street. We reporters had gotten off the bus and were following on foot as his car went slowly along. Suddenly there were several loud popping sounds—like gunfire—close to the car. Kennedy turned pale and his knees buckled. But these were firecrackers. Kennedy composed himself, and the motorcade moved slowly forward through a cheering crowd.

All was strangely quiet as we got back on the bus and headed for the airport. That afternoon in San Diego, Kennedy was midway through a speech when he sagged to his knees from exhaustion. He was helped off the platform and to his dressing room by two major black athletes, the pro football player Roosevelt Grier and Olympic decathlon champion Rafer Johnson. There he threw up and then went back to the platform and finished.

The next morning, he went bodysurfing with some of his children in Malibu, where he was staying, and got to his fifth-floor suite at the Ambassador Hotel just as the returns started coming in. I got to the Ambassador Hotel early in the evening and talked my way into his room to be with him as he watched the returns and collect "color" for my story. It wasn't easy getting in. Reporters close to Kennedy were jealous of anyone else's access to him. Pudgy New York columnist Jimmy Breslin argued to Kennedy's press secretary Frank Mankiewicz that I should be barred from the inner sanctum. "Why the hell should he get in," Breslin said. I'd seen plenty of competitive reporters before, but this was a new low. I finally got in, pointing out that this was the critical moment in Kennedy's quest for the nomination and *Newsweek* ought to be there. Just the week before, Senator Gene McCarthy had defeated Kennedy in the Oregon primary, and if he didn't win California, all was lost. Breslin and I, as it turned out, were the only reporters in his room as Kennedy stood quietly in front of a television set, sleeves partially rolled up, tie loosened. He said little as the numbers came in, occasionally ducking into the bathroom for some privacy to discuss some issue with an aide.

Finally, as the returns were heading toward the ultimate 46 to 42 percent Kennedy win, somebody said, "OK, it's time to go down now." A thousand supporters were packed in the ballroom waiting for him to come down and give a victory speech. There were no police downstairs, only private security guards. Kennedy had steadfastly spurned police protection everywhere, although he had often said he expected to be shot at. "I play Russian roulette every time I get up in the morning," he had told reporters. "But I just don't care. If they want you, they can get you."

"Do we know enough yet?" asked Kennedy when told it was time to go down to the ballroom.

"Oh, yeah, there's no doubt about a victory," said Jesse "Big Daddy" Unruh, the speaker of the California Assembly, who had helped talk Kennedy into the race.

Almost at the stroke of midnight, Kennedy put on his suit

coat, collected his wife, Ethel, and they and his aides left to go down to the ballroom to declare victory. I decided to stay in his room and avoid what would be a mob scene. And so I watched his television set as Kennedy made his victory speech.

"I think we can end the divisions within the United States," he said, to wild cheers. "What I think is quite clear is that we can work together. We are a great country. A selfless and a compassionate country. And so, my thanks to all of you, and now, on to Chicago." He left the stage and within seconds, there was madness. Gunshots rang out. People screamed. "Jesus Christ, oh, Jesus Christ," someone cried. I raced for the stairwell and flew down the stairs. I hit the lobby just as Sirhan Sirhan was being rushed out of the building by cops, as Kennedy supporters screamed, "Kill him, Kill him," and Unruh yelled, "Keep him alive! Don't kill him! We want him alive. Slow down. If you don't slow down and be careful somebody's gonna shoot this bastard." The cops shoved Sirhan into a squad car and raced away.

I went back to the ballroom. Kennedy was on his back, his eyes glazed, in a dingy pantry just off the podium. His staff had tried to take him through there to an impromptu press conference rather than fight their way through the crowd and Sirhan had been waiting with a .22 pistol concealed in a folded campaign poster. All around me, people were crying and screaming. I followed—it was now 12:30 A.M.—as Kennedy was lifted onto a litter and loaded into an ambulance. The ambulance then rushed him two and a half miles to Central Receiving Hospital on Sixth Street. I raced over there in my car. I called the three members of my Los Angeles bureau staff at home and quickly gave them assignments: Nolan Davis to do the medical story, Phil Hager to do the police investigation, Jim Bishop to do the background on Sirhan. This is where I would need—and use—all of my experience and training. I knew *Newsweek* would need every possible scrap of information that we could dig up about every single aspect of this story. Detail, detail, detail. I called Oz Elliot to tell him we were all on the case.

I called my wife. She had seen it all on television. I told her not to expect me home that night. She understood. And then began a long vigil. We reporters—there were about fifty of us—stood on the street outside the hospital, waiting for any news. Inside, as Nolan Davis was able to piece together as the week went along, nurses had cut off Kennedy's clothes to prepare him for a heart-lung resuscitator. Blood was leaking from his head wound and his blood pressure was almost undetectable. His eyes were blank. A priest delivered last rites, but a doctor got a breathing tube down Kennedy's throat, pounded his chest, gave him adrenaline, albumin, and Dextra, and his blood pressure soared to 150 over 90. Frank Mankiewicz came out to tell us there appeared to be a chance Kennedy might live. I called Oz back to give him the update.

Central Receiving was not properly equipped. It had neither blood plasma nor X-ray machines, so Kennedy was transferred four blocks east to Good Samaritan Hospital. A bullet was lodged in his brain. At 2:30 A.M., he was prepared for surgery on the ninth floor to stop the bleeding and to get the bone and bullet fragments out of his brain. At 6:30 A.M., someone came out to tell us Kennedy had been moved to intensive care from surgery. His brain stem had been severely damaged. Brain cells were dying. But he lived on all through that day and into the night. Few of us reporters had left the sidewalk and the iron fence around the front of the hospital for more than a few minutes. Shortly after 1:45 A.M. on June 6, 1968, more than twenty-five hours after the shooting, Dick Drayne, one of Kennedy's aides, came out of the front of the hospital and down the lawn toward us, carrying Kennedy's black shoes in his hand, tears coming down his cheeks. He didn't say a word. Nor did any of us. I looked around. Several reporters were crying.

I went back to the bureau to coordinate our coverage. I hadn't slept in two days, had eaten practically nothing. This was a Thursday and the magazine would close Saturday night, *Newsweek*'s regular lock-up time. My colleagues and I stayed there all that day—talking and typing. Together we sent in 50,000 words that were boiled down and became part of *Newsweek*'s ten-page cover story. I was physically and emotionally exhausted, but pleased that I had been able to do my own reporting and mentor my younger colleagues at a time of such high stakes and high stress. I did not cover the funeral because it was back east. Instead, I took my young boys—in our new camping trailer—to Big Sur up on the Northern California coast, where we slept out, cooked, played cards, pitched rocks, and had food fights beside the Big Sur River. Long-haired hippies giving the peace sign and carrying hand-scrawled "Food," "Spare Change?" and "Dope?" signs were everywhere. This was the new California and a whole new world for me. It was a dope-smoking, free-loving, war-hating vanguard in VW vans that floated up and down the Pacific Coast Highway with their "old ladies" and dogs. I would, in the months ahead, start to cover them, along with the escalating antiwar movement and marches.

In August I flew to Chicago for the Democratic National Convention. It was a bitter week, inside and outside the convention hall. Antiwar demonstrators massed in parks and marched in the streets. Chicago police waded into them swinging clubs and firing tear gas, and a shocked national TV audience—and delegates in the convention hall—watched the cops club, handcuff, and push kids into paddy wagons. A nonpartisan investigative commission later called it "a police riot." The ghosts of the Kennedys hung over the hall and there was no particular joy when Hubert

Humphrey won the nomination—later to be beaten by Richard Nixon, who had run a "law-and-order" campaign and talked about "the forgotten middle class" (translation: white people). Nixon handily won the South, playing on whites' resentment of the civil rights movement and the Democratic Party's support of it. From then on, the region the Democrats had always banked on as the Solid South became, in fact, solidly Republican.

I went to the Republican convention in Miami late in August and then covered Nixon through the election. There was no levity on this campaign, at least with Nixon and his staff, headed by John Erlichman, Bob Haldeman, and PR man Ron Ziegler. We reporters taped motel room keys to our campaign plane roof, played poker nightly, told jokes and tried mightily to stay attentive through day after day of hearing the same speech over and over. One day when it was my turn to represent the news magazines as the "pool" man on Nixon's plane, I went up to Ziegler, who was seated with Haldeman and Erlichman, and said, "Ron, I've been deputized by the press corps to inquire what it is that Nixon does upon the occasion of his semi-annual erection. The rumor is that he smuggles it to Tijuana." I got hard blank stares, but a lot of laughs from my fellow reporters.

It was not a year of many laughs, to be sure. After it I would always wonder how different things might have been had King and Kennedy not been killed. What I did know at the end of 1968 was that I was sick of hatred, violence, and bloodshed. In a four-year stretch, I had covered four assassinations—John F. Kennedy, Martin Luther King Jr., Robert Kennedy, and Medgar Evers. I had covered the murders of the three civil rights workers in Philadelphia, Mississippi. I had covered the bombing murder of the four little girls in Birmingham. I had seen hundreds of black people beaten by white cops and angry mobs. I was just sick of it all. I was totally burned out.

Chapter *14*

A Fall from Grace

AFTER MY INTENSE involvement in the Martin Luther King and Bobby Kennedy murders and the tumult of the 1968 political year, my own career and life began to unravel. The complicated and often bitter, angry, and shame-filled feelings that I had carried out of my hard-scrabble childhood, into the orphanage, and into my successful career began to resurface as the work quieted down. While the civil rights drama had called forth the best in me and made use of those tangled feelings, it had also served to sidetrack them and keep buried some dark issues that I had not resolved.

The blow to my head in Watts jolted something loose in my heart, and the big result within a couple of years was that I fell desperately, irretrievably in love with an aspiring young journalist and writer, Anne Taylor, a California private school girl I met on a colleague's tennis court. She was a friend of his daughter's and the child of two long-divorced actors, Don Taylor and Phyllis Avery. We came from worlds as different as possible, and yet seemed, from the beginning, elementally tethered—by our love of words, of California, of food, of conversation, of Patsy Cline, Beethoven, Brahms, and Nat King Cole, and of so much more. Part of me hoped this was just a mid-life crisis (I was forty) and I would get over it, for it was agonizing thinking about leaving the family my first wife and I had built together over sixteen years. She was a good woman in every way, had been a good wife, good partner, good supporter, good mother. She did not deserve to have her marriage shattered. And the thought of leaving my boys, especially given my own fatherless past, was painful in the extreme. I loved them right to my core. But I could not deny the pull on my heart. So I moved out and into a small apartment on the beach in Malibu.

There was another dividend from Watts, this one with no upside: The mild asthma that I had had through my adulthood, often dormant for long stretches, kicked up severely. No one knew precisely what had triggered it, whether it was physical or emotional trauma, but I went gasping and panicked to the Saint John's Hospital emergency room in Santa Monica on quite a few occasions and was hospitalized there at least three different times when only intravenous adrenaline, breathing machines, vacuuming my lungs, and cortisone could restore near normal breathing. I was, in fact, put on massive doses of cortisone: forty milligrams a day in order to breathe on my own. I was not warned that cortisone use could cause serious mood swings, even psychotic side effects. Not that it would have mattered then, for I literally couldn't breathe without it. But these pills induced erratic thinking and behavior in me, and wild rushes of energy and euphoria, followed by bouts of extreme lassitude and depression. In tandem with my new home state of California, in thrall to its own late

1960s euphoria and outbursts of energy, I was riding high—heading for a fall, though you couldn't have made me believe it then.

In 1970, I threw another mood-altering substance into the mix when I was introduced to marijuana. I had not been drinking after the Watts injury, but now with everything else going on I started doing that again, too. I was as always not a chronic drunk, but when I did drink, I drank too much and the alcohol—given everything else I was taking—now frequently had a Jekyll and Hyde effect on me, leading to unpredictable outbursts of anger that caused embarrassing public scenes and fear in my children. My oldest son, Charles, later told me that he and his brothers waited apprehensively for me to come home from work and listened to how the car door slammed to ascertain what kind of mood I would be in.

I had been introduced to dope one day in early 1970 when I went to San Francisco to report on a massive anti–Vietnam War demonstration in Golden Gate Park and ran into my old colleague Nick Von Hoffman. We went to a party that night on Telegraph Hill at the home of the *Newsweek* San Francisco bureau chief, Gerald Lubenow, and the heavy smell of weed was in the air. Coming out of the South, where marijuana was practically unheard of, I knew nothing about it except rumors that it was a powerful aphrodisiac used by the likes of drummer Gene Krupa and movie star Robert Mitchum. I had begun to see it openly smoked by the long-haired flower children who claimed to be rebelling against the straight-laced bonds of their fifties parents and unleashing their natural creative powers. "Free Love" and "Peace Now" were their rallying cry. I got in line, joined the party—even as I dutifully still covered it. Everybody on the West Coast seemed to be smoking marijuana—and making love in hot tubs. It was rare to go to a party and not have marijuana passed around, and I became a periodic user.

That summer I let my hair grow long, grew a beard, bought a sleeping bag, and hitchhiked from Malibu up U.S. 1 to Big Sur—the so-called Hippie Highway—sleeping in abandoned buildings and the woods and interviewing and photographing dozens of dope-smoking "love children" in their VW vans with their "old ladies" and dogs. When I got to Big Sur, where hundreds of hippies were encamped and soliciting motorists, I ran into two teenage boys and a girl I had gotten to know while doing a story about a Salvation Army drug recovery center in Los Angeles, one of the first such in the country. These three were getting money for drugs by charging tourists to watch them swim nude in the icy Big Sur River. My report and photographs made a two-page spread in *Newsweek*, entitled "Tripping Down The Hippie Highway," but Oz Elliott flew out and expressed concern that I was spending too much time on lifestyle subjects such as this and not enough on the hard news that they had come to depend on from me. The unspoken message was that I had "gone California." But it seemed to me that the culture was changing fast, and that once again I had a front row seat. This was another kind of revolution.

I soon asked to step aside as bureau chief. I was burned out and bored—certainly with the managerial part. I had never had any ambition to go to Washington or New York and climb the corporate ladder. I was a reporter. So I opted to become what they called a full-time contributing editor with a mandate to travel the country doing special reporting of the long stories called take-outs. I briefly flirted with the idea of going to Vietnam, as this was now the biggest story, and two of my friends, Jack Langguth and David Halberstam, were there. But there was no way *Newsweek* would have let me go given what had happened in Watts, and there was no way I was going to leave my children. Instead I did home-front stories. I traveled across

Canada and did a long article, illustrated by my photographs, on the Vietnam draft evaders hiding out there. I traveled across America doing a piece on the "forgotten middle class" that Nixon talked about. I went to several military bases and West Point for a piece on the Army officer corps. I met a young soldier discharged in Oakland, California, after serving in Vietnam, flew home to his small Ohio town with him, and did a story chronicling his difficulty trying to readjust to life there.

My favorite story of this time, though, awful as it was, captured those old civil rights undertones. It was the story of a black soldier killed in Vietnam whose body was carried by train from Oakland, California, back to his small hometown of Hemphill, Texas, for burial. The Hemphill funeral home wouldn't handle a black body, so he had to be prepared for burial at a black funeral home twenty miles down the road.

This was a period of some of my best reporting and certainly my best writing. I had learned to be more concise and to write in a more novelistic, narrative style. But by late 1971, I was beginning to feel restless and increasingly unmoored from *Newsweek*. I had covered most of the big events of the civil rights movement, four national political conventions, a string of presidential campaigns, a lot of marquee trials, including that of Charles Manson, whose drug-crazed "family" murdered starlet Sharon Tate, many antiwar demonstrations, drug stories, the Hell's Angels, the Beach Boys, and myriad other topics. I was watching some of my old colleagues at *Newsweek* settle in for the long haul toward retirement and my instincts told me I didn't want to end like that. I felt as if my big moments there had passed and I didn't want to sit around and become a mediocrity who dined out on past glories. I knew deep down I would never again feel so in the right place, at the right time, doing the right thing as I had during the civil rights movement.

I came up with the idea to start a new weekly newspaper in Los Angeles, which did not have a good one. I knew it was a roll of the dice, of course, but it seemed exciting and new and bold, something I myself could create. I found a bankrolling angel in a wealthy local entrepreneur named Max Palevsky after laying out to him my vision of what a new weekly paper in Los Angeles could be—a cross between the *Village Voice*, *New York* magazine, and the *New York Review of Books*. Active in a small group of liberal Democrats called the Malibu Mafia, Palevsky had put up some of the money with which Jann Wenner had started *Rolling Stone* in San Francisco. So I quit *Newsweek* in early 1972. It had been a great run. I knew I would miss the collegiality and the company of a core of great national reporters I had worked, laughed, drank, and played poker with. I knew I would be leaving the security of a professional family. But I felt ready to cut the cord.

For the paper, which I named *LA*, I recruited a talented young group of reporters, photographers, and graphic artists, among them graphic designer Roger Black, who would go on to redesign the *New York Times Magazine* and *Newsweek*, Terry McDonnell, later to be editor of *Esquire*, *Rolling Stone*, *US*, and *Sports Illustrated*, and Barry Siegel, later to win a Pulitzer writing for the *Los Angeles Times*. By mid-June we were up and running. It was a handsome paper, full of good writing and imaginative ideas. It got good reviews and was selling well. I was wearing jeans. My hair had gotten even longer. I was smoking marijuana with my young staff every Thursday night after the paper closed. I was still flying high. One night I had dinner with Palevsky in his modernistic house atop a hill in Bel Air. Watching me down second and third helpings of dinner served up by his uniformed factotum, Palevsky said, "Karl, the way you eat it's a good thing you're going to be rich."

Anne and I had married in March 1972, three months before the first issue the newspaper came out. It was an exhilarating time. I was full of life, plans, new beginnings. We married on the back patio of Anne's father's big house. Anne, a baby-faced twenty-two-year-old, was in a long white fitted dress with a wreath of flowers in her hair and I wore a double-breasted blue blazer and tan twill pants. All our many friends were there, and at least half of them, I was sure, were betting this would never last. Of course, my four still young sons were there as well. Not being under the same roof with them was painful. I made a $15,000 down payment on a small white cottage with a rose arbor and a picket fence in Brentwood—just like the one my mother always imagined she and I would live in one day—and we set about making a nest for my boys. They came and went with great regularity and ease, not least because Anne, herself a child of divorce, was a natural stepmother, and because my ex-wife behaved with great dignity and civility. I brought my mother out to meet my new wife and stay with us in our new house. "If only I had ever had a house like this," she said. She stayed for a week and remained tactfully silent about my divorce and was polite to Anne, though plainly she was disconcerted.

In the middle of all these dramatic changes—new newspaper, new marriage, lots of steroids, booze, and marijuana, not to mention a healthy dose of hubris—I now made the biggest blunder of my life. I fell for a pair of con men. On Thanksgiving eve in 1971, as Northwest Airlines Flight 305 from Portland to Seattle took to the air, a passenger midway back in the plane, wearing a dark suit and sunglasses, handed a stewardess a note saying he had a bomb. He demanded $200,000 in unmarked twenty-dollar bills and four parachutes. When the money was delivered at the Seattle-Tacoma airport, he released the passengers and ordered the crew to set the Boeing 727 on a course for Mexico at 200 knots and 10,000 feet. Somewhere between Seattle and Portland, he opened the door in the tail of the plane and parachuted out.

Anne and I soon after we were married in March 1972, when she was twenty-two and I forty-four. Many of our friends thought it wouldn't last. It has.

He gave his name as D. B. Cooper, and no trace of him could be found despite hundreds of FBI and state and local cops searching the forests north of Portland. He became a legend overnight. I decided to try to find him. I figured the story would be a great parting gift for *Newsweek* and a great attention-grabber for my new newspaper. I placed small ads in papers on the West Coast asking D. B. Cooper to get in touch with me and promising that I would tell his story honestly, protect his anonymity, and give him money for his legal defense if he would turn himself in.

Two weeks went by and then I got a call at my office from a man who said he was acting as Cooper's intermediary. I had worked it out that if a call came, I would direct it to a nearby pay phone. I was sure the FBI would be listening. When I took the call at the pay phone, I arranged for the intermediary to call us at Palevsky's house that night and let Palevsky hear what they had to say. The intermediary said Cooper was willing to tell his story, under certain conditions. The guts of the story, he said, was that Cooper, a faithful husband and father, Nixon supporter, and hater of welfare recipients, had been unfairly fired by Boeing and betrayed by Northwest, which had reneged on a job offer, and that the hijacking was the vendetta of a righteously aggrieved man. The FBI had circulated the numbers of the bills given to Cooper, and I had gotten the list. I told the intermediary I would insist on seeing some of the ransom money to verify that it was part of the loot. He agreed, but said Cooper would have to be paid if we believed his story. I told him we could work something out.

I soon flew up to Seattle to meet them, carrying $30,000 of Max Palevsky's money in a tennis racket cover. The man who said he was Cooper looked remarkably like the composite drawing that the FBI had circulated——medium build, slightly balding, thin eyebrows, a narrow turned-down mouth on a heart-shaped face. His confederate was a larger man, dark-haired, quiet-voiced, a real estate broker, he said, and a lifelong friend of Cooper. He showed me two of the twenty-dollar bills, and the numbers matched those on the list.

Cooper described himself as a good man done wrong by a heartless corporation, and so he had plotted his revenge. He concluded that $200,000 was what he would have gotten in salary and retirement benefits had he hoed out his row to the end and that was how he fixed the amount of the ransom he would demand from Northwest. I stayed around Seattle for three days interviewing Cooper. He and his confederate drove me down to a remote area just north of Portland and Cooper showed he where he said he had stashed a car before the hijacking and set up three radio transmitters in a wide triangle as a target to hit in his parachute. He had a receiver with him on the 727 and when the signals came in showing he was over his target, he parachuted out, landed, retrieved his car, and drove home. Now, he said, he needed money because he couldn't spend the marked bills. Satisfied, I gave him the $30,000 for the rights to his story, plus his promise to surrender himself, and went home, convinced I had a great yarn.

Two weeks later two FBI agents came to my office and told me it was all a hoax. The two men had been arrested on fraud charges. Their arrests hit the papers, including the *New York Times*, with my name prominently mentioned as the hoax victim.

I was devastated. I had exercised the worst journalistic judgment and become, I felt, a laughingstock. It was the first time in my career that I had failed at anything, and it had been a widely publicized failure. All the old long-buried feelings of shame and fear of humiliation, of not being a real man, resurfaced. Palevsky was furious at being drawn into the mess. He withdrew his financial support from the paper, and a week later it went down the tubes. Just before Christmas, I had to tell my staff members they were out of their jobs. On December 18, I was back in Seattle in federal court testifying against the hoaxers. They were easy to convict because of all my tapes and films but they claimed I was part of their conspiracy to defraud Palevsky. I testified that I had believed the story, that I had "swallowed the whole thing—contents, bottle, cork and label." The judge called a recess when I broke down describing my newspaper's sudden death.

After that I fought hard to stay afloat, but began a slow painful descent. My confidence was shattered. I was deeply ashamed and depressed. I cut myself off from my old reporter friends. Anne and I both did freelance magazine work to try to bring in money, but it was tough. I didn't have the appetite for it, and she was just getting up and running. Money got very tight. I slid into a dark depression, spending hours prone on the sofa in my little office, unable to function, often in tears, begging for night to come so that I could sleep. I often thought of suicide and considered how to go about it. I didn't like heights and a gun would be too messy. A pill overdose would do it.

I was now smoking marijuana constantly to numb the pain but it didn't help much. The depression deepened, especially when the doctors took me off the cortisone cold turkey. There were new asthma drugs that were less physically and psychologically disturbing. But the net effect of my instant withdrawal was to sink me even farther. Finally I broke down completely—I was blabbering incoherently—and on a rainy spring night, Anne and her father drove me to a nearby mental health facility. I was committed and put on a gurney in a straitjacket. As I lay there with a partially free hand I tried to stuff the corner of a sheet down my throat to kill myself.

Heavy doses of powerful anti-depressants, as well as therapy, didn't seem to help. I tried round after round. There was a little flower bed outside the small building where I was housed. I asked Anne to bring me a trowel and some vegetable seeds and I sat in the dirt planting them—a vegetable garden for me and my fellow nuts. Finally, after much discussion with me and Anne—who did all kinds of research of her own—it was decided that I should try electroshock treatment. It wasn't, the doctors assured us, the old *Cuckoo's Nest* stuff. The doses were small, expertly administered, no lingering side effects except occasional, minor, and usually transitory memory loss. I signed on. I didn't have a choice and I was too far down to be scared. Indeed, the shock treatments did seem to work. Finally, slowly, I began to get better, began to see the sun shine again. But it was a long, slow way back up. Six months after my release from the mental hospital, I went back to North Carolina to visit my mother. I burst into tears as she opened the door. She stood frozen, unable to embrace me. Her own need to see me as the strong care-taking "husband" rendered her incapable of comforting me, or so I thought. I tried to explain what had happened, but she was uncomprehending. I left and walked my old haunts of the streets of Wilson for hours thinking about the days when I had been young and full of hope.

I started doing some freelance magazine articles again, including a piece for the *Atlantic Monthly* about my orphanage years, the first time I had ever written about it. I was still pretty fragile and still taking anti-depressants, but was grateful—able to be grateful—for the tenacious love of my wife and sons. We tried to protect the boys from knowing how seriously ill I was, but they knew enough to be worried and to stay closely in touch.

In 1978, Van Gordon Sauter, whom I had met in Philadelphia, Mississippi, in 1964 when he was a reporter covering the Chaney, Goodman, and Schwerner murders for the *Detroit Free Press*, came to Los Angeles to manage the CBS affiliate television station and hired me as its managing editor in charge of editorial content. TV—certainly local TV news—was a whole new world for me. The values were different from the print world. You had to tell a story in a minute and thirty seconds. I had been hired to make sense of the editorial content, to give it some depth, clear writing, and, among other things, come up with series ideas for the all-important ratings periods, the sweeps. In my old *Newsweek* fashion, I came up with a long list of what I thought were good ideas and presented them to the news director. He glanced through them, laughed, and said, "Karl, we can't put any of this stuff on the air. This is journalism. Let me tell you what makes a good television story. It has to contain one or more of the following elements: vets, pets, tots, tears, or tits."

Local television news was more interested in trucks on fire on freeways ("crispy critters"), earthquakes, mudslides, brush fires, youth gang shootings, and "freak stories" about courageous cripples than in thoughtful reporting on serious issues. Brush fires that came in the fall dry season shot billowing flames into the air as they swept through the hills. They made great television and as I sat one night in the news director's office watching live coverage of a huge fire in the Malibu hills, he shouted, "Burn, baby, burn!" Even so, we did a lot of good work. The writing and reporting improved, and we did investigative pieces that resulted in the shutting down of Southern California's largest Ford dealer after we exposed them for bait-and-switch tactics.

I continued to secretly smoke marijuana and take anti-depressants during this time. When my friend Van Sauter left for New York to become head of CBS Sports and then of CBS News, I decided I wanted to be an on-air reporter and started reporting on politics. Pretty quickly I was not happy in this role. Trying to boil down a political story into the one minute thirty went against all of my natural curiosity and training as a reporter. Also, I was not comfortable on air, and sometimes sneaked out to my 1967 Mustang convertible to smoke a joint before going on live.

I decided to quit the role of TV reporter one day when I was walking on the Santa Monica pier and found myself, to my utter shame, looking around to see if people recognized me. After that I moved over to the network at CBS's Television City and became a producer for the *Morning News*. But I was not happy there either, and quit in 1986 to become editor and publisher of a struggling magazine, *California Business*, owned by a close businessman friend, Martin Stone. On my watch, we improved its writing, reporting, and graphic appearance, but couldn't pull it out of financial trouble, and I quit when Stone brought in someone else as publisher. I felt slightly embarrassed bouncing around the way I was, so far from my serious reporting days and my serious reporting friends. At the same time Anne's writing career was on the rise. She had become a gifted writer and reporter, with cover stories in places like the *New York Times Magazine*, and a network radio commentator for CBS. I nurtured her and supported her, but I felt like a has-been.

For my sixtieth birthday, August 30, 1987, Anne gave me a big party at her father's house, complete with live music, barbecue, square-dancing, and a large live (Hollywood-trained) pig with a bandanna around its neck. That night, I decided to stop the marijuana once and for all. Sixty was a significant birthday and I had just had enough, but it was not until January that I finally committed to doing so. On January 4, after close to a lifetime of using some substance or another, I walked into my first Twelve-Step recovery meeting. It didn't matter that my recent drug of choice was pot. To that program, it was all the same.

The meeting was held in a synagogue on Sunset Boulevard not far from our house and it was jammed, a thousand people. I hated it. I had always shunned joining and joiners and I hated the idea of being there, hated all the platitudes of "one day at a time," "keep coming back," and "let go and let God." All the talk about a higher power filled me with contempt. There were clean-cut people in suits, ties, and pretty dresses, as well as those bedraggled and just off the streets, but I was certainly not like any of them.

But I kept going to meetings because I had tried everything else to quit and be happy and nothing had worked. I was extremely angry and hostile at first, so much so that when I sat down at a communal table at a men's meeting at Uncle John's Pancake House in Santa Monica, people would get up and move away. I was told I had to face up to my defects, to what I had contributed to my misery, to get rid of my secrets and apologize to all the people I had hurt. And one day I blurted out my deepest secret, the story of my childhood sexual molestation when I was five and that group of boys forced me to suck another kids' penis and laughed at me. It was the first time I had ever told anyone and I immediately felt better. I kept going to meetings, kept facing up to my past, and the anger and resentments slowly began to melt away.

As I continued to feel better and stronger, I flipped my lifetime reportorial skills and starting training people in how to deal with the media and how to make speeches. I ran my small, fledgling business out of our garage, which I had converted to an office, and while it was still odd and a little discomfiting not to go to work somewhere, not to have a tether, I began to like my independence. Word got around that I was good at this and calls came in, a stream of money began, and I was pleased to be helping people feel more confident in public. I also began to write opinion articles for newspapers and to make speeches myself. Despite all the upheaval, I was still deeply in love with my wife, our marriage was intact and getting healthier, and I was closer to my children than ever. And at the end of my first year of sobriety, I began to feel hopeful that I might at long last find the peace and happiness that despite all my success had eluded me for so many years.

Chapter 15

Coda

ON FEBRUARY 15, 1990, I flew across the country to bury my mother. She died as she had lived most of her life, alone. She was eighty-nine years old and had been living in a nursing home near Smithfield, North Carolina, not far from my sister's house. The official cause of death was pneumonia, but a colon cancer she had been treated for back in 1975 had also returned and spread.

As I flew South from my home in Los Angeles, I was sadly aware that even her death had not and would not completely alter my complicated feelings about her. Through the years, those feelings had gyrated between love, forgiveness, anger, resentment, and frustration. For the last fifteen years of her life, my mother lived in unit A3, Oettinger Apartments, a two-story old brick building with faded wood columns and a swing on the front porch, next to the fire station in Wilson and a few blocks from the tracks where the North–South trains blew their mournful dirges through the night. She had quit working at the popcorn stand after she got cancer and had subsisted thereafter on a meager Social Security check and money I sent every month. The firemen at the station next door collected, sorted, and distributed clothes for poor people, and I urged her to get involved—or to volunteer to do something at the Methodist Church. But she always had an excuse, and I finally gave up. As with the rest of her life, it was as if she were waiting for somebody to come to her and make it at long last all right.

She had come out to visit us once a year, and I had always visited her at least once a year, usually when I went back for the Easter orphanage reunion. She would insist on getting out her cast iron pan, frying chicken, and making buttermilk biscuits, accompanied in the Southern manner with iced tea sweetened while it was hot. We would sit at her oilcloth-covered kitchen table and I'd tell her about her grandchildren and my life back home.

She paid a last visit to our California bungalow and her grandchildren to celebrate her eighty-ninth birthday on September 8, 1989. By that time, her four brothers and two sisters were all dead, as were her few close friends. We were it. She sat at the end of our dining room table, with a pointed paper hat on her head, a Dixie Cup beside her to spit her snuff in, surrounded by our large family. She and my sister had brought that vinegary Eastern Carolina barbecue from Parker's in Wilson and she had done the thing she always first wanted to do when she came to visit: make her buttermilk biscuits. There was a pile of presents and a cake with candles and the singing of "Happy Birthday." She had the one alcoholic drink she liked, a finger of Dubonnet mixed with soda, and I danced with her in our dining room, she moving with teenage awkwardness to the sound of Glenn Miller with a smile on her thin face.

She was a big hit that visit. I took her to see some of the more famous friends I had made while at *Newsweek*, including the actress Jennifer Jones, now married to the big industrialist and art collector Norton Simon. In fact, I had, in my capacity as bureau chief, fixed Jones and Simon up on their first date to attend a *Newsweek* party for the visiting Oz Elliot and we had become friends. Jennifer was much taken with my tall, cracked-voice mom from another world.

"She looks just like herself," my mother whispered to me, spitting snuff into her Dixie Cup. Jennifer could not have been more gracious. She recognized the authenticity in my mother. She had often told me she herself was just a hick girl from Oklahoma whose mother had tried to teach her good table manners when she was a little girl. She said that when she had eaten and commented that she was "stuffed" her mother would reply, "Don't say I'm stuffed. A turkey is stuffed. Say, 'I've had sufficient.'"

When my mother and I were alone that last time, I told her I was sorry for all the anger I had felt at her over the years. But she did not understand, or want to understand. Sending me and my sister to the orphanage was her heartbreak, not ours. I was sure she was wondering how I could be angry at her, after all she had sacrificed. "I've had the worst life of anybody I ever heard of," she told me, sitting at our kitchen table. I felt the old surge of anger, but kept my mouth shut.

She began to decline shortly after she went home. The cancer had returned and she was unable to look after herself so we found a nursing home near where my sister lived. My sister asked the doctor to give us a heads-up near the end so that I could make it back for a last visit. But suddenly there was pneumonia, and she was gone. I flew back to help with arrangements. We had her

My mother, my four sons, and me in 1963 at the swamp-side tenant shack my mother, my sister, and I lived in before she sent us to the orphanage.

cremated and arranged for a memorial service at the Methodist Church in Wilson. My wife and three of my children (the fourth was ill) flew back and attended with my sister. The six of us plus a woman I had dated thirty years before when I was a reporter on the *Daily Times* were the only people who attended. It was a brief service. I talked about her essential honesty and her lifelong absence of prejudice, her love of good food, and the way she ate enormous meals all the while complaining that she could "hardly eat a mouthful."

Afterwards, we went to Parker's for barbecue and drove over to Smithfield to my sister's. We reminisced and played poker and looked through a box of my mother's photos, including a picture of her with me and my boys—when they were still fairly young—in front of that now-abandoned tenant shack on Mauls Swamp. Then we all flew home.

In the spring I went back. I collected her ashes from a mortuary in Raleigh, picked up my sister, and we drove to Wilson and stood silently as they were buried beside those of her sister Belle in the Maplewood Cemetery. I had ordered up a simple stone plaque with her name, dates of birth and death, and an inscription: "A Good Woman."

I stayed around Wilson for a few days taking notes for a memoir I hoped I would write. The memories of my early reporting years there were intense and vivid. The town I had known so well was not much changed, though it had grown a little. There was a new police station and the *Daily Times* had moved to fancy new quarters on the edge of town. Nash Street looked physically just the same, but the human landscape was drastically altered. The old courthouse was still there, but the "White" and "Colored" water fountains were gone. The Cherry Hotel was now a senior citizens residence with a satellite dish on the roof. Tobacco still ruled, but had declined, and many of the old warehouses lay in burned and rusted rubble. My mom's popcorn stand and the two old movie theaters were shut, one occupied by a fitness club, and the old brick Charles L. Coon High School lay vacated and bare. Wimpy's Pool Parlor was long gone. Oettinger's Men's Store and Churchwell's Jewelers were gone, and nearly all of the other solid old businesses had died or moved to the malls in the suburbs. In their place had come wig stores, finance companies, storefront churches, a "King of New York Fashions" store, and video rental outlets catering to a black population that, after integration came in the 1970s, had migrated west across the railroad tracks from the segregated "niggertown." The old elite white families had moved further west to modern air-conditioned new houses in the suburbs. Their stately old homes out on Nash Street were now occupied by law offices, insurance companies, CPA's, and sorority and fraternity houses belonging to Atlantic Christian College.

The only cop surviving from my era at the *Daily Times* was A. J. Hayes, the old fingerprint sergeant from my first capital punishment case, who had made it finally to chief and then retired. I went out to visit him, past the old public library where a half-dozen white and black kids were playing on the wide lawn. Hayes was now an enfeebled and thin widower living alone in a small house off West Nash Street near the still-going Dick's Hot Dogs. A black family lived catty-corner from him. Two black kids were in the street, throwing a baseball back and forth.

"Those niggers don't bother me, and I don't bother them," he said. "Everybody gets along OK."

I decided it was time to try to find out what little more I could about a father I had never known, so I drove east forty miles to Greenville where his family was from and where my mother said he was buried. I had never known exactly when he died. I went to the office of the *Greenville Reflector* and began searching through the microfilm and finally came upon his obituary, in the lower corner of the front page. "Former Pitt Man Dies In Florence," the small headline said.

"Mr. David Henry Fleming Sr., age 54, a native of Pitt County, died suddenly in Florence, S.C. at 2 o'clock Saturday afternoon, March 24, (1928) after an illness of just a few hours," it said.

"The remains will be buried in the Fleming burial ground a few miles north of Greenville."

Aside from my sister, I had one surviving relative, Hazel Jackson, an eighty-seven-year-old first cousin, daughter of one of my father's two brothers. I found her and her aged husband living in a small house on the edge of town and they led me, driving their old Cadillac, through downtown Greenville across the Tar River and out the Bethel Highway and onto a dirt road and stopped in front of a small brick house. This, my aunt told me, was the old Fleming farm. She led me past a collapsed tobacco barn across a sandy field and to the edge of a small pine wood, where in a tangle of honeysuckle and blackberry vines were a dozen Fleming gravestones.

I searched for my father's stone, but couldn't find it, although my aunt assured me he was there, for she had attended the burial service. There was, though, a worn and badly rusted old steel temporary marker stuck in the ground, and this, she said, must be the place. I asked her if I could be there alone for a few minutes and she and her husband went on back to their car. I sat down on a gravestone beside his marker. I felt a wave of pity come over me for him. What a small, trapped life his must have been—an alcoholic in failing health in the middle of the Great Depression with a brand new baby and disappointed young wife. How lucky I was in comparison to have gotten out, to have escaped poverty, to have gone on and been part of a huge world in which I had been able to do work I cared deeply about and build a family I loved.

I drove back up to Raleigh to fly home to California and stopped again at the old Methodist Orphanage. I wasn't going back there much anymore. The orphanage as I had known it was no more. The land had been sold off and all the old buildings except one, which was preserved as a little museum, had been razed and replaced by condos. The "Methodist Home For Children" still existed as an institution, but now it served only to place children in temporary foster care in private homes. The farm was long since gone, too, converted into an industrial park. The grove in front of the old Vann Building was now a city park. I walked down into it. The two old giant pecan trees were still there, budding out along with the oak and hickory trees. The dogwoods were in bloom and the clear blue sky was filled with the familiar cries of robins and blue jays.

A young black man was kicking a soccer ball back and forth with his son. A young white man and his girlfriend were sitting beneath one of the pecan trees, holding hands. "I used to climb these pecan trees when I was a boy," I said to them. They looked at me blankly and turned away, and I walked down to the creek and the weeping willow tree where with my boyhood friends I had waded and collected frog jelly all those springs before.

As always when I went back there, I was overcome with a mix of exquisite pleasure and pain. But the old feelings of bitterness were gone. Though there was by necessity a lack of personal love in the orphanage, it had in most all ways served me and thousands of other children well. I had learned many valuable life lessons there: pride in hard work done well, however menial, honesty, loyalty, punctuality, keeping my word, respect for my elders, a love of sports, games, and good manners, fair play, self-reliance—and sympathy for life's underdogs. That sympathy had defined my professional and personal life.

I realized that though I had endured much pain in the orphanage and in my later life, I had had a lot more joy than misery. I had been lucky in my life, very lucky, and had few regrets. The main one was that I had not been able to completely forgive my mother before she died. She had ended up alone and unhappy. I was surrounded by love—my wife, my four fine sons and their wives, eight grandchildren, many good friends, old and new.

Anne and I were happier than ever, still joined at the hip as we had been from the start, though there had been turbulent times. In the years of my downward spiral, she had become a nationally known print journalist, a network TV commentator, and a regular essayist for the *NewsHour with Jim Lehrer*. She had written a successful and well-reviewed novel, *Marriage: A Duet*, and was well-launched into another. I was proud of her, as she was of me.

I didn't go to church at all, but I had more or less made my peace with religion. I still rankled at the dogmatic and punitive God that the Rev. Albert Sydney Barnes and others stuffed down my throat when I was a child. I rankled, too, and will forever be ashamed of, the hatred and violence visited on blacks by whites in the South in the name of God. But I remained inspired by the memory of all those "mass meetings" and all that stirring music in all those little Southern black churches where faith in a kinder and more just God kept hope alive. And I had seen my own bitterness at organized religion replaced by a sense of awe and wonder at the good that people could do.

I remained skeptical of politicians, suspicious of concentrated power, and intolerant of intolerance, but I was not the gruff and tough guy I once was. I walked with a pronounced limp as a result of spinal nerve damage from the Watts injury and I had therefore had to give up all the running sports that I had loved since childhood. The asthma had abated and was under control with new and better drugs. I cooked a lot, delighted in telling the hundreds of jokes I knew, played golf—the Republican game—exercised regularly, did a lot of volunteer work, and told people who asked how I was, "I'm great from the eyebrows up."

Amid all this, my boyhood chums were dying off. Fatty Clark, who had gone on to serve thirty years in the Army and had only returned once to the orphanage—very bitter about his boyhood there, I was told—was gone. So were both Charles "Big Jeebie" and Russell "Little Jeebie" Clay, both of whom, like me, had become newspaper reporters. So were the Jordan brothers, Monkey and Shorty, both of whom had served years with the CIA. Gone, too, were Snake Driver, Cootie and Snot-Eye Roach, Pisspot Brown, Pumpy Peacock, Sleepy Williams, Preacher Weeks, Susie and Link Tilley, Big Nigger and Little Nigger Rogers, Pussy Leathers, Greasy Brooks, Pooty Parker, Skinny Boston, Skunk Bradford, and Chin Lee. Old Man Barnes had died in 1961 at eighty-seven. And so had Muh Brown, matron of the first building I was in at the orphanage. She died August 3, 1995, in a nursing home near Raleigh, still very much connected to the institution that had been her life. I flew back to North Carolina for her funeral. The little Methodist church where her services were held was packed. Many people cried, including me.

I'd had a final letter from her in early 1990, which began, "My dear little boy, You will always be my little boy, for I love you just as much as I did when you were my little boy."

I had not been back to the South of my civil rights reporting days for a long time. But I had kept in touch through old friends, reporters, and activists. There had been huge changes. Across Georgia, Louisiana, Alabama, and Mississippi, once the fiercest bastions of segregation, blacks were now legislators, mayors, police chiefs, and sheriffs. By 2004, there were 250 elected black officials in Mississippi alone, and 400,000 blacks were registered to vote, as opposed to 15,000 in the early sixties. All across the South, black people could now register to vote without fear of injury, death, or intimidation, and they had done so by the hundreds of thousands. Martin Luther King had predicted it, and it had come true: The South was now more integrated, and contentedly so, than any other part of the country. Blacks were moving there from the North. The main change was that the fear that blacks had once constantly lived under was now gone. The Klan was in tatters and the Citizens Council was gone. White sheriffs and cops could no longer intimidate, beat, and kill blacks with impunity. A white man could no longer get away with killing a black man for looking the wrong way at a white woman—or just for presuming to try to vote.

A new generation of white and black people, though, wouldn't see, or wouldn't admit, that much had changed. On my last official visit to the South for *Newsweek* in 1970, I had gone back to the major battlegrounds of the civil rights movement—Montgomery, Birmingham, Philadelphia, Greenwood, Selma, Jackson—for a take-out called "The South Revisited."

In a fancy new Jackson mall, two fiery two young black women having lunch at Primo's Restaurant lectured me at passionate length on how nothing was better. A decade earlier they might have been beaten or killed but here they were, eating stuffed flounder surrounded by white patrons not paying any attention, with a white waitress asking, "Can I get you ladies anything else?"

I went back to Philadelphia where the three kids were murdered by the Klan in 1964 with the help of Sheriff Rainey and Deputy Price. Rainey had been acquitted at a federal trial, but couldn't find a job locally and had moved to Kentucky. Price and three Klansmen went to prison. The local schools were totally integrated and the star of the local high school basketball team was a black youth who had been carried on the shoulders of his white teammates around the gym at the end of a winning season.

I managed to find the man who had led the mob that had threatened Claude Sitton and me in the courthouse lobby when we went to interview Rainey and Price about the murders. His name was Clarence Mitchell. I found him at the local golf course in sunglasses and loud pants. This time, he was as friendly as could be.

"You must have changed a lot to be able to accept all this integration," I said.

"Naw, I'm the same good ol' Southern boy I always was: ready to fuck or fight on sixty seconds' notice," he said.

"If the niggers want to come to white schools, let 'em be. We don't care. We resent this forcing but there's no way to resist. It's like looking down the barrel of a cannon: You can't fight back with a pea shooter," he said.

And this time when I left town, of my own volition, Mitchell shook my hand, grinned, and said, "Come on back anytime, boy. I won't let nobody hurt you."

Later, as I looked back on the worst of the earlier years, I remembered being sick with rage and shame over things that I saw—the murders, beatings, bombings, burnings, and humiliations visited upon black people. It had been painful to watch. But those years had been inspiring, too. Led mainly by Martin Luther King and Bob Moses, a tiny band of kids, mostly black and Jewish, had literally changed America. And they had done it without the use of violence.

Out of their sacrifices and their stubborn commitment to an idea came many new laws advancing black rights. What they did had spawned, as well, the Vietnam antiwar movement, the women's movement, and the gay rights movement. As a result, as the new century came—less than four decades after the Freedom Rides—more people in more places had more rights than ever before. Stubborn problems of race and poverty persisted, but much of King's dream had come true.

In the spring of 2004 I attended a retrospective symposium of civil rights reporters at Syracuse University in New York. I sat on a stage beside my old friend Claude Sitton telling stories about what we had shared. I didn't say it to the big audience that attended, but I could look back on my reporting career and not be apologetic in any way that I had been unabashedly on the side of the black people in their struggles. I never hid my feelings. But I was also proud that those feelings had never tainted my reporting. I had sought always to be scrupulously fair and objective. I had reported on literally thousands of stories, and I had never once been accused of bias. That was a badge of honor.

The night before this symposium began, I had been in New York and spent a convivial evening reminiscing with John Doar, one of the truly heroic white figures of the civil rights movement. He was eighty-one years old and still practicing law. I got him to tell me again a story he'd told me some years earlier.

A decade after the Ole Miss riot, Doar had spent a boozy Chicago evening with retired federal judge John Minor Wisdom, a Republican native of New Orleans, who, as a member of the U.S. Fifth Circuit Court of Appeals, had in the early 1960s ruled in favor of blacks in many voter registration and school integration cases. As a result, Wisdom was threatened, had crosses burned on his lawn, and was ostracized by most of his friends.

This night, as he and Doar were retiring upstairs in the club where they were staying, Wisdom, carrying the remainder of a bottle of bourbon in his hand, looked down at Doar and said, "Well, John, we didn't do anything to be ashamed of."

What a great epitaph for a life that was, I thought, to have done nothing to be ashamed of. And as I looked back on my own life and especially at my years as a reporter covering the civil rights movement, I could say with a mixture of gratitude and humility and, yes, some pride, too, neither had I.

Index

PublicAffairs is a publishing house founded in 1997. It is a tribute to the standards, values, and flair of three persons who have served as mentors to countless reporters, writers, editors, and book people of all kinds, including me.

I.F. STONE, proprietor of *I. F. Stone's Weekly*, combined a commitment to the First Amendment with entrepreneurial zeal and reporting skill and became one of the great independent journalists in American history. At the age of eighty, Izzy published *The Trial of Socrates,* which was a national bestseller. He wrote the book after he taught himself ancient Greek.

BENJAMIN C. BRADLEE was for nearly thirty years the charismatic editorial leader of *The Washington Post.* It was Ben who gave the *Post* the range and courage to pursue such historic issues as Watergate. He supported his reporters with a tenacity that made them fearless and it is no accident that so many became authors of influential, best-selling books.

ROBERT L. BERNSTEIN, the chief executive of Random House for more than a quarter century, guided one of the nation's premier publishing houses. Bob was personally responsible for many books of political dissent and argument that challenged tyranny around the globe. He is also the founder and longtime chair of Human Rights Watch, one of the most respected human rights organizations in the world.

For fifty years, the banner of Public Affairs Press was carried by its owner Morris B. Schnapper, who published Gandhi, Nasser, Toynbee, Truman and about 1,500 other authors. In 1983, Schnapper was described by *The Washington Post* as "a redoubtable gadfly." His legacy will endure in the books to come.

Peter Osnos, *Publisher*